THE POLITICS OF ALGERIA

This book brings together Algerian-based scholars and Algerians in the diaspora to address the many, salient issues facing Algeria, the largest country in Africa and the Middle East. Until February 22, 2019, Algeria looked like the beacon of stability in the region, for the authoritarian regime eluded the so-called Arab Spring, which resulted in chaos in a number of countries in the Middle East and North Africa (MENA).

The authors of the chapters in this book are a mix of sociologists, economists, political scientists, linguists, and international relations specialists who have used the theoretical and methodological instruments in their respective fields to decipher the complexities that characterise the Algerian political system. In the domestic part, some of the chapters deal with issues seldom tackled in Maghreb studies, namely, the language and identities issues, which are at the forefront of the protest movement since February 2019. Other chapters analyse the role of the elites, the emergence of the new entrepreneurs, the future of energy, gender, media, and human rights, the predicament of the rentier state, gender, language, identity issues, and the resource curse. The international relations part examines Algeria's roles in the Mediterranean and in the Sahel, the strategic partnership with China, the complicated relations with France, and the relations with Iran and the Gulf Cooperation Council (GCC).

Exploring Algeria's transformation, this collection is an original addition to the books on the Maghreb that will be a key resource to students and scholars interested in the developing world, the Middle East and North Africa (MENA).

Yahia H. Zoubir is professor of international studies and international management and director of research in geopolitics at KEDGE Business School, France. He has taught at various universities in China, Europe, the United States, Indonesia, India, South Korea, and the Middle East and North Africa (MENA). He has published numerous books and articles internationally.

Picture of Hirak's demonstration in Algiers taken by Adel Hamaizia

THE POLITICS OF ALGERIA

Domestic Issues and International Relations

Edited by Yahia H. Zoubir

Routledge
Taylor & Francis Group

LONDON AND NEW YORK

First published 2020
by Routledge
2 Park Square, Milton Park, Abingdon, Oxon OX14 4RN

and by Routledge
52 Vanderbilt Avenue, New York, NY 10017

Routledge is an imprint of the Taylor & Francis Group, an informa business

British Library Cataloguing-in-Publication Data
A catalogue record for this book is available from the British Library

Library of Congress Cataloging-in-Publication Data
Names: Zoubir, Yahia H., editor.
Title: The politics of Algeria : domestic issues and international
    relations / edited by Yahia H. Zoubir.
Description: London ; New York, NY : Routledge/Taylor & Francis Group,
    2020. | Includes bibliographical references and index.
Identifiers: LCCN 2019030518 (print) | LCCN 2019030519 (ebook) | ISBN
    9781138330962 (hardback) | ISBN 9781138331006 (paperback) | ISBN
    9780429824876 (adobe pdf) | ISBN 9780429824869 (ebook) | ISBN
    9780429824852 (mobi)
Subjects: LCSH: Algeria--Politics and government--1990- | Algeria--Foreign
    relations--21st century. | Algeria--Social conditions--21st century.
Classification: LCC DT295.6 .P65 2020 (print) | LCC DT295.6 (ebook) | DDC
    965.05/4--dc23
LC record available at https://lccn.loc.gov/2019030518
LC ebook record available at https://lccn.loc.gov/2019030519

ISBN: 978-1-138-33096-2 (hbk)
ISBN: 978-1-138-33100-6 (pbk)
ISBN: 978-0-429-44749-5 (ebk)

Typeset in Bembo
by Lumina Datamatics Limited

To my adored grandchildren Haizam and Tilelli.

To my sister Dalila.

To the Martyrs of the Algerian Revolution
who sacrificed their lives for freedom.

To the Algerian people for their struggle
for a free and democratic state.

CONTENTS

LIST OF FIGURES

LIST OF TABLES

PREFACE

The Politics of Algeria: Domestic Issues and International Relations is the first book of its kind, at least in the English language, because it brings together Algerian experts both in Algeria and in the diaspora. The objective was not the exclusion of non-Algerians; the main reason was to provide Algerian scholars with the opportunity to examine issues in their own country (or country of origin) from their specific standpoint. Algerians in the diaspora remain attached to their country of origin and committed to contribute, through their acquired knowledge and experience, to Algeria's development and better governance and the eradication of the current corrupt system in place. To repair the damage that Abdelaziz Bouteflika's twenty-year rule has engendered, Algeria will need the contribution and solidarity of all its citizens, especially that of its intellectuals.

To tackle the most significant issues related to Algeria, I invited leading Algerian experts in their respective fields. The book is divided into two parts: (1) Domestic issues and (2) Regional and international relations. Belguidoum's chapter sits astride both parts, so I included it in the second part.

The first part addresses numerous issues for which the best experts, sociologists, economists, and political scientists, in their respective areas in the social sciences, have agreed to contribute. The first part contains chapters dealing with state and social relations, the youth, gender, identities, language, Jihadism, political power, the media and human rights, energy policy, and political economy. For readers interested in the issues that could not be treated in this book, such as civilian-military relations, political economy, or security sector reforms, albeit from a comparative perspective, they can refer to Zoubir and White (2016).

The main questions I asked the contributors to address relate to the transformations, or lack thereof, Algeria experienced 6 years after the "Arab Spring" and whether the country was still in a state of "perpetual transition." I asked them more generally to focus on the continuities and changes in the last 20 years of Abdelaziz Bouteflika's presidency and how his regime tackled the major challenges it faced. Although the contributors wrote the chapters in the middle or the end of 2018, the content of their texts provide the causes that ultimately triggered the nationwide protests that began on February 22, 2019 (and on a lesser scale earlier), which might result in the construction of a democratic polity, what Algerians refer to as the "second republic," which would put an end to the usurped revolutionary legitimacy and the rentier state that successive regimes have relied on to impose their authoritarian rule whatever its forms. I have provided a lengthy Introduction to consider current developments and thus bring events up to date.

The second part focuses on Algeria's policies in its neighbourhood and internationally. The chapters in this second part focus on the country's position in the Mediterranean, its relations with France, its position on Western Sahara, its relations with China, transnational trade, the policy in the Sahel, and the relations with the Gulf and Iran. This second part does not deal with Algeria's relations with the United States, Russia, the European Union, or Africa. This was due to reasons of space, but also because there has been little change in those relations. Scholars interested in academic works on Algeria's relations with the United States and with Russia can refer to Zoubir and Zunes (2016) and to Zoubir (Zoubir 2011, 2020), respectively. On relations with the European Union, they can refer to Joffé (2016). With respect to Africa, which Bouteflika neglected, they can check Zoubir (2015).

The chapters in this book will provide objective analyses of Algeria, a country that is of significance for the Maghreb region, Africa, Europe, and for major powers.

References

Joffé, George. 2016. "Barcelona, Twenty Years On," *North African Politics: Change and Continuity*, edited by Yahia H. Zoubir and Gregory White. London & New York: Routledge.

Zoubir, Yahia H. 2011. "Russia and Algeria: Reconciling Contrasting Interests," *The Maghreb Review*, 36 (3): 99–126.

Zoubir, Yahia H. 2015. "Algeria's Roles in the OAU/African Union: From National Liberation Promoter to Leader in the Global War on Terrorism," *Mediterranean Politics*, 21 (1): 55–75.

Zoubir, Yahia H. 2020. "Making Up Lost Time: Russia and the Maghreb." Oxford University Press (forthcoming).

Zoubir, Yahia H. and White, Gregory (Eds.). 2016. *North African Politics: Change and Continuity*. London & New York: Routledge.

Zoubir, Yahia H. and Zunes, Stephen. 2016. "The United States and North Africa," *North African Politics: Change and Continuity*, edited by Yahia H. Zoubir and Gregory White. London & New York: Routledge, pp. 277–308.

ACKNOWLEDGEMENTS

Putting together an edited volume is no easy task; however, the commitment and close collaboration of dedicated scholars makes the endeavour worthwhile. I would like to thank the contributors for their trust in me and their dedication to the project, which went beyond mere academic exercise; most of the contributors to this book believe that their chapters will contribute in some way to a better understanding of Algeria and to sharing that knowledge with Algerian scholars everywhere. They also believe, like I did when I decided to go through the arduous process, that this book will hopefully influence Algeria's policymakers and academics in not only analysing the root causes of the long-lasting crisis, but also in encouraging the emergence of a free and democratic nation that millions of Algerians have been calling for and for which hundreds of thousands have lost their lives to free this complex yet so amazing country.

I would like to thank and express my immense appreciation to James "Joe" Whiting, acquisitions editor at Routledge, for believing in me. I feel privileged to have worked with him on three edited volumes, two on North Africa and this one on Algeria.

My sincere thanks to Miss Titanilla Panczel, editorial assistant at Routledge, for her dedication and patience in my carrying out this project to fruition.

My greatest gratitude goes to Mrs. Heather Ascott, in South Africa, who served as my consultant and editorial counsellor for this book. Her editorial skills are simply superb; this acknowledgement is a modest expression of my immense indebtedness.

I would also like to thank the blind reviewers who provided valuable comments on some of the chapters.

Last, but by no means least, my everlasting indebtedness goes to my wife Cynthia, my children Nadia, Jamel, and Malek, who have always supported me, even when they objected to my long working hours. I owe them my most sincere eternal gratitude.

NOTES ON CONTRIBUTORS

Sarin Abado is an expert in the field of energy and draws on extensive international experience in North Africa, the EU, and Central Asia. In her most recent assignment, she was based in Algiers as the leader of an EU-funded project with the Algerian Ministry of Energy in the field of energy regulation. Her career started as an energy consultant in Kazakhstan covering the regional electricity and gas sector. She then worked many years for Austria's Energy Regulatory Authority E–Control as its attaché in Brussels and closely followed EU energy policy in the field of energy infrastructure, security of supply, renewable energy, and consumer protection. She is a graduate of Johns Hopkins University, SAIS in Washington, DC, with a specialisation in economics and international energy policy and holds an MBA from Vienna University of Economics and Business Administration.

Abdelkader Abderrahmane is a researcher and international consultant on African peace and security issues. He previously held a senior research position with the Institute for Security Studies in Addis Ababa, Ethiopia. Abderrahmane has written extensively on peace and security in the Sahel and Northwest Africa. He is also part of the London-based Brehon Advisory Ltd Board. He is the author of numerous articles and analyses such as "The Sahel: A Crossroads between Criminality and Terrorism (IFRI)" and "How Security Vacuum provided terrorists and Traffickers Fertile Ground in the Sahel" (Africa Center for the Study and Research on Terrorism).

Mohammed Akacem teaches economics at MSU Denver, Colorado, USA. His areas of research interests and teaching are political economy of the Middle East and North Africa as well as the geopolitics and economics of world oil markets. In addition to teaching, Dr. Akacem has published Op. Ed articles in

The Rocky Mountain News, The Denver Post, The Wall Street Journal, The Los Angeles Times, The Washington Times, and *The Christian Science Monitor*. He published his research in refereed and policy journals, such as the *Journal of South Asian and Middle Eastern Studies, Business Education Innovation Journal, Middle East Policy, Review of Islamic Economics, The Journal of Private Enterprise, OPEC Review*, and *Journal of Energy and Development*. He is currently jointly working on a book *"Why the status quo is unsustainable in MENA and how to address it."*

Mohamed Farid Azzi holds a PhD in Political Sociology and has been a senior researcher at the Emirates Center for Policy, Abu Dhabi, UAE, since 2003, where he supervises the department of public policy and opinion survey. In this quality, he initiates and coordinates project development, analyses findings, and provides recommendations aimed at informing public policies in the UAE. In this position, he carried out more than a hundred surveys and wrote numerous confidential and policy papers related to educational, political, and social issues. In addition to his research agenda, he contributed to chapters in edited books published under the name of the Emirates Center for Strategic Studies and Research, where he worked before joining the Emirates Policy Center. He previously taught at the department of sociology, the University of Oran, where he served as head of research at the Center of Social and Cultural Anthropology (CRASC).

Aomar Baghzouz is professor of political science at Tizi Ouzou University, Algeria, and president of the doctoral school at the Department of Politics. He is also an expert in the evaluation of research projects with the Ministry of Higher Education. He has taught, for many years at Batna and Algiers Universities as well as at the Institute of Diplomatic and International Relations (IDRI) of the Ministry of Foreign Affairs in Algiers. In 2015, he was a visiting fellow at Paul Cezanne University in Marseille (France). From 2007 to 2017, he was associate researcher at the Institute for Research and Study on the Arab and Muslim World (IREMAM-Aix-en-Provence). He has been a member since 2003 to date of the scientific committee and contributor to the French geopolitical journal, *Outre-Terre*. His research fields include Euro-Mediterranean relations, security and integration problems of the Maghreb, and democratisation processes in North Africa. He is the author of numerous works on these topics in scholarly journals, such as *L'Année du Maghreb*; *Outre-Terre*; *Maghreb-Machrek*; *Questions internationales*; and *Cahiers de la Méditerranée*, among others.

Saïd Belguidoum is associate professor in sociology at Aix Marseille University and researcher at the French National Center for Scientific Research (CNRS), IREMAM UMR 7310, 13094, Aix-en-Provence, France. He is the head coordinator of the Urban Research Center in Algeria (Pôle de la Recherche Urbaine en Algérie—PRUA), a multidisciplinary and cross-sectional network for researchers working in the city. He also manages several research programmes *Inconspicuous Globalization* in the Maghreb. His publications include books, review dossiers, and articles such as, "Made in China: Transnational trade and urban spaces around the Mediterranean basin," in *Les Cahiers d'EMAM*, 2015; "The Cities and Urbanity in the Maghreb," in *L'Année du Maghreb*, 2015; "Yiwu: The Creation of a Global Market Town in China," *Articulo—Journal of Urban Research*, 2015; *Les migrations vues du Sud*, 2017; and *La ville algérienne dans tous ses états: transition urbaine et nouvelles urbanités*, 2018.

Fatiha Dazi-Héni holds a PhD from the Institute of Political Studies in Paris. She obtained an MA in Political Studies on the Arab-Muslim World, from the Institute of Political Studies in Paris, a master's degree in the Arabic language and Civilisation, and another master's degree in Contemporary History of the Arab and Muslim World at the University of Sorbonne Paris III. Since October 2014, she has been a researcher on the Arabian Peninsula and the Gulf's regional and security issues at the IRSEM: Institute for Strategic Research of the Ecole Militaire (Military School) in Paris. She is an associate professor at the Political Institute of Lille. She is the author of numerous publications, such as "Saudi internal uncertainty and divergent GCC strategy"; "Rebuilding security in Libya, Syria, Iraq, and Yemen, in the Arab Reform initiative"; "Picking a quarrel with Qatar"; "The smaller GCC states' foreign policy and regional role," in *Orient IV/2016, Gulf Politics one year after JCPOA*.

Chérif Dris is professor at the National Higher Education School of Journalism and Information Sciences. He holds a PhD in Political Science; his areas of research include power and opposition parties in Algeria, Algerian media, and Algeria's political communication and regional policy. He published many articles in peer-reviewed journals and book chapters. Among his publications, one can cite "Rethinking Maghrebi security: The challenge of multilateralism." In Zoubir and Amirah Fernandez (Eds), *North Africa in Transition*, Routledge, 2008; "Maghreb: Internal security." In Zoubir and Dris-Aït-Hamadouche (Eds), *Global Security Watch*, 2013; "Algeria 2014: 'From the presidential election to the emergence of tycoons in the political game'." *L'Année du Maghreb*, 2015, "Politische Parteien In Algerien: Pluralismus In Einem Dominanten Präsidialsystem," In Fath, *Politische Parteien in Nordafrika. Ideologische Vielfalt – Aktivitäten- Einfluss*, 2017. Other articles were published in *l'Année du Maghreb, Maghreb-Machrek, Global Brief Magazine,* and *Question de Communication*.

Nardjes Flici is Associate Professor at the National Higher School of Political Science in Algiers, Algeria. Specialising in the management of international conflicts, her doctoral thesis, defended at the University of Bucharest, was entitled "Western Sahara: Last Colony of Africa"; her fields of research focus on the Mediterranean area and geopolitics. She has led, since 2016, a team of researchers as part of a broad research project, supported by the Ministry of Higher Education and Scientific Research; the theme of the research is preparing national defence in the face of new security threats, using Algeria as a case study. Her research focuses also on the study of different conflicts as well as on the security challenges in the Sahel Saharan band, and on terrorism and how and where against it, and defining the security priorities in the region. Her other research centres on international interactions around the Mediterranean.

Dalia Ghanem is resident scholar/researcher at the Carnegie Endowment for International Peace, Carnegie Middle East Center in Beirut. Prior to that, she was *El Erian* Fellow at the Carnegie after serving for 3 years as a political analyst at the same institution. Ghanem holds a PhD from the University of Versailles Saint-Quentin-en-Yvelines (France) and two master's degrees in political science, one of which was obtained from the Sorbonne (Paris I. France). She is an expert on political violence, Islamism, and the radicalisation process, with focus on Jihadism. She worked as a research assistant at the Center for Political Analysis and Regulation at the University of Versailles (France) and taught at Williams College (United States) prior to joining Carnegie. She has published extensively on political and extremist violence, Jihadism, and on Algeria. She has been a regular commentator on such issues in different Arab and international print and audio-visual media.

Youcef Hamitouche is professor of political science and international relations and president of the scientific committee of the Department of Political and Administrative Sciences at the University of Algiers 3, Algeria. His academic interests focus on international public policies, China in North Africa, security in the Sahara-Sahel region, as well the history, politics, society, and culture of the Middle East and North Africa. He authored many articles on Algerian civil society, Arabisation in Algeria, the hegemony of the English language in the world, and Algerian nationalism. His publications include, *Les sources de la culture politique et du discours politique d'après Messali El Hadj et Ferhat Abbas* and a book published in Italy on the *Impact of Illegal Immigration on Security in the Mediterranean Sea Region*. He has participated in many conferences around the world, including China, Italy, Finland, Belgium, France, Uppsala, Sweden, and Switzerland.

Aissa Kadri is professor emeritus of sociology, currently associate professor at EPN 12 CNAM and researcher at Laboratory UMR-LISE-CNAM/CNRS, Paris, France. He directed the Institute "Maghreb Europe" at University Paris 8 (2000–2012). He was a member of the National Commission of Universities (CNU) and the National French Committee of Research Evaluation (AERES) and member of the administrative board of the University Paris 8 (2000–2005). He directed the master's degree Euro-Mediterranean Relations/Maghreb World and research laboratory ERASME 3389. He authored and co-authored many books, such as *Enseignants et Instituteurs en Algérie* (2015), *Parcours d'intellectuels maghrébins* (1999), *Le retour de l'histoire, nationalisme et internationalisme en immigration: Messali Hadj* (2002), *Mémoires algériennes* (2004), *Enseignants issus des immigrations:*

l'effet génération (2006), *Lyon capitale des Outre-Mers: immigration des Suds et culture coloniale en Rhône – Alpes et Auvergne* (2007), *La guerre d'Algérie, revisitée, nouvelle génération nouveaux regards* (2015), as well as dozens of journal articles and book chapters.

Smail Khennas holds a PhD in Energy Economics from the Energy Institute of Economics and Energy Policy of Grenoble University, France. He has more than 35 years' experience in the field of energy policies and planning, renewable energy, and climate change. He has an in-depth theoretical and practical knowledge of the energy sector in Algeria and its evolution since the 1970s, notably as senior lecturer on energy economics at the Faculty of Economics of the University of Algiers, the coordination of the research group on alternative energies of the Research Center in Applied Economics for Development (CREAD, Algeria), and consultancies for leading national and international research centres and institutions. He was the coordinator of the UNDP regional programme on energy and poverty in Sub-Saharan Africa. He has authored or co-authored 10 books on energy policy in Algeria and developing countries and published more than 40 articles on this topic.

Souadou Lagdaf is assistant professor in the history of Islamic countries and the contemporary history of Arabic countries at the University of Catania in Ragusa (Italy). Her research interests include the history of the Western Sahara, the *sanusiyya* brotherhood in Libya, the social anthropology of customs, traditions, and religious commandment in Mauritanian society, as well as gender issues. She has published a book on the Western Sahara, entitled *La colonizzazione irrisolta, il Sahara Occidentale dalla Spagna al Marocco* (Unresolved colonisation, Western Sahara from Spain to Morocco), book chapters, and articles in scholarly journals. She is the co-author with Yahia H. Zoubir of "The Struggle of the Women's Movements in Neopatriarchal Libya" (2018), and the author of "The cult of the dead in Mauritania: between traditions and religious commandments," in the *Journal of North African Studies*. Her current research focuses on social rituals and religious commandments in Islamic religious schools in some Arab countries.

Ahmed Mahiou is professor of law, retired, former dean of the faculty of law and economics at the University of Algiers, former president of the International Law Commission of the United Nations, and member of the Institute of International Law. He has taught at many universities in several countries, including Algeria, France, Morocco, Tunisia, Lebanon, Egypt, Switzerland, Madagascar, Ivory Coast, Spain, and Italy. He is the author of a dozen works in domestic law (Administrative Institutions, Administrative Litigation, Office of University Publications, Algiers), international law [The Hague Academy of International Law (South-South Cooperation: Some Experiences of Integration, 1993, General Course on International Law, 2008], of more than one hundred articles in international law and International relations, 20 articles in administrative law and administrative science, and a dozen articles in constitutional law and science policy.

Hayat Messekher is associate professor of English at the Ecole Normale Supérieure of Bouzaréah, Algiers, Algeria, where she teaches pre-service teacher-trainees. Hayat holds a BA in English, an MA in Applied Linguistics, ELT from the University of Constantine (Algeria), a PhD in English Composition, and TESOL from Indiana University of Pennsylvania as a Fulbright Scholar. Her research interests include teacher education, TEFL/TESOL, second language writing, and quality assurance in higher education. Her publications include articles and book chapters on teacher identity, humanising pedagogy, cultural representations in Algerian English textbooks, linguistic landscape, education in Algeria, teaching research writing, and writing for publication. Hayat also serves as a consultant for the British Council Algeria where she manages a large portfolio of education and society programmes, including projects on the internalisation of higher education, social inclusion of youth, and governance.

Mohamed Miliani is professor of English at the University of Oran 2, Algeria. He holds a BA in English, a diploma in TEFL, an MEd, and a PhD from the University of Wales. He has been teaching at the University of Oran since 1974. He specialises in education, TEFL, and ESP. His research interests include sociolinguistics; education/training; TEFL; and languages in education. He published widely in these areas. He has contributed to numerous book chapters (about pre-schooling, languages in education, and education systems). He is research project lead in university ethics at the Centre for Research in Cultural and Social Anthropology (CRASC). He also serves as president of the Algerian Technical Committee for Education (UNESCO-Algeria). Currently, he is working on a project introducing a cross-cutting module on professional ethics for future teachers of foreign languages. He is a Higher Education Reform Expert (HERE) for the Erasmus+ programme in Algeria.

Fatma Oussedik is professor of sociology and urban sociology at the Department of Sociology, University of Algiers 2. She has taught at numerous universities in Europe, the United States, Africa, Pakistan, and the Middle East. Her publications include various books, most notably *Identité Féminine à Alger* (Female Identities in Algiers), *Relire les Ittifaqat* (Rereading the Ittifaqat) 2007, *Raconte-moi ta Ville* (Tell me about your City) 2008, *Mutations Familiales en Milieu Urbain* (Changing Families in Urban Environments) 2017, and others. Her research focuses on political minorities in Algeria, including Ibadis, gender issues, demographic transitions and their impact on women, and the youth. She is a member of various scientific committees across the Mediterranean. Her articles were published in the scholarly NAQD in Algiers. She has also contributed extensive studies on these issues in leading newspapers in Algeria and abroad. In 2019, she was the recipient of the Shared Knowledge Prize from Manouba University in Tunisia.

Nadji Safir is a sociologist who has conducted research in the social sciences since 1968, particularly at the Algerian Association for Demographic, Economic, and Social Research in Algeria. He taught sociology at the University of Algiers from 1979 onwards. From 1984 to 1995, he was Head of Department in the Office of the President, then at the National Institute of Global Strategy Studies. In 1996, he joined the African Development Bank. He has been a consultant since 2007. He has published books in Algeria and abroad, including *Essais d'Analyse Sociologique* (2 volumes). He contributed chapters to *Les Arabes du message à l'histoire, Le développement économique de l'Algérie, expériences et perspectives,* and *Le Maghreb à l'épreuve de la mondialisation* (co-editor). He published articles in *Revue des Mondes Musulmans et de la Méditerranée, Maghreb-Machrek, Futuribles, Alternatives Internationales, IEMed Papers, Confluences Méditerranée,* and *Les Clés du Moyen-Orient*. His current research focuses on transitions in the Maghreb, especially in Algeria.

Mohand Tilmatine is a professor of Berber languages and culture at the University of Cádiz, Spain, and has led since 2000 the research group HUM 685 *Arab and Berber Languages and Societies*. He holds professorships in various universities, such as The Free University of Berlin, the University of Cologne, the Universitat Autònoma of Barcelona, the School of Advanced Studies in the Social Sciences (EHESS), and completed different research stays in Paris (INALCO and EHESS), Canada (Toronto), and Oxford. His publications include books, such as *Les revendications amazighes dans la tourmente des "printemps arabes"* (2017), and articles in scholarly journals, such as *Études et Documents Berbères, Awal – Cahier d'Études berbères, Studi Africanistici, Studi magrebini, Revista Internacional de Lingüística Iberoamericana, Revista de Estudios Internacionales Mediterráneos,* and *International Journal of the Sociology of Language*. His current research focuses on identity and social movements in North Africa.

Rachid Tlemçani holds a PhD in Political Economy/Comparative Politics from Boston University, where he obtained his PhD in the 1980s. He has been teaching political science and world politics at the University of Algiers ever since. He has contributed regularly important studies to *El Watan* and *Le Soir d'Algérie,* leading newspapers in Algeria. His numerous publications include books, such as *State and Revolution in Algeria* (London), *Etat, Bazar et Globalization: L'aventure de l'Infitah en Algérie* (Algiers), and *Elections et Elites en Algérie* (Algiers), as well as scholarly articles. He has been visiting scholar at Harvard University, the European University Institute, Florence, Georgetown University, Carnegie, and the Nordic Africa Institute, Uppsala (Sweden). His current research focuses on civil-military relations in the MENA.

Yahia H. Zoubir is professor of international studies and international management and director of research in geopolitics at KEDGE Business School, France. He holds a PhD from the American University and coursework at Georgetown University in Washington, DC. He has taught in various universities in China, Europe, the United States, South Korea, Indonesia, India, and the MENA. His publications include books, such as *North African Politics*; *Building a New Silk Road: China & the Middle East*; *Global Security Watch—The Maghreb*; and *North Africa: Politics, Region, and the Limits of Transformation* and articles in scholarly journals, such as *Third World Quarterly, Mediterranean Politics, International Affairs, Journal of North African Studies, Middle East Journal, Journal of Contemporary China, Maghreb-Machrek*, etc. In 2019, he completed an extensive study, "Civil Strife, Politics, and Religion in Algeria," for the *Oxford Research Encyclopedia of Politics*. His current research focuses on China's and Russia's relations with the Maghreb countries and on Algeria's domestic and foreign policy.

INTRODUCTION

The making of a new republic?

Yahia H. Zoubir

Algeria is the largest country in the Arab world, Africa, and the Mediterranean basin, ranking 10th in the world in size; in the Islamic world, only Kazakhstan is bigger. It has the third-largest oil reserves in Africa and the world's tenth-largest gas reserves. Algeria has powerful, modern armed forces totalling 300,000, not counting the reserves. With a total annual spending of $10.4 billion, Algeria has the largest defence budget in Africa. The total boundaries with the seven neighbouring countries cover square 6,734 km, while it has a Mediterranean coast of more than 1,000 km. Although Algeria is not a regional hegemonic power, it is indisputably a middle power, as defined by some scholars of international relations (Cooper 2013, 25). The country has gone through a decade-long crisis in the 1990s; the civil strife claimed the lives of at least 100,000 people and caused more than 7,000 disappearances. However, it was able to elude the so-called "Arab Spring" (Aghrout and Zoubir 2016) that resulted in the collapse of some regimes and/or continued civil wars. While escaping the uprisings that swept through the region, Algeria faces instability along its long borders, not only in the Maghreb, but also in the Sahel. Algerian security forces have deployed along those borders to thwart threats from Al-Qaida in the Islamic Maghreb (AQIM) and the organisation of the Islamic State, among other terrorist organisations that continue to mushroom in the Maghreb-Sahel region.

Despite the seeming stability that prevailed in Algeria, on the eve of the February 22, 2019, powerful, unceasing nation-wide protests, the country still faces considerable political, economic, and security challenges. From 2012 onward, the Algeria system had not found a successor to the ailing ex-President Abdelaziz Bouteflika, an anomaly that had sclerotised Algeria's institutions as well as its diplomacy. The restructuration in 2015 of the intelligence services, one of the pillars of the regime, has yet to reveal the manoeuvrings inside the "black box," due to the well-known opacity that has characterised the system since the country's independence in 1962 (Zoubir 2019a). There have been important changes in the armed forces, which remained legalistic despite the increasing predominance of the self-styled presidential clan that ostensibly ruled the country in the shadows since the illness of the president who had not addressed the nation from May 2012 to his forced resignation on April 2, 2019.

Algeria has experienced a perpetual transition (Dris-Aït-Hamadouche and Zoubir 2009), highlighting a unique type of resilience of the regime in the region. Its economy is a rentier one; hydrocarbons represent more than 90% of the country's revenues. The redistribution of part of the rent allowed the regime to buy social peace and enable it to survive for some time. However, this peace rested on continued, regular, relatively high prices of oil. The drop of oil prices, coupled with the absence of a genuine productive economy, has enfeebled the stability of the system and the successive regimes. Unemployment among the youth remains high and the temptation of joining violent extremist groups, although latent, represents a genuine threat. In addition, while the appeal of Islamism and Jihadism had dwindled following the end of the armed insurrection and the policy of national reconciliation (1994, 1999, and 2005), this has not eliminated the root causes that have instigated the momentous uprising of 1988 and its aftermath. The country also faces questions of identities and human rights. Despite some liberal measures, the regime resorts to repressive measures when it feels threatened by civil society organisations. The political parties have little anchorage in society, even if they occasionally exerted a degree of pressure on the regime and denounced its obsolescence. The Bouteflika regime, though, had succeeded in co-opting many opposition parties and even the parasitic emerging business class, the so-called "oligarchs," who have made alliances within the structures of the state and increasingly influenced the state's domestic and foreign policy.

Events in the neighbourhood have strongly affected Algeria's national security. This has resulted in the continuous increase of the military budget. Indeed, with a total annual spending of more than $10 billion, Algeria has the biggest defence budget in Africa. Taking advantage of the hike in oil prices, its military spending more than doubled in the period 2004–2013, with an increase of 176%; the drop in the oil prices did not affect the defence budget allocation although a prolonged drop in oil prices might eventually influence military spending.

Given its regional importance, Algeria has succeeded in readjusting its multilateral and bilateral relations. Because of its experience in fighting terrorism, it has been able to work with a multitude of regional and international organisations in the prevention of terrorism. The fight against terrorism has become an important part of Algeria's relations with the United States, Russia, and European countries. Although relations with the West have been among the most important priorities of the regime, relations with China have increased considerably. China is today Algeria's main trading partner, supplanting France, the country's traditional economic supplier. The regime neglected the important relations with Africa for some time, although a resurgence of policies in Africa to counter the policies of its main regional rival, Morocco, following Bouteflika's disgrace, seems in the making.

Algeria experts do not all agree on what Algeria's future might be. This has triggered a rich debate regarding all aspects of this middle power. Scholars and non-scholars alike have shown, until the February 2019 events, a fascination for the robustness of the regime, especially since predictions about its downfall have each time proven wrong.

The idea for this book was germinating for many years. When the contributors were invited to contribute to this book in fall 2017, they were far from imagining the events that have unfolded since February 22, 2019. Although the crisis of the regime was unmistakable, few had expected Algerian society to be so robust as to compel the military's high command (État-Major Général), under the leadership of strongman Ahmed Gaïd Salah (AGS), to remove Bouteflika from power. Neither did they expect the launch of an anti-corruption campaign against Bouteflika's most powerful cronies, including the mighty head of intelligence, Mohamed "Tewfik" Médiène (1990–2015) and his successor Bachir "Tartag" Sahraoui.

Because the chapters in this book were written before those events, it is only rational that this Introduction provide an analytical overview of the origins of the crisis that has the potential of leading to what the Algerian protestors have dubbed the "second republic" (Zoubir 2019b). Analysing the current Algeria crisis is challenging, particularly due to Algeria's complex history. Yet, examining its genesis from a critical, historical viewpoint might enable one to decode at least some of the intricacies of the Algerian state and society and elucidate the current unfolding episodes without falling into the trap of journalistic narration. Such a method is essential in comprehending the progresses and wasted prospects, as well as the obstacles that Algeria has undergone since its independence in 1962. I will provide first a succinct synopsis of the period that preceded the existing crisis. I will also assess the twenty-year calamitous reign of Abdelaziz Bouteflika and scrutinise the root causes that have prompted the gigantic weekly marches since February 2019. The essay will also highlight the demands/grievances of the millions of demonstrators. I will also discuss how demonstrators enunciated those exigencies, which matured in response to the actions of the fragile government and the decisions of the military's high command, through its spokesperson, AGS. I will then focus on the issues regarding the prospects for a peaceful transition.

A misappropriated revolution

The conception of the Algerian political system, which Algerians today would like to see dismantled, saw its conceptualisation prior to the country's independence. No matter the variations that it might have taken, the foundation of the system has been fundamentally authoritarian; it reflected the nationalist movement's narrow vision, which made independence its exclusive slogan, without conceiving a rational, democratic socioeconomic programme for post-independence Because of the specific nature of the nationalist movement, the *Front de Libération Nationale* (FLN), whose claim to authority rested solely on historic rather than democratic legitimacy, became in 1963 the only lawful party. In this system, however, the FLN, officially entrusted with the task of controlling civil society, remained a mere transmission belt to the group (known as clan) or clans in power. Progressively, the FLN resorted to "inheritance capture" (see Safir's chapter in this volume); all kinds of opportunists usurped its historical legitimacy and filled its membership without regard to the interests of the nation. The FLN has served as a mere vehicle of control and repression in the hands of the ruling bloc (in the Gramscian sense), which wrested the reality of power. Lacking popular legitimacy and being suspicious of the masses, the regime instituted an entire administrative and political machinery to generate unanimous approval of its policies (*unanimism*) and repressed any type of opposition to its rule. Successive regimes sought to exert complete domination over every aspect of state and society (Zoubir 1999), for it needed to remain in power through an assortment of methods to preserve its rule, including seemingly liberal policies (Kilavuz 2017). The bloc in power (*le pouvoir* or the "deep state") was not only distrustful of institutions, but was also apprehensive of other rival clans, as well as society. Yet, notwithstanding the clan's totalitarian attempts, concurrent mechanisms (e.g., development of an informal sector—in which some dignitaries of the regime were and still are involved—dissidence in the guise of cultural demands, such as Islamism, Berberism, etc.) contested overtly and covertly the regime's policies, particularly during periods when the prices of oil dwindled (e.g., 1986, and since 2014) and the distribution of the rent became more difficult. A polarisation between state and civil society was the most perceptible corollary of the policies various regimes have practiced. The institutions in place have rarely represented the real interests of society. Instead, their real purpose has been to give the illusion of legitimacy and to prolong the power of the incumbent regime and of the nascent local oligarchy whose interests, linked to their patrons in the regime, were opposed to the masses. The power in place empowered clienteles within these institutions because of the factionalism that has been the hallmark of the system. Corruption, clientelism, nepotism, and favouritism best typify the system, which has also permeated society. Bouteflika's rule, in fact, represented the apex of the degeneracy of the system and at the same time the beginning of its downfall. The revelations of corruption following Bouteflika's removal from office on April 2, 2019, highlighted the unimaginable levels of corruption and illicit enrichment of officials and their collusion with the oligarchs.

The institutionalisation of this political system has had a persisting, damaging effect on any attempt of a genuine transition to a more democratic state and society. The regime's legitimacy of its continued rule drew from both the war of liberation (1954–1962), which had been eroded by the late 1980s (Zoubir 1996) and from the hydrocarbons revenues that served to co-opt society and political "opposition." Algeria is a rentier state that rebuffed introducing true economic reforms, for the rent ensured both social and political peace. Unsurprisingly, upheavals usually follow the drop of the oil prices when the regime can no longer keep its part of the bargain of the social contract or rather of the "rentier social pact" (Safir 2019; Safir in this volume) that ties it to society, i.e., the redistribution of part of the rent to the population and to the clienteles. Although the popular masses experienced substantial improvement in their standards of living, due to the large revenues from hydrocarbon earnings and an initially successful industrialisation programme (mainly in the 1970s), the gap between the masses and the wealthy class resulted in recurrent social discontent. The absence of democratic mechanisms forced Algerians to adopt attitudes of apathy towards the regime and its populist discourse, and to political life in general, thus strengthening the growing suspicions vis-à-vis the state and to totally mistrust the élites in power. The prevalent expression of this general dissatisfaction came in the form of passive resistance: complete apathy towards public affairs, strikes, riots, absenteeism, lack of civism, disrespect for state symbols, brain-drain, and illegal and legal migration of the youth. The low level of participation at the polls during presidential, municipal, and legislative elections since 2004 were proof, if need be, of this mistrust towards the system and indifference towards the regime in place.

The lost opportunities of negotiated pact transitions

The contention in this essay is that successive regimes have wasted opportunities to initiate genuine transitions to a more democratic state and a modern economy. I will argue that before Bouteflika's twenty-year rule (1999–2019), Algeria had missed two opportunities for a democratic transition, or at least for establishing a system based on good governance, rule of law, and political participation. The first was in 1976 when President Houari Boumedienne's regime had, despite its failings and its authoritarianism, fairly decent accomplishments, especially in the socioeconomic realm and when it elaborated a National Charter after relatively "democratic" public debates. Unfortunately, the regime reverted to authoritarianism soon thereafter; after his death, the process of de-Boumediennisation did not aim at ending the system, but at maintaining it through a different tactic. The second, more promising occasion happened after the October 1988 bloody riots. Similar to today, the rioters, though much less politicised than the generation of February 22, had called for the eviction of all officials whom they believed had betrayed the promises of the struggle for independence. They also demanded justice, the end of the *hogra* (bullying/injustice), and insisted on respect of their dignity (*karama*) and the enjoyment of full citizenship (Zoubir 1996). The liberalisation process that ensued in 1989, led by "reformers", what *transitologists* call "softliners" was quite promising since the authorities allowed for the creation of political parties and associations. That potential transition, however, failed mainly because the actors did not participate in a negotiated pact which would have clearly delineated the roles of the government and of the opposition parties, which had been legalised following the riots, and the military. A negotiated pact, as *transitologists* theorised in the 1980s (O'Donnell and Schmitter 1986, 40), would have made such transition possible, perhaps one unique in the Arab world. The absence of a negotiated pact before the fateful elections of 1990 and 1991, which saw the overwhelming victories of the unconstitutional, yet authorised, Islamic Salvation Front, was one of the primary reasons for the military's intervention in January 1992 and the civil strife that followed (Zoubir 1998). The strategy that the regime had pursued after the October events consisted of ousting a few of the most detested public figures and using the all too familiar stratagem: whereas the whole political system was de-legitimised, the regime sacrificed a few figures (the secretary-general of the FLN and the head of intelligence services), while the political system remained intact, notwithstanding the push of the softliners. The few alterations that the softliners had introduced remained superficial mainly because the regime obeyed the same logic: how to preserve the rule of the bloc (or clans) in power. Moreover, the reforms arrived at through a democratic, consultative debate; the few changes that the hardliners conceded resulted from the pressure emanating from "street" and the momentary tenacity of the softliners. The *pouvoir* (deep state) foremost objective in allowing them was to thwart further outbreaks from happening. Therefore, the reforms were rather fragile. More importantly, the burgeoning civil society was virtually ignored (Zoubir 1999). The reforms, from above, were part and parcel of the power struggle inside the regime and were launched, therefore, to help the perpetuation of the same old system. Overall, the changes could not result in the institutionalisation of a genuinely democratic state; their objective was simply to preserve the old one by giving it a "democratic" façade. In other words, the regime used the multiparty system it put in place in 1989 as a stratagem for survival and a shrewd way of controlling any opposition (Dris-Aït-Hamadouche and Zoubir 2009). The Islamist radicalism and the explosion of terrorist violence gave the regime the opportunity to reverse the progress made in 1989–1991. Indeed, the 5 years following the cancellation of the electoral process in 1992 witnessed a high level of political violence. To break the deadlock of violence, from the end of 1995 onward, the rulers implemented institutional normalisation (e.g., new Constitution in 1996, legislative elections in 1997, etc.). The regime alternated between authoritarianism and fragile, limited forms of "democracy." The ostensible transition period in which Algeria engaged lasted indefinitely; it had become a protracted "transition" with no end in sight, while the system remained unscathed. Since then, the Algerian political system has thus been neither democratic nor authoritarian in the strict definition of the concept. It was at best an illiberal democracy. Like many other regimes in the region, it corresponds to the hybrid types with different appellations, such as competitive, electoral, hegemonic, or semi authoritarian, although Bouteflika reintroduced into the system many characteristics of classical authoritarianism and neopatrimonialism.

Bouteflika's sultanistic power

While he was credited with re-establishing peace in the country through the Civil Concord (September 1999) soon after his questionable election in April 1999—the military had imposed him as the candidate; aware of the manoeuvre, the six presidential contenders withdrew on the eve of the election—and the Charter on National Reconciliation in 2005, it was in reality his predecessor President Liamine Zeroual, who had begun the *Rahma* policy (1994) whose objective was for the Islamist fighters to surrender and obtain amnesty. As well as the reinstatement of revolutionary legitimacy and the redistribution of the hydrocarbons revenues, restoration of peace and security served as the main sources of legitimacy of the Bouteflika regime. However, Bouteflika never intended on serving only two terms in office, as inscribed in the 1996 Constitution; neither was a genuine transition to democratic governance part of his plan (Zoubir 2000). Being confident about his "achievements," an expression that had become the mantra of his cronies, during his first and part of his second terms, Bouteflika introduced in 2008 amendments to the 1996 Constitution, adopted overwhelmingly by parliament, which removed the limit on the number of presidential terms, thus making Bouteflika a president for life (Aghrout and Zoubir 2009). As both commander in chief of the armed forces and defence minister, Bouteflika gradually forced to retirement senior officers and replaced them with officers loyal to him; he succeeded in reducing the military's political role not because he sought the erection of a civilian state, but because he wanted to increase his power vis-à-vis the military. His re-election in 2004 confirmed that, at least in appearance, he had succeeded in prevailing over the military and reducing greatly their role in politics. Unquestionably, perhaps unwittingly, after a while, the armed forces had become more professional, a professionalisation that, in fact, had begun in the 1990s. The armed forces gained from modernisation of their equipment, obtained thanks to a substantial budget, which reached more ten billion dollars almost annually. Nevertheless, while he seemingly imposed his power over the military, he did not fully control the intelligence services (Roberts 2007), although he managed to remove in late 2015 powerful Major-General Mohamed Médiene, alias "Toufik," who had headed the Directorate of Security and Intelligence (DRS) for 25 years.

Bouteflika ruled Algeria virtually unrestrained. From a conceptual perspective, his rule fell within the definition of neo-sultanistic regimes (Chehabi and Linz 1998), that is, neo-patrimonial regimes marked by personal rulership. Here, we retain the definition of Erdmann and Engel (2006, 18):

> Neopatrimonial rule takes place within the framework of, and with the claim to, legal-rational bureaucracy or 'modern' stateness. Formal structures and rules do exist, although in practice, the separation of the private and public sphere is not always observed. In other words, two systems exist next to each other, the patrimonial of the personal relations, and the legal-rational of the bureaucracy.

Indeed, Bouteflika used his power without restraint, at his own discretion, and above all uninhibited by rules or by any dedication to an ideology or value system. He surrounded himself largely with people he had chosen directly; those people were mainly members of his family, individuals from his (western) region, friends, business associates, or individuals who ensured that the system sustained itself. The position of Bouteflika's entourage grew from their total personal submission and allegiance to his person. Government officials acted as the personal servants of Bouteflika despite his incapacity to oversee government affairs, and they obtained their power solely from this relationship with Bouteflika or his brother from 2013 onward. The absence of rule of law and utter corruption were the hallmark of Bouteflika's regime. The responsibility of Bouteflika is considerable for these unlawful lootings, misappropriations, thefts, squandering, and illicit enrichment. Through his actions or inactions, he was primarily responsible for the corruption practices that pervaded the whole polity. The security services always informed Bouteflika about the investigations they carried out on his own ministers and other dignitaries connected to him. When he did not protect these associates, he encouraged them with his silence and complicity. When he saved them from justice, he encouraged them to continue dilapidating willingly or passively the country's assets. Under his sultanistic rule, corruption of ministers, senior civilian, or military officials had turned into an instrument of governance. There are abundant cases to support such observations. For instance, when security services submitted to him corruption files of various ministers, such as Chakib Khellil, the powerful Minister of Energy, he ignored those files and retained ministers who were involved in huge cases of corruption. In fact, officials who refused to drop charges against Khellil, for instance, were fired, as was the case in 2013 of Dr. Mohamed Charfi, Minister of Justice for issuing an international warrant against Khellil and insisting on keeping the charges against him (Mahmoudi 2013).

Bouteflika generally used the parliament as a rubber stamp for his policies, which the deputies, elected through mostly rigged elections and through clientelism, used it for the acquisition of privileges. To ensure their loyalty, support for the constitutional revisions, and for his candidacy for a third term (2009–2014), for instance, parliamentary deputies—and later governors and high government officials—received a 300% salary increase 2 months prior to the election, even though their salaries and benefits were already considerable compared to those of the average citizen. Opposition political parties—secular and religious—existed under his reign, but they have shown no proclivity for acceding to power. They were content with having representatives in the parliament in part because a portion of their salaries went to the parties' coffers. This explains why the population did not see the political parties as playing a consequential role in politics or their power to produce any change; the low turnout for the May 2012 and 2017 legislative elections and the 2014 presidential election confirmed this apathy towards the political system and incapacity to effect far-reaching transformation. Throughout his rule, Bouteflika endeavoured to domesticate civil society and tolerated only those organisations that championed his continued rule. Bouteflika ensured that he would remain president for life, although in 2016 an amendment to the Constitution reinstituted the two-term limit, which did not affect him. He created a total void around him and eradicated any authentic challenge to his power. Bouteflika succeeded in fragmenting political parties to thwart them from ever building a mass party like the Islamic Salvation Front, which was the first ever force to challenge the life of the regime (Zoubir and Aghrout 2012).

However, it would be erroneous to contend that there was no opposition to Bouteflika's régime. In fact, Algerians resisted in diverse methods (Zoubir and Dris-Aït-Hamadouche 2018), through autonomous unions or through dissents within the regime itself, as well as through limited riots or through low participation at the polls during elections; yet, Bouteflika and his cronies believed that they could co-opt Algerians through a redistribution of the oil revenues (cheap housing, food subsidies,…). Bouteflikists still held to this scenario even when the economy was at a dead end. While political analysts predicted the explosive situation (Zoubir 2016), and despite warnings from experts, the regime had no inkling as to the massive demonstrations that broke out in February 2019 and have continued until now (September 2019). Bouteflika's cronies were persuaded that since the country succeeded in dodging the so-called "Arab Spring" (Zoubir 2011), Algeria would overcome the economic predicament and control any wave of protests (about 500 riots a month). In fact, through their speeches, it became evident that officials were of the opinion that Algerians were uninterested in politics and would thus not attempt to launch massive demonstrations. Additionally, the regime warned Algerians continuously that any upheaval would result in catastrophic consequences. It referred to countries, such as Libya, Syria, or Yemen, overlooking the fact that more than 70% of Algeria's population is below 35 years old and that most of them have not experienced the bloody decade of the 1990s. Algerians had decided that it was time to overthrow the regime, cognizant that violence would be to the advantage of the regime, which could use the state of emergency to crush any rebellion.

The end of Bouteflikism or the end of the system?

As often happens in an oil rentier economy, the drop of prices mostly causes suffering for the people, especially the middle class and the underprivileged. The regime's disinclination all these years to transform a rentier economy into a productive one has come back to haunt it in exactly the way experts had predicted. The government had no other choice but to cut budgets, increase the prices of some goods, and reduce imports, almost similar to what the regime did after the oil slump in 1986 that resulted in the 1988 riots. After the collapse of the oil prices in 2014, the challenges worsened due to other factors, such as the extreme level of corruption and lack of accountability. Indeed, Transparency International's Corruption Perceptions Index 2018 ranked Algeria in the 105th place out of 180 countries (Transparency International 2019), and the World

Bank's *Doing Business 2019* puts Algeria at 157 out of 190 (World Bank 2019). Corruption scandals had rocketed, occasioning heavy costs for the country's economy, while angering the citizens. Bouteflika failed in transforming the rentier economy into a productive economy or diversifying it, maintaining Algeria as a one-commodity producer (hydrocarbons)—revenue from hydrocarbons account for about 60% of Algeria's Gross Domestic Product and 97% of foreign earnings. The regime resorted to the printing of money to survive the economic crisis, but this did not alleviate the impoverishment of the population. Regardless, officials continued to claim that under Bouteflika Algeria has been a beacon of stability and that the programme of austerity put in place would help overcome the crisis.

The demonstrations that broke out throughout the country in February 2019 merit an explanation. I posit that Bouteflika seeking a fifth term in office was only the spark; however, Algerians had accumulated grievances against the kleptocratic regime whose corruption had attained staggering proportions for years. Already in 2014, Algerians opposed Bouteflika's running the country. Despite his poor health (he suffered a stroke in April 2013), the regime maintained Bouteflika for a fourth term in April 2014; he campaigned for re-election through proxies (his cronies) since he could not walk or give speeches (his last speech to the nation was on May 8, 2012). Undoubtedly, the regime magnified Bouteflika's re-election results for a fourth presidential term; the alleged 51.7% rate of participation was much higher than it really was, as most observers asserted that the rate did not exceed 20%–25%. During the fourth term, the prospects of Bouteflika, whose health had deteriorated considerably—he moved on a wheelchair and seemed unconscious—seeking yet a fifth five-year term in office in 2019, was a perspective that shamed the regime and humiliated Algerians. Those loyal to his person because they profited from his rule wished that he would seek a fifth term despite calls in 2018 from many quarters that he should not; anyone who opposed the fifth term experienced reprisal. Through his powerful brother and special advisor Saïd Bouteflika and a constellation of cronies, including bureaucrats, government party members (National Liberation Front, National Rally for Democracy, Rally of Algerian Hope (TAJ), and Algerian Popular Movement), a few senior military commanders, the government workers' Union Générale des Travailleurs Algériens, all part of the so-called presidential clan that ran the country, Bouteflika declared on February 10 that he would run for a fifth term. This was in violation of the Constitution and an aberration considering his worsening health.

Disapproval to his candidacy for a fifth term did not derive from his violation of the Constitution—the regime has violated it at will—but mainly from the humiliation that Algerians had been suffering throughout his fourth term. It would be a grave mistake to underrate this element in decrypting the protests that began in Bordj Bou Arreridj on February 13 (with the slogan "Makach ouhda khamsa," "no 5th term"), then in Kherrata and Khenchela on February 16, 2019 (with the call "no to the 5th term of shame") before taking on a national dimension by the millions. In the Algerian mind, this form of shame or assault on their self-respect (as was the case under colonialism) has always prompted uprisings, though the timing is often unanticipated as was the case of the Berber Spring in April 1980 and in April 2001, or the October Riots in 1988, which had been preceded by limited demonstrations in 1986. In the social media, Algerians criticised harshly the president's appalling sporadic appearances (one or two a year). They were exasperated seeing officials offering a painting to Bouteflika's frame. The indignant conduct of his cronies disgusted Algerians who understood nonetheless that such insistence in keeping Bouteflika in power derived from the predation they were enjoying (access to contracts, high pay, and other privileges). In sum, Algerians felt that they had become the joke of the world.

The massive protests from February 22 onwards were striking by their peacefulness; the role of social media was considerable in passing the message of nonviolence. Obviously, the presidency would have preferred violent riots, so that hostility could force the military to intervene, as in October 1988, and impose a state of emergency. This was a serious miscalculation of the presidential clan for two main reasons. One, the military had made it clear that it would not intervene, signifying that the military institution had decided to forsake Bouteflika's regime. Two, the millions of marchers decided to conduct the demonstrations peacefully ("silmiya"), denying any justification for the security services to use force—the security forces themselves avoided the use of force. Actually, the most striking development was the advent of a powerful civil society, with incredible organisational, non-violent skills. No less astounding was the increasing politicisation of the movement. The determination of the regime to maintain the election strengthened the resolve of the protesters to oppose a fifth term for Bouteflika. Fissures within the regime multiplied; even state employees began denouncing the regime. More importantly, the armed forces showed signs of impatience with the Bouteflika clique. The head of the military Ahmed Gaïd Salah, although a long-time ally of Bouteflika, even raised the spectre of Art. 28 of the Constitution, part of which stipulates that, "[the National People's Army] shall also assume the task of protecting the unity of the country and the integrity of its land..." (Algerian Constitution 2016). One could only infer from this that the stubbornness of the president not to resign constituted a threat to the country's national security and therefore the armed forces would hold even his entourage accountable. Ahmed Gaïd Salah had now changed his position, claiming to be siding with the protesters who had kept the pressure to prevent a fifth term for Bouteflika. In fact, without this pressure and AGS' change of position, which was unmistakably the result of consensus inside the high military command to see Bouteflika renounce his candidacy of a fifth term, Bouteflika and his supporters would have clung to power indefinitely since his cronies had so many interests at stake. On March 26, AGS called for the application of Article 102 of the Constitution to force Bouteflika to resign. The article stipulates that, "When the President of the Republic, because of a serious and lasting illness, is totally unable to perform his functions, the Constitutional Council shall meet de jure and, after having verified the reality of the impediment by all appropriate means, it shall propose, unanimously, to Parliament to declare the state of impediment." The next day, the parties of the so-called Presidential Alliance, such as the FLN and RND, supported this call, hence confirming the fractures inside the regime. On April 2, under extreme pressure from the military, Bouteflika announced his resignation, not without seeking a last minute ruse to prolong his fourth term in lieu of the fifth one he had sought. Bouteflika's resignation did not stop the millions of protesters to persist in their weekly marches on Fridays and the students on Tuesdays.

Whilst the demonstrators focused on political issues, they have not ignored the economic demands. Indeed, the slogans include condemnation of corruption, inducement, and the rents that profit the regime's clienteles. Obviously, this raises the issue of the economy, which the Bouteflika regime has ruined, mostly due to its mismanagement. The oligarchs and high officials in the administration had swindled billions of dollars. Today, Algerians face challenging socioeconomic concerns; whatever the type of the government that will gain power, it will have to face the economic challenges. The economy is in dire need of diversification. The population has grown considerably in the last decades, while unemployment, especially among the youth, remains high. Since 2014, the government's ability to keep its end of the social contract has been broken because of the low oil prices, which have strained the country's public finances and reduced Algeria's reserves from $178 bn in 2014 to approximately $75 bn in 2019. In 2018, the budget deficit had reached 10.2% of the GDP and projected to be equal to 9.2% in 2019 (Ghanmi 2018). When the crisis erupted in 1988, Algeria's population was about 25 million; in 2019, it has reached 43 million, which means that it would be difficult to alleviate the grievances of Algerians through printing money that causes inflation. One of the major tasks of the new government will definitely be to engage in authentic reforms that would entice foreign direct investments and create jobs through a diversification of the economy. The Algerian crisis is multifaceted and better governance, perceptible enough by the population, is undoubtedly the best remedy. Civil society, which seemed weary before February 22, has understood the importance of sustained struggle for a more democratic system. Certainly, civil society, through representatives, has already produced proposals for a transition that would end the old regime which continues to resist and institute one based on genuine popular legitimacy. For instance, on June 12, 2019, civil society organisations met in Algiers and adopted a common roadmap for ending the crisis. Participants from different backgrounds opted for a transition period of 6 months to 1 year. They suggested the appointment of a presidential body or an agreed upon person to manage the transition. They also suggested the constitution of a government of national competence to manage daily affairs. The establishment of an independent commission to organise elections and proclaim the results would follow. The participants urged the opening of a global national dialogue involving the political class, civil society, national personalities, and activists of the popular movement. They asserted the necessity for a broad dialogue that would be "a prelude to a national conference to initiate a peaceful democratic transition on the basis of an electoral process that would represent the rupture with the existing system." To achieve a successful process, the participants insisted on the "preparation of a favourable climate, through the respect of individual and collective freedoms and the free practice of human rights" (Lina 2019; Makedhi 2019a). Other initiatives emerged since then and many proposals have come into sight. Lively debates are taking place in the media and even in the streets, occurrences that Algerians have not seen since the country's independence. On June 26, 2019, members of political parties, civil society organisations, independent trade unions, and intellectuals, held a meeting in Algiers to agree on a common platform for a transition to democracy. The meeting resulted in the issuance of a political resolution, entitled Political Pact for a Genuine Democratic Transition, in which the drafters denounced "the maneuvers of the government in the sole hope of defeating the flood of citizens and preventing any credible political alternative for radical democratic change" (Amir 2019). The signatories underlined the fact that, today, real power is assumed and exercised entirely by the army's general staff. The participants highlighted the preconditions for negotiations (with the authorities) and a genuine transition to democracy, which cannot happen without:

- The immediate release of all political and opinion detainees;
- The liberation of the political and media field;
- An immediate end to judicial harassment and threats against citizens, activists of political parties and their organisations, independent associations, trade unionists, human rights activists, and journalists;
- The immediate cessation of the squandering of national wealth and the recovery of looted property.

Furthermore, the signatories declared that this requires the organisation of a transition period that brings together the political means to express the true sovereignty of the people and the building of a democratic rule of law based on (*Pacte Politique* 2019):

- Independence of the judiciary;
- Separation and balance of powers;
- Non-use of religion, national heritage, and symbols of the nation for political purposes;
- Equality of rights between men and women;
- Non-use of violence for the conquest and exercise of power;
- Right of association and trade union organisation subject only to the declaratory regime;
- Right of assembly, organisation, and demonstration;
- The state's guarantee of citizens' fundamental social and economic rights;
- Recognition of individual, collective, and trade union freedoms and the right to strike;

- Popular sovereignty over the nation's natural resources;
- Recognition of the role of the state in the conduct of national development and the fight against socio-economic inequalities and poverty; and,
- Respect for all pluralisms.

This, of course, represents only one of the many attempts Algerians have initiated with the hope that the military institution would support the transition, without, however, interfering in the process whose main objective is to erect a democratic, civilian state.

The forum on national dialogue

On July 5, 2019, which also marked the fifty-seventh anniversary of the country's independence, an estimated twenty million Algerians took to the streets throughout the country. In addition to the earlier demands, they called for the freeing of those arrested the previous weeks, including a hero of the war of independence. The most repeated slogans referred to the capture of the state by fake revolutionaries who usurped the Algerian Revolution for their own economic interests. They reiterated that no transition would be possible while those who were responsible for Algeria's predicament are still in the government. Thus, most Algerians rejected the holding of the forum on national dialogue, which brought together some political parties that had collaborated with the old regime; unsurprisingly, the forum received negative feedback from the movement as was evident through the social networks. This despite the forum's participants' call for the "recognition [by the regime] of the legitimate demands of the popular movement, the exclusion of the symbols of the former regime, the opening of the political and media field with the lifting of all constraints." In the text which the participants published also listed other crucial actions, including securing the popular marches [some limited police brutality was evident on July 5] and stopping the harassment of demonstrators [seizure of the Amazigh flag], respecting individual and collective freedoms, stopping arrests, and respecting the principle of free and independent justice. The conference participants also insisted on the need to establish a government of national competence and the exclusion of political officials involved in corruption (Makedhi 2019b). The perception, however, among the general public is that the regime concocted the conference since the participants espoused, at different degrees, the roadmap that AGS and the interim president of the state have supported. The leader of the forum, Abdelaziz Rahabi, a former, well-respected diplomat, was fully aware of the difficulties that the potential transition faces:

> "Algeria is in a political deadlock with unpredictable consequences," says Rahabi, who was one of the architects of the national dialogue conference held Saturday in Algiers. "No authority in Algeria, neither the presidency of the Republic, nor ourselves, nor the political forces, is in a position to set a date for the holding of the presidential elections."

He also added that,

> The election date is not the key to the solution. The key to the solution is the overall political agreement between the political forces and an environment that gives Algerians the feeling that they are going into a clean election, that their votes will not be diverted, that things have changed and that the country is truly entering a democratic electoral process (*Algérie Patriotique* 2019).

Rahabi insisted, like do transitologists, that Algeria needs "a political, negotiated, consensual and peaceful solution" (Cited in *Radio Algérie* 2019); this presupposes that a minimum of trust between the popular movement and the authorities be established. It remains to be seen whether the social movement (*Hirak*) can trust the authorities and whether the latter are willing to reach compromises and to initiate a genuine transition to a democratic political system. It remains also to be seen whether these conditions are met and whether the *hirak* will eventually produce its own representatives to negotiate a transition with the holders of real power, that is, the high command of the armed forces. As of this writing (late August 2019), the protest movement has gone unabated and the deadlock between civil society and the high military command has continued.

Conclusion

The ongoing peaceful revolution marks an extraordinary turning point in Algeria's post-independent history. Algerians have shattered the hybrid, yet robust, authoritarian regime that had wounded their dignity and defamed the reputation of their nation. They are now fighting for a genuinely democratic republic. Certainly, today, the most important challenge is to keep the momentum in the movement's demands and to continue addressing the difficult questions of the transition to this second republic. Protesters have made radical demands, but, like most successful transitions have shown, they still need to dialogue with some members of the old regime, that is, those that have simply served the state and did not engage in corrupt practices. Lively debates are frequently held in universities—which had lost their role of centres of knowledge and ideas in the last 20 years—and among some respected national figures to work out transition strategies. Since one of the pillars of the system has been the military, the main question is what role the armed forces will play during this transition. Some Algerian intellectuals are convinced that the "ANP is determined not to supervise, control or supervise the profound social change that Algerians are undergoing (because that is not its role) but to guarantee its effectiveness and success" (Mebroukine 2019). Should Algeria succeed in this transition, it would certainly disprove the *transitologists* who have focused on the so-called "Arab exceptionalism" (Goldsmith 2007; Stepan and Robertson 2005). For the moment, this seems to be the case. But, undoubtedly, Algerians will certainly have to prevent the old regime from stealing the revolution like it did prior to independence (the coup against the Provisional Government of the Algerian Republic in 1961), at independence in 1962 when the so-called Group of Oujda captured the independent state, and after the riots of October 1988, when the system concocted a façade democracy to guarantee its endurance.

References

Aghrout, Ahmed and Zoubir, Yahia H. 2009 (April 1). "Introducing Algeria's President for Life." *Middle East Report Online.* https://merip.org/2009/04/introducing-algerias-president-for-life/.

Aghrout, Ahmed and Zoubir, Yahia H. 2016. "Algeria: Reforms without change?" In *North African Politics: Change and Continuity*, edited by Yahia H. Zoubir and Gregory White. London: Routledge, pp. 145–155.

Algerian Constitution. 2016. http://www.conseil-constitutionnel.dz/pdf/Constitutioneng. pdf.

Algérie Patriotique. 2019 (July 7). "Abdelaziz Rahabi: Aucune autorité ne peut fixer la date de la présidentielle dans le contexte actuel." https://www.algeriepatriotique. com/2019/07/07/abdelaziz-rahabi-aucune-autorite-ne-peut-fixer-la-date-de-la-presidentielle-dans-le-contexte-actuel/ (accessed July 7, 2019).

Amir, Nabila 2019. *"Les forces politiques plaident pour une transition: Le pacte des democrats."* El Watan. 2019 (June 27). https://www.elwatan.com/a-la-une/les-forces-politiques-plaident-pour-une-transition-le-pacte-des-democrates-2-27-06-2019 (accessed June 28, 2019).

Chehabi, Houchang E. and Linz, Juan J. (Eds.). (1998). *Sultanistic Regimes.* Baltimore, MD: Johns Hopkins University Press.

Cooper, David A. 2013. "Somewhere Between Great and Small: Disentangling the Conceptual Jumble of Middle, Regional, and 'Niche' Powers," *Journal of Diplomacy & International Relations*, 14 (2): 23–35.

Dris-Aït-Hamadouche, Louisa and Zoubir, Yahia H. 2009. "Pouvoir et opposition en Algérie: Vers une transition prolongée," *L'Année du Maghreb* 2009. Paris: CNRS, pp. 111–127.

Erdmann, Gero and Engel, Ulf. 2006. "Neopatrimonialism Revisited-Beyond a Catch-All Concept." GIGA Research Program: Legitimacy and Efficiency of Political Systems, N° 16 February 2006. https://core.ac.uk/download/pdf/71729549.pdf (accessed June 26, 2019).

Ghanmi, Lamine. 2018. "Algerian Government Pursues High Spending for 2019 as It Eyes Elections." *Arab Weekly.* (September 16). https://thearabweekly.com/algerian-government-pursues-high-spending-2019-it-eyes-elections (accessed June 5, 2019).

Goldsmith, Arthur A. 2007. "Muslim Exceptionalism? Measuring the 'Democracy Gap.'" *Middle East Policy*, 14 (3): 86–96.

Kilavuz, T. 2017 (May 2). "Reconfiguring the Algerian Regime: On the Stability and Robustness of Authoritarianism in Algeria." *Al-Sharq Forum.* https://research. sharqforum.org/2017/05/02/reconfiguring-the-algerian-regime-on-the-stability-and-robustness-of-authoritarianism-in-algeria/.

Lina, Sarra. 2019 (June 16). "La société civile adopte sa feuille de route et se prépare pour le dialogue." *Algérie Patriotique.* https://www.algeriepatriotique.com/2019/06/16/la-societe-civile-adopte-sa-feuille-de-route-et-se-prepare-pour-le-dialogue/.

Mahmoudi, R. 2013 (September 16). "Limogé pour avoir assumé l'affaire Khelil et refusé de mêler la Justice aux chamailleries du FLN." [Fired for taking on the Khelil case and refusing to involve Justice in the FLN's squabbles] *Algérie Patriotique*. https://www.algeriepatriotique.com/2013/09/16/limoge-pour-avoir-assume-laffaire-khe-lil-et-refuse-de-meler-la-justice-aux-chamailleries-du-fln/ (accessed September 17, 2013).

Makedhi, Madjid. 2019a (June 16). "La société civile adopte son initiative consensuelle: Quatre étapes pour sortir de l'impasse actuelle." *El Watan*. https://www.elwatan.com/edition/actualite/la-societe-civile-adopte-son-initiative-consensuelle-quatre-etapes-pour-sortir-de-limpasse-actuelle-16-06-2019 (accessed June 16, 2019).

Makedhi, Madjid. 2019b (July 7). "La présidentielle comme moyen de sortie de crise: Les partisans du dialogue posent leurs conditions." *El Watan*. https://www.elwatan.com/a-la-une/la-presidentielle-comme-moyen-de-sortie-de-crise-les-partisans-du-dialogue-posent-leurs-conditions-07-07-2019 (accessed July 7, 2019).

Mebroukine, A. 2019 (April 17). "L'Armée accompagnera le changement voulu par les Algériens." *Le Matin d'Algérie*. https://www.lematindalgerie.com/larmee-accompagnera-le-changement-voulu-par-les-algeriens (accessed April 18, 2019).

O'Donnell, Guillermo and Schmitter, Philippe C. 1986. *Transitions from Authoritarian Rule-Tentative Conclusions about Uncertain Democracies*. Baltimore, MD: The Johns Hopkins University Press.

"Pacte politique pour une véritable transition démocratique." *El Watan*. 2019. https://www.elwatan.com/edition/actualite/pacte-politique-pour-une-veritable-transition-democratique-27-06-2019 (accessed June 27, 2019).

Radio Algérie. 2019 (July 7). "M. Abdelaziz Rahabi: face « aux conséquences imprévisibles » de l'impasse politique, il y a urgence à parvenir à un accord global." http://radioalgerie.dz/news/fr/article/20190707/174043.html (accessed July 7, 2019).

Roberts, Hugh. 2007. "Demilitarizing Algeria." *Carnegie Paper No. 86*. Washington, DC: Carnegie Endowment for International Peace, p. 15. https://carnegieendowment.org/files/cp_86_final1.pdf (accessed May 31, 2007).

Safir, Nadji. 2019 (April 3). "Algérie 2019: une crise majeure." *Diploweb.com: La Revue géopolitique*. https://www.diploweb.com/Algerie-2019-une-crise-majeure.html (accessed April 4, 2019).

Stepan, Alfred and Robertson, Graeme B. 2005. "Arab, Not Muslim Exceptionalism," *The Journal of Democracy*, 15 (4): 140–146.

Transparency International. 2019. "Corruption Perceptions Index 2018." https://www.transparency.org/country/DZA (accessed June 25, 2019).

World Bank. 2019. "Doing Business In 2019—Training for Reform: Economy Profile Algeria." https://www.doingbusiness.org/content/dam/doingBusiness/country/a/algeria/DZA.pdf (accessed June 23, 2019).

Zoubir, Yahia H. 1996. "The Failure of Authoritarian Developmentalist Regimes and the Emergence of Radical Protest Movements in the Middle East and Africa: The Case of Algeria," *Journal of Third World Studies*, 13 (1): 127–184.

Zoubir, Yahia H. 1998. "The Algerian Political Crisis: Origins and Prospects for Democracy," *Journal of North African Studies*, 3 (1): 75–100.

Zoubir, Yahia H. 1999. "State and Civil Society in Algeria," In *North Africa in Transition: State, Society, and Economic Transformation in the 1990s*, edited by Zoubir, Yahia H. Gainesville, FL: University Press of Florida, pp. 29–42.

Zoubir, Yahia H. 2000. "Algerian Democratic Transition under Bouteflika's Rule: One Step Forward or Two Steps Back?" *Civil Society* (Cairo, Egypt), 9 (101): 4–9

Zoubir, Yahia H. 2011 (October 20). "Arab Spring: Is Algeria the Exception." *EuroMeSCo-IEMed Policy Brief*, No. 17. https://www.euromesco.net/publication/the-arab-spring-is-algeria-the-exception/.

Zoubir, Yahia H. 2016 (February). "Algeria after the Arab Spring." *Foreign Affairs*. https://www.foreignaffairs.com/articles/algeria/2016-02-09/algeria-after-arab-spring.

Zoubir, Yahia H. 2019a. "Algeria." in *Politics & Society in The Contemporary Middle East*, Edited by Michele Penner Angrist, 3rd Edition, Lynne Rienner Publisher, pp. 189–216.

Zoubir, Yahia. 2019b (May 21). "The Algerian Crisis: Origins and Prospects for a 'Second Republic'". *Al Jazeera Centre for Studies*. http://studies.aljazeera.net/en/reports/2019/05/algerian-crisis-origins-prospects-republic-190520100257161.html.

Zoubir, Yahia H. and Aghrout, Ahmed. 2012. "Algeria's Path to Political Reforms: Authentic Change?" *Middle East Policy*, 19 (2): 66–83.

Zoubir, Yahia H. and Dris-Aït Hamadouche, Louisa. 2018. "Algérie: résistances et contre-résistances," *Alternatives Sud. État des luttes-Moyen-Orient et Afrique du Nord: Points de vue du Sud*, 25 (4): 109–116.

PART I

Domestic issues

1

ALGERIA IN THE 2000s

A rentier system in crisis

Nadji Safir

Introduction

The social movement that began in Algeria in mid-February 2019 is in all respects a decisive turning point in the country's life since it constitutes a direct form of challenge to the authoritarian system that has prevailed since the country's independence in 1962. To be better understood, the events currently underway must be placed in the context of the rentier model that can be identified and that is structured around the functioning of two systemic rents: one linked to the international valuation of hydrocarbons and the other to the instrumentalisation of national history. After a long phase of latent crisis, this model has now entered into an open crisis and directly raises the question of what prospects are currently, that is in 2019, available to Algerian society.

Since the early 2000s, Algeria entered a new phase in its post-independence history, one marked by political and economic uncertainty. This is due to the combination of three factors: firstly, the sharp decline in the different manifestations of armed violence that characterised the 1990s, most of which had their origins in the actions of various Islamist terrorist groups which had been operating in the country for a long time. This process culminated in the adoption by referendum of fundamental texts, such as Dutour (2008), promoting the emergence of the conditions for a national consensus in favour of civil peace (Zoubir & Dris-Aït-Hamadouche 2013, 104). Secondly, a significant increase in the state's financial resources (the fiscus) linked to a better valorisation of hydrocarbons. These were exported to a world market which had a strong demand for raw materials until the economic downturn in mid-2014. Thirdly, the election in April 1999 of Abdelaziz Bouteflika, who had created a personality cult and whose management of state affairs was authoritarian.

The dynamics of these three factors distinguish the 2000s as a critical phase in the country's history.

In addition, certain modalities of the Algerian political system must also be analysed because of their unique specificities and their direct consequences on the issue of the relationship between society and the state. These include the exceptional conditions under which President Bouteflika was able to stand for a fourth term in the April 2014 presidential election. That election took place not only after the 2008 constitutional revision, which had removed the two-term presidential term limit; but also, and quite extraordinarily, allowed him to stand after the stroke he suffered in April 2013. This was an important event, which, because of the obvious deterioration in his health and with regard to the constitutional and legal provisions in force, should have led to his disqualification as a candidate. However, not only was his candidacy accepted by the Constitutional Council, but because of the severe limitations on President Bouteflika's ability to engage in the electoral debate as an autonomous political actor, this validation resulted in an unprecedented electoral campaign during which he made no public appearance.

After having had a stroke, Bouteflika appeared unable to assume his official duties. Despite this uncertain context and against all probability, on February 2, 2019, the four parties forming the Presidential Alliance officially announced that they supported Bouteflika's candidacy for a fifth presidential term in April 2019. He would therefore be able to assume the presidency.

The effect of the events since mid-February 2019 resulted in the emergence of conditions ripe for an ongoing popular revolt against the authoritarian political system. It is therefore necessary to consider all the conditions that have enabled such a unique political opportunity for Algerian society and that contribute to Algerian reactions.

A paradigm fundamentally structured by two systemic rents

The central hypothesis in this chapter, part of an approach to deconstructing the existing model, is based on the economic rent dynamics that underlie the development of Algerian society. These stem from the logical functioning of two closely linked systemic patterns of rent: the first is exogenous, energetic, economic in nature, and of extractive origin and the second is endogenous, political, symbolic in nature and of historical origin.

If we try to deconstruct the relationship between society and the state, we are dealing with a model structured by all the dynamics and synergies generated by these two logical patterns of systemic rent.[1] They permeate the social dynamics operating within the society as a whole, and not only the economy, and the state, as well as in the close relations they maintain. They are characterised by the existence of an implicit social rentier pact that has been active since the 1970s. During the 2000s, this would be strengthened and function as a structuring paradigm at the heart of all the issues denoting the country's developments. In any event, the main identifiable logic and dynamic make it possible to qualify both the state as a rentier, within the meaning of the problems defining the notion of "rentier state" (Mahdavy 1970; Beblawi 1990); and also society as "seeking a rent, within the meaning of the notion of 'rent seeking society'" (Krueger 1974). The political problem here is that the logic underlying the real functioning of the state is neopatrimonial (Eisenstadt 1973).

A systemic, exogenous, and energetic rent, economic in nature and of extractive origin

The extraction and exploitation of oil and gas and their export are the economic bedrock of Algeria. Recalling the productive and imperishable capacities of natural agents that the eighteenth century economist David Ricardo mentions—from the difference between the direct and indirect costs linked to the extraction and exploitation of oil and gas—are factors linked to the conditions of the country in which production takes place and therefore, of an endogenous nature. Added to those are transport issues, that is their transport to the places of consumption. The selling price, that is the price at which the products concerned will finally be sold, is in the context of the contemporary economy, a necessarily exogenous variable, since it evolves according to the conditions in the world market. Hydrocarbons dominate Algeria's economy and have formed a major part of the country's macroeconomic balance. During the period from 2000 to 2014, that is until the decline in oil prices on the international market, they represented a significant percentage: from 30% to 40% of the gross domestic product per annum, about 65% of the financial resources of the state budget, and around 97% of the total value of exports. Over the entire period considered, this constitutes revenues to the order of 800 million to 1,000 billion current US dollars, according to various estimates. Because of the predominant role of public spending in macroeconomic policy, as well as the predominant role it plays in actions initiated and implemented by a private sector that is dependent on this same expenditure because of structural mechanisms, a large part of the gross domestic product is driven by hydrocarbons. At the same time, hydrocarbons are practically the only product that allows the country to access international markets to obtain supplies for its domestic demand, including essential needs for the population (medical supplies, foodstuffs, etc.).

A systemic, endogenous, and political rent, symbolic in nature and of historic origin

Though this may seem less obvious than in the case of energy, it is equally real and identifiable. As with hydrocarbons, this rent will follow a logic according to which it uses an existing source of this type of capital to accumulate symbolic, not economic capital. The process of formation and development is linked to the demand generated within the framework of an essentially national market. In this case, it will be all the symbolic capital accumulated by the entire Algerian people during two successive historical phases, the National Movement (in the twentieth century, before 1954) and, in particular, the National Liberation War (1954–1962) because of the resistance to and struggle against French colonial rule conducted in those periods. Through successive processes of memorisation, accumulation, and valorisation, these have been both transformed within individual and collective consciences and memories into equivalent sources of a socially significant, legitimate, and valued symbolic capital, as well as necessarily discriminating in terms of positions, strategies, and social practices (Bourdieu 1994). As in the case of rents from hydrocarbons, the potential source from which the symbolic political rent of historical origin is built is also a non-renewable source, consisting of historical events that cannot be replicated. In both cases, the non-renewable nature of the resource is a core value and therefore of a high level of the rent thus generated. Thus, all the participants establishing or seeking to establish a direct and significant link to the War of National Liberation will do everything possible to obtain an increase in the capacity for symbolic capital accumulation. As an important source of social legitimacy, this aims to strengthen their negotiating power in various activities in order to facilitate their access to more wealth (mainly in the economic field) and/or more power (mainly in the political field).

Political power may be analysed as a state bureaucracy which, from the point of view of this elite, benefits from two rents. This has political importance as it guarantees their legitimacy and therefore the sustainability of their power and is also of an economic nature, as a means to achieve the ultimate objective of controlling political power for as long as possible.

In this respect, one of the best illustrations is the situation of the National Liberation Front (FLN) party, whose successive leaders have long since been instrumentalising national history, positioning themselves in a completely abusive way. This is the true logic of "inheritance capture,"[2] and the embodiment of what the FLN was able to represent during the historical phase 1954–1962.[3] However, there is a clear distinction between the revolutionary FLN which the Algerian people have "sworn in," to use the terms used in the text of the poem "Kassamen" (adopted as the national anthem after independence) and the FLN which, since 1962, has functioned as a state party. In fact, the interim secretary-general of the National Organization of the Mujahideen War Veterans, Mohand Ouamar Benlhadj, called on June 12, 2019, to return the acronym of the National Liberation Front (FLN) to Algerians, and thus put the former single party in the museum. He accused members of the FLN of having usurped the acronym to serve their own interests (Métaoui 2019). Since 1989, this FLN has become one of the many political parties operating in the country and the main component of the "presidential majority," the basis of the ruling political regime. There remains only a tenuous thread between these two iterations that offers little basis for the official thesis of continuity, which is increasingly contested among younger generations[4] and genuine war veterans.

In much the same way, as a direct beneficiary of political rent, another institution that should also be mentioned is the National People's Army (ANP), which fundamentally positions itself as the direct heir of the National Liberation Army. By continuing to benefit from the positions acquired since the various institutional *coups de force* in which its representatives were involved, both during the National Liberation War and in the summer crises of 1962, the ANP still holds a dominant position in the political field. In fact, this gives it the status of a major political player acting, since 1962, as the true holder of political power of last resort.

Codifying the relations between the state and society, these foundations will be laid in a rentier ecosystem essentially determined by the logic linked to the two systemic rents of energy and politics. This pact, which involves a triad of society, rent, and government, can be summarised as follows: firstly, with regard to energy rent, the state has the exclusive monopoly on the modalities of its management and undertakes to ensure the widest and most equitable redistribution possible of energy rent to society in various forms. This approach is effectively aimed at establishing a kind of welfare state. In exchange for this policy the state ensures, as delegated manager, a broad and equitable redistribution of resources which, by definition, are supposed to belong to the whole society. Thus society, as the principal beneficiary, cannot easily contest the way in which the state defines the main public policies that guide the country.

Secondly, as far as political rent is concerned, the state poses itself as its own ultimate regulator. Indeed, since national independence, it has presented itself as the legitimate direct heir to all national history, as considered on the "long term." This has particular reference to the two founding phases of the twentieth century: the National Movement and the War of National Liberation. Consequently, the state considers that at the very heart of its sovereign powers, there exists a set of issues postulated as part of its monopoly and, even today, still presented as part of its various prerogatives and privileges which all revolve around the central objective of preserving the social legitimacy of political rent.

A society built around a broad rent consensus

Because of the rentier logic irrigating both society and the state as well as their mutual relationship, there is a gradual process of social metastasis. The effect of this logic extends to all sectors of activity and to a large extent determines the behaviour of all the actors. Each of them, directly or indirectly, lives in an environment affected by these different rentier logics, and they end up internalising these principles, assuming them as their own, and integrating them into their practices. The basic principle remains that of minimising efforts and maximising the results obtained, because all the rentier logics have contributed decisively to the way in which individuals and groups have developed during successive socialisation processes. These are the *"habitus"* (Bourdieu 2000), which will singularise them and characterise their social practices.

Origins of the popular revolt against the authoritarian system

The operating conditions of the long-standing dual-rentier pact had ensured relative stability for the political system since the early 2000s. Nevertheless, its positive effects were exhausted because of the direct and indirect effects of two sets of interrelated factors.

First, those linked to a structural evolution led to the inevitable exhaustion of the dual rentier model. By definition, these were engaged in a race against time because of the exhaustion of its two sources of income, energy and historical legacy. The effect was declining social efficiency, both non-renewable and affected by a sustainable scissors effect. In terms of energy supply, the stock of hydrocarbons in the country has only limited prospects for significant positive development. In terms of demand, the potentially profitable population can only grow from around 43 million in 2019 to 57.5 million inhabitants in 2050, greatly limiting the margins for political power to manoeuvre in terms of redistributing the rent to meet the demands of society. The second factor is that of history, and in terms of supply, the stock of historical legitimacy, too, can only decrease irreversibly. It has fewer tangible realities assumed by living carriers and is more and more a symbolic register of collective and individual memories. In terms of demand, the historical legacy has a decreasing hold on a young population—today, half of the population is under 27 years of age—which is less and less sensitive to the official discourse. This official history evokes realities that the youth has never really known, and, for their part, they express a strong demand for a future dispensation that they cannot envisage in real terms.

However, this structural evolution, which is moving towards a gradual exhaustion of the positive effects of the dual rentier model, accelerated due to the direct and indirect consequences of the drastic drop in oil prices in 2014. This counter-shock saw the level of the country's energy income drastically reduced with dramatic consequences for the social efficiency of the redistribution processes that had been undertaken.

The emergence of a deep social malaise was particularly noticeable among the youth. It was driven by an economic and social policy that seriously underestimated the challenges around diversifying the national economy and, ipso facto, creating jobs, particularly for young people. However, in addition to the phenomenon of unemployment, many categories of the population exist in a precariat position on the economic fringes. Official statistics indicate that in 2015 there was a work-force of 4,347,000 marginalised people consisting of non-permanent and apprentice employees, live-in caregivers, and the unemployed whose economic status is unstable. This is an important youth component, and they can be essentially defined as living in a situation of greater or lesser vulnerability in terms of employment, whatever the various forms this vulnerability may actually take—unemployment, underemployment, non-permanent employment, or employment in the informal economy. This includes work that is more or less formalised, but that is poorly paid and justifies the designation of the working poor.

The social group thus constituted is composed mainly of young people, whose social status can be designated as precariat.[5] The current (2019) estimate, based on the various data available and personal estimates, is that this group consists of around 5 million people, mostly young males.

The growing importance of this precariat presence in society can be seen, in particular, in everything related to football competitions, one of the main leisure activities of the social groups in question. And so, in the absence of a public space open to democratic expression, football club supporters' organisations and their stadiums have become the new forums in which a very strong hostility to the regime's policy is expressed. Most young people, and in particular those living in precarious circumstances on the fringes, consider the political regime to be a gerontocratic entity taking no account of the aspirations of youth. This antipathy has been expressed regularly by various means, including songs that have become a genuine social phenomenon.

The two main sets of factors identified thus far are linked and consist of unemployment in general, and youth unemployment in particular. With all the consequences these entail, they are the direct products of an economic and social policy which, in a short-term vision favouring redistribution with a view to buying social peace at all costs, has neglected the necessary investments in the productive sectors. These alone can create conditions leading to the sustainable emergence of viable jobs so badly needed.

In this increasingly unstable economic and social context, and even as an already highly hypothetical fourth term was coming to an end, the announcement on February 10, 2019, of President Bouteflika's candidacy for a fifth presidential term appeared to the vast majority of the population as an obvious form of hubris. Above all, it appeared to be a strictly private appropriation of the highest institutional levels of the state and was an unacceptable provocation that had to be clearly rejected, and was precisely what individual human rights activists such as Hadj Ghermoul, who lives in the Mascara province, have done. Ghermoul's stance has resulted in his imprisonment.

The first local popular demonstrations in three medium-sized cities took place in the east of the country, Bordj Bou Arreridj on February 13, Kherrata on February 16, and Khenchela on February 19. Following numerous slogans launched on social networks, the first clearly articulated national opposition demonstration to the fifth term project took place on Friday, February 22, 2019. This was a hugely popular success throughout the country. Since then, in addition to the major regular demonstrations held on every Friday throughout the month, various other categories of citizens—students, lawyers, teachers, intellectuals, journalists, doctors, workers, and trade unionists—have continued to make strong political demands that gradually broadened the scope of their objectives.

Since the resignation of President Bouteflika, which was finally announced on April 2, 2019, the demands of the social movement thus born have increasingly focused on the need for regime change. In Arabic, the word used is that of *harak* or *hirak* whose root refers to that of movement, as often expressed by the slogan "they must all go," starting from a clearly *dégagiste* [get out] inspiration seeking the establishment of a democratic regime. Three months after the start of the protest, a national demonstration resulted in an exceptional mobilisation throughout the country at the end of the month of Ramadhan. This has in no way affected the willingness of the majority of citizens to change, and the strength of the social movement is clearly embedded in both the duration and logic of satisfying its demands.

Dynamics of the social movement

The disproportionate scale of the social movement was illustrated by the millions of citizens—including the active participation by women, which must be emphasised. What was equally remarkable about this movement was that it regularly engaged in peaceful demonstrations across all regions of the country, and that its social composition takes the form of a rich mosaic that is highly representative of the whole society. This is in fact a deeply interclass movement which aims to be as broad a popular gathering as possible. It makes no demands in terms of any particular social category—class, gender, income', or education—and, even less so, does it propose a conflict between opposing social groups. The importance of the precariat does not mean that it plays a major role in leadership, for example, but that, because of its broad weight, its widespread coverage, and its capacity to demand, particularly in terms of symbolic violence, it constitutes an immense potential for mobilisation that directly increases the capacities of the social movement as a whole.

Regarding the political content of the social movement, it is first of all a profoundly moral revolt against a political power widely considered to be authoritarian, cynical, incompetent, and corrupt, whose draft fifth mandate was perceived as a deep contempt for the people. Or, by using an absolutely central term in the problem of inter-individual relations in Algerian society, as a true *hogra* [bullying/injustice]. As such, according to an implicit, but very present code of honour in Algerian society, this requires from the people a response commensurate with the insult that had been delivered to them. In addition, the moral dimension of the revolt was considerably strengthened by the corruption that characterised the functioning of the political system in place at the time. As the social movement progressed and with it the revelations it helped to uncover, these continued to reveal its most sordid and shocking aspects, as elements that regularly fed popular anger.

That being said, it is clear that the social movement covers the entire spectrum of political currents or is assimilated and operating in Algerian society. From this point of view, four main trends can be mentioned, in particular:

•   An Islamist trend, with the full range of its sensitivities, including those expressing its most extremist forms and ideologically linked to those of the 1980s and 1990s;

- A modernist democratic trend, which sees in the current social movement an opportunity to restore vigour to its proposal on the need to establish a democratic regime;
- Amazigh (Berber) identity, committed to regional establishment of conditions for the expression of the various cultural and particularly indigenous claims;
- Nationalist-bureaucratic, determined to continue the FLN as it has functioned as a state party, despite its heavy legacy, but determined to ensure its continuity by making the necessary changes in accordance with the changed context.

In addition, within the social movement there are many citizens who are not directly linked to particular political structures and who can be either totally independent or part of a logic linked to civil society organisations.

To these political or civil society movements, which take place in the public domain, must be added various actions carried out by less formal networks. These include those linked to the former structure in charge of security services, the Department of Intelligence and Security which was dissolved in 2015. Some of its agents may have considered that the current social movement provides an opportunity to take their revenge against the reorganisation of 2015. This had been decided by Bouteflika, and from their point of view undermined their power, which had long been decisive within the political system and towards society in general.

Despite the social, cultural, and political heterogeneity of the citizens who participate in its activities, it is remarkable that, for the most part, the social movement has managed to maintain a remarkable unity of action This unity is concentrated around its initial objectives of regime change, in line with the affirmation of democratic principles.

The ANP in the social movement

At the beginning of the social movement, the ANP confined itself to its initial position supporting the continuity of the regime. At any rate, this was as expressed through its Chief of Staff, Ahmed Gaïd Salah, who, at the same time, exercised the function of Deputy Minister of Defence—that of Minister of Defence being exercised by the President of the Republic himself. ANP's stance was, in particular, explicit support for the assumption of the presidential fifth term. Once faced with the reality of increasingly firm demands of the social movement during its first few weeks, and, in particular, the absolute rejection of the fifth term, Gaïd Salah changed course by deciding to obtain the resignation of Bouteflika, which was announced on April 2, 2019.

From that date, the country entered into an exceptional political situation. By strictly applying the provisions of the Constitution, the President of the Council of the Nation has become head of state and is expected to organise presidential elections within 90 days. At the same time, the social movement refuses to participate in any discussion with representatives of the old regime. The proposed timetable initially centred on a presidential election that was supposed to be held on July 4, 2019, but this was cancelled due to the lack of credible candidates, and increasingly appears to be in need of reconsideration. Indeed, the social movement is calling for a transition period, the duration of which remains to be determined and which necessarily implies a distance from the strict provisions of the Constitution, coupled with intelligent political negotiation between all national role players.

Since April 2, 2019, and with a head of state who has no real powers, it is the Chief of Staff of the ANP who has become the main voice expressing the political positions of the regime, as reconfigured. This is through a succession of speeches, generally weekly, and expressed in military forums. In the final analysis, these operate in a more or less direct form of dialogue with the demands of the social movement that they usually reject, reaffirming the primacy of the strict application of the provisions of the Constitution.

Nonetheless, the various forms of dialogue which seem to have been established regardless, raise a fundamental question as to which side is legitimate in terms of popular sovereignty. The two opposing points of view are expressed, on the one hand, by the Chief of Staff of the ANP, who is certainly supposed to express the position of the military, but who seems to do so in the name of the principle that "authority comes from above and trust from below." On the other hand is a very broad social movement in which millions of citizens activate and identify with each other. Each of them has repeatedly rejected, with remarkable constancy and in a peaceful manner in a form of an everyday referendum, the approach involved in the formal implementation of the Constitution. In the process, they call for specific reforms for a regime change as part of a national dialogue between the authorities, civil society, and political parties.

Once again in Algeria's contemporary history, the fundamental question raised is that of the status and role of the military in the functioning of the political system. The first formal position on the subject appeared in the text of the Soummam Congress in August 1956 (Harbi 1981), which is the primacy of politics over the military. This was modified the following year at a meeting held in Cairo in August 1957 by the National Council of the Algerian Revolution (CNRA): "The CNRA reaffirmed: all those who participate in the liberation struggle, with or without uniform, are equal. As a result, there is no primacy of politics over the military, nor is there any difference between inside and outside."

The year 1957 ended in a tragic way with the assassination of the main initiator of the 1956 Soummam Congress thesis, Ramdane Abane, by his comrades-in-arms. However, since these events, and apart from the serious crises of the summer of 1962, the challenges around the relationship between political power and the military institution continue, depending on various circumstances, to constitute sources of tension within Algerian society.

This is clearly the case today, at a time when the country is at a turning point in its history, since there is a disagreement between distinctly different visions:

on the one hand, the vast majority of citizens are mobilised within the current social movement and are deeply attached to democratic principles; on the other hand, the ANP General Military staff operate as if they were attempting to preserve the authoritarian system that had long been in place, which was certainly shaken, but is still persistent.

This situation gave rise to a deadlock which necessarily leads to the question of who, within the society, and in the last instance, holds legitimate authority for any political action: the military institution or the people? The only possible answer is that this is stipulated in the current Constitution, in particular in its Preamble, as well as in its Articles 7 and 8, and is often recalled by citizens and many political actors: it is only the people who are the legitimate source of sovereignty.

If, on the basis of special considerations that need to be justified, the military institution requests an exceptional status, that status can no longer be acquired automatically on the basis of a logic that no longer has any place in Algerian society. This political privilege must be openly negotiated with current society in the context of a broad democratic debate excluding any form of argument for authority and/or against taboo.

Perspectives

The complex crisis that Algeria is currently experiencing is above all that of a dual-rentier model, in which the two main systemic rent dynamics, of energy and of politics, are becoming increasingly exhausted. In this overall process, the deterioration in the president's health has also played a role; however, this has only served to precipitate events that were already part of unavoidable systemic processes.[6]

In the short term, Algerian society must find a way out of the crisis it is currently experiencing. Beyond its obvious political dimension, this crisis also has direct negative consequences on the country's economy. The country must within a reasonable timeframe create the conditions for a new social consensus through various forms of inclusive dialogue, enabling the country to regain the conditions for an efficient functioning of its institutions and economic apparatus.

In the medium and long term, Algerian society will then necessarily have to face choices to be made between two main hypotheses of a political and economic model: one, the rentier, of which it has already had bitter experience, and the other, "productive," in the sense of both tangible production (outside hydrocarbons) and intangible values, which the heavy national and international constraints called for tomorrow impose on the country's developments. In terms of the necessary political transition, the purpose is to create conditions for the emergence of a representative political system excluding any rentier logic in which legitimacy can only come from open competition (i.e., elections), in which informed citizens freely participate and make their choices based on reason. In any case, the country's experience of an ineffective authoritarian system and the blockages it has generated in many areas suggest that the required transition should move towards a democratically inspired political system.

In terms of economic transition, this is nothing new and has for decades been recycled as the post-oil economy. However, for more than 40 years, hydrocarbon has continued to represent around 97% of the value of the country's total exports. This is as if a number of bottlenecks were at work, a kind of glass ceiling of a necessarily systemic nature, given the long period during which this export structure has been maintained as it stands. A lengthy blockage of this kind can only lead to the possibility of an identifiable "natural resource curse" as is the case of many other hydrocarbon-producing countries (Humphreys et al. 2007).

Whatever the answers are to these questions, the challenge in the coming years will be to know how and at what cost, such persistent obstructive situations will be overcome. This is in order to bring them effectively into line with an efficient and socially legitimate political system as well as a truly diversified and internationally competitive economy.

Notes

1 It should be understood here that within Algerian society there are also other rentier logics at work which contribute directly to forging and strengthening its rentier character and of which the most significant are those underlying various forms of land, urban, and entrepreneurial rents.

2 Inheritance capture: this appellation refers to a situation when an elderly person's state of weakness is abused to divert part of his or her inheritance by someone else's own benefit. In this chapter, this refers to current FLN's capture, or exploitation, of the historical FLN's name and symbols for own ends.

3 On the occasion of public meetings organised by the FLN party, banners are hung up using a highly symbolic verse in Arabic from the text of the poem by Moufdi Zakaria (1908–1977). Translated into English, this solemnly proclaims: "Front de Libération, we have sworn to you."

4 As illustrated in a 2014 text by the Algerian writer, Kamel Daoud, entitled "FLN, I hate you! "who writes in conclusion: 'I dream of freeing Larbi Ben M'Hidi's memory from the present of Belkhadem and Saadani. It [FLN] is my enemy. The insult that is being made to me. My first shame." (Daoud 2014). Or, in the field of French literature, a Kafkaesque novel, such as Toumi (2016).

5 Built through merging precariousness with the proletariat, the notion of precariat is increasingly used by sociologists and economists in their analyses of the evolutions of contemporary societies. Thus, the British economist Guy Standing refers to it as a new class, both "emerging and dangerous"; Standing (2011).

6 In 2012, while the formal performance of the *model* was certainly at its best, notably because of a particularly high oil price per barrel, I mentioned in a published article the systemic crisis already underway which was negatively affecting the prospects of the "model" Nadji Safir (2012).

References

Algérie Patriotique 2019 (June 12).

Beblawi, H. 1990. "The Rentier State in the Arab World," in H. Beblawi & G. Luciani (eds.), *The Rentier State*, pp. 49–62, University of California Press, New York.

Bourdieu, P. 1994. *Raisons pratiques*, Editions du Seuil, Paris.

Bourdieu, P. 2000. *Esquisse d'une théorie de la pratique*, Editions du Seuil, Paris.

Daoud, K. 2014 (June 25). "FLN, je te déteste!" https://www.algerie-focus.com/2014/06/fln-je-te-deteste-par-kamel-daoud/. Retrieved September 5, 2019.

Dutour, N. 2008. "Algérie : de la Concorde civile à la Charte pour la Paix et la Réconciliation nationale : Amnistie, amnésie, impunité," *Mouvements*, 53: 144–149.

Eisenstadt, S. N. 1973. *Traditional Patrimonialism and Modern Neopatrimonialism*, Sage Publications, Beverly Hills.

Harbi, M. (1981). *Les archives de la Révolution Algérienne*, Editions Jeune Afrique, Paris.

Humphreys, M., Sachs J. D. and Stiglitz J. E. 2007. *Escaping the Resource Curse*, Columbia University Press, New York.

Krueger, A. O. 1974. "The Political Economy of the Rent-Seeking Society," *The American Economic Review*, 64 (3): 291–303.

Mahdavy, H. 1970. "The Patterns and Problems of Economic Development in a Rentier State: The Case of Iran," in M. A. Cook (ed.), *Studies in Economic History of the Middle East*, pp. 428–467, Oxford University Press, London.

Métaoui, F. 2019 (June 12). "La charge de l'Organisation nationale des Moudjahidines contre le FLN," *TSA*, https://www.tsa-algerie.com/la-charge-de-lorganisation-nationale-des-moudjahidines-contre-le-fln/. Retrieved September 5, 2019.

Safir, N. 2012. "Algérie 2012": Contribution à l'analyse d'une crise complexe », in *Réflexions et Perspectives, Revue scientifique et académique de l'Université d'Alger 2*, Cinquantenaire de l'Algérie indépendante, Juin; pp. 45–71.

Standing, G. 2011. *The Precariat—The New Dangerous Class*, Bloomsbury Academic, New York.

Toumi, S. (2016). *L'effacement*, Editions Barzakh, Algiers.

Zoubir, Y. H. and Dris-Aït-Hamadouche, L. (2013). *Global Security Watch: The Maghreb, Algeria, Libya, Morocco, and Tunisia*. ABC-Clio, Santa Barbara, California.

2

THE MISUSE OF OIL WEALTH IN ECONOMIC DEVELOPMENT AND WHY INSTITUTIONS MATTER

An Algerian case study

Mohammed Akacem

Introduction

Much has been written and debated about the resource curse, and its negative impact on economic growth and development (Sachs and Warner 1995). Some authors go as far as suggesting that a negative linkage exists between the presence of resource wealth and democracy. Michael Ross (2011: 2–7) stated that "There is no getting around the fact that countries in the region are less free because they produced and sell oil" (Ross 2011: 2). However, in a subsequent publication in 2012 (Ross 2012), he modulated his views about the certainty of the causation. The purpose of this chapter is to refute the view that oil, or any resource wealth for that matter, retards either economic development or the rise of democratic governments.

"Petroleum after all, is nothing but a black viscous material" (Karl 1997: 6). How can it derail attempts to grow an economy or to plant the seed of democracy? We will present institutional data to support our main argument, but more importantly, will use two countries as counter arguments to add weight to our thesis. The two countries are Singapore and Norway. Singapore is a city state. It has no resource wealth. Yet it has done extremely well on the economic development front—perhaps not as well on the democratic score, but it still does better than Algeria, as our data will show.

Norway, on the other hand, is an oil economy *and* a democracy. The presence of oil did not impede Norway from achieving a high per capita income as well as being first or near the top of all of the institutional indices. Algeria, which discovered oil

The chapter draws on past research by the author on this topic and mainly from the following: Akacem (2015), Akacem and Cachanosky (2017), Akacem and Miller (2015), Akacem and Geng (2015).

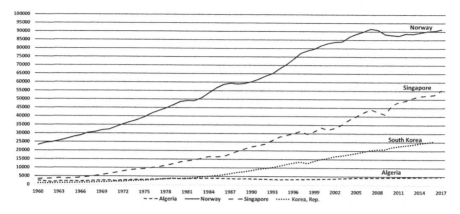

FIGURE 2.1 GDP per capita Algeria, Norway, Singapore, and South Korea. (From World Development Indicators.)

in the mid-1950s, long before Norway, has lagged considerably behind. The difference is the institutional deficit, that even after more than half a century after gaining independence, Algeria has yet to meet the aspirations of its growing population. Finally, Singapore and South Korea[1] with no natural resource wealth managed to outperform Algeria on a per capita basis (see Figure 2.1).

As can be observed from the above figure, Algeria's per capita Gross Domestic Product remained almost flat with timid growth for almost 60 years, while that of Norway started at a much higher level (almost 10 times that of Algeria's) in 1960 and took off after that. It is important to note that Algeria discovered oil in 1956 with oil production starting in 1958[2] and Norway in 1969.[3] GDP per capita for Singapore started at the about the same level as Algeria's in 1960, but took off in the early 1970s and continued on that trajectory. Figure 2.1 highlights the fundamental problems facing the Algerian economy. It has remained hostage to the oil and gas sector for more than half a century and failed to diversify its economy or build the necessary institutions that are conducive to a faster rate of economic growth. In a nutshell, despite the oil wealth, it has not delivered to its people, the biggest hurdle facing the country at the moment is time. It takes miles to turn an oil tanker, but it takes decades to change the economic course of a country.

Literature review

The topic of resource curse has been widely covered in the academic literature. A search on Google produces 31 million hits. We will limit ourselves to the main sources and more importantly to those that are consistent with the main thesis of this chapter. While the main focus of the analysis is on Algeria, many oil

producing countries in and outside of the Organization of Petroleum Exporting
Countries have not taken advantage of their resource wealth. This does not mean
that oil[4] is to blame.

Saudi Arabia's former oil minister wished that his country had never
discovered oil. He would have preferred that they had discovered water
instead (Okere 2013), while a Venezuelan oil minister as far back as 1975
foresaw the downside of oil riches when he stated that: "I call petroleum the
devil's excrement. It brings trouble...Look at this locura—waste, corruption,
consumption, our public services falling apart. And debt, debt we shall have
for Years" (*The Economist* 2003). The oil minister was correct in pointing out
the *potential* ills of oil wealth, and looking at the current state of the Venezuelan
economy, he was certainly right. However, trouble need not necessarily follow
the discovery of oil wealth, nor does the lack of such riches, as we will show in
the case of Singapore.

The research on the oil curse started with the work of Sachs and Warner
(1995) as an attempt to show the adverse effect of natural resource wealth on
those economies that were endowed with such riches. The authors concluded
that their research has "documented a statistically significant, inverse, and robust
association between natural resource intensity and growth over the past twenty
years." However, they add that the results "are far from definitive." The authors
state:

> The oddity of resource-poor economies outperforming resource-
> rich economies has been a constant motif of economic history. In the
> seventeenth century, resource-poor Netherlands eclipsed Spain, despite the
> overflow of gold and silver from the Spanish colonies in the New World.
> In the nineteenth and twentieth centuries, resource-poor countries such as
> Switzerland and Japan surged ahead of resource-abundant economies such
> as Russia. In the past thirty years, the world's star performers have been
> the resource-poor Newly Industrializing Economies (NIEs) of East Asia—
> Korea, Taiwan, Hong Kong, Singapore—while many resource-rich econo-
> mies such as the oil-rich countries of Mexico, Nigeria, Venezuela, have gone
> bankrupt.

The authors' observation points to the heart of our main argument: the
importance of institutions[5] and their role in shaping not only the development of economies, but also the nurturing and preservation of democracies. There is nothing peculiar as to why the resource rich countries such as
Mexico, Nigeria and Venezuela cited above did not do well. In addition to
the presence of oil riches, one should also note the timing of the oil discovery

and its exploitation as having happened before or after the establishment of institutions.

In an attempt to replicate the work of Sachs and Warner, but in a more limited way and with a much smaller sample of countries,[6] we ran a regression analysis specifically for countries in the Middle East and North Africa region (from here on MENA) (Akacem & Geng 2015). The regression analysis did not find evidence of the resource curse. Moreover, when testing for Norway as the control variable, there was no evidence that the presence of oil negatively impacted its economy. In fact, the results appeared to point to a positive impact. A more specific test for Algeria (Akacem & Cachanosky 2017) was conducted, and there again, no robust or negative correlation between the presence of oil wealth and economic growth, but institutional shocks did impact the economy.

Alexeev and Conrad's results (2009) did not agree with those of Sachs and Warner. Their findings supported the thesis that oil riches helped, not hindered, the prospects of countries that were endowed with it. They further point to a "phenomenon X" and state:

> The role of X has been played by the Dutch disease, civil conflict, rent seeking, neglect of human capital development, decline in saving and investment, and increase in income inequality, among other factors. Recently, deterioration of institutions appears to have emerged as the most popular interpretation of phenomenon X (586).

This provides support for main our argument that the presence or absence of institutions is the primary area of focus for resource-rich countries. Nothing else comes close to explaining the failure of either Algeria or other oil producing countries in MENA to excel on the economic and political front as the data in the next pages of this chapter will show.

Acemoglu and Robertson (2012) put the focus squarely on the importance of institutions in trying to explain why some countries do well while others fail. The quote below relates to all of the resource-endowed countries, including Algeria.

> Nations fail today because their extractive economic institutions do not create the incentives needed for people to save, invest and innovate. Extractive political institutions support these economic institutions by cementing the power of those who benefit from the extraction. Extractive economic and political institutions, though their details vary under different circumstances, are always at the root of this failure (372).

On the inclusiveness of economic and political institutions, the authors go on to state that:

> Inclusive economic institutions, such as those in South Korea or in the United States, are those that allow and encourage participation by the great mass of people in economic activities that make the best use of their talents and skills and that enable individuals to make the choices they wish. To be inclusive, economic institutions must feature secure private property, an unbiased system of law, and a provision of public services that provides a level playing field in which people can exchange and contract; it also must permit the entry of new businesses and allow people to choose their careers (68–69).

Karl (1997: 6) adds to the argument that institutions are the key. He argues that the problem is not some oil curse.

> ...the fate of oil-exporting countries must be understood in a context in which economies shape institutions and, in turn, are shaped by them. .... Because the causal arrow between economic development and institutional change constantly runs in both directions, the accumulated outcomes give form to divergent long-run national trajectories.

Michael Ross (2012: 223) recalibrated his main thesis regarding the presence of oil and its impact on countries. He admits that his research "...finds little evidence for some of the more dire claims in the resource curse literature: that extracting oil slows down a country's economic growth, or makes governments weaker or less effective."[7]

Ross' arguments above have yet to apply to the MENA region as a whole. In fact, governments in that area have not been able to meet the aspiration of their citizens on the economic front. Data on unemployment for the region as a whole and in particular for the youth segment of the population is substantial and in the long run unsustainable. Ross goes on to argue that despite these shortcomings, the presence of oil riches can be a positive since it can enlarge the size of public goods such as in education and health.

Unfortunately, the evidence does not support such as a claim. Spending on these sectors does not correlate with the final product. Both of these sectors have, on the whole, failed to deliver in the region as a whole and in Algeria in particular. Algeria ranks 120th for the skillset of university graduates, while Singapore is 4th and Norway 21st. Such a ranking does not bode well for the economy and is evidence of the disconnect between the education sector and the needs of the economy. The low skillset explains the relatively higher levels of unemployment given the inability of either the public or private sectors to employ these graduates, which results in a high rate of unemployment (see Figure 2.2).

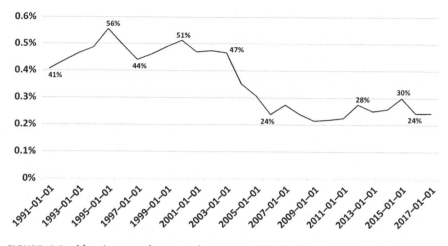

FIGURE 2.2 Algerian youth unemployment: 1991–2017. (From Federal Reserve Bank of Saint Louis, St. Louis, MO.)

Despite Ross' argument that one can find redemption for the oil economies given their attention to health and education, the evidence does not support it. The Human Capital Index is a measure that puts a value on the health and education sectors and how they contribute to elevating the productivity of future workers. According to the World Bank, Algeria's score is .52, lower than either Norway or Singapore with scores of .77 and .88, respectively (World Bank 2002).

The fundamental problem has to do with who controls the flow of oil revenue. Being an oil producer does not necessarily produce bad results. Norway is an oil producer and yet it does not experience the rent-seeking so prevalent in the oil MENA region. One reason, as we have argued, is the presence of solid institutions. Even though the oil revenues flow to the government, as they do in MENA, Norway has checks and balances and allows for feedback and accountability. The latter has been addressed by the Arab Human Development Report (2004: 152) of the United Nations Development Programme that explains why Arab countries suffer from the rentier effect. It states

> In the rentier state, therefore, government is absolved of any periodic accountability, not to mention representation. As long as the rent continues to flow, there is no need for citizens to finance government and thus expect it to be accountable to them. On the contrary, when the flow of rent depends on the good will of influential outside forces, as in the case of some Arab countries, the right to accountability passes to those who control the flow of rent, instead of remaining with citizens, who are turned into subjects (1522).

Adding emphasis to the dire straits of rentier economies in the Arab world, it continues by referring to them as "black hole" countries. In these states, "the executive apparatus resembles a 'black hole' which converts its surrounding social environment into a setting in which nothing moves and from which nothing escapes" (15).

What has been shown so far is that the resource curse theory is a myth. Norway, an oil economy, and Singapore, a city state with no resource wealth, outperform the oil economies of the MENA region. Why? Because institutions matter. The other extreme is Venezuela with the largest oil reserves in the world and yet fails to provide the most basic services to this people that prompted a large exodus of its citizens. Once again, the absence of institutions in the presence of massive oil wealth leads to ruins.

The challenge for Algeria, however, is how to move from an institutional deficit environment to a state where institutions function properly. We submit that it is not an easy task. But we nevertheless maintain that the status quo is unsustainable in the long run. We will present a radical approach at the end of this chapter that may be a catalyst to the required institutional change.

Empirical evidence

There are ample data on the institutional indices, but we will limit ourselves to a few that relate to the core indices that are in play and shed light on the suboptimal rates of growth of the Algerian economy. We begin with the fiscal balance with forecasts up to 2020. The fiscal balance is the difference between total spending and total revenue. Given the dependence of Algeria on oil receipts, oil prices are a primary determinant of this measure.

Figure 2.3 plots Algeria, along with MENA and oil exporters within it. Algeria's fiscal deficits as a percentage of the GDP are larger for each of the years shown and forward to 2019 and 2020. The figure for 2018 is an estimate and those for 2019 and 2020 are forecasts. This is driven by the difference between the prevailing oil price and the price needed to balance the budget. In 2018, the difference between the market oil price and the fiscal

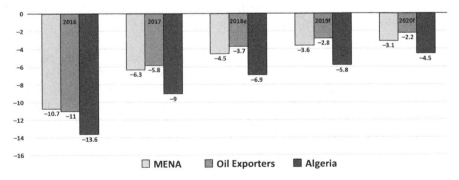

FIGURE 2.3 Fiscal Balance as a % of GDP. Fiscal balance difference between spending and revenue. (From The World Bank, MENA Economic Monitor.)

breakeven oil price was—$44.49 dollars, higher than its fellow Gulf oil pro-
ducers. A number of factors led to this dire fiscal picture and among them,
waste, corruption, a lack of coherent long-term economic strategy, as well
as a non-inviting attitude towards foreign direct investments. To make matters worse, an increasing population and in particular the youth bulge exert
pressure on the country's labour market. Consequently, a number of Algerian
youth (Harraga) risk their lives crossing the Mediterranean Sea in search of
better lives.

To further explore the data to add weight to our argument that oil wealth is
a blessing rather than a curse, we turn to the correlation between income per
capita and resource rent for a number of countries. Figure 2.4 shows the GDP
per capita and resource rent as a percentage of the GDP. What is remarkable is
the inverse relationship between those two variables, further adding to the idea
that what matters in the long run are good institutions. The richer the country is
in natural resources, the lower the per capita GDP. Looking at Algeria, Kuwait,
and Saudi Arabia and comparing these oil exporters to Singapore, Norway, and
the USA, we see the difference that good institutions make. Singapore is by
far the best example with zero resource rent and a higher GDP per capita than
Kuwait and even Saudi Arabia. Norway, with far less oil wealth and having
started exploiting its oil later, has the highest per capita GDP with less resource
rent (see Figure 2.4).

Lately, the International Monetary Fund and the World Bank have begun
to use the term governance (or the lack of it) as a factor that explains poor
economic performances among natural resource-rich countries. Governance
covers a number of indicators such as corruption and the rule of law. The figure
below plots the governance indicators for Algeria and our two control countries. Algeria scores poorly (negative score) in each one of them for the year
2017, while Norway and Singapore are positive with some closer to the maxi-
mum score of 2.50. Voice and accountability are key indicators because without
feedback and receptiveness to the views of others and the general population,

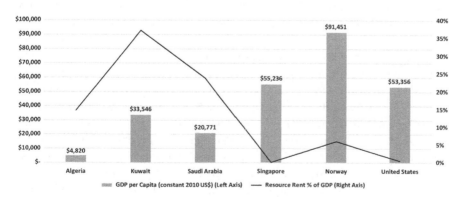

FIGURE 2.4 Natural resource rent and GDP per capita updated to 2017.

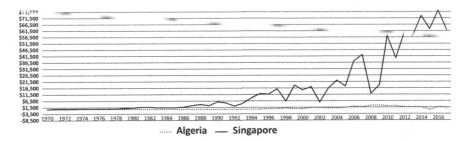

...... **Algeria** — **Singapore**

FIGURE 2.5 Inward foreign direct investments: 1970–2017 in millions of US$. (Courtesy of UNCTAD, Geneva, Switzerland.)

the government is robbed of the chance to make the necessary policy correction. The rule of law is an important measure incorporating the enforcement of contracts, the protection of property rights, and to the extent that the judiciary is independent, inspires trust in the country and its economy. The latter translates into foreign direct investments (Singapore), and Algeria has lost ground in that area largely due to the low score for that measure. Figure 2.5 shows the gap between Singapore and Algeria.

The resource curse literature notes the excessive spending on the military in resource-rich countries. Humphreys, Sachs, and Stiglitz (2007: 12) point to the idea that these countries generally have "weak and unaccountable states":

> Since a resource-rich country's revenue is largely independent of the strengths and success of the overall economy, the government of the resource-rich country has less of a need to engage in activities that support the economy. Without a broad support base in the economy, a government can instead invest its earnings in an oppressive capacity.

According to the authors, there is not much of an incentive to move towards a system of government that allows for feedback and accountability and instead tend to allocate more of the country's resources to the military. The best measure to capture this is defence spending as a fraction of the GDP. In 2017, Saudi Arabia, for example, spent just over 10.29% of its GDP on defence, while Norway, the USA, and Singapore spent: 1.64%, 3.15%, and 3.32% of the GDP, respectively. In other words, Saudi Arabia spend over three times more on defence than the USA, the largest economy and a super power. Algeria, spent 5.71% of its GDP, more than the USA and Norway combined. These relatively large spends relative to other larger and developed economies point to a significant amount of loss. It is important to note that in the post-9/11 environment as well as the Arab Spring, spending on defence, security, and counter-terrorism measures may have increased, but the scale of spending in the oil economies is still far higher than in the established democracies that have checks and balances.

Finally, another characteristic of the oil economies where the institutions are either absent or weak, is the prevalence of corruption. Algeria ranked 112th out of 180 countries in the Corruption Perception Index in 2017 (Transparency International 2017),[8] while Norway and Singapore and ranked 3rd and 6th. This is proof that an oil economy such as Norway can do very well despite the presence of oil, as can an economy such as Singapore without a drop of the black gold.

Radical policy as path to institutional change

In this chapter, we attempted to expose the myth that a black liquid such as oil could by itself cause those economies who were blessed with it to miss out on its benefits. The data showed such is not the case unless countries fail, wilfully, by design or by accident, to build and encourage the necessary institutions to maximise the benefits of the oil riches. We used Norway and Singapore to reject the notion that either the presence of oil or its absence is detrimental to an economy.

Now we turn our attention to a path to institutional change that would help oil economies transition to an inclusive economic and political institution. Since the primary cause of the rent seeking is due to centralisation of oil revenues in the hands of governments, we propose that oil revenues be rerouted directly to the citizens. Instead of the benefits of the oil wealth trickling down to the general population which represents the shareholders' base, why not distribute the oil revenue directly to them.

This model is not necessarily new[9] and not difficult to implement provided the *will for change* is there. The state of Alaska has been engaged in direct distribution of dividends for years. The annual dividend payment for 2017 was $1,100 per resident.[10] The situation is so dire not only in Algeria, but in most of the Arab oil exporting countries due to corruption, waste, unaccountability, lack of due process, etc. that nothing short of a radical approach would do. One approach proposed by van der Ploeg (2011: 366–420) recommends a constitutional amendment.

> An interesting option is to change the constitution to guarantee that resource revenues are handed to the public. The government has to subsequently tax its citizens to finance its spending programs. The advantage is that the burden of proof for spending resource revenues is with the government.

Others have made the same case for cash transfers to the rightful stakeholders (Moss, Lambert, & Majerowicz 2015). Their approach is not as radical as ours because they advocate a split of oil revenue between the state and the citizens. Such an approach is not likely to address the fundamental cause for the waste and the misappropriation of funds so prevalent in the MENA region.

Given that we have established that the problem is not natural resource wealth, but rather who collects and distributes the oil wealth, a rerouting of these funds directly to the people would be a start in breaking the link between despotism and oil. Milton Friedman, while referencing the case of Iraq post-invasion in the context of oil and despotism stated the following:

> One reason, and one reason only—the oil is owned by the governments in question. If that oil were privately owned and thus someone's private property, the political outcome would be freedom rather than tyranny. This is why I believe the first step following the 2003 invasion of Iraq should have been the privatization of the oil fields. If the government had given every individual over 21 years of age equal shares in a corporation that had the right and responsibility to make appropriate arrangements with foreign oil companies for the purpose of discovering and developing Iraq's oil reserves, the oil income would have flowed in the form of dividends to the people—the shareholders—rather than into government coffers. This would have provided an income to the whole people of Iraq and thereby prevented the current disputes over oil between the Sunnis, Shiites, and Kurds, because oil income would have been distributed on an individual rather than a group basis.[11]

In the case of Algeria, this could be a share distribution system that would guarantee each citizen an annual payment based on the oil revenue generated less the cost of the oil operations. The national oil company would transition into a citizen-owned company run by a board responsive to the shareholders instead of the government.[12] Data on oil revenues by oil exporters are already in the public domain and citizens can easily establish what their approximate share is (Figure 2.6).

The per capita share for the Algerian citizen varies with oil prices and reached its highest level in 2008 at $1,931. In Dinar terms and using the parallel exchange rate which better reflects what the market exchange would be if it were free floating, the amount is substantial and a multiple of the minimum

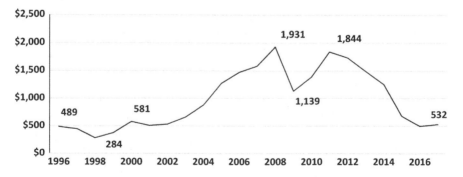

FIGURE 2.6 Algeria's per capita net oil export revenue: 1996–2017 (2017$). (From https://www.eia.gov/beta/international/regions-topics.php?RegionTopicID=OPEC.)

monthly wage. The distributed oil shares should not be sold by their owners for fear that others would buy them back and corner the market. It is conceivable that a poor family, not completely aware of the full discounted value of the future streams of income that will last until the oil runs out, can be tempted to sell outright because of needs.

In a market economy and with the proper safeguards, investors would get a sense of the value of their oil shares. However, there is not much of a stock market or a bond market in Algeria to help guide the average citizen to properly assess the value of their share of the country's oil wealth. As such, our proposal recommends that the shares remain with their original owners.[13]

A question that is often asked in opposition to such a scheme is how the government would fund itself if it were prevented from controlling control of oil revenues? The answer is the same as Singapore, without any oil wealth, its funds meet its obligations to its population, or the same as most countries which are not so well endowed. Economic literature refers to this as "starving the beast" theory (Romer & Romer 2009), the beast being the government. The argument behind this theory is that if governments are starved of funds, they will be forced to cut spending. The problem with this is that in the Western world, with its mature financial markets, governments faced with deficits simply issue debt and borrow.

We submit, however, that starving the beast may work in countries like Algeria. Given its underdeveloped financial market, it is not able to borrow or issue debt in the international market like the USA or other economies with advanced capital markets. In fact, in the recent past, the government resorted to literally printing money to fund some of its expenditure. In this case, the budget constraint facing the government becomes binding and the next step in our plan calls for the government to simply raise revenue through taxes. That will slowly bring back some modicum of accountability and feedback from the part of the electorate who can then inquire as to the purpose of the tax and where the proceeds will go, just as in mature and emerging democracies.

We admit that neither Algeria nor the MENA region has reached the stage of emerging democracies, but this does not prevent the ideas, and this approach in particular, to be at least considered and discussed. *The Economist* addressed this issue in one its special reports (January 14, 2019):

> Arab countries have not yet succeeded in fostering the institutional prerequisites of democracy—the give-and-take of parliamentary discourse, protection for minorities, the emancipation of women, a free press, independent courts and universities and trade unions.[14]

The status quo is unstainable in the long run, and Figure 2.1 shows that on a per capita basis, Algeria has stagnated, while Singapore flourished without a single drop of oil. The failure to undertake economic reforms very early on only increases the cost of implementing them, the longer Algeria waits.

Conclusion

Our proposal to nudge Algeria towards institutional change through a reallocation of oil revenues away from the state and to the citizens is, we hope, a catalyst that could spur a change towards inclusive institutions. It could, if done right and over time, make the government more accountable and would free government from blame when oil markets are soft, since the citizens now receive all the revenue.

Despite our proposed approach to deal with the negative impact of oil and the institutional deficit, and radical as it is, there is one constraint facing Algeria that is difficult to overcome unless action is taken: time. The country has literally muddled through for over half a century without a coherent or a rational vision on both the economic and the political front. "The confusion and lack of transparency is typical of Algeria. Of all the main sources of oil and gas in the world, the North African giant has one of the most opaque political systems, and one of the most confused and confusing economies" (Peel 2007).

The result is widespread discontent that has morphed into an Algerian Spring with millions of Algerians marching[15] and demanding an end to the status quo. This led to the resignation of president Bouteflika, an event not thought possible just a few months ago. Despite this, the population is adamant in its demand that the whole "system" must go and a new model be instituted where the citizens are the source of power. The authorities were taken by surprise by the widespread and national expression of rejection. But the data and evidence have long pointed to the undercurrent of misery, unhappiness, and more importantly the contempt shown to the population by the successive governments. Figure 2.7 shows

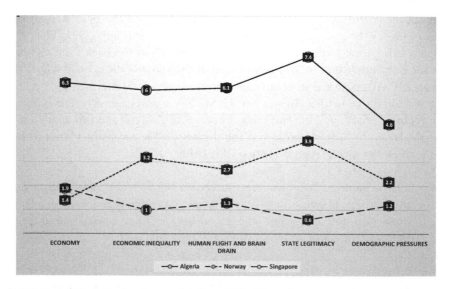

FIGURE 2.7 Algeria's fragile state's index: 2019. (From https://fragilestatesindex.org/excel/, Fragile States Index, The Fund for Peace.)

the fragile state's index and captures the essence of the problem. For the plotted indices, Algeria scores worse that our two benchmark countries, Singapore and Norway. Note the state of legitimacy score which is highest among all of the scores (the worst score is 10), while the rest are all higher than the benchmark countries. The country needs a fundamental change in governance if it is to regain the people's trust.

First, the incentives have to be right. Rent seeking cannot dominate the Algerian landscape forever and oil will run out. Then what? Second, the oil markets have already been upended by the shale oil revolution with less dependence on oil by the USA—and no doubt others in the future—while Algeria is still hostage to it. The economy must extricate itself from the socialist model that has not delivered, as well as inward-looking policies that discourage foreign direct investments. It should be designed as a "beyond oil" strategy. Without it, the future will remain uncertain.

Notes

1 The chapter will use Norway and Singapore as the two reference countries. We are referencing South Korea for the purpose of Figure 2.1, to highlight the different paths in economic growth of countries with no oil that did well.
2 See https://www.opec.org/opec_web/en/about_us/146.htm, accessed on January 4, 2019. It is important to note that Algeria went through a war of independence from France from 1954 to 1962 when it gained its independence from France. It is natural for the economy to experience a few years of stagnation as it adjusts to the post-independence environment and the per capital GDP would reflect this in the early years. However, as the Figure shows, per capita GDP did not improve as expected given the presence of oil and in particular in the early years, a much smaller population as in the present. Contrast this with the Singapore and South Korea.
3 See https://www.regjeringen.no/en/topics/energy/oil-and-gas/norways-oil-history-in-5-minutes/id440538/, accessed on January 4, 2018.
4 While we are referring to oil only, we are not excluding natural gas. The analysis deals with all hydrocarbons. Algeria has natural gas reserves and so do Qatar, Iran, and others in the Middle East.
5 "Institutions are the rules and enforcement mechanisms that govern economic, social and political interactions" Islam (2018).
6 These were Algeria and Libya from North Africa and Saudi Arabia, the United Arab Emirates, and Kuwait from the Gulf.
7 The author admits in footnote 1, on the same page that "…some of my own previous studies supported several of these claims."
8 Transparency International, https://www.transparency.org/news/feature/corruption_perceptions_index_2017?gclid=EAIaIQobChMIwcaxus7k3wIVVrjACh3lRgGyEAAYASAAEgIHkvD_BwE.
9 The ideas presented here rest on past unpublished research papers by Mohammed Akacem and Dennis D. Miller and later in Let it Flow, *The Washington Times,* 21 February 2003, https://www.washingtontimes.com/news/2003/feb/21/20030221-085612-4813r/, as well as in Oil as the Path to Institutional change in the Oil-Exporting Middle East and North Africa, ASPJ, Volume 6, Issue 4, Winter 2015, English version URL https://www.airuniversity.af.edu/Portals/10/ASPJ_French/journals_E/Volume-06_Issue-4/akacemmiller_e.pdf, both accessed on January 13, 2019.
10 https://pfd.alaska.gov/Division-Info/Summary-of-Applications-and-Payments.

11 A Conversation with Milton Friedman, in Imprimis, July 2006, Volume 35, Number 7, https://imprimis.hillsdale.edu/emfree-to-chooseem-a-conversation-with-milton-friedman/, accessed on 14 January 2019.

12 Detailed exposition of the approach is in a forthcoming book by Akacem, Faulkner, and Miller, by Springer, expected in 2019.

13 The decision as to the distribution should be on a per capita basis or to citizens 18 years and older is a difficult one. Distribution on a per capita basis is more just from a constitutional standpoint. Citizenship is not a function of age and if every citizen has a right to a claim of the oil wealth, then that would be the appropriate course of action. The downside is that one would have to trust the parents, guardians, and whoever is the legal person responsible for those under 18 years of age to do the right thing and invest the oil payments until they are adults. A quick fix would be to have the new oil citizen oil company deposit the funds for the minors in accounts that are legally only accessed by the appropriate owners after they are 18 years old.

14 *The Economist* in a survey of the Arab world looks at the state of the Arab world, where it states that, "A civilisation that used to lead the world is in ruins—and only the locals can rebuild it." In "The tragedy of the Arabs," in *The Economist*, https://www.economist.com/news/leaders/21606284-civilisation-used-lead-world-ruinsand-only-locals-can-rebuild-it, accessed on January 14, 2019.

15 By the end of April 2019, the marches have taken place for nine consecutive weeks with students marching on Tuesdays as well.

References

Acemoglu, Daron & James A. Robinson. 2012. *Why Nations Fail: The Origins of Power, Prosperity and Poverty*, 1st ed. New York: Crown Publishers.

Akacem, Mohammed. 2015. *The Myth of the Oil Curse in Arab Oil Exporting Economies: Evidence from Norway and Singapore* (No. 13). Middle East Paper Series, Middle East Institute, National University of Singapore.

Akacem, Mohammed & Nicolas Cachanosky. 2017. "The Myth of the Resource Curse: A Case study of Algeria." *The Journal of Private Enterprise* 32 (2): 1–15.

Akacem, Mohammed & Xin Geng. 2015. "The Fallacy of the Resource Curse in Arab Oil Economies: Why Institutions Matter." *Journal of South Asian and Middle Eastern Studies* XXXVIII (2): 27–43.

Akacem, Mohammed & Dennis D. Miller. 2015. "Oil as the Path to Institutional Change in Oil-Exporting MENA." *Air and Space Power Journal (ASPJ)* 6 (4): 46–62.

Alexeev, Michael and Robert Conrad. 2009. "The Elusive Curse of Oil." *The Review of Economics and Statistics* 91 (3): 586–589.

Busse, Matthias & Steffen Groening. 2013. "The Resource Curse Revisited: Governance and Natural Resources." *Public Choice* 154 (1–2): 1–20.

The Economist, "The Devil's Excrement: Is Oil Wealth a Blessing or a Curse." *The Economist*, May 22, 2003. https://www.economist.com/finance-and-economics/2003/05/22/the-devils-excrement.

Humphreys, Macartan, Jeffrey D. Sachs, & Joseph E. Stiglitz, eds. 2007. *Escaping the Resource Curse*. New York: Columbia University Press.

Islam, Roumeen. 2018. "One More Time: What Are Institutions and How Do They Change?" Policy Research Working Paper 8422, The World Bank, April 2018.

Karl, Terry Lynn. *The Paradox of Plenty: Oil Booms and Petro-States*. London: University of California Press, 1997.

Moss, Todd, Caroline Lambert, & Stephanie Majerowicz. 2015. *Oil to Cash: Fighting the Resource Curse through Cash Transfers*. Center for Global Development.

Okere, Roseline. 2013. "Oil Resource Curse and the Yamani Syndrome." *The Guardian*, October 30. Available at http://oilrevenueng.org/revenews/oil-resource-curse-and-the-yamani-syndrome-the-guardian/ (accessed on January 4, 2018).

Peel, Quentin. 2007. "Algeria Confusion Typical of Socialist Time-Warp." *The Financial Times*, December 12. Available at https://www.ft.com/content/dad75b2a-a8e1-11dc-ad9e-0000779fd2ac (accessed on January 11, 2018).

Romer, David H. & Christina D. Romer. 2009. *Do Tax Cuts Starve the Beast? The Effect of Tax Changes on Government Spending,* Berkeley: University of California, Revised May 2009.

Ross, Michael L. 2011. "Will Oil Drown the Arab Spring? Democracy and the Resource Curse." *Foreign Affairs* 90 (5): 2–7. Available at http://www.jstor.org/stable/23041770.

Ross, Michael L. 2012. *The Oil Curse: How Petroleum Wealth Shapes the Development of Nations.* Princeton: Princeton University Press.

Sachs, Jeffrey D., & Andrew M. Warner. 1995. "Natural Resource Abundance and Economic Growth." Working Paper 5398. Cambridge, MA: National Bureau of Economic Research. https://www.nber.org/papers/w5398

United Nations Development Program. 2004. *Arab Human Development Report 2004.* Available at http://hdr.undp.org/sites/default/files/rbas_ahdr2004_en.pdf (accessed December 14, 2018).

Van der Ploeg, Frederick. 2011. "Natural Resources: Curse or Blessing?" *Journal of Economic Literature* 49 (2): 366–420.

World Bank. 2002. *World Development Report 2002: Building Institutions for Markets,* Oxford University Press.

3

ALGERIA BEYOND OIL AND NATURAL GAS

Challenges and options

Sarin Abado and Smail Khennas

Algeria is known for its rich hydrocarbon reserves, particularly natural gas, and is among the leading energy producing and exporting countries in the world. It supplies crude oil and natural gas to international markets and generates almost all of its state revenues from this sector. Energy is therefore of utmost strategic importance to the country and shapes Algeria's political, economic, and social landscape more than any other sector.

Algeria's energy: ample resources, growing demand

The oil and gas dimension

Currently, oil, natural gas, and petroleum products account for more than 95% of Algeria's total exports. The importance of hydrocarbons has emerged in the 1970s as a result of the "first oil shock" and the relative decline of other sectors, particularly the agricultural sector.

As at the end of 2016, Algeria holds Africa's second largest gas reserves after Nigeria with a total of 4.5 billion cubic meters (bcm) of proved gas reserves. However, the trend observed since 2010 shows a relative stagnation in gas reserves which can be explained by the lack of significant new discoveries and rapidly growing domestic demand (British Petroleum 2017).

Algeria's strategy has consisted mainly of maximising the use of natural gas to meet domestic demand in order to optimise export revenues from oil which generate higher profits. Compared to natural gas, oil exports are more lucrative mainly due to the high investment, processing, and trans-portation costs associated with the natural gas value chain, particularly

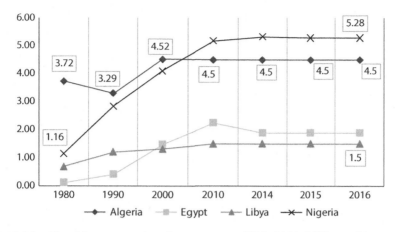

FIGURE 3.1 Algeria's proven natural gas reserves 1980–2016 (billion cubic metres). (From British Petroleum 2017, Statistical Review of World Energy, https://www.bp.com/content/dam/bp/en/corporate/pdf/energy-economics/statistical-review-2017/bp-statistical-review-of-world-energy-2017-full-report.pdf, 2017.)

liquefied natural gas. Consequently, natural gas is used as the main source of energy for almost all domestic power plants and other domestic end uses such as heating and cooking. Even in the transport sector, liquefied petroleum gas is increasingly used in order to limit gasoline and diesel imports. As a result, domestic natural gas consumption doubled between 2000 and 2016. (British Petroleum 2017) (Figure 3.1).

Despite this approach, it is important to note that natural and liquefied natural gas exports still accounted for 48% of Algeria's hydrocarbon net exports in 2016 and 56% including liquefied petroleum gas[1] (Algerian Ministry of Energy 2016, 2017) (Figure 3.2).

The elevated level of domestic gas demand can be further explained by widespread access to modern energy services and heavy subsidies that have led to inefficient and wasteful consumption. As a result, Algeria's overall energy consumption per capita is relatively high.

Natural gas also predominates Algeria's energy balance because its proved oil reserves are substantially lower than its gas reserves. However, within Africa, Algeria still holds the third-largest proved crude oil reserves after Nigeria and Libya with 12.2 billion barrels/1.5 billion tons oil equivalent (British Petroleum 2017). Similar to natural gas, oil reserves are likely to experience a sharp decline over the next 20 years given rising demand, inefficient consumption, and the absence of major new discoveries (Figure 3.3).

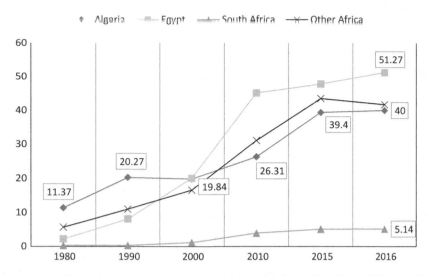

FIGURE 3.2 Natural gas consumption in Algeria and Africa 1980–2016 (billion cubic metres). (From British Petroleum 2017, Statistical Review of World Energy, https://www.bp.com/content/dam/bp/en/corporate/pdf/energy-economics/statistical-review-2017/bp-statistical-review-of-world-energy-2017-full-report.pdf, 2017.)

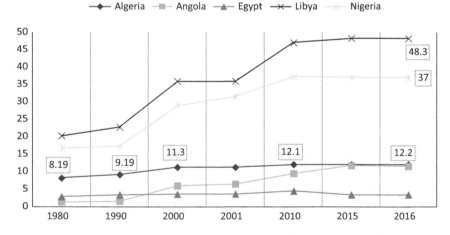

FIGURE 3.3 Algeria's proven oil reserves 1980–2016 (billion barrels). (From British Petroleum 2017, Statistical Review of World Energy, https://www.bp.com/content/dam/bp/en/corporate/pdf/energy-economics/statistical-review-2017/bp-statistical-review-of-world-energy-2017-full-report.pdf, 2017.)

Green energy trends and potential

The heavy reliance on hydrocarbons and their continuous decline coupled with the vulnerability of Algeria's economy are key factors for Algeria's increasing interest in deploying renewable energy on a large scale. Due to its geographical location, Algeria holds considerable potential for renewable energy, notably solar and, to a lesser extent, wind (Table 3.1).

TABLE 3.1 Algeria's solar energy potential

	Coastal region	High plateau	Sahara
Area (%)	4	10	86
Average sunshine (hours/year)	2650	3000	3500
Average amount of energy received (kWh/m²/year)	1700	1900	2650

Source: Algerian Ministry of Energy, "Potentiels des Energies Renouvelables," http://www.energy.gov.dz/francais/index.php?page=potentiels, 2018.

To deploy this potential, Algeria adopted a major national renewable energy plan approved by the government in February 2011 and revised in May 2015. The programme foresees a production target of 22,000 megawatts of renewable energy by 2030. Through this target, 27% of electricity should be produced from renewables by 2030 (Algerian Ministry of Energy 2015a) (Figure 3.4).

Initially, solar photovoltaics and wind energy will be the main technologies accounting for approximately 84% of production according to the national renewable energy plan. At a later stage, it is likely that other technologies, especially concentrated solar power will gain substantial importance. Concentrated solar power has indeed experienced major technology progress over the last 5 years, particularly with regard to storage. Further development of concentrated solar power will therefore dramatically reduce the intermittency constraint associated with renewables. Moreover, the levelised costs of concentrated solar power have significantly decreased. A high share of concentrated solar power in the renewable energy mix could thus prove to significantly benefit Algeria. A first step in this direction

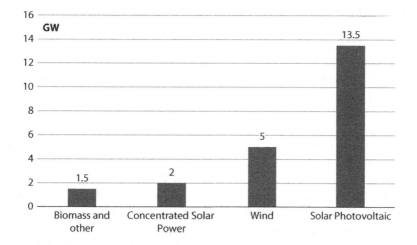

FIGURE 3.4 Algeria's renewable energy plan and foreseen technologies (megawatt). Biomass includes residues and municipal waste; other includes cogeneration and geothermal. (From Algerian Ministry of Energy, "Programme National des Energies Nouvelles et Renouvelables," http://www.energy.gov.dz/francais/uploads/2016/Programme-National/Programme-National-Energies-Nouvelles-Renouvelables.pdf, 2015a.)

has already been taken with a hybrid concentrated solar power/natural gas power plant in Hassi R'Mel which came on stream in July 2011 (El Gharbi 2011).

Strategies for coping with the energy dilemma

Algeria's energy dilemma consists of meeting its rapidly rising domestic demand without having to compromise on lucrative export volumes that keep the economy alive. Solving this dilemma is paramount not only to ensure energy security in the future, but also for the country's economic survival if the hydrocarbon sector remains the backbone of the economy. Unless forward-looking policies are implemented, Algeria's position as major hydrocarbon exporter is increasingly at risk as its oil and gas fields are maturing in the face of fast-growing energy consumption and long-standing European clients (ICIS 2017).

Based on this outlook, Algeria will need to find ways to increase its energy production in order to both serve its population and keep enough volumes available to sell abroad for the purpose of filling its state budget. At the same time, it can ensure that growth rates are kept under control by inducing a more conscious and efficient use of energy among its consumers.

Possible strategies and options that can help pull Algeria out of its energy dilemma are outlined in the following paragraphs.

The case for renewables in Algeria

Countries around the world are transitioning from hydrocarbon intensive economies towards greener solutions to mitigate climate change, reduce dependence on fossil fuel imports, or provide energy access to populations in remote areas. In Algeria, renewable energy sources, especially solar and wind, are well positioned to add extra volumes of electricity to the system to help cover rising consumer demand. With close to 100% of electricity produced from natural gas, the exploitation of renewable energy could free up significant volumes of gas for export and thereby ease the energy dilemma.

The idea of introducing renewable energy in Algeria is not new. Policy makers have been considering renewables since the late 1990s in various pieces of legislation.[2] These allow for priority access of renewables to the grid and oblige distribution companies to purchase electricity from renewable or cogeneration plants. The government's latest action involved the issuing of a long-term national renewable energy strategy including the already mentioned central target of bringing 22,000 megawatts of installed renewable capacity online by 2030 (Algerian Ministry of Energy 2015a).

Despite these ambitious goals and laws, the production of electricity from renewable sources still constitutes less than 1% of the domestic energy mix (Algerian Ministry of Energy 2015b). Fortunately, wind and solar photovoltaics are among the fastest growing renewable energy sources worldwide due to the drastic cost reductions and rapid technological advances that have taken place over the past decade. As a result, wind and solar have never been more competitive at any time in history and are continuously developing into a real alternative to conventional sources in economic terms (IRENA 2018). In light of these developments, Algeria is facing an optimal moment to invest in renewable energy, but has yet to take concrete steps to bring new capacities online.

One step that has been taken to facilitate the achievement of the renewable targets is the establishment of a feed-in tariff system in 2014.[3] Yet before this system could take effect, a new policy introducing auctions as the main support mechanism for renewables[4] was established in 2017.

In an auction system, investors bid a price they desire to receive per kilowatt hour of electricity produced in contrast to feed-in tariffs which are set beforehand by the national regulatory authority for each renewable technology. Both mechanisms certainly represent legitimate approaches to increase renewable energy production. However, for auctions to be most successful, a competitive market setting with a multitude of bidders should be ensured. In the absence of such conditions, there is an increased risk of strategic behaviour among bidders. Participants may collude and agree on prices in advance or drastically under-bid to push others out of the market. Experience in Europe has shown that for these reasons, many countries apply feed-in tariffs or similar systems first before moving to auctions (Klessmann 2014).

So far, competition in Algeria's energy sector has been virtually non-existent despite the liberalisation of the energy market in the early 2000s.[5] It thus remains to be seen whether a sizable number of bidders can be attracted to the first-ever planned auction of 4,000 megawatts for utility-scale solar in Algeria (Portail Algérien des Energies Renouvelables 2018a). At this point, no reference examples are available as neither feed-in tariffs nor renewable auctions have been tried out in Algeria.

Overall, the announcement of the tender caused mixed reactions within the local and global solar sector due to strict domestic content requirements embedded in the draft tender rules. It is, however, likely that these requirements will loosen up significantly given a decision taken by the Council of Ministers in June 2018. This decision questions the government's original intention to oblige investors to manufacture the equipment used for renewable electricity production in Algeria.

At a broad level, the key ingredients to bring renewable energy online are fulfilled in Algeria. There is sizable solar and wind potential, a rough regulatory framework, and an advantageous economic prospect for renewable energy. The deployment of renewables is thus a realistic option for the country to increase its domestic electricity production in the medium term. Any further delay will put the country's energy future at even more risk and aggravate the energy dilemma.

Will shale gas be part of the future energy mix?

Alongside Algeria's renewable potential, the country also needs to assess whether it can count on its shale gas reserves as a realistic source to mitigate its energy dilemma. The technically recoverable shale gas reserves in Algeria have been estimated to account for more than 20,000 billion cubic meters which represent the third largest recoverable shale gas resources worldwide (EIA 2013).

This number can hardly be neglected as it represents around four to seven times the country's proven conventional gas reserves. The fluctuation ratio is a direct result of the depleting conventional gas reserve base for which estimates keep being revised downwards (Aissaoui 2016). Yet the impressive magnitude of Algeria's shale deposits alone still does not reveal whether they are recoverable in a profitable, environmentally safe, and socially acceptable manner (Figure 3.5).

Discussions about the role of shale gas in Algeria are as controversial as in the rest of the world with proponents and opponents on either side of the spectrum. Broadly speaking, the government has promoted a pro-shale agenda (Official Journal of the Republic of Algeria 2013) hoping to free up more gas to close the looming energy gap while the majority population in the concerned areas have fiercely protested these plans over health and safety concerns stemming from the hydraulic fracking process applied during extraction. While the government suspended its test drillings in 2015 in response to popular grievances, the appetite for shale gas revived in 2017 when the government ordered the state oil company Sonatrach to re-launch shale gas development claiming that the situation would not leave any other choice to the country in light of the dwindling conventional reserves.

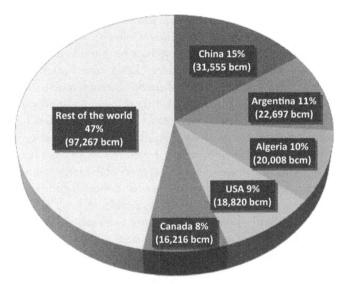

FIGURE 3.5 Top five countries with technically recoverable shale gas resources (billion cubic metres). (From EIA, "Technically Recoverable Shale Oil and Shale Gas Resources: An Assessment of 137 Shale Formations in 41 Countries Outside the United States," https://www.eia.gov/analysis/studies/worldshalegas/pdf/overview. pdf, 2013.)

Apart from social protests, there is uncertainty as to whether exploiting Algeria's shale gas is profitable in economic terms. In fact, apart from some initial test drillings, there are no insights on how lucrative the extraction process will be, i.e., how many wells need to be drilled annually to reach the break-even point factoring in the additional costs for equipment, infrastructure, and logistics. Rough calculations using average shale gas output in the USA have led a number of experts to express doubts regarding the profitability in the short to medium-term, especially in times of low prices. Overall, it is difficult to determine a break-even price for shale gas fields given the differences in geological characteristics, the amount of reserves, and other factors. However, when oil prices dropped below 50 USD, a sharp decrease in global shale gas production was observed (Kemp 2017). An additional argument voiced is that China and Argentina which are blessed with even more shale gas reserves than Algeria (according to 2013 data from the US Energy Information Administration) have not opted for extraction despite being net importers of energy due to the lack of profitability. Shale gas is also associated with other risks, particularly ground water contamination. These risks must be thoroughly assessed before granting licenses for commercial shale gas exploitation (Table 3.2).

In the south of Algeria where the country's shale gas deposits are located and rainfall is particularly low, ground water is the main source for competing end uses including agriculture. Consequently, contamination of ground water will have a huge social and economic impact on the local population. Moreover,

TABLE 3.2 Shale gas and environmental risks

Environmental aspect	Individual production site		Cumulative production sites	
	Fracturing	Overall project	Fracturing	Overall project
Groundwater contamination	Moderate-high	High	Moderate-high	High
Surface water contamination	Moderate-high	High	Moderate-high	High
Water resources	Moderate	Moderate	High	High
Release to air	Moderate	Moderate	High	High
Land use	Not applicable	Moderate	Not applicable	High
Risk to biodiversity	Low	Moderate	Moderate	High
Noise-related impact	Moderate	Moderate-high	Moderate	High
Visual impact	Low	Low-moderate	Moderate	Moderate
Seismicity	Low	Low	Low	Low
Traffic	Moderate	Moderate	High	High

Source: Jackson, R., et al., *Annu. Rev. Env. Resour.*, 39, 327–362, https://jacksonlab.stanford.edu/sites/default/files/jackson_et_al._arer_2014.pdf, 2014.

TABLE 3.3 Water intensity in extracting and processing of different energy sources (litres per MMBTU)

Energy source	Water for extraction and processing
Natural gas, conventional	7.2
Natural gas, unconventional	15.5
Pulverised coal (once through)	28.4
Saudi Arabia crude	121.1
Nuclear (once through)	49.2
Corn ethanol (unirrigated)	450.5
Corn ethanol (irrigated)	14384.6
Solar PV	0
Wind	0

Source: EIA, "Technically Recoverable Shale Oil and Shale Gas Resources: An Assessment of 137 Shale Formations in 41 Countries Outside the United States," https://www.eia.gov/analysis/studies/worldshalegas/pdf/overview.pdf, 2013.

Abbreviations: MMBTU, One Million British Thermal Units; PV, photovoltaic.

extracting and processing shale gas requires more than twice the amount of water compared to conventional gas (Jackson et al. 2014).

Notwithstanding the uncertainties and grievances, the prospect for (Table 3.3) shale gas in Algeria remains real even if the first volumes will probably appear on the surface only in the very long-term. With technology and research advancing over time, the extraction process may become more efficient, less costly, and less environmentally invasive. However, until the conditions for a profitable business case fall into place, a rush to extract shale gas in the short to medium term risks bringing more loss than gain, both economically and politically. Regarding the latter, an effort must be made to re-assure and engage local communities in Algeria's southern desert regions from early on. This includes presenting real solutions to the people's concerns such as how water supply is made safe once extraction starts on a large scale.

In sum, the moment to benefit from the tremendous shale gas reserves in Algeria is yet to come. Until then, the country will have time to carefully study its potential in more detail and lay the ground for shale gas to possibly become part of the equation. However, in the short to medium term, shale gas does not seem to be a reliable option to fix the energy dilemma.

The challenge of doing business in Algeria

An important precondition for renewable energy and shale gas to succeed in Algeria is the attraction of foreign investments and know-how. At present, a number of obstacles keep hampering investors to get profitably engaged in Algeria.

In the hydrocarbon sector, one major reason for investors to shy away from Algeria is the fact that all oil and gas projects must be majority owned by Sonatrach. Protectionist policies like these are highly counterintuitive when complex ventures such as the exploitation of shale gas form part of the national agenda. The situation is even more worrying as Algeria had previously abandoned the majority ownership rule in 2005, only to revise it back to the previous status quo shortly thereafter (Boersma, Vandendriessche, & Leber 2015). In order to unlock Algeria's vast shale gas potential, a more inviting approach towards investors will be necessary. Given that the exploitation of unconventional gas remains one of the most challenging undertakings in the energy sector, Algeria will need foreign support if it seriously wants to pursue this path.

In relation to renewable energy, the government has contemplated obliging investors to manufacture the equipment they intend to use for renewable energy production inside Algeria. Thus, compared to most countries, the auction system adopted in Algeria in 2017[6] foresees that bidders develop a full industrial project alongside electricity production. This is a major constraint as most independent power producers are not necessarily involved in solar manufacturing. Furthermore, solar manufacturing is still a risky business which may deter many potential bidders interested solely in the deployment of renewable energy capacity. While the intention behind this is to build up an industry for renewable equipment in Algeria, such an "all-or-nothing" approach seems unnecessarily rigid considering the strategic importance of renewables for Algeria's future. If such a conditionality is pursued in the course of the planned 4,000 megawatts auction, it may be a decisive element for some investors not to bid. The industrial component should thus ideally be dealt with outside the framework of the renewable auctions in order not to diminish the pool of investors interested in developing renewable energy projects in Algeria.

Another important aspect for market development is policy continuity. The relatively sudden nature of government reshuffles that took place between 2015 and 2017 can pose an additional element of discouragement to investors. In fact, Algeria has seen a total of four different energy ministers within the two-year period from 2015 to 2017. During this time, shale gas drillings were promoted by one minister, completely abandoned by another minister, and back on the agenda with yet another minister. Similarly, the shift from feed-in tariffs to an auction-based system for renewable energy took place virtually overnight with the arrival of a new minister. Frequent changes in top government officials risk leading to legal uncertainty and send conflicting signals to investors. Stability in the regulatory framework is a key aspect for investors to have confidence to engage.

Curbing demand through economic measures and consumer policies

The analysis so far provided solutions for Algeria's energy dilemma from a supply side perspective. This section shall focus on possible demand side measures that can be implemented to help control rapidly increasing electricity consumption.

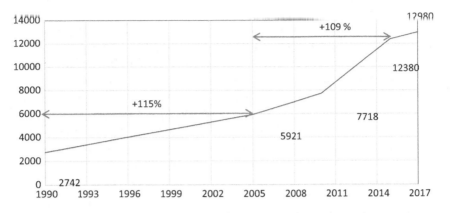

FIGURE 3.6 Northern Algerian electricity network, peak demand, 1990–2017 (megawatt). (From Sonelgaz, Various Data Reports and Statistics, 1990–2017.)

Algerian households and businesses have benefitted from generous energy subsidies allowing for their electricity bills to remain well below the actual cost of service. Consequently, most consumers lack awareness of the real value of energy as a commodity. This has largely resulted in inefficient consumption behaviours across sectors. With peak demand growing rapidly, mainly due to increased cooling during summer months, a more conscious consumption is vital to curtail the energy dilemma and optimise infrastructure investments in the electricity sector (Figure 3.6).

It is very likely that the upward trend in electricity peak demand will continue, although at a slower pace. In 2017, electricity peak demand reached 12,981 megawatts which represents an approximate 5% increase between 2015 and 2017.

Considering the overall structure of the Algerian economy as a rentier state with an extensive subsidy policy, an upward revision of energy prices for final consumers would have a double effect: on the one hand, higher end-user prices would induce consumers to save energy; on the other hand, the state budget would be under less pressure through reduced energy subsidies.

The increase of energy prices remains a highly sensitive political subject. So far, the government has largely refrained from measures in this regard as the distribution of subsidies has worked well in keeping social unrest under control. This approach has been the regime's central mechanism to maintaining legitimacy and ensure loyalty from the population (Achy 2013). For example, during the Arab Spring, the government raised overall subsidies by 60% in 2011 and increased civil servant salaries by 9% the year thereafter (Werenfels 2014). As a result, social grievances did not heat up as they did in neighbouring Tunisia and other countries in the region. Overall, explicit and implicit subsidies devoted to energy account for approximately 8% of the GDP (IMF 2016) (Table 3.4).

TABLE 3.4 Explicit and implicit subsidies in Algeria in 2015

	Billion Algerian Dinars (DZD)	% GDP
Explicit	926 of which	5.5
Housing	357	2.1
Education	109	0.7
Food	225	1
Electricity, natural gas, water	74	8.1
Interest rate	160	1
Implicit	1367 of which	8.1
Housing (2013)	67	0.4
Energy (fuel, natural gas, electricity)	1300	7.7
Total	2293	13.6

Source: IMF, 2016, "Algeria, Selected Issues," Country Report 16/128, April 29, viewed 22 July 2018, from https://www.imf.org/external/pubs/ft/scr/2016/cr16128.pdf, 2016.

With revenues from hydrocarbon exports decreasing due to an extended period of low oil prices, the subsidy policy has, however, become more difficult to sustain. In fact, the country's financial situation has worsened so dramatically that the government was forced to reduce subsidies on a variety of goods to protect the state budget from depletion. To this end, new taxes on petroleum products were introduced in 2016.[7] Moreover, significant increases in electricity and gas tariffs were enacted further to a decision of the regulator taken at the end of December 2015 (CREG 2015). This constituted the first raise in electricity and gas tariffs in 10 years which is an unusually long timeframe for a tariff review. While average household customers remained exempted (from electricity and gas price increases, not from fuel), prices for larger consumers as well as business and industrial consumers were raised. While this first tariff adaptation has been a step in the right direction, end user prices still remain comparatively low and should therefore be further adjusted over the coming years. Domestic consumers must gradually become part of the equation as well, notably to reduce the inequality between wealthier and poorer parts of the population. While subsidies for poor households are legitimate and necessary, there is no reason to provide these benefits to those who are able to afford their energy bills. A subsidy reform that stops supporting those who do not require help could therefore significantly improve the budgetary situation.

Due to the possibility of implementing price increases quite rapidly, these will have a more immediate impact on Algeria's energy balance as opposed to the long-term effects expected from renewable energy and shale gas development. Economic reforms in this direction are therefore vital to bridge the gap until solar, wind, and possibly, in the long term, shale gas come online to curtail the energy dilemma from a supply side perspective.

For the subsidy reform to be effective, policy makers must also ensure that consumers are not saddled with higher bills and no further assistance. In fact, consumers must be educated on how to save energy in their daily lives, empowering them to influence their consumption levels and keep their bills as low as possible. Large-scale programmes are needed in this regard considering that the average Algerian citizen plays a crucial role in fixing the country's energy dilemma.

Is Algeria on the road to an energy transition?

Algeria's energy landscape is set to change drastically if the options outlined are put into practice. The introduction of renewable energy would mark a particular paradigm shift in this regard, providing for a more diversified and climate-friendly future energy mix. Despite the favourable conditions for renewables in Algeria, a real transition has not yet taken effect. The development of concrete projects has been delayed although the political framework has been delivered successfully. Yet for a real transition to take place, the renewable tenders planned by the government, notably a 4,000 megawatts tender as well as a smaller 200 megawatts solar auction[8] must effectively be launched (Portail Algérien des Energies Renouvelables 2018b). So far, these auctions have been repeatedly announced with no official call for bids following. Considering this status quo, Algeria is extremely close to making a key step towards a national energy transition involving renewables and should seize this moment to invite suitable investors. As long as renewable energy remains offline, the energy dilemma will, however, persist.

Assessing a potential energy transition in Algeria also requires a look at the broader economic context. The dominance of the hydrocarbons sector in generating state income has created a situation whereby the latter carries the entire burden of Algeria's economic survival. The lack of economic diversification also represents one of the root causes for the energy dilemma. In fact, the dilemma is fuelled by Algeria's economic dependence on export revenues and not by the lack of energy as such. The paradox of a major oil and gas producer fearing to be unable to meet domestic demand demonstrates that energy security is not the main issue at stake. It shows even more that the country has plunged into a vicious economic circle as a result of its vulnerable economic set-up. An energy transition without an economic transition will therefore not be sustainable. Only economic diversification will provide for Algeria's energy security in the long-run.

Overall, Algeria seems well aware of the structural problems that have led to the looming crisis. It has started adopting targeted policies to ease the energy dilemma, be it by preparing for the introduction of renewables and shale gas or through a first reduction of energy subsidies. Policies are, however, implemented rather slowly. Considering the urgency to resolve the energy dilemma, more concrete and immediate action will be needed to take the energy transition to the next level.

So far, efforts to move towards an energy transition have been particularly high in periods of low oil and gas prices. It therefore remains to be seen how serious the government stands behind its declarations when prices remain high over longer periods of time. At this point, the motivation to embark on an energy transition has probably reached an unprecedented height compared to previous years.

Conclusion

Algeria's hydrocarbon wealth has secured the country's position as major oil and gas exporter since the 1970s. Almost half a century later, this position is increasingly endangered given the competition between growing domestic demand and export commitments. Shrinking reserves and heavy dependence on hydrocarbon revenues exacerbate this dilemma.

Algeria has several alternatives to address the challenges ahead. In the short-run, the gradual reduction of subsidies seems the most effective way to reign in consumption and increase the state budget. Such economic reforms coupled with more targeted social transfers will lead to a healthier and more energy efficient economy.

In the medium-term, the development of renewable energy, especially solar and wind, can provide additional volumes of electricity to satisfy domestic demand and diversify the energy mix. The exploitation of shale gas is yet another option to bring more energy online, albeit in the long-run as economic, social, and environmental feasibility still needs to be ensured.

While these solutions focus solely on the transformation of the energy sector, a more profound economic reform would be necessary to establish a truly resilient Algerian economy. The energy sector will not be able to fix it all. For a healthy, prosperous, and flourishing Algeria, the economy needs more than one sector to move the country forward.

Notes

1 Authors' calculations based on data retrieved from the Algerian Ministry of Energy's Energy Balances 2015 and 2016 (*Bilan énérgetique national 2015* and *Bilan énérgetique national 2016*).
2 Law n°99-09 dated July 28, 1999 *(Loi n°99-09 relative à la maîtrise de l'énergie)*; Law n°04-09 dated August 14, 2004 *(Loi n°04-09 relative à la promotion des énergies renouvelables dans le cadre du développement durable)*; Decree n°13–218 dated June 18, 2013 *(Décret exécutif n°13-218 fixant les conditions d'octroi des primes au titre des coûts de diversification de la production d'électricité)*.
3 Decree n°13-218 dated June 18, 2013 *(Décret exécutif n°13-218 fixant les conditions d'octroi des primes au titre des coûts de diversification de la production d'électricité)*; Ministerial Orders of February 2, 2014 *(Arrêtés fixant les tarifs d'achat garantis et les conditions de leur application pour l'électricité produite à partir des installations utilisant la filière solaire photovoltaïque et éolienne)*.
4 Decree n°17-98 dated February 26, 2017 *(Décret exécutif n°17-98 définissant la procédure d'appel d'offres pour la production des énergies renouvelables ou de cogénération et leur intégration dans le système national d'approvisionnement en énergie électrique)*.

5 Law n°02-01 dated February 5, 2002 *(Loi n°02-01 relative à l'électricité et à la distribution du gaz par canalisations).*
6 Decree n°17-98 dated February 26, 2017, Article 5 *(Décret exécutif n°17-98 définissant la procédure d'appel d'offres pour la production des énergies renouvelables ou de cogénération et leur intégration dans le système national d'approvisionnement en énergie électrique).*
7 Law n°16-14 dated December 28, 2016, Article 28 bis *(Loi n°16-14 portant loi de finances pour 2017).*
8 The 200 megawatts auction to be launched in 2019 shall be the first auction open to national, foreign, public, and private investors. This auction is aimed at drawing lessons from this mechanism before larger-scale auctions are offered.

References

Achy, L., 2013, "The price of stability in Algeria," Carnegie Endowment for International Peace, viewed April 29, 2018, from https://carnegieendowment.org/files/price_stability_algeria.pdf.

Aissaoui, A., 2016, "Algerian Gas: Troubling Trends, Troubled Policies," Oxford Institute for Energy Studies Paper NG 108, viewed May 22, 2018, from https://www.oxfordenergy.org/wpcms/wp-content/uploads/2016/05/Algerian-Gas-Troubling-Trends-Troubled-Policies-NG-108.pdf.

Algerian Ministry of Energy, 2015a, "Programme National des Energies Nouvelles et Renouvelables," viewed May 12, 2018, from http://www.energy.gov.dz/francais/uploads/2016/Programme-National/Programme-National-Energies-Nouvelles-Renouvelables.pdf.

Algerian Ministry of Energy, 2015b, "Electricité et Gaz," viewed May 2, 2018, from http://www.energy.gov.dz/francais/uploads/2016/Energie/electricite-gaz-maj.pdf.

Algerian Ministry of Energy, 2016, "Bilan énérgétique national 2015," viewed July 25, 2018, from http://www.energy.gov.dz/francais/uploads/2016/Bilans_et_statistiques_du_secteur/Bilan_Energetique_National/Bilan_Energitique_National_2015_last.pdf.

Algerian Ministry of Energy, 2017, "Bilan énérgétique national 2016," viewed July 25, 2018, from http://www.energy.gov.dz/francais/uploads/2017/Bilans_et_statistiques_du_secteur/Bilan-Energetique/Bilan_Energetique_National_2016_edition_2017.pdf.

Algerian Ministry of Energy, 2018, "Potentiels des Energies Renouvelables," viewed July 25, 2018, from http://www.energy.gov.dz/francais/index.php?page=potentiels.

Boersma, T., Vandendriessche, M., & Leber, A., 2015, "Shale gas in Algeria: No quick fix," Brookings Institution, *Policy Brief* 15-01, viewed May 5, 2018, from https://www.brookings.edu/wp-content/uploads/2016/07/no_quick_fix_final-2.pdf.

British Petroleum, 2017, Statistical Review of World Energy, viewed July 25, 2018, from https://www.bp.com/content/dam/bp/en/corporate/pdf/energy-economics/statistical-review-2017/bp-statistical-review-of-world-energy-2017-full-report.pdf.

CREG, 2015, "Décision D/22-15/CD du 29 décembre 2015 portant fixation des tarifs de l'électricité et du gaz," viewed May 30, 2018, from http://www.energy.gov.dz/francais/uploads/2016/Energie/decision%20tarification.pdf.

EIA, 2013, "Technically Recoverable Shale Oil and Shale Gas Resources: An Assessment of 137 Shale Formations in 41 Countries Outside the United States," viewed June 12, 2018, from https://www.eia.gov/analysis/studies/worldshalegas/pdf/overview.pdf.

EIA, 2015, "Technically Recoverable Shale Oil and Shale Gas Resources: Algeria," viewed June 12, 2018, from https://www.eia.gov/analysis/studies/worldshalegas/pdf/Algeria_2013.pdf.

El Gharbi, N., 2011, "La centrale hybride de Hassi R'Mel," CDER, *Bulletin* 21, viewed July 28, 2018, from https://www.cder.dz/vlib/bulletin/pdf/bulletin_021_11.pdf.

ICIS, 2017, "Shifting sands of Algeria," *European Gas Markets* 24, 21, p. 5.

IMF, 2016, "Algeria, Selected Issues," *Country Report* 16/128, April 29, viewed July 22, 2018, from https://www.imf.org/external/pubs/ft/scr/2016/cr16128.pdf.

IRENA, 2018, "Renewable Power Generation Costs in 2017," viewed May 20, 2018, http://www.irena.org/-/media/Files/IRENA/Agency/Publication/2018/Jan/IRENA_2017_Power_Costs_2018.pdf.

Jackson, R., Vengosh, A., Carey, W., Davies, R., Darrah, T., O'Sullivan, F. & Petron, G., 2014, "The environmental costs and benefits of fracking," *Annual Review of Environment and Resources* 39, 327–362, viewed July 22, 2018, from https://jacksonlab.stanford.edu/sites/default/files/jackson_et_al._arer_2014.pdf.

Kemp, J., 2017, "U.S. shale breakeven price revealed around $50: Kemp," Reuters, viewed June 8, 2018, from https://www.reuters.com/article/us-usa-shale-kemp/u-s-shale-breakeven-price-revealed-around-50-kemp-idUSKBN1AP25M.

Klessmann, C., 2014, "Experience with renewable electricity (RES-E) support schemes in Europe: Current status and recent trends," Ecofys presentation, viewed May 3, 2018, from https://de.slideshare.net/Ecofys/ecofys-2014webinarrese-supportpoliciesineurope.

Official Journal of the Republic of Algeria, 2013, Loi n° 13-01 du 20 février 2013 modifiant et complétant la loi n° 05-07 du 28 avril 2005 relative aux hydrocarbures, viewed May 5, 2018, from http://www.energy.gov.dz/francais/uploads/Loi_13-01_modifiant_loi_hydro_05-07-2013.pdf.

Portail Algérien des Energies Renouvelables, 2018a, "ENR: en attendant le déploiement à grande échelle," viewed June 18, 2018, from https://portail.cder.dz/spip.php?article6571.

Portail Algérien des Energies Renouvelables, 2018b, "Energie solaire: appels d'offres pour la production de 200 mégawatts," viewed June 18, 2018, from https://portail.cder.dz/spip.php?article6573.

Sonelgaz, 1990–2017, Various Data Reports and Statistics.

UNCTAD, 2018, "Shale Gas," *Commodities at a Glance, Special Issue on Shale Gas* No 9, viewed July 22, 2018, from http://unctad.org/en/PublicationsLibrary/suc2017d10_en.pdf.

Werenfels, I., 2014, "The risk of playing for time in Algeria," German Institute for International and Security Affairs (Stiftung Wissenschaft und Politik), viewed May 31, 2018, from https://www.swp-berlin.org/fileadmin/contents/products/comments/2014C23_wrf.pdf.

4

ALGERIA'S ELITES AND INTELLECTUALS

Aissa Kadri

The downward spiral of the Algerian political system, its blockage, and its resilience to change need to be considered in terms of the role and responsibility of the Algerian elites,[1] intellectuals, and intelligentsias. The failure of the Algerian political system is above all a failure of opportunistic elites who have become increasingly mediocre, submissive to the existing political power, and unable to support the current transformations and the dynamics the society is witnessing. This inability of the elite to emancipate themselves from a Caesarist-type plebeian power is not only a matter of cyclical conditions related to the role and policies of an independent national state, but goes back in history to the country's social formation.

The origins of the different categories of Algerian elite are to be found firstly in the colonial situation.

Imposing a colonial education system in Algeria was at base a production strategy, with intermediate elites sandwiched between the dominated and the dominant, between a subservient class and the colonial power. These intermediate elites were divided, but complementary, based on a duality of training defined essentially by the logic of controlling the indigenous society. The colonial education system was divided into two networks from primary school. These comprised a specific network of indigenous primary, higher primary, complementary courses, Medersas, Ecole normale [Teachers's school], and special certificates especially for Algerians; and an elite network for European children consisting of elementary school, college, high school, normal school, and universities, which a few selected indigenous Algerians could attend. The free Muslim education itself, which wanted to offer an educational alternative, was from the start relegated to an inferior position assigned to it in the Algerian system. Born out of questioning French education, the cultural initiative proposed by the religious reform movement proposed by religious elites breaking with the Brotherhood movement, has paradoxically put itself in its school. However, the limits imposed on it by the colonial authorities (school closures, convictions) prevented its development especially after the decree March 1938.

This differentiation of the elite is based on a policy of divide and rule, a domination strategy aimed at exercising power through both assimilation and differentiation. One demonstrates what the colonial power could for the few elected members of the elite, the other turned to local society to implement colonial directives, but in vernacular languages and codes. These express the difference of the assigned functions and the similarity of ideological prerequisites between the teacher and the Medersian [medersa graduates] and on a different note, the products of the mosque. The essential feedback that illuminates both the permanent divisions and specific solidarities (of group or class) seems to be located in the relations that were formed between cultural, identity, national, and political claims (Djeghloul 1988). It is in their relation to the colonial power that these categories are specified and differentiated.

The political element had a paradoxical effect on the formation of the Algerian intelligentsia and the structuring of the cultural and political field during the colonial period. As a driving force in the process of empowering the various factions of the elite, this turned into a barrier that halted the antagonisms between the French-educated and the Arab-educated. This changed soon after independence.

The formation of the Algerian elite

This politicisation of the Algerian intellectual movement appears as a factor of blockage, of fossilising its cultural development. Trapped in the society-state binary antagonism, it did not carry out its cultural revolution: in turning to politics, it appears to have had "a low impact on society" (Djeghloul 1988). Merad notes that the modernisation from the Middle East turned out to have a weak influence as much on the French-educated youth as on the Arabic-educated (Merad 1967: 307–309), "whose modernism depended on the times and was nothing less than lukewarm."

Algeria appears in this respect to be typical of a good part of the Muslim world, especially in cases like Turkey, Egypt (Malek 1969: 140), or Tunisia (Smida 1970: 318); it bears witness to the incompleteness of the cultural restructuring process. When the Badisian movement experienced its expansion (1931–1932) a few decades prior (1850s), cultural renewal had affected Egypt and Tunisia; this did not help them escape the imperialist economy, but it was nonetheless from the start a relatively homogeneous national elite rooted in its own culture.

The immaturity of the Algerian intellectual movement and its present characteristics emerged under colonial conditions. The colonial enterprise has, therefore, absorbed the dynamics initiated at a local level, particularly in other Maghreb countries which prior to colonial intrusion had engaged in modest reforms, and which nevertheless had the potential for change. Science was thus put to the service of colonisation, as evidenced by the instrumental and utilitarian vision of knowledge mobilisation.

Whcn the Algerian national movement supported the Algerian elites, it did so with all based on their training, with all the contradictions (Pervillé 1984); however, they were overshadowed by the political nationalisation of the intelligentsia operated by the independence movement.

The Algerian national movement thus supported these Algerian elites by merging them into a fundamentally plebeian movement with the scars and contradictions of their training. Those would continue throughout the maturation of the movement and sometimes break out in events, such as the so-called Berber crisis (1949), the centralist break, the emblematic confrontation around the Union Générale des Étudiants Musulmans Algériens UGEMA), etc. These would resurface throughout the national liberation struggle when the anti-intellectual syndrome, manipulated by the colonial forces of repression, turned into a form of purification in some regions. Many historians and witnesses account for dissensions born within the mountains during the national liberation struggle, as the result of an anti-intellectual movement. Some of the rural guerrillas were almost illiterate, possessing at best a limited Arabic, and were opposed to French-educated intellectuals, graduates, students, and high school students perceived as privileged and considered suspect because of their training and social background.

After independence, there was a resurgence of the cultural problem and more specifically the problem of cultural antagonism born of the colonial period. Immediately after national liberation, a political class with its largely French-educated leadership, but Islamic and Arabic references that had prevailed in the armed struggle, and was still dominant in the civil society, thought in terms of conciliation and synergy. For a long time Arabisation seemed to have gone underground, and its supporters are precisely the heirs of the reforming leaders of the past'[2] (Peneff 1982). Nevertheless, with social development and, more precisely, the progress of Arabisation, the problem of antagonisms tended to gain in sharpness and, in recent decades, it has dominated all the others. In addition, it is paradoxical that the processes that followed independence and which intensify the fractures of today are like a reverse image of what happened during the colonial era. The cultural equation remains the same: Westernisation or self-recovery of society; cultural forces, or even their social component, are similar, even if they have expanded. The presuppositions associated with them are the same: the French-educated elite has its pro-Western ideology and the Arabic-educated elite its Middle Eastern influences. Even the effects of global geopolitics would be identical: on the one hand, the dominant and acculturating will of French imperialism, modernisation perceived as Westernisation and as American hegemony; and a return to the tradition, national values, and resurgence of a new Islamic revolution on the other.

Post-independence Algeria: an identical cultural equation

The immediate post-independence years would indeed immediately raise the cultural and linguistic issue and more precisely the problem of cultural antagonisms born of the colonial period. This was especially through the debate on bilingualism and the primacy of vernacular languages by some intellectuals like Abdallah Mazouni or later Mostefa Lacheraf, who was quickly called into question by Arabisers like Abdallah Cheriet—"bilingualism is a bourgeois way," said one of the advocates of forced Arabisation.

From the perspective of these processes, independence did not constitute a break. The triumphant developmentalism of the 1960s and 1970s intensified reforms that harnessed the sciences and intelligentsia in the service of a technocratic project, dressed in the "clothes" of a specific socialism, tailor-made by a Caesarist power. This project aimed to reconcile formally an Arabisation as the foundation of a re-appropriation, with authenticity, of national (chauvinist) values and an opening on progress through the French language.

The national education system will thus deepen the antagonisms and intensify the contradictions until the rupture. Both school and university, through curricula, pedagogies, and supervision, will develop different, but complementary modes of socialisation. These categories of the elite were also scheduled and socialised by a global environment, by a society that has two versions, two registers, two levels—Arabic or French speakers—but which remains fundamentally unifying, homogenising, and whose dominant thought patterns, beyond their differences in referencing and affiliation, refine the same stereotypes.

The political presuppositions that will form the basis of the definition of the elite production's institution during the years of specific socialism's implementation are those of integrating the latter into the political project. The elite that the state wants to produce is not so much one that would be technically competent, but one that has internalised the political principles that could manage for the state, for civil society. The student volunteering for the agrarian revolution, for example, could constitute in this respect a junction between political speech, educational speech, and the expectations of a large part of the student population.

Colonial and national systems: elective affinities

The central hypothesis here is that the formation and place envisaged for the elites by the colonial power and the national power are mirror images, echoing each other. They operate homologically in the two historical situations.

In both cases, the educational system only makes sense if it is instrumentalised by politics in a domination process. This would probably be nothing more than a matter of evidence if the educational system assumed a function of broad social reproduction which would affect the whole society, and which would involve the inclusion or exclusion of all social groups in relation to the actual exercise of political economic or cultural powers. Yet, the historical analysis for the colonial case and the sociological analysis for the national case show that the two systems of education operated freely. In the first case, Algerian Muslims were largely unconcerned and those few members of the elite in the system had not, with the exception of a few individuals, been integrated into the restricted circles of power. It is the same in the current system; despite a massive development of schooling, the failing educational system has produced graduates rather than elites, or even intellectuals; the political and social system has worked since independence until today with an old political class, which is due more to a historical legitimacy than a scientific one. Even if one admits that the educational system produced an elite, it is noteworthy that, in much the same way as in the colonial situation, the indigenous elite did not participate in the exercise of political and economic powers. Similarly, the current system, at least until the beginning of the decade, remained outside the sphere of decisions. Thus, the two situations are characterised by a closed circle of elites at least until the irruption of civil society in the political game.

This may be the case because the state is extraneous to the educational system; the latter only exists in order to and in so far as it is possible to control society and keep it at a distance from the power bloc. In this respect, access to political resources appears only as a result of co-option practices: in the two historical situations, the state selecting, according to subjective criteria, from the fishpond of the education system's products.

Keeping this distance was bound in the colonial case to a dilemma: to acculturate is at the same time to raise awareness and can be referred, in the national case, to the old suspicious atavism of a rural core of power about those bearing knowledge, especially in a foreign language.

This foreignness leads to doubts about the effect of political socialisation of the institution in the two historical situations; in both cases, political integration does not seem to have taken on the products of the school system, and barely affected the rural, uneducated society, which clung to its traditional anchors. In the colonial case, this is explained by the Malthusianism effect, rarely denied in indigenous education and an ambiguity constitutive of the dominated society's control strategy. In the national case, this is the perverse effect of the mass education system development, which led to a deep deculturation, or at least, to "an impoverishment of what used to be the elements of peasant or community culture or urban neighbourhoods, to leave room for a dual incapacity of expression and thought" (Gallissot 1984: 52). This similarity was not simply borne by different modes of development of the educational system; this was also the result of the misunderstandings that accompanied the definitions of the place of Arabic language and the religion, which is consubstantial with it in society. In each case, it has been thought more "in terms of alibis to complex processes of domination than to the implementation of concrete modalities of modernization."

The second characteristic, which also expresses the comparability of the two historical situations, colonial and national, is that of the permanence of the Algerian cultural equation which has remained much the same after decades. Because of the imposition of the French school system in Algeria, the French-speaking/Arabic-speaking division at the root of this equation thus crosses all the intellectual, cultural, and political history of contemporary Algeria.

In this respect, independence did not transform the nature of this opposition, but rather deepened it to the point of rupture; contradictions at the basis of the formation and development of the Algerian elite. Arabisation has developed in this order of ideas, less as an implementation of intellectual learning and of openness, than an ideologisation with a religious connotation substituting a strongly simplified and stereotyped neo-religious education for a traditional religious teaching more or less articulated on learned cultures (Leca 1990: 2). On the other hand, teaching in the French language deepened in a neo-Marxist rhetoric of rupture all the more assertive because its bearers felt guilt about the colonial past. "The ideological apparatus," that the university had never ceased to be, was further refined in the modulation of a deeply unitary and homogenising discourse, a discourse that would soon reach its limits before the disenchantment set in that characterises the developmental reflux. From then, the stakes have become radicalised, the illusions were unveiled, the institution lost its aims of social promotion. Arabisation appeared for what it has always been, a vast movement of widening social declassification. At the same time, it ended in a widespread process of deinstitutionalisation, the deskilling of the institution's products, expressing their limits at establishing a meaningful intelligentsia which would have relative autonomy from the state.

These general historical characteristics of the elite's division, like the instrumentalisation of the university institution, did not allow for the empowerment of an intellectual field nor the empowerment of an intelligentsia, nor those of specific categories of the elite, which would break with a normative double language speech.

With the general regression and marginalisation of an intelligentsia that had until then only followed the movement of history, often forming an appendage of established powers, proletarian intellectuals emerged[3] (Weber 1971: 480, 525) who were even more demanding as they had nothing to lose. This movement, coinciding with the groundswell of those marginalised from intellectual society, asserted itself in the rupture. This was a definitive return of the pendulum restoring them to their role in the vanguard and linking them more to the company of intellectuals whom history had ignored.

This means that because of the misunderstanding they had learned in their training from a bankrupt education system, they carry the same scars and have the same limits as those who had occupied, but in a different context, on the frontline of the political scene. Behind the sociological mutation, the mode of acquisition of what was given as knowledge had hardly changed and the young Islamist guard formed of engineers, doctors, and lawyers, had nothing to envy in its predecessor. In opposite referencing systems and often by borrowing the conceptual tools and approaches of the previous decade, the same thought patterns and the same stereotypes continued to operate. An entire reuse by "replacing its head," Marxism could develop; from the reverse Marxism paradigm a new thought system ensued:

[A] demonization of the bourgeoisie and idealization of the proletariat ... a Manichean vision of the world where capitalism—i.e. the entire West—is substituted for destiny, where exploitation becomes the original stain, the

bourgeois the symbol of the Ahrimanic forces, the proletariat, the liberat-
ing angel, the revolution a resurrection, and the classless society paradise
lost and found [...]. (Shayegan 1990)

At the same time of the affirmation of this new utopia, the transformation of
the general conditions of society as well as the democratic progress even in its
juridical formalism can work to make the society emerge at another level of self-
consciousness and establish real alternatives to authoritarian or totalitarian forms
of political exercise. For the moment, if the inversion appears strongly engaged,
it does not yet erase the reality of permanently anchored oppositions whose radicalisation is troubled with an implosion of the national society.

The radicalisation of such an opposition has expanded to the point of constituting coherent universes between which communication appears impossible
and whose contradictions have developed until the rupture. This has also been
underpinned and carried by the permanent confrontation in the history of contemporary Algeria of two normative orders with a hegemonic vocation: Islamic
law and positivist law.

From this point of view, there are conflicting relations that may have developed in one or the other historical phase; this is the third characteristic of comparative analysis. Indeed, here too, independence has not been a rupture; the
national state has defined itself in its relationship to Islamic law in much the same
way as the colonial state had done. The suppression of Islamic law after independence was almost as strong as in the colonial period. It took about 20 years
to see the promulgation of Islamic family law—a code, which was, by the way,
contested. Similarly, ambiguities have been at least as marked. At the same time,
the law of the land asserted itself in an all-out voluntarism and the institution of
instrumentalised teaching recorded in the exegesis of the new law.

This imposition of state law and subjection of Islamic law had similar consequences: "Today, as yesterday, the resistance of Islamic law to the logic of the
modern state seems to correspond to the refusal by part of the social body of
something that is 'foreign' or external to its historical experience as well as its
aspirations" (Henry 1990).

This challenge is all the more profound because the failure of the state as a
vector of progress and modernisation is here even more obvious; especially as
the contestation tends to target politics and the exercise of power. Although it
widens to include all civil society in the face of the state, it nevertheless appears
differentiated into secular and religious (Badie 1987: 261f). However, whereas
the first movement, if not exhausted by committing itself, at least developed on
a segmental basis by submitting to the categories and rules of the political game
that the state defines, the second movement is rooted more in the search for
identity and the denunciation of the foreign and authoritarian character of the
state and its rights. It is true that until then the rule of law had functioned like
the exercise of a law of the state and the many readjustments to social demands,
in their ambiguities, fed the process of counter-legitimation.

This contest rests on a traditional order that has been shaken, but which persists; the religious reference, eroded, but still a permanent substrate of this society, appears to synthesise the different dimensions of the protest. According to Badie (ibid), "it serves as a legitimation for any protest practice … it offers a symbolic repertoire provided and diversified to structure the mobilization movements." Especially in its desire to challenge the state, it presents an alternative based on the application of the supreme (Islamic) law, Sharia; in this, it competes with the state for its legitimacy.

In doing so, the insertion of the religious aspect into the student's action becomes a political act. The area of protest tends to be constructed in a political order of legality superior to that of the state; "the law" appears as the essential vector of this statement; the anomie of society predisposes this; the social rules lose their efficacy, undermined by the social changes they become obsolete (Boudon online). Into this void, in this "generalized ideological despair" (Rodinson 1984), the new utopia of a return to the golden age here and now proves to be an outlet for all frustrations.

In this society in crisis, the law thus becomes the crystalliser, the place of expression of the clash between "the modernist reason and the emotion of identity" (Ben-Achour 1989); it thus manifests the fundamental cultural challenge that runs through the society and expresses itself in the irreducibility of the one to the other referenciation.

This double logic founds a double structure: the affirmation of an original society and that of a new political entity (Ben-Achour 1989: 60) which is informal and unfinished, increases the contradictions of law and legal practices, weakens the state, and feeds the process of counter-legitimisation. The transmutation of the law is thus quite formal; the democratic legal paradigm is retranslated without taking into account all its philosophy, its requirements, as well as its culture: "modern law and in a general way the philosophy of the Western legal model were the subject, in Islam of a superficial graft," noted J. Deprez, before continuing, "[that is] sufficient to give this right positive value to the detriment of the right Muslim but not deep enough to impose all the requirements" (Deprez 1987).

Some of these have found in the historical order the emancipation of the economic from the political individualisation of the social relations constitutive of individual rights, and the public/private distinction. Yet, it is clear that the conditions that prevailed in "the great transformation" (Polanyi 1983) that affected Western Europe, do not apply here. The market categories, like the economic rationality peculiar to capitalism, do not quite take over in a still rentier society, which remains marked by a distributive and non-productive economy; the market economy is not rooted in a culture that would reinforce its functioning; the sphere of private interest is not entirely free from the public interest, the state not quite free from society; "public space" (Habermas 1986), the locus of citizenship, constitutive of a dialectic between the private and the public like the "new sphere" of the relationship between civil society and the state in Western societies, is here inconsistent and opaque (ibid.: 59). It is because here the state tends to merge with society. Three decades of domination by a one-party culture that combines authoritarianism and paternalism has profoundly affected the representations of its debates, discourses, and the actions it produces. At the same time, the state implements processes of atomising the community, functioning in a system of community allegiances and a unified and unifying representation of the society. Nationalism and its avatar populism were the main elements that froze and thwarted the emergence of the citizen consciousness. In this movement, the process of counter-legitimisation will feed both the resources of legitimation implemented by the national populist state and its inadequacies:

- the essential characteristics of the functioning of the state and the production of the law;
- the formal integration of the state and society, ethnic and religious foundations in the enunciation of the norm, and identity or positivism in its definition, stalling the norm in relation to realities,

are the very ones that will be created under Islamic revivalism.

An ideology based on the representation of a non-antagonistic conception of the components of the society, will respond by reviving and beyond it a "holistic" conception of an undivided community, the "Umma Islamya" sealed through religious solidarity.

Islamism appears in this respect as the continuation, in another form, of the populist ideology. It appears "inseparable from a nationalist dynamic; that is not new, but whose permanence and perhaps reactivation is a problem" (Dakhlia 1990). In the same way, that the law rests on ethico-religious categories—in the threefold sense of morality, religion, and the religious truth of an authoritarian state. The challenge of the state is in categories of the same nature.

The thrust of contestation is thus, in terms of current legal formalism, both a breeding ground and a framework for affirmation; stalling the legal norm with respect to reality, the contradictory referencing in the definition of the rule, the ineffectiveness of the latter, and, subsequently, its depreciation making the law a hollow shell which becomes the main stake of the societal redefinitions in progress.

If the balance of power was radicalised through the affirmation of an identity emotion about the erosion of rationalistic thought, this was inevitable because the educational institution proved unable to produce a legal culture of synthesis carried out by critical intellectuals, restoring to law its historicity and its temporality. The cathartic upheavals that periodically shake Algerian society mark, above all, the failure of the national developmental state's educational project. This failure carried, accompanied, and reinforced a wider process of re-traditionalisation and de-institutionalisation.

The phase that begins in the 1990s appears to be the completion of an era that started with colonialism and has always denied rational (intellectual) society. It thus participated in the obliteration of a historical stage at the same time as it was expressed in the transparency of contradictions brought to their pic in the societal projects. By posing the conditions' terms of the civic compromise in instability, it repositioned those conditions that could give it meaning; because of the urgency with which it was carried out, it set the question of the ends of an educational system adrift. Yet, the educational question was apparently not a priority.

The disenchantment that follows puts other options at the centre of the debate, other commitments brought by actors who are the products of these aborted processes. These appear as true clones of their predecessors, but in different systems of representation, different registers, practices, and actions. It is from them, the graduates of mass universities, proletarian intellectuals, methodically indoctrinated, with the declared constant values of an exclusive nation-party-state, and sociologically de-structured by truncated formations, that the contestation develops the legitimacy of the states that were built after independence.

In the decades of the 1970s and 1980s, two major categories of intellectuals took centre stage: French-speaking intellectuals fed with a more or less assimilated Marxism, and traditional *lumpen* intelligentsias—both proletarianised, more or less controlled, more or less joined to state powers that combined socialism and authenticity, openness to the world, and re-rooting in national values. The categories that would emerge in the 1990s represent a whole heterogeneous aggregation of both graduates of mass universities, those excluded from these institutions, and the semi-literates left behind in a deep socio-economic crisis.

At the end of the twentieth decade, we can observe the fragmentation of the intellectual field, its weak empowerment, and the division of the elites. These contribute to the centrality of the state, which has paralysed and corrupted many of the elite. This is in a society where the private sector is dependent on a state, which has not allowed the construction and empowerment of an intellectual field capable of debates, of producing meaning, and of proposing and allowing alternatives other than authoritarianism to emerge.

The foundation of this weak empowerment thus appears to be largely related to the mode of production of the intelligentsia in a colonial situation and to the structuring of an independent national state and its role in the arrangement and control of knowledge and culture. Despite or thanks to social movements, this arrangement has tended to leave all the space to an authoritarian state inscribed as out of sync with the society where there is a void, behind the reinforcement of control. This is a bankruptcy of the socio-political mode of regulation, together with an intergenerational fracture, a bankruptcy of socialising bodies, and a gaping fracture between society and the state, where poor governance and endemic corruption, characteristics of a prebendary system, reproduce through the production of new elites cloned on the model of the old ones. They are always at the apex of the state, arousing the despair of the younger generations.

In the absence of collective registers of meanings through which they could give meaning to their social life, this younger generation is deprived of the possibilities to build a sense of personal esteem, to assert themselves, and to be recognised, testifying to a domination, which subsumes their emergence as free and responsible individuals.

For both the elite and many intellectuals, questions and answers to the current problems do not address the issue of nationalism in its different forms. A heuristic typology distinguishes between pioneers, founders, builders, heirs, or intellectual generations of succession. It appears, nonetheless, that the affirmation of these categories in connection with precise moments and historical events is effected by crystallising a certain relationship between the state and society. Thus, one can see the weak empowerment of intellectuals as much in relation to the socio-political framework defined by the state as in relation to the values and norms of the society. A long-term departure from populist nationalism does not seem to be on the agenda. The importance of the dual state/society relationship seems to confuse the clarification of the moments and the different types of intellectuals who echo each other's formations and registers.

Intellectuals and diasporic intelligentsias

The balance of power became radicalised between a state folded around clientelist and prebendary groups, increasingly authoritarian and repressive as its disintegration is advanced, and social categories that became ever more demanding as they have nothing more to lose. This situation derives from total confinement and leaves plenty of space for other alternatives.

Therefore, this obliteration of the future means that many members of the intelligentsia and alternative elites would exist only in the marginal zones, in the established or underground protest, or in exile. The state will have to work more and more with opportunistic, corrupt elites from a strongly ideological mass education system. These are the only guarantors of stable social control and everything related to development is subcontracted by conglomerates abroad: construction by the Chinese, water and transport by the French, and hydrocarbons by the Americans and Europeans.

From a local point of view, the situation seems to completely paralysed, and the rebound by the state is late and always awkward. They claim ownership of the contestation only to return in a headlong rush to their claimants, hence deepening the crisis.

The new situations and conditions favour the redeployment, or emigration, of these social groups to European spaces where they move in search of jobs. There they experience new encounters with secularised societies where many different groups live in the same cultural area, and this redefines in new terms the problem of secularisation and the construction of democracy. However, in this respect, there is already a moving and closing of the economic, political, and cultural borders, the deepening of intellectual, cultural, and political divisions, between the intelligentsia who remain at home base in Algeria and those in the diasporas, between categories of the intelligentsia, and between the intelligentsia and society.

Notes

1 Understood here, in the broad sense of the notion. In this chapter, we will not discuss the definitions, different perceptions, and theoretical foundations of what people often accept commonly as elites in the generic sense. We refer here to different categories of elites with social, cultural, and economic capitals, meaning producers for some of them and participating in the management of the state's institutions.
2 Thus, it would be interesting to produce social biographies, family histories, and even tribal histories to identify, decades later, the connection that would exist between the social components of the main socio-cultural and economic forces that work in the society. We can cite as an example the National Education Minister's case, 1963–1966, Taleb El Ibrahim, adopted son of the reformer Bachir El Ibrahimi; the minister had a very voluntarist Arabisation policy in the primary stage during the first years after the independence.
3 In the sense that Max Weber (1971) described these, "layers [...] with an education considered mostly inferior [...] which are not bound by social conventions in terms of the meaning to be given to the cosmos, and the intense ethical and religious passion that animates them is not hindered by material considerations."

References

Badie, B. 1987. *Les deux états, pouvoir et société en occident et en Terre d'Islam*. Paris Fayard.

Ben-Achour, Y. 1989. "Droit et environnement politique, le cas de la Tunisie," *in*: *Droit et environnement social au Maghreb, seminar of Décembre 10–12, 1987*.

Boudon, R.A., *Encyclopædia Universalis*, http://www.universalis.fr/encyclopedie/anomie/.

Dakhlia, J. 1990. "Islam et nationalisme, la fin des états de grâce." *Le genre humain* (23), Paris: Le Seuil.

Deprez, J. 1987. "Environnement social et droit international privé, le droit international privé marocain entre la fidélité à l'Umma et l'appartenance à la communauté internationale." *Droit et environnement social au Maghreb, seminar of December 10, 1987*.

Djeghloul, A. 1988. *"La formation des intellectuels algériens modernes, 1880–1930,"* In, Carlier, Omar, Colonna, Fanny, et al. *Lettrés intellectuels et militants en Algérie 1880–1950*, Algiers: OPU.

Gallissot, R. 1984. Les limites de la culture nationale, enjeux culturels et avènement étatique au Maghreb, *Annuaire de l'Afrique du Nord* (AAN) Paris: CNRS, pp. 24–41.

Habermas, J. 1993. *L'espace public, archéologie de la publicité comme dimension constitutive de la société bourgeoise*. Paris: Payot.

Leca, J. 1990. *Le Maghreb à la fin du siècle*. Paris: Institut d'études politiques. Unpublished manuscript.

Malek, A.A. 1969. *Idéologies et renaissance nationale, l'Egypte modern*. Paris: Maspéro.

Merad, A. 1967. *Le réformisme musulman de 1925 à 1960. Essai d'histoire religieuse et sociale*. Paris-The Hague: Mouton, pp. 307–309.

Peneff, J. 1982. *Industriels algériens*. Algiers: OPU.

Purvillé, G. 1984, *Les étudiants algériens de l'université française 1880–962*. Paris: Editions du CNRS.

Polanyi, K. 1983. *La grande transformation, aux origines économiques et politiques de notre temps*. Paris: Gallimard.

Rodinson, M. 1984. "L'intégrisme musulman et l'intégrisme de toujours," *Raison présente* (72), 4th quarter.

Shayegan, D. 1990. *Qu'est-ce qu'une révolution religieuse*. Paris: Bibliothèque Albin Michel des Idées.

Smida, M. 1970. *Kheïreddine, Ministre réformateur*. Tunis: Maison tunisienne d'édition.

Weber, M. 1971. *Économie et société*, French Translation. Paris: Plon, pp. 480 et 525.

5

POLICING ALGERIA UNDER BOUTEFLIKA

From police state to civil state

Rachid Tlemçani

Introduction

In May 2012, former President Abdelaziz Bouteflika made a strong call for the post-independence generation to take over; since by then his health had deteriorated daily. Despite being in a wheelchair, he ran for office for a fourth term. After suffering a stroke he was unable to speak during the 2014 presidential campaign, and, then more critically, during his entire fourth mandate.

The day after Algeria celebrated 56 years of independence, the political class pledged to support the ailing President Bouteflika's bid for a fifth term in April 2019.[1] This pledge was made in spite of the fact that his 20-year programme has not been depicted in a new development paradigm integrated in a national project. The $1.100 billion public expenditure balance sheet is at best ambiguous and controversial. Mismanagement, embezzlement, and corruption account for more than 30 percent of the budget.

The Algerian political system has been exceedingly resistant to democracy and economic development. Authoritarianism was consolidated under President Bouteflika (1999–2019), although he has changed everything so as everything can stay the same, to paraphrase Giuseppe Tomasi di Lampedusa, in the world-famous movie, *The Leopard*.

The demilitarisation of the state currently under way aims at establishing a civil state in place of the *moukhabarate* state headed by the *Département du renseignement et de la sécurité* (DRS). This police state emerged while neopatrimonial politics and corruption were promoted to the detriment of national interest. The institutionalising of power is still an empty slogan that nobody believes in. The parliament has no control over the structure of the budget and more particularly of military and security expenses. Decisions on all the levels of social fabric are made by fiat.

Army and state-building

Among countries in the Middle East and North Africa, Algeria holds a distinctive position, largely due to its historic experience in which political violence was the most decisive action in the armed struggle against colonial rule. As Algeria's strongest feature, the army took part directly in the formation of the state at the very start of this process. The state does not own the army, it is, on the contrary, the army that owns the state, as historian Mohammed Harbi has pointed out.

At the time of independence, the army emerged as the only efficient powerbroker in a shattered political landscape dominated by weak and competing political factions. *L'armée des frontières* then rose to prominence in a fragmented society as the sole organised force capable of taking over what remained of the colonial infrastructure. Post-colonial modernisation has been a great instrument in developing the security and military apparatus to the detriment of an independent public sphere and civil society. State-building has emerged as a stronger force than nation-building in post-colonial societies (Tlemçani 2019). This process has led to the prominence of a specific authoritarianism in which security forces have played a critical function in decision-making. The military society headed by a powerful personality has been at the expense of civil society and the autonomy of the public sphere.

Between independence in 1962 and the 1988 riots, Algeria was a one-party state. The post-colonial Front de Libération Nationale (FLN) was not established on the basis of any particular ideology, but rather by administrative measures (Roberts 2007: 5). It was, from the outset, an ideological state apparatus rather than a genuine political party. In contradistinction to other authoritarian regimes, the FLN was not itself a source of decision-making. Instead, the power structure is vested in the military and security groups. Ironically, democratic groups frequently call on the army to intervene in the political arena in order to address the profound crisis of legitimacy.

As soon as Abdelaziz Bouteflika rose to prominence in April 1999, he started to modernise the military. In 2005, Algeria decided to build a military-industrial complex, as did Egypt under Hosni Moubarak (Tlemçani 2014). In addition, Bouteflika increased the number of police officers from 90,000 in 2009 to 209,000 in 2014 and 220,000 in 2018, and they are now well equipped and trained. The security ratio per capita is one of the highest in the world, with military and security expenses at around one third of the national budget. This build-up was pursued even when the oil revenues dropped drastically in 2014. The Kalashnikov still occupies a crucial function in national security to the detriment of the citizenry. Citizenship is not viewed as the heart of the security sector reform.

October 1988 riots

In 1989, Algeria undertook a great democratic breakthrough, seen as unique in the Middle East and North Africa and Muslim world. After over two decades of one-party rule, the government, in a pre-emptive response to the 1988 October riots, liberalised its political system overnight. A new constitution was enacted in February 1989 which marked the end of the FNL monopoly and the legitimisation of political parties and non-governmental organisations (NGOs). More fundamentally, press restrictions were lifted with the result that over 40 new newspapers and political parties started up and elections at the municipal and national level were rapidly scheduled. The DRS set up a special office to handle formal relations with political parties, NGOs, and a free press. With the blessing of the élites (cadres, intellectuals, party leaders, and so on), the intelligence service[2] thus infiltrated democratic institutions and the promotion of civil society. There is consensus on the whys and wherefores of the crisis.

First, the élites rushed into the democratic breach under the direction of the intelligence service, instead of investing in the public sphere and fighting for a new order which would inevitably build the second republic.

However, the October 1988 rioters, mostly youngsters between 17 and 25, simply sought the departure of officials who had betrayed the egalitarian promises contained in the official discourse of socialism. In opposition to strong media belief, democracy was not on the rioters' agenda. The real issue was the power struggles between the conservative and the reformist wings of the single party. The overnight uprising developed its own dynamic and spiralled out of control, ending in street battles. The protests were violently suppressed so as to impose a new balance of power. As a result, more than 200 young people were killed and many more injured. *L'Armée nationale populaire*, "the heiress of the glorious *Armée de libération nationale*," fired for the first time on Algerian protesters. Their historic legitimacy was shattered overnight not in a border war, but in the streets of Algeria. The military authorities clearly displayed that they would go far for the sake of regime maintenance. In so doing, a new legitimacy needed to be built as soon as possible before the emerging social movement could threaten the political establishment and the security order under construction.

Corrupt multipartism and Islamism

The Islamic Salvation Front, or FIS *(Front islamique du salut)*, was able to integrate the emerging social protest in its programme. This party proved to be the most effective and well-organised opposition party although it opposed the 1989 Constitution and the Law on Associations. This is not the first paradox of the Algerian transition to democracy. The FIS campaigned in a confusing context with the simplistic slogan "Islam is the solution" in a society marked by a profound identity crisis in the context of a drop in oil revenues. Western balloting can hardly be free and fair when there is a deep crisis of legitimacy. Electoral behaviour, such as intimidation, vote rigging, misrecording, electorate manipulation, and violence were viewed as natural behaviour. According to Islamists, the ends justified the means in order to oust the *taghout* (unholy) power. The FIS manipulated the FLN's fraud devices and captured a majority of seats in the local elections (June 1990) and subsequently in the first round of legislative elections (December 1991). This victory took everybody by surprise, first and foremost the FIS leaders themselves. Algerians were fed up with authoritarian politics and *hogra* (rule of arbitrariness). They were ready to follow any group promising radical change.

The army's General Staff realised that democratisation had begun to escape its control, as the FIS was about to take state power for itself without sharing with the other actors. The army's General Staff moved first to remove President Chadli Bendjedid. This assumed that Islamism is not alien to democracy although Islamist leaders declared that democracy is *kofr*, a blasphemy, a sin. The FIS viewed itself as the only legitimate group holding people's sovereignty with God's blessing (Zoubir 1995). The army thus annulled the elections and banned the FIS and arrested its leaders; violent confrontations ensued between the security forces and armed Islamic bands. Notorious groups such as l'*Armée Islamique du Salut*, le *Groupe Islamique Armé*, and le *Groupe Salafiste pour la Prédication et le Combat* launched a ruthless campaign against the government, the military, and the civilians, on the one hand, and on the other, committed violent acts abroad, namely, in France. In this armed conflict, around 150,000 people were killed, 9,000 disappeared, 1 million were displaced, and economic and infrastructural damage was estimated at $20 billion. This balance-sheet does encourage people to rebel for a second time.

Strangely, the modern and well-equipped security forces took nearly a decade to crush the military wing of Islamism made up of poorly trained and armed bands. The economic situation was meanwhile leading to structural adjustment reforms the Bretton Woods institutions had imposed. By the end of this conflict, or civil war, new fortunes appeared while Algerians had not yet healed old wounds. The overnight increase in oil revenues in the 2000s has engendered, under Bouteflika, the "Islam of market," a prosperous bazaar economy.

The failure of co-optation in 1994

The security establishment realised that it was stuck in a quagmire. The military had no control over the conflict as Algeria's image abroad tarnished. Bouteflika, the talented minister of foreign affairs under Boumediène (1965–1978), was believed to be the right person to help, though the concern was more with the image of the regime than the violence perpetrated on Algerians. As a skilled diplomat, Bouteflika was not in a rush to accept the army's proposal in January 1994 to succeed the assassinated President Mohamed Boudiaf June 1992.[3] To do so, he had to ask the formal support of the political parties and civil society which he had previously disregarded. More fundamentally, he would not be granted full authority over the armed forces. In addition, his return from abroad would be organised through a big welcome, as a *zaïm*, or leader. Finally, he declined the invitation made by a quarter of the military generals as if the country was their private property.

To recall, in 1979, Bouteflika was tipped to succeed President Boumediène as head of state, but the General Staff, under the direction of the intelligence department, the *securité militaire*, decided otherwise. Colonel Chadli Bendjedid, an unknown entity without political ambition or experience in state affairs, found himself overnight as the head of state where he stayed for 13 years. Bouteflika was unhappy with this decision and held a grudge against the military which he viewed as incompetent and responsible for the civil war. He then left the country.

The 1996 constitution

Liamine Zeroual, another little-known retired army general, was then co-opted as head of state and then elected president in the midst of civil war. The 1995 November election initiated the first pluralistic presidential balloting in post-colonial history. Against all expectations, this historic election witnessed a large turnout. *Le Groupe Islamique Armé* threatened to kill anyone who attempted to vote, with the slogan "one vote, one bullet." Zeroual won 68.54% of the votes, but, in 1999, Bouteflika did achieve the same election turnout as Zeroual. According to people close to the top, Bouteflika blackmailed the military with a request for a larger majority than Zeroual, threatening to go home otherwise. Strong media opinion called on Zeroual to run for the 2009 presidential election, which he declined, fearing the voting would be rigged, as before. He had been head of state when Bouteflika won in a contentious election in 1999 and was not able to secure fair and free voting, as he had promised. "An invisible hand" has always managed elections. Bouteflika was finally granted 74.92% of the presidential vote.

In reality, Algerians, tired of violence, were willing to elect any candidate who promised to restore peace and security. Before being elected in November 1995, Zeroual was able to deliver this message during the campaign, a problematic adopted later by Bouteflika during the 1999 presidential campaign. The electoral legitimacy led Zeroual to adopt a new constitution in 1996. The new law was viewed as a great breakthrough in Arab constitutional history since its Article 74 limited the presidential mandate to two terms; Bouteflika lifted that limit in 2008 to allow himself to run for a third term (Aghrout and Zoubir 2009) before reinstituting the two-term mandate in another amendment of the Constitution in 2016.

The 1996 Constitution introduced a bicameral legislature in which one third of members of the senate, appointed by the president of the Republic, can prevent any unwanted law from being passed. This text virtually removes the role of parliament, in which the legislative institution becomes a mere recording room. The main thrust of this new constitution was to concentrate far more power in the office of the presidency. It was further consolidated in the "profound political reform" initiated under President Bouteflika as a pre-emptive strike against the Arab Spring. This reform enacted several bills on labour, trade unions, multipartism, NGOS, and media. The ultimate goal of this legislative revolution is to eradicate any genuine intermediate political organ so as to tighten the grip of the regime on the public sphere and civil society.

Surprisingly, Zeroual cut short his mandate on September 11, 1998. His authority was contested by the General Staff under General Mohammed Lamari, previously head of special forces. Like the six presidential candidates in 1999, President Zeroual returned to business as usual, expecting to confront those opposed to his peace plan.

The rise of Abdelaziz Bouteflika

The 1999 presidential vote had all the makings of a free and fair contestation between seven candidates, including two Islamists and a Trotskyite woman. Though considerable mobilisation of voters and candidates characterised the campaign, on the eve of the election six of the seven candidates withdrew from the race on the assumption that the election was rigged from the start. They were convinced that the General Staff would allow Bouteflika to win the first round. As Bouteflika remained the sole candidate, this democratic election turned out to be a mere plebiscite. Had this election not been corrupted and rigged, democracy would most likely have prevailed in Algeria. The six candidates who refused to run returned to their usual business. The political ethic should have been to pursue the struggle in the political arena. One of the main traits of the Algerian political elite is that it does not invest in the political sphere. The constitutional opposition, fearful of losing its privileges, does not consider it useful to confront state power so it was easy for Bouteflika to manipulate the political class as he pleased. A new political dynamic could hardly be launched in the fragmented political field regarding the acceptance of a fifth term for the incumbent.

When he rose again to prominence as head of state in a contentious election, Bouteflika pursued a twofold strategy. At the local level, he was willing to grab full constitutional authority, as he awarded himself the position of minister of defence. In world politics, he pursued non-stop public relations and policy offensives involving global initiatives during the first term. The apex of his popularity with the world media was when he greeted Israeli Prime Minister Ehud Barak at the funeral of King Hassan II of Morocco in July 1999. This was the first ever gesture by an Algerian leader towards Israel. Against both left and right populists, he was even ready to take the next step to normalising Algerian-Israeli relations (Tlemçani 1999). The assumption was that Zionism has the upper hand in the world finance market and that Israel would most probably help Algeria's reconstruction in the event of full diplomatic normalisation. This naïve view is very strong in Arab opinion and among élites (Tlemçani 2018). To recall, the international community perceived the Algerian fight against armed Islamist bands as a mere violation of human rights. As retaliation, heavy financial pressures had been applied against Algeria which was constrained to undertake a structural adjustment programme. Algeria's war against terrorism, however, was praised in the aftermath of 9/11 by the United States and the European Union.

To recall, Algeria eradicated radical Islamism on its own without international assistance. President Bouteflika played this card neatly though he was abroad during this entire period. President Bouteflika and the General Staff military had a mutual interest in showing that Algeria was trustworthy as an international partner. Still, President Bouteflika hinted several times that he might send the military generals accountable for violence to the International Criminal Court (Nezzar 2003).

From the rule of colonels to the rule of generals

Bouteflika played an important role in independence in forging a heteroclite military alliance which paved the way for the army under Colonel Houari Boumedine to take over the colonial infrastructure. The failure of the provisional government, *le Gouvernement Provisoire de la République Algerienne*, 1958–1962, to assert its supremacy as a civilian authority over the General Staff constituted a turning point in Algerian military development.

The General Staff was abolished after the abortive putsch in December 1967. The defence minister consequently became the unrivalled head of the military power structure in the absence of General Staff. It was re-established in 1984, which institution diluted President Chadli Bendjedid's personal authority in the course of professionalising the armed forces. Eight colonels were promoted to become the first generals in post-colonial period. In 2005, General Ahmed Gaid Salah, a war veteran, was appointed to the General Staff to replace Mohammed Lamari. This seems to contradict the expressed wish to rejuvenate the leadership of the army. In July 2006, President Bouteflika elevated Major-General Ahmed Gaïd Salah, Abbas Gheziel, Gendarmerie head, and Mohamed Mediène, DRS head, to the rank of general corps army. Algeria has rapidly moved from the rule of colonels to the rule of generals.

Military's fatal error

When Bouteflika declined the invitation to be co-opted in 1994, the General Staff should have thought twice before doing it for the second time. In vain. The military decided against all odds to support his candidacy in the first pluralistic presidential elections in Algeria's post-colonial history. As soon as he was co-opted, Bouteflika waged a struggle on all fronts to sever the traditional link between the presidency of the Republic and the army. The total withdrawal of the military from the political stage has ultimately been his chief goal. Even during the 1999 presidential campaign, Bouteflika sent many contradictory messages to the army. At one point, he declared that according to the Constitution, the army is a mere state institution whose function is clearly defined as it is depends on the presidency. According to Bouteflika, the army has acquired important extra-constitutional responsibilities in exceptional circumstances which no longer apply.

A few months after he took power, President Bouteflika addressed Algerians, calling on them to help him curtail the influence of "the fifteen," referring to fifteen army generals who at the time controlled foreign trade and the bazaar economy. Also, he clearly stated that he needed full control to extricate the country from the national crisis. Bouteflika was unambiguous that he would not be a "quarter of a president" in defiance of the country's military and intelligence institution, as were the previous presidents. From the start, he decided to cling to state power to the detriment of national interest. Bouteflika made no secret of his disdain for parliament, for democratic politics, or for a free press. He centralised power and changed the Constitution three times and was ready to do it again during his fifth term. This problematic candidacy was forcing him into the same humiliating resignation that ended Hosni Moubarak's 30-year rule. Clinging to power is not peculiar to Bouteflika or to Moubarak or any other autocrat. The intelligence service was directed by the same person for 25 years despite the security crisis that marked this entire period. This phenomenon characterises Muslim elites prior to the advent of good governance and the rule of law. Political parties that profess democracy and political turnover remain headed by the same people.

The constant reshuffling of officials

It took President Bouteflika more than 6 months to reshuffle his first executive branch of state. The General Staff wanted to keep key departments, but Bouteflika managed to co-opt his close political friends in key positions in the security apparatus, executive branch, diplomacy, and public firms. These included Chakib Khelil in energy, Abdellatif Benachenhou in finance, and Hamid Temmarin in industry. Their experience in multilateral institutions was viewed by neo-liberal groups as a great asset although they were disconnected from local reality. However, the DRS, a pivotal institution, remained under the direction of Mohamed Médiène, a general who originally came from the central part of the country. The security apparatus had secret power; from its rise during the liberation war up until the early 2000s, it had been dominated by people originally from the eastern part of the country, particularly the Batna-Tebessa-Souk Ahras region. By the end of the first mandate, the heart of the power structure started to move from the eastern towards the western part of the country. The re-ordering of officials has been a constant feature of Algeria under President Bouteflika and has destabilised the government and the other institutions, creating a confusing situation propitious to embezzlement, mismanagement, and corruption.

The In Amenas hostage crisis resulted in the second re-ordering of state structure.[4] Eighteen government ministers were replaced, including those who had opposed the election of the FLN's new Secretary-General Amar Saïdani. More fundamentally, President Bouteflika, after his return from the hospital, launched a sweeping re-ordering of the *L'Armée nationale populaire*. A *coup de force*, such as a medical crisis that would have let the President leave with dignity and pride, was ruled out. Those accustomed to taking important decisions behind closed doors did not seem to have taken the historic decision as in 1992.

Doing business as usual was more secure than an adventure in a changing geopolitical environment. However, a parliamentary coup was undertaken in October 2018 to oust the Assemblée Nationale Populaire's (APN) president. FLN's deputies locked the entrance door of the building.

The dissolution of the police state

The most important feature of the Algerian political system is that it is a civil state on the surface, but military in its heart. There is no clear division between the formal power exercised by the president and the executive branch of the state, on the one hand, and on the other, the hidden power is held by the high military command and top security officers. This situation is unique in Africa and the Middle East and North Africa.

The military has exercised great power behind closed doors. The post-independence presidents and heads of state have either come from a military background or enjoyed the full support of the army. Leaders in all other institutions also have the blessing of the security services. The military intervene in all stages of the decision-making process over foreign trade and the bazaar economy. *La police politique* intervenes directly in political parties, NGOs, and other institutions, assisting some, weakening others. In 1976, only 6 months after its birth, the Rassemblement National Démocratique (RND) took control of parliament. An unconstitutional power became the kingmaker in both single party rule and multiparty politics.

The precarious balance of power made up of three poles, i.e., six military regions, the presidency, and the intelligence service, broke up at the end of the fight on terror. The DRS had meanwhile managed to rise as a security leviathan, a state within a state.

The DRS has woven a complex network of client relations in government, administration, universities, the economic sector (public and private), and civil society. A security clearance is mandatory for an appointment to a high state position. The stakes in factional struggles are not ideological, but rather rent-seeking, privilege, and honours. The allegiance of the ruling class is virtually total in one way or another. The failure of the Arab Spring is associated with the strength of this deep state in the society. The relationship of domination has, as Max Weber argues, a minimum of obeisance and the will of submission under authoritarianism.

Before President Bouteflika declared his candidacy to stand for a fourth term, a battle raged between the president's office and the DRS. The head of the DRS is said to have objected to the fourth term as his unit had exposed major corruption involving Bouteflika's associates, including the ministries of energy and of public works. The juridical unit in charge of corruption probe was dissolved in this shake-up.

The international community pushed for a deal for the sake of regional and political stability. A deal was thus struck to re-enlist Bouteflika for a fourth term, even though he was virtually unable to speak or to act during the presidential campaign. To that end, General Gaid Salah, a war veteran and chief of the army's General Staff, became vice minister of defence. During Bouteflika's last period of rule, this general rose to prominence and was viewed as an emerging Marechal Fatah el-Sissi in Algeria.

A few months after his election, President Bouteflika issued a series of decrees removing several civilian associates and senior military officers from government and army positions. These included the president's defence associate, General Mohammed Touati, who formally retired from the army in 2005, but was co-opted in the presidency in 2011. General Touati was viewed as a Trojan horse for the military establishment. His removal was described as a sign that Bouteflika was pushing back against the influence of the military elite, namely, its radical group, called "eradicators" versus the "reconciliators" during the fight against Islamist extremism.

In an interview on February 2, 2014, Amar Saïdani, the FLN's secretary-general and a close ally of Bouteflika, demanded General Mediène's resignation and the removal of the DRS from the political stage. Saïdani launched an unprecedented attack against Mediène, saying what others only whispered. This department had infiltrated all the institutions of the country, its economic enterprises, universities, NGOs, political parties, elections, local administration, trade unions, and private firms. He was responsible for the security crisis that has had a devastating effect on the political and economic environment. Neither did this department deter the attempt to assassinate president Bouteflika in Batna in September 2007. Saïdani also recollected the major terrorist acts of the 1990s that shocked the world, such as the kidnapping and killing of the Tibehirine monks, the attack on the government palace, and on the gas site in Tiguentourine. He concluded by saying that "Toufik should have resigned, he failed in his job." Strangely enough, Toufik did not react to these charges, and it was clear that the kingmaker's days in office were numbered.

In July 2015, the heads of three groups responsible for providing protection for Bouteflika were dismissed after a lapse in security at the presidential residence. Fearing a "medical putsch," as was the case of Tunisian President Habib Bourguiba in 1987, Bouteflika removed those in charge of his bodyguards.

In September 2015, President Bouteflika finally succeeded in removing his powerful intelligence chief. General Mediene had been head of the DRS from 1990 to 2015 despite the tricky security crisis that characterised the regime. Nicknamed "Toufik," he has been described as the world's longest serving intelligence chief. Little is known of him. No-one knows his birthday or his birthplace. His photograph was published for the first time after his removal from office. On the eve of independence, Toufik was sent in a group, "*tapis* rouge," to study at a Russian Komitet gosudarstvennoy bezopasnosti (KGB), or Committee for State Security, school in the USSR. All members of this group have a played a crucial role in Algeria after independence. He became a feared figure as he built the department into an immensely powerful institution and was Algeria's undisputed strong man after the April 2004 elections.

A few weeks after Toufik's dismissal, retired General Hocine Benhadid was arrested and jailed for 8 months for speaking out against the political system. No one ever expected that a retired military general, a war veteran of the fight against France, would be jailed for denouncing neo-patrimonial politics. The regime decided to pass a bill forbidding retired military officials from speaking out on politics.

In January 2016, President Bouteflika finally succeeded in his long fight to dissolve the country's powerful security service, the DRS, which dominated the fight against terrorism. A new agency, the Security Affairs Department (DRS) replaced it. The DSS aims to merge security information coming from different services, including the police, military, and *la gendarmerie* (rural police). The DSS would no longer be under the authority of the minister of defence, as was the DRS, but was to answer to the head of state, as were the entire security and intelligence cluster. Lastly, the institute of higher national security studies (*l'Institut des hautes études de sécurité nationale* IHESN) was established in May 2017. This institute would have more research credibility if it were run by a civilian. The re-structuration allegedly aimed at enabling the intelligence services to move from being "*une police politique*" (secret political police) to a more conventional intelligence agency.

Cocainegate

The reshuffling of the security and military departments reached a turning point in the summer of 2018, on the eve of the presidential electoral campaign, as in the case of 2014. It coincided with the seizure of 701 kg cocaine in boxes marked "halal meat" together with other important seizures reported in the media. The crucial issue that remains to be investigated is the role of Algeria in international drug trafficking and smuggling. These affairs and others have unravelled a large network of corruption involving top officials and their families.

The departmental reshuffling included the dismissal of most military commanders, as well as several security officials. The powerful heads of the military regions, in addition to other generals in the military high command, in the police and gendarmerie, have been removed in this coup de force. The powerful police chief, General Abdelghani Hamel, was seen as a loyal ally of Bouteflika, but recently displayed presidential ambitions and was also dismissed.

Algerians are accustomed to reading in the media that high-ranking officials such as ministers, governors, bank managers, and economic firms are fired by fiat. But nobody could have imagined that the untouchables of the régime, such as top military officers, would also be fired by fiat along with the oligarchs. Over the past few years more than 100 of the army's top officers have been sacked or retired. Some have had their homes confiscated, others were forbidden to leave the country, or were jailed for corruption. This phenomenon is unique in Algeria's political history. The army is unlikely to play a crucial role in the election of the next head of state, but the new régime has not altered the decision-making process. It has not extended political participation so as to increase national interest at the expense of business groups and oligarchs. Corruption has meanwhile become a key instrument in governance.

The ailing President Bouteflika finally turned out to be the only player building a new régime type. This new state has resembled far more the police state of Tunisian President Ben Ali (1987–2011), than the declared civil state. This latter is not ruled by fiat and nepotism, but by transparency, meritocracy, and widespread political participation. Like the previous regime the new order is marked by nepotism as a fundamental method in the management of the polity. As a result, the *hogra* (officialdom's contempt for the citizens) of the Justice Department and the abuse of power have become major topics of conversation. More critically, Algerians do not feel directly concerned with the fights at the heights of power as long as *la lutte des clans* (clannish struggles) do not reverberate on the streets as they did in 1988. Deputies locked the APN gateway in October 2018 so as to oust the president of the parliament. Such thug-like behaviour has further humiliated Algerians.

Prosecutions against journalists, bloggers, and human rights activists have increased recently, mainly in defiance of the principle of the presumption of innocence. The economic situation is also deteriorating to a great degree as the foreign exchange reserves that secure social programmes will be exhausted in about 2 years. The new finance configuration will not be adequate for the growing social demand. The police state is sitting on a powder keg, as was the case in Venezuela.

It is in this troubled context that in February 2019, Bouteflika announced his candidacy for a fifth term. After suffering a stroke in 2013, he had been in no physical or intellectual condition to lead the country. Executing article 102 to remove him from office constitutionally should have been invoked well before it was finally invoked in April 2019. Instead, an unconstitutional group headed by his brother, Saïd, took over the reigns of power. Algerians across the country, including women, children, the elderly, and the diaspora, spontaneously took to the streets. The public threat of the head of government to transform Algeria into another Syria was the final straw. Algerians from different social walks of life and political stripes demanded peacefully "no for the fifth term" and "regime change." Ongoing mass protests unexpectedly opposed Bouteflika's fifth term and the rule of the old élite.

The groundswell of opposition since February 22, 2019, has had three main traits: national, peaceful, and non-corporatist (Bourenane 2019). This unprecedented revolutionary movement opposes the ruling group, the government, the oligarchy, the élites, the political opposition, and the political system. Modern social networks have taken over the traditional ones institutionalised under Bouteflika. The strength of the movement is paradoxically the absence of leadership. The traditional elite, including both the ruling class and opposition groups, became overwhelmed by the magnitude, the spontaneity, the pacifist character, and the genuine improvisation of this ongoing movement. This movement expressed the need for renewal, for new faces that would not rely on the legitimacy of the war of independence nor be involved in the rule of the (secret) political police. Instead, the new elite should spring from within the social movement representing the post-colonial generation, and lead the country to modernity and social progress.

Algerians, as both nation and state, feel deeply and profoundly humiliated in world affairs. Algerians have not made economic demands; they called for dignity and liberty. History has shown that humiliation can be a driving force and is often more crucial than economic factors. Algerians have been exasperated with the *hogra*—or the rule of arbitrariness. They are no longer afraid of state coercion and blackmail and are now fighting for a change of political system so that the country can regain its dignity, national pride, and the influential regional role it had in the past.

Notes

1 President Bouteflika was admitted to a hospital in Paris on November 26, 2005, reportedly suffering from a gastric ulcer haemorrhage. This 19-day stay in a clinic was followed by others in 2006 and 2007. In spite of that, he was co-opted for a third mandate although the Constitution limited presidents to two terms. In April 2013, he was again hospitalised for having "a mini-stroke without serious complications." Against all odds, he was co-opted for a fourth term. In a wheelchair, he was unable to articulate a single a word during the entire mandate. According to Bajolet (2018), French ambassador (2006–2008) in Algiers, President Bouteflika was kept alive artificially. On the eve of the fifth term, he was again hospitalised in Switzerland from where he sent his candidacy.

2 The intelligence service was set up as an important structure in the Ministère de l'Armement et des Liaisons Générales during the Revolution (1954–1962). "The men of the shadow" played a crucial role in the victory. After independence, the Ministère de l'Armement et des Liaisons Générales was renamed, Sécurité militaire and reorganised on the Eastern bloc model. President Chadli Bendjedid (1979–1992) mistrusted the Securite militaire and dismantled it in 1987, renaming it the *Délégation générale de la prévention et la sécurité* which became the DRS in 1990 (Sifaoui 2012).

3 Mohamed Boudiaf was one of the genuine fathers of the liberation war. At independence, he broke with the new regime and went into exile. Surprisingly, General Staff brought him back during the civil strife to lead le Haut Conseil d'Etat that would govern for an interim government to the end of 1993. He rapidly attempted to change the rules of the game. Six months later, he was assassinated while delivering a speech in Annaba. One of his security guards was arrested and charged with this assassination.

4 The In Amenas crisis took place in January 2013 at the Tiguentourine gas facility in the Algerian Sahara. A terrorist group took 700 people hostage. The Special Intervention Group raided the site in an effort to free the hostages, during which 37 foreign nationals and 32 terrorists were killed. Several Western officials bemoaned Algeria's failure to minimise casualties. What happened at the Tiguentourine plant is still unclear. Several changes in the military and security establishment occurred in the aftermath.

References

Aghrout, Ahmed and Zoubir, Yahia. 2009. (May). "Introducing Algeria's President for Life." *Middle East Report Online*, April 2009. https://merip.org/2009/04/introducing-algerias-president-for-life/.

Bourenane, N. 2019. (March 10). "Mouvement de contestation politique. Le rôle des universitaires dans la résolution de la crise." *El Watan*. https://www.elwatan.com/edition/contributions/mouvement-de-contestation-politique-le-role-des-universitaires-dans-la-resolution-de-la-crise-10-03-2019.

Nezzar, Khaled. 2003. *Algérie: Le sultanat de Bouteflika*. Algiers: *Apic*. pp. 42–44.

Roberts, Hugh. 2007. "Demilitarizing Algeria," Carnegie Papers. No. 86. https://carnegieendowment.org/files/cp_86_final1.pdf.

Sifaoui, Mohamed. 2012. *Histoire secréte de l'Algérie indépendante. L'Etat-DRS*, Paris, Nouveau Monde Editions.

Tlemçani, Rachid. 1999. (July 30). "Algérie–Israël: Vers la normalisation." *El Watan* (no longer available).

Tlemçani, Rachid. 2014. (November 11). "Le complexe militaro-industriel. Bouteflika et la croissance économique," *Le Matin*.https://www.lematindz.net/news/15691-le-complexe-militaro-industriel-bouteflika-et-la-croissance-economique.html.

Tlemçani, Rachid. 2018. (June 5–6). "Relation triangulaire: USA, lobbies et Israêl, le système sioniste part 1 et 'La fin dy mythe de l'Etat palestinien.' part 2. 'Le système sioniste.'" *El Watan* (no longer available).

Tlemçani, Rachid. 2019. (February 26). "Modernisation et modernité: Etat contre Société." *El Watan*, https://www.elwatan.com/edition/contributions/modernisation-et-modernite-etat-contre-societe-26-02-2019.

Zoubir, Yahia H. 1995. "Stalled Democratization of an Authoritarian Regime: The Case of Algeria," *Democratization*, 2, 2, pp. 109–139.

6

SOCIAL AND POLITICAL ATTITUDES OF THE ALGERIAN YOUTH

A longitudinal study

Mohamed Farid Azzi

Introduction

Until a decade ago, youth played an important social and political role in Algeria. They had fuelled one of the most of the significant events in the country's recent history (the October 1988 uprising, followed by mass participation in the short-lived political opening from 1989 to 1991, took an active part in the bloody events that have deeply affected Algerian society, and have played a considerable role in the protest movement since 2019).

Since the end of the internal armed conflict in the early 2000s, the youth have adopted a relatively low profile; they were not part of the large movement, the so-called Arab Spring that swept across the region from in late 2010.

Some analysts have attributed this to the surge in social and religious conservatism in the society in general. Among the youth, this has manifested in quietist forms of Salafism and Sufism, along with a rise in popular archaic practices, such as magic, Rokia,[1] etc. Social and religious conservatism has been accompanied by a massive withdrawal of young people from political participation, thus indicating political apathy.

Observing this trend one writer states: "By many accounts, Algerian society is increasingly 'Islamizing', despite the (apparent) collective disdain for Islamism. This is not to say Algerians are any more religious-spiritual than a decade ago, rather that outward displays of piety are of growing significance. Public attitudes are growing more socially conservative, to the extent that even the wider political class and members of the (non-Islamist) nationalist centrist parties have been progressively more conspicuous in their displays" (Sakthivel 2017: 31).

So, how much of this is due to changes in outlook and attitudes?

This chapter aims to explore the nature and evolution of the social and political attitudes of the Algerian youth and their determinants, drawing data from the Arab Barometer. The latter allows a longitudinal investigation as it provides a time series set of data covering a period of more than 10 years.

The first part of the study consists of a descriptive account of the social and political attitudes of the youth. Social attitudes reveal the views of the youth concerning family and gender issues; political attitudes encompass views and opinions on elements of political culture, i.e., democracy, political Islam, and political participation. A comparison of the findings on the above-mentioned issues will be undertaken through exploiting data of the four waves of the Arab Barometer.

The second part introduces explanatory intervening, contextual, attitudinal, and socio-demographic variables to account for variance. Some general questions and hypotheses that guide the study include whether there is an observed increase in social conservatism of the youth corroborated by data, and, if so, does it influence the political outlook. Also considered is whether there is a generational effect on social and political attitudes in Algeria.

The relevance of a generational approach to the Algerian case

Age is one of the primary social classifications in human societies. It is an essential factor in the distribution of roles, privileges, and power between individuals and groups in society. Relations between age groups have implications for stability and social change.

It is well established in the literature on socialisation and generational studies (Mannheim 1952; Braungart & Braungart 1993; Kohli 1996; Tessler 2004) that the succession of generations and the substitution of one by another is a common driver of socio-political change. The generational effects are mediated and enhanced by major historical events, especially those taking place during the formative years (17–25 years)[2] of the individuals witnessing those events. Permanent attitudes may ensue, which are distinct from the attitudes of other individuals and groups in society; their tendencies and attitudes are seen as generational.

Not only are these effects on the political arena, but there are researchers who consider that "human generations are the basis of social mobility at all levels of social life—not only in politics but also in the economy and in the family" (Kohli 1996: 10).

Previous studies on the Algerian youth (Azzi 1999; Tessler, Konold, & Reif 2004) found that they played an active role and were at the forefront of major events that characterised the last two decades of the twentieth century. The Algerian social and political scenes have witnessed watershed moments during the 1980s and 1990s in which the youth actively participated.

The interventions of the successive cohort of youth onto Algeria's social and political stages have occurred at a regular pace since the beginning of the 1980s. Different sets of values motivated the actions of the waves of youth through the decades: progressive nationalist and socialist values captivated youth elites throughout the 1960s and 1970s, while the 1980s and 1990s were more propitious to Islamist values and activism.

Youth movements in Algeria in the decades following independence played integrative and functional roles in the newly formed state (Azzi 1999). Then, youth were viewed as great assets and precious human capital necessary for social and economic development. Considerable efforts were exerted by the state to prepare the new generation for its new roles.

The Algerian politico-economic model depended solely on oil and gas revenues, of which an important part was assigned to the social sector. This started to crack under the pressure of the economic crisis caused by plummeting oil prices in 1986 and started a wave of protests that culminated in the uprising of 1988, in which the youth played a major role.

The youth cohort of the new millennium has been socialised in very different social, political, and economic contexts than those who made the news in previous decades. Sharp economic crises, scarce opportunities, social dislocation, and generalised violence were conditions in which youth of previous generations were raised.

The millennial generation has benefited from more clement life conditions, notably more peaceful domestic space (internal peace), and more favourable economic conditions thanks to the increase in the oil price for more than a decade. This study considers the extent to which these living conditions and formative experiences have influenced younger generations in endorsing particular norms and values (Spates 1983) that have determined in their turn the quietist/conservative attitudes.

This chapter tests the fundamental hypothesis that the millennium generation is politically non-participant and socially conservative. Similarly, and through longitudinal and cross-sectional study, we examine changes and variations in values.

Data and methodology

For the purpose of this study, data collected in the Arab Barometer project on Algeria were used. They cover a 10-year time span represented in four waves (2006, 2011, 2013, and 2016) surveying nationally representative samples. The survey instruments were administered as face-to-face interviews.

The present work will first explore changes over time in four sets of values (economic, social, political, and religious); secondly, an age and sex-related variation in the values will be examined using the data of the last Arab Barometer in 2016.

To this end, four age cohorts will be studied and compared. Accounting for variance according to age and gender entails the construction of attitudinal scales in order to measure political, social, religious, and economic dimensions.

The values chosen for this study constitute part of the debate among intel-lectuals and politicians, and sometimes involve public opinion as well. Central to these values are:

- The relationships between politics and religion;
- The status of women;
- The nature of the political regime;
- The introduction of modern socio-political values, such as democracy and political activism, to the elites and subsequently to the general populace in the second half of the twentieth century.

There are certain of these values that have some historical precedents. This is particularly from the second half of the nineteenth-century contemporary to the Islamist renewal, *al-Nahda*, where notions such as despotism, consultation, constitution, politics, and religion were debated among the intellectuals (Moaddel 2017).

These values include:

- Interpersonal trust;
- Women's status and gender issues;
- Political values;
- Political trust;
- Democracy;
- Political interest;
- Political Islam;
- Personal religiosity.

In the first part of the study, a longitudinal comparison will be made from the first to the fourth wave in the above-mentioned values. In the second part, an age and gender analysis will be attempted based solely on the finding of the fourth wave. To this end, a conservative/liberal index will be constructed which will subsequently incorporate social and political components.

Social and political attitudes of the Algerian youth: a longitudinal study

Social values

Trust

The value of trust, according to classics of civic culture (Almond & Verba 1963; Putnam et al. 1993) was related to a strong society and stable democ-racy. Interpersonal trust, it was argued, leads to cooperation, and this in turn contributes to maintaining democracy. In their surveys, the authors revealed that democracy was stable in the UK and the USA because these countries demonstrated a higher level of trust than, for example, Italy and Mexico.

Interpersonal trust results from the extent and quality of the associative life; where it is scarce and weak, democracy is either non-existent or fragile (Putnam et al. 1993). Following in the footsteps of his predecessors, Inglehart (1999) used a large set of data gathered from 60 countries and found that there was a statistically positive relationship between trust and democracy.

Most of the renowned authors of political culture such as Almond, Verba, and Inglehart demonstrate that interpersonal trust and other features of political culture enhance citizen involvement in politics. Recent theories of social capital also emphasise the role of generalised interpersonal trust, membership in voluntary associations, and norms of reciprocity in enhancing political participation and democracy.

Table 6.1 reveals that no clear trend regarding interpersonal trust can be detected through the 11 years and four waves of survey. There has been rather a pronounced fluctuation in attitudes.

Barely two respondents out of ten on average for the four waves do trust each other. Interpersonal trust is even lower among the youngest generation (15.8%). A low level of social trust is not confined to Algerians, but it is common in most of the countries surveyed by the Arab Barometer where interpersonal trust registered 18% on average.

The troubles and violence in Algeria in recent decades cannot alone explain the low level of trust, as an analyst has rightly pointed out (Tessler 2016). Other economic, social, and historic-cultural elements may be at play in explaining the lack of trust among Algerians.

Another aspect that may partially explain the trust deficit is firstly, that interpersonal trust is a consequence and not a cause; secondly, it results from the ascendance of survival values in society, in the sense that Inglehart gives to these concepts.

In their struggle to fulfil their basic needs, food, shelter, and security, and faced with the relative scarcity of these goods and services, people tend to do everything possible to achieve their objectives. This struggle for survival creates tensions between the people and the state and between people themselves, a condition that erodes interpersonal trust. In other words, economic underdevelopment is not propitious for trust.

TABLE 6.1 Interpersonal trust

	2006	*2011*	*2013*	*2016*
% Interpersonal trust	33.6	7.3	21.9	18.3

Source: Calculations by the author from the Arab Barometer data, https://www.arabbarometer.org/survey-data/data-analysis-tool/.

TABLE 6.2 Interpersonal trust, age, and gender

	18–24			25–34			35–44		
	All	*Male*	*Female*	*All*	*Male*	*Female*	*All*	*Male*	*Female*
% Trust	15.8	13.3	18.4	20.5	20.7	20.3	20.2	21.8	18.7
% Don't trust	82.6	85.9	79.4	75.6	73.3	78	77.6	75.9	79.4

Source: Calculations by the author from the Arab Barometer data, https://www.arabbarometer.org/survey-data/data-analysis-tool/.

Another contributor to the trust deficit is that in order to maintain their grip over society, totalitarian political regimes spread suspicion, divisiveness, espionage, and paranoia among their people, which have an adverse effect on interpersonal trust and social cohesion (Table 6.2).

Women: status and gender issues

Women in the Western Hemisphere have had a long struggle to gain a legal status guaranteeing them equality to men. However, in the Middle East and North Africa (MENA) region comprising countries in the Middle East and North Africa, the status of women continues to be a much debated and controversial topic. Although there have been some women writers, intellectuals, and women's rights activists since early in the twentieth century (such as Amin Kassim in Egypt), patriarchal ideology and practices continue to be hegemonic.

Moaddel (2017) portrays the context in which issues of women rights emerge in the Arab and Islamic countries as follows:

> encountering Western modernity during the 19th century, maltreatment of women in historical Islam became the subject of considerable debate among diverse intellectual leaders, political activists, and the ruling class [....] intellectual debates among the proponents and opponents of greater freedom for women shaped the intellectual context within which Islamic feminism emerged during the late 19th and early 20th centuries.

The relationship between men and women in private or public spheres in Algeria since independence has taken disproportionate dimensions, involving political, ideological, and, inevitably, religious arguments.

Political Islam has contributed to the moulding of the discourse and to the debate around the status of women. The Salafist non-political brand of Islamism leads the chorus at present; they claim that the social role and the legal status has been definitively settled by the holy book and there is nothing to negotiate.

Opposing the Salafist view are numerous social and political activists in civil society association. They struggle for a change in family law which they judge to be totally inspired by the Sharia which they view as unsuitable for present-day Algeria and for the problems and constraints women face.

Notwithstanding the activism of an elite group of militant women, the majority of Algerian women are portrayed by Gray (2009) as follows:

> Traumatized by the more recent decade of the violence, the majority of younger women today stay away from public activism. Most women in Algeria today wear the veil, if not always for religious reasons so as to afford them some protection when moving in the public sphere. They rather focus on professional advancement or engage in social service projects. Encapsulating some of the most pressing global tensions within its borders, the way Algeria resolves issues of gender inequalities, will determine Algeria's position in the Muslim world and on the global stage.

Many questions on gender issues were asked in the survey. In order to capture the ordinary citizens' attitudes and perceptions, the answers to selected questions on the issue from the fourth wave.

There seems to be a trend concerning women's status and gender issues as shown in Table 6.3. Respondents belonging to the fourth wave have the most conservative attitudes with a mere 38.1% of them agreeing to the notion that a woman can become the president or prime minister of a Muslim country against 62.7% in the first wave respondents; similarly, a high percentage (78%) of the fourth wave respondents believe that men make better leaders than women.

The two values concerning the status of women that appear to have some consensus are equal rights for higher education and the right for women to work after marriage. However, Algerians are still conservative when it comes to allowing women an active role in public and political life (Figure 6.1).

TABLE 6.3 Percentage of agreement on questions relating to the perception of women's status, four waves

	2006	2011	2013	2016
A woman can become prime minister or president in Muslim country	62.7	41.9	na	38.1
A married woman can work outside the home if she wishes	79.9	80.4	87	76
In general, men are better at political leadership than women	77.6	67	62.5	78
University education for men is more important than university education for women	35	19.7	4.5	23.5

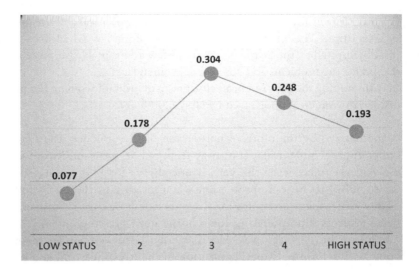

FIGURE 6.1 Perceptions about the status of women. (Calculated by the author from the Arab Barometer Data, https://www.arabbarometer.org/survey-data/data-analysis-tool/.)

Age, gender, and the status of women

A women's status index was constructed after running a factorisation where the entire item pertaining to women's status formed one factor. We formed the index by taking the mean average of five among six variables related to women's status, then the resulting new variable was recoded into five values, where 1 represents a low status and 5 a high status.

The following result was noted: around 25.5% of respondents assign a low status to women, 30.4% ascribe a moderate status, while 44.1% allot women a high status. As expected, there is a gender divide around women's status; 38.7% of men attribute a low status to women, only 12.3% of this latter did. While six in ten women credit themselves with high status, only three in ten men did so.

Though there is no significant age variation among men's opinions of the status of women, young men seem to confer a lower status to women then older men, as Table 6.4 demonstrates. Among women respondents, age has some statistically significant effects as to their perception of their status; it is the young cohort of women, 63.8% of the age group 18–24 years and 56.9% of 25–34 years who claim a high status, whereas only 54.2% of the eldest age group have that attitude.

It is not clear why young men have a low perception of women's status, whether this is the effect of age or generation. A possible explanation is that their attitude is age-related, because most young men in Algeria of between 18 and 24 have little experience involving women. At a later stage, when they start families, they have to make concessions and adjustments that could somehow change their attitudes to women's role and status.

TABLE 6.4 Women status by age and gender

Women status by age and gender

	18–24			25–34			35–44			45+		
	All	*Male*	*Female*	*All*	*Male*	*Female*	*All*	*Male*	*Female*	*All*	*Male*	*Female*
% High status	44.4	25	63.8	42.5	28	56.9	47.4	32.2	62.6	43.2	32.3	54.2
% Moderate status	28.2	33.5	22.9	32.8	37.8	35.8	50	24.1	25.2	57.4	29.2	28.2
% Low status	27.3	41.5	13.2	20.6	34	7.3	27.9	43.7	12.2	27.8	38.5	17.2

Source: Calculations by the author from the Arab Barometer data, https://www.arabbarometer.org/survey-data/data-analysis-tool/.

Pulitical values

Political interest

On average, only one respondent in five in the four surveys declared an interest in politics. The highest marks (28.1%) were attained in the first wave in 2006, a period where the country was just coming out of a costly internal military conflict, and the hopes were high for political reform and economic recovery. Age and gender do have some influence on individual interest in public life.

The findings of the 2016 survey, displayed in Table 6.5, reveal that the older cohort show more political interest than the younger, the under-35 years scored 16.9% versus 27.3% for those over 35 years of age. In general, women are less interested in public affairs, with a low percentage of 13.6% and no statistically significant differences between female age groups.

Low turnout in different local and national elections (McAllister 2016: 138)[3] is one indication of the lack of interest in politics, but many reasons were put forward to explain the low interest in Algerian political life. Chief among these is the sclerotic, non-competitive, authoritarian political system.

Some analysts argue that if Algerians and especially the youth are alienated from official politics, it doesn't mean that they don't have political principles and preferences. As one author noted "granted, many felt at best cautiousness and at worst deep cynicism about the possibility of lasting political change, but this neither implied apathy, nor a lack of political principles [...] Young people in Bab el Oued[4] cared about injustice, often passionately, and were extremely vociferous in their defence of principles such as freedom of speech, political integrity, and accountability" (Boserup 2016).

Democracy and governance

Despite a varying understanding of the meaning of democracy,[5] support for it is constantly high across all four waves. As democracy is a multidimensional concept, there are several questions in all four waves of the surveys to measure it.

A question relating to the content of democracy was posed in which the respondents emphasised the law and order and socioeconomic aspects of democracy. Another question asked interviewees to assess how democratic Algeria is and how fit is it for democracy.

Table 6.6 illustrates that more Algerians think that the country is suited for democracy (median 6) than those who think it is democratic (median 5). It should be noted that for both measures there has been a statistically significant decrease in the 2016 survey (Arab Barometer 2016: 14).[6]

On a more abstract level, and in reaction to the statement in the questionnaire "a democratic system may have problems, yet it is better than other systems," 71.3% agreed. The lowest support (66.1%) for democracy was registered in the second wave in 2011, coinciding with the debut of the Arab Spring (Figure 6.2).

TABLE 6.5 Interest in politics

Interest in politics

	18–24			25–34			35–44			45+		
	All	*Male*	*Female*	*All*	*Male*	*Female*	*All*	*Male*	*Female*	*All*	*Male*	*Female*
% Interested	13.7	14.2	13.2	20.2	28.1	11.1	24.4	36.8	14.2	30.2	45.7	15.9
% Not interested	86.3	85.8	86.8	79.8	71.9	88.6	75.6	63.2	85.8	69.8	54.6	84.1

Source: Calculations by the author from the Arab Barometer data, https://www.arabbarometer.org/survey-data/data-analysis-tool/.

TABLE 6.6 Democratic systems are better

Democratic systems have problems, yet are better than other systems		2006	2011	2013	2016
	Agree	73.3	66.1	69.4	78.8
	Disagree	12.3	12.4	15.1	13.6

Source: Calculations by the author from the Arab Barometer data, https://www.arabbarometer.org/survey-data/data-analysis-tool/.

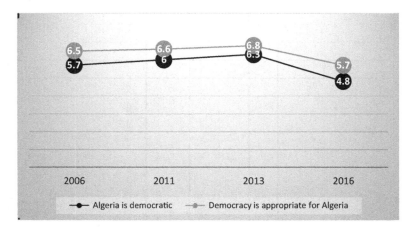

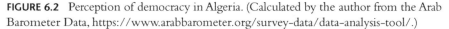

FIGURE 6.2 Perception of democracy in Algeria. (Calculated by the author from the Arab Barometer Data, https://www.arabbarometer.org/survey-data/data-analysis-tool/.)

The culmination (78.8%) of support for democracy was displayed by those in the fourth wave. The observed variation in support for democracy, although high in general, could be partly dependent on context.

In Algeria, and after the fear of unpredictable change and the chaos that may follow, as was the case in most of the Arab countries that experienced the events of the Arab Spring, have dissipated, and democratic demands are on the rise again.

Related to this is also the persistence and resilience of the governing elite in place for decades and the lack of any meaningful political change. Attitudes to democracy are contingent upon individuals' attributes like age and gender.

Support for democracy by age and gender

A statistically significant relationship was uncovered between the support for democracy and age, as expressed in Table 6.7, the most supportive are respondents belonging to the eldest cohort (83.9%) and those in the youngest (79.5%). Men are slightly more in favour of democracy than women, except for the age group 35–44 years, where women scored 5 percentage points higher.

TABLE 6.7 Support for democracy by age and gender

	18–24			25–34			35–44			45+		
	All	*Male*	*Female*	*All*	*Male*	*Female*	*All*	*Male*	*Female*	*All*	*Male*	*Female*
% Support democracy	79.5	81.4	77.7	76.8	76.1	77.6	72	69.8	74.3	83.8	86.2	81.5
% Do not support democracy	20.4	18.6	22.3	23.1	23.9	22.4	27.9	30.2	25.7	16.1	13.8	18.5

Source: Calculations by the author from the Arab Barometer data, https://www.arabbarometer.org/survey-data/data-analysis-tool/.

In a related question, respondents were asked to express their views on a suit able form of government for the country. A large majority in the three waves of the survey were in favour of a parliamentary system in which nationalists, left wing, right wing, and Islamists parties compete in a parliamentary election as shown in the findings of the three Arab Barometer waves,[7] with the exception of the fourth wave where those in favour of a representative democracy had a slim majority (51.4%). At the same time, an important minority (22%) of the fourth wave survey, believe that a system governed by Islamic law in which there are no political parties or elections would be suitable.

Institutional trust

Institutional trust varies according to the institution in question and how it is perceived according to the historical context. The general observation is that there seems to be a hierarchy of trust as shown in Table 6.8, the security apparatus (the army and the police) enjoy a relatively high trust among the population where seven individuals among ten on average for the four survey's waves do trust the army and the police forces.

The lowest percentage of trust for those two institutions and, especially the police, was obtained in 2011. This coincided with the Arab Spring movements that have spilled over to Algeria where many demonstrations took place, but failed to gain momentum, due to some extent to the strong and pre-emptive intervention of the police force.

The least trusted among the political institutions are the representative and civilian ones, which is quite a paradox as the political parties, the parliament, and to some degree the courts are seen as less legitimate than the security apparatus. Muslim brothers and the religious leaders display declining trust; however, for the latter, it is still higher than the other political institutions.

TABLE 6.8 Institutional trust: longitudinal view

	2006	2011	2013	2016
Trust in government	65.9	27.5	69.7	30.8
Trust in court	76.1	42.6	na	35.4
Trust in army	na	52.5	90.1	73.6
Trust in the police	86.2	47	89.5	65.7
Trust in parliament	54.9	18.1	40.1	16.5
Trust in political parties	29.2	17.5	na	12.8
Trust in Muslim Brotherhood	na	43.7	47.5	16.8
Trust in religious leaders	na	86.5	52.6	44

Source: Calculations by the author from the Arab Barometer data, https://www.arabbarometer.org/survey-data/data-analysis-tool/.

Political trust varied from one wave to another, it seems at its lowest in 2016 during the fourth wave and in 2011, except for religious leaders. The geopolitical context as mentioned earlier explained the lack of trust in the political system as a whole. In 2016, in addition to the absence of any meaningful political reform and the persistence of the opaque political practices and personnel, there was a sharp drop in the country's revenues due to the plummeting of the oil prices on which Algeria's economy and budget depend heavily. This had repercussions on the lives of ordinary citizens as they have to pay more taxes to make up for the state budget deficit and spend more money on necessary commodities due to inflation.

Trust and age

Table 6.9 exposes an index of institutional trust computed of the seven items for the fourth wave survey and crossed with age and with a p value >005, it was found that the younger age cohorts (18–24 years and 25–34 years) demonstrate less political trust (27.5%) than the older cohorts (35–44 years and 45+ years) who scored 37.4% and 36.9% successively.

Trust and gender

Though institutional trust is low in general, women are found to have more trust than men, surpassing them by 12 percentage points. On the individual trust items, it was on items pertaining to religion that they marked off the highest difference to men. This finding confirms the results of several studies on religious practices and religiosity where women were found to be more religious than men.

Political Islam

In relation to political Islam, the majority (55.8%) opinion is not Islamist in the last survey, and this is the case throughout all the four waves where the average of non-Islamist was 56.63%. According to an index of political Islam we constructed through the selection of six items[8] among many questions relevant to political Islam,[9] 55.8% of the opinions are non-Islamist, only a small minority (around 16%) are diehard Islamists, with a large minority of 28.4% moderately Islamist (Figure 6.3).

Although the findings of the fourth wave concerning political Islam are not fundamentally different from the previous waves, some items of the index and others which are not included in the index clearly indicate a more conservative outlook.

When asked which party they prefer, a religious or no religious one, 52.1% of respondents of the fourth wave prefer religious parties versus only 25.1% of respondents from the previous survey. Moreover, only a third of the last survey considers religious practice a private matter versus an average of 51.6% of the three previous surveys.

TABLE 6.9 Political trust by age and gender

	18–24			25–34			35–44			45+		
	All	*Male*	*Female*	*All*	*Male*	*Female*	*All*	*Male*	*Female*	*All*	*Male*	*Female*
% Political trust	27.8	19.1	36.5	28.2	21	35.5	36.9	28.6	45.3	36.9	39.5	34.3
% No political trust	72.2	80.9	63.5	71.7	79	64.5	62.8	71	54.7	63.1	60.5	65.7

Source: Calculations by the author from the Arab Barometer data, https://www.arabbarometer.org/survey-data/data-analysis-tool/.

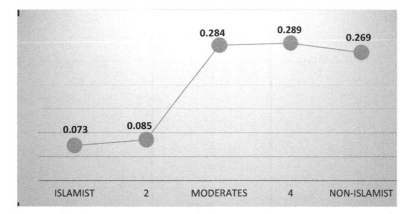

FIGURE 6.3 Political Islam. (Calculated by the author from the Arab Barometer Data, https://www.arabbarometer.org/survey-data/data-analysis-tool/.)

Islamism by age and gender

The relationships between age, gender, and Islamism is complex and not linear. Table 6.10 indicates that although barely two in ten individuals are hard Islamist, males tend to be more Islamist than women, except for the eldest age group where the percentage of female Islamists is double that of men (27.2% for the former and 14.3% for the latter). Whereas, in the non-Islamist category and among the youngest age group, it is the females who constitute the largest group with 63.2%, versus 49.4% for men.

Liberal conservative continuum

In order to support further my claim that nowadays Algerians tend to express more conservative social and religious attitudes, I proceeded to the construction of a general index representing the attitudes of the respondents of the four waves on four dimensions: political, social, moral, and political Islam.

Each of these dimensions was denoted by an index, as shown in Table 6.11 for the fourth wave, and the indexes were aggregated to form a general index measuring a continuum of liberal/conservative attitudes on the values constituting the dimensions studied.

The liberal/conservative index comprises seven values, where 1 depicts an extremely conservative attitude and 7 an extremely liberal attitude. Subsequently, the scale was divided into three categories: liberal, moderate, and conservative, where the values from 1 to 3 stand for the first category (conservatives), 4 for the second (moderates), and from 5 to 7 for the third (liberals).

TABLE 6.10 Political Islam by age and gender

	18–24			25–34			35–44			45+		
	All	*Male*	*Female*	*All*	*Male*	*Female*	*All*	*Male*	*Female*	*All*	*Male*	*Female*
% Islamist	15.3	20	10.7	10.7	11.7	9.2	17.4	23.1	11.7	20.7	14.3	27.2
% Moderate Islamist	28.4	30.5	26.3	32.2	28.2	36.2	28.7	26.2	31.2	26	29.2	22.8
% Non Islamist	56.3	49.4	63.2	57.1	60.2	54	53.9	50.7	57.2	55.2	60.5	50

Source: Calculations by the author from the Arab Barometer data, https://www.arabbarometer.org/survey–data/data–analysis–tool/.

TABLE 6.11 Conservative/liberal scale, 1 = very conservative; 7 = very liberal

scale	wave1	wave2	wave3	wave4
1	4.3	8.6	1	15.4
2	15.7	14	4.1	13.2
3	5.2	9.6	14.1	15.3
4	34	34.7	23.2	15.9
5	5.1	6.7	27.4	14.5
6	27.6	20.8	24	15.6
7	8.1	5.5	6.3	10.1

Source: Calculations by the author from the Arab Barometer data, https://www.arabbarometer.org/survey-data/data-analysis-tool/.

Conclusions

From the tables and charts above, a number of remarks and conclusions can be made:

- Overall, liberal attitudes are more widespread among the population than conservative ones (see Table 6.12);
- It is within the third wave, implemented in the year 2013, that the highest percentage of liberal outlooks was reached (57.7%), followed by the first wave (40.8%), then the fourth wave (40.2%), and lastly the second wave (33%);
- The findings related to the distribution of conservative attitudes partly support our working hypothesis that the respondents of the fourth wave of surveys carried out in the year 2016 conveyed more conservative views and attitudes than those of the previous waves. 43.9% of the respondents in the fourth wave expressed conservative attitudes, compared to only 19.2% in the third wave. However, and paradoxically, the percentage of respondents in the fourth wave who had liberal attitudes is also high (40.2%), therefore, we face here a polarised opinion, where almost the same numbers of people express opposing views;
- As has been demonstrated in the previous sections, respondents of the fourth wave survey differed from respondents of preceding waves on a number of issues: they hold a pessimistic economic outlook for the country and exhibit low interpersonal and political trust. The trust in government has never been lower, except in 2011 coinciding with the Arab Spring. Their disenchantments reached even the religious leaders. Nonetheless, they are still attached to the Islamist ideal more than the previous waves. A majority of them prefers a religious party and do not consider religious practice as a private matter that can be separated from socio-economic life. They also hold quite conservative views on some aspects regarding women's roles in

TABLE 6.12 Liberal/conservative scale by gender and age

	18–24			25–34			35–44			45+		
	All	*Male*	*Female*	*All*	*Male*	*Female*	*All*	*Male*	*Female*	*All*	*Male*	*Female*
% Conservative	35.9	34	39.9	40	39.4	40.6	41.8	42.1	41.5	43.7	43	44.5
% Moderate	16.4	16.9	16	15.7	16.2	15.3	15	14.1	15.9	14.3	14.8	13.9
% Liberal	46.5	49.1	44	44.3	44.5	44.1	43.1	43.8	42.5	41.9	42.2	41.5

$p > 0.10$.

the family and in society at large; for instance, a large majority believes that men make better political leaders, and that husbands should have the final say in all decisions concerning the family. Furthermore, they show to some extent more intolerance, especially vis-à-vis other religions. Nonetheless, they scored high on democracy, only a small majority chose a free and open political system;

- The youngest generation (18–24 years) of the fourth wave survey has shown different and less conservative attitudes on some issues, did not differ on others, and even was more conservative on a few. The young cohort is particularly low on interpersonal trust, but higher on the scale of social tolerance;

- The young cohort marked a high score on the women status scale, and this is thanks to young women's strong attitude concerning their status in society. This concurs with that of Tessler (2016) in analysing the data of the 2013 Arab Barometer survey for Algeria: "Accordingly, among Algerians in the 18–24 age group, women are much more likely than men to support gender equality and to agree with less restrictive interpretations of Islam";

- Although the youth display little interest in political matters, they massively subscribe to democratic values (at least as they conceive of it), men are slightly more democratic than women. Young men are less secular than older ones, but young women are more secular than older women. However, and as a group, the 18–24 years are to some extent more liberal than the oldest age group;

- We are seeing a young generation that is more conservative, less Islamist, and more religious in the sense of popular religion.[10] Algeria's political-religious landscape has become more complex since the post-conflict era, which has witnessed the resurgence of two quietist forms of Islam: Sufism and Salafism. This requires us to reconsider how Islamism can be defined, as well as conventional wisdom about Islamist behaviour, which seems to obey more an individual approach than to a collective bound. Also, this young generation, as Boserup (2016: 65) puts it, has adopted a more pragmatic mode of action, unfettered by the conflict of the recent past, focused on bringing and practicing change in everyday life, and in so doing changing their social world.

Notes

1 A kind of exorcism widely practiced as an alternative medicine.
2 Formation years: a term used by the authors of political formation and generations to indicate the stage between the end of adolescence and the beginning of youth. The idea here is that experiences at this stage have significant implications in shaping the attitudes and values of individuals and whether some of these values and political attitudes that individuals have during the early stages of their lives, during adolescence or early youth, continue with them later in life. See, Braungart (1984); Erlich (1997).

3 Only around 1% of Algerian young people are members of political parties or trade unions and turnout in elections is routinely 30%. Cited in McAllister (2016: 138).
4 Bab el Oued is a popular quarter of Algiers.
5 According to the report of the findings from the fourth Arab Barometer, "the concept of democracy contains multiple elements, and Algerians tend to conceptualize its most essential characteristics in primarily socioeconomic terms."
6 Statistics for the two questions were borrowed from the findings from the Arab Barometer entitled "Algeria five years after the Arab Uprisings," April 15, 2017, P14.
7 For more details consult the Arab Barometer online at http://www.arabbarometer.org/survey-data/data-analysis-tool/.
8 The survey questions constituting the index: (1) religious leaders (imams, preachers, priests) should not interfere in voters' decisions in elections. (2) Your country is better off if religious people hold public positions in the state. (3) Religious clerics should have influence over the decisions of government. (4) Religious practice is a private matter and should be separated from socio-economic life. (5) It is acceptable in Islam for male and female university students to attend classes together. (6) A women should dress modestly, but Islam does not require that she wears a hijab.
9 The choice of these variables for an index for political Islam could be defended on the grounds that it has been already used by scholars and specialists of Islamism (see Tessler) and proven to be reliable and valid.
10 Popular religion, in the sense that Ernest Gellner gave to concept.

References

Almond, G.A., and Sidney, V. 1963. *The Civic Culture: Political Attitudes and Democracy in Five Nations*. Princeton: Princeton University Press.
Arab Barometer. 2016. http://www.arabbarometer.org/survey-data/data-analysis-tool/.
Azzi, M.F. 1999. *Maghribi Youth: Between Alienation and Integration*. In Y.H. Zoubir (Ed.), *North Africa in Transition*. Gainesville: University Press of Florida.
Boserup, A.R. 2016. Contention and Order. In L. Martinez & R.A. Boserup (Eds.), *Algeria Modern*. London: Hurst.
Braungart, R.G. 1984. Historical Generations and Youth Movements: A Theoretical Perspective. In R. Ratcliff (Ed.), *Research in Social Movements, Conflict and Change*. Greenwich: JAI Press.
Braungart, R.G., & Braungart, M.M. Eds. 1993. *Life Course and Generation Politics*. Lanham, MD: University Press of America.
Erlich, H. 1997. "Generational Conflicts in the 20th Century in the Middle East." *Paper Presented at a Conference on Youth in the Middle East and North Africa*, Amsterdam, the Netherlands, organized by the European Commission for Culture, November 8–10, 1997.
Gray, D.H. 2009. Women in Algeria Today and the Debate Over Family Law. http://commandtheraven.com/women-in-algeria-today-and-the-debate-over-family-law/ (no longer available).
Inglehart, R. 1999. Trust, Well-Being and Democracy." In M.E. Warren (Ed.), *Democracy and Trust*. Cambridge: Cambridge University Press.
Kluckhohn, C. 1951. Values and Value-Orientations in the Theory of Action: An Exploration in Definition and Classification. In T. Parsons & E. Shils (Eds.), *Toward a General Theory of Action*. Cambridge, MA: Harvard University Press.
Kohli, M. 1996. The Problem of Generations: Family, Economy, Politics. Public Lectures N0 14, Budapest, www.colbud.hu.
Mannheim, K. 1952. "The Problem of Generation." In K. Mannheim (Ed.), *Essays on the Sociology of Knowledge*. London: Routledge & Kegan Paul.

McAllister, Ed. 2016. "Youth, Social injustice and Cynicism in Bab el-Oued." In L.L. Martinez & R.A. Boserup (Eds.), *Algeria Modern*. London: Hurst & Company.

Moaddel, M. 2017. "Youth Perceptions and Values During the Arab Spring: Cross-national Variation and Trends." In M. Moaddel & Michele J. Gelfand (Eds.), *Values, Political Action, and Change in the Middle East and the Arab Spring*. Oxford: Oxford University Press.

Parsons, T. 1949. *The Structure of Social Action: A Study in Social Theory*. Glencoe: Free Press.

Putnam, R.D., with Leonardi, R. and Nanetti, R.V. 1993. *Making Democracy Work: Civic Tradition in Modern Italy*. Princeton: Princeton University Press.

Sakthivel, V. 2017. Political Islam in Post-Conflict Algeria—Analysis. Hudson Institute. https://www.eurasiareview.com/14102017-political-islam-in-post-conflict-algeria-analysis/.

Spates, J. 1983. The Sociology of Values. *Annual Review of Sociology*, 9 (1), 27–49.

Tessler, M., & Gonzalez, M.L. 2016. "Maghribi Youth in the Wake of the Arab Spring." In Y.H. Zoubir & G. White (Eds.), *North African Politics: Change and Continuity*. London & New York: Routledge.

Tessler, M., Konold, C., & Reif, M. 2004. Political Generations in Developing Countries: Evidence and Insights from Algeria. *Public Opinion Quarterly*, 68 (2), 184–216. doi:10.1093/poq/nfh011.

7

JIHADISM IN ALGERIA

From lethal to manageable

Dalia Ghanem

Algeria has had a long history with jihadism.[1] Aside from those in Egypt, Algerian jihadist groups were among the first to appear in the Arab world and the African continent. The origins of radical Islamist groups are to be found at the independence of the country in 1962. Back then, conflicts between the regime and Islamists erupted challenging the monopoly of the religious realm. Throughout the 1980s, the dialogue between the government and the Islamists hardened, especially in 1982, when Mustafa Bouyali established the first Algerian jihadist group called the Armed Islamic Movement (MIA).[2] It was the premise of the long and bloody war that the country witnessed from 1991 until 2001 claiming some 150,000 lives ('Algérie: Dix ans après la Charte, où en est la réconciliation' 2015), 7,000 missing, 1 million internally displaced (Daoud 2015), and more than $20 billion of material damages.

Even though most Algerian jihadist groups in the 1990s were defeated and disbanded, one group internationalised in the 2000s and became known as Al Qaeda in the Islamic Maghreb (AQIM). With its old lineage, pragmatic leadership, sophisticated recruitment tactics, and sturdy base, AQIM was able to adapt to the new regional realities by changing its scope of action from focusing on the Algerian hinterlands to instead targeting the Sahelian states. Despite the group status as a dominant player in the Sahel region, it lost its momentum at home. AQIM's downfall can be attributed to its extreme violent methods, its organisational woes, coupled with the state's repression methods and conciliatory policies towards jihadists. Furthermore, losing several leaders, assets, and facing significant challenges with recruiting militants locally, AQIM has recently lost its historical bastion in the Berber hinterland. AQIM seems to have failed in passing its dream of an Algerian Caliphate to a new generation of Algerians. The same can be said about the Islamic State affiliate in Algeria, *Jund El Khilafa* [The soldiers of the Caliphate], who did not constitute a serious threat to the country, but rather a publicity stunt

(Ghanem 2014). While it is true that these groups remain a nuisance for the state, they do not constitute an existential threat as shown vividly by the data of the latest Global Terrorism Index. Indeed, the number of fatalities from terrorism in Algeria fell from 153 in 2009 to 9 in 2016 (Institute for Economics and Peace 2017).

From ballots to guns

Algeria's transition from a one-party system to a multi-party system in 1989 prominently benefited the Islamist movement. The most popular party at the time of the democratic opening was the Islamic Salvation Front (FIS), led by Abassi Madani and his acolyte, Ali Belhadj. The FIS has a diversified membership composed of radical Islamists, some Algerian-Afghan veterans, members of a traditionally conservative urban class, and a substantial number of the alienated youth. With the support of this diverse constituency, the FIS won the local elections in June 1990.[3] After the first round of legislative elections in December 1991, the FIS proved to be a strong social force by securing 188 out of 232 seats in Parliament.

However, the second round of elections, scheduled for January 1992, never took place. The military interrupted the electoral process and took effective control of the country. They ousted then-President Chadli Bendjedid, banned the FIS, and jailed thousands of its sympathisers.[4] Nonetheless, it is important to note that the armed violence and call for jihadism started before the interruption of the electoral process in 1992 as witnessed by the attack of Guemmar on November 29, 1991. The cessation of the electoral process offered the supporters of violence, such as the FIS extremist faction, an opportunity to prove the that the only viable way was violence.

A plethora of jihadist groups emerged throughout the country to fight what they called *dawlet El Tagut* [the impious state]. The most formidable group, the Groupe Islamique armé (GIA) "liberated" entire villages and claimed the "*Khalifa*" [Caliphate] across several localities in the country and called these regions "*El Manatik El muharara*" [liberated areas]. The liberated areas were governed as a parallel-state with the launch of GIA's social programmes, justice, administration, social assistance, tax collection, and so on. Consequently, many villages became a support base for the GIA. However, the group's local support was short-lived, since most groups eventually lost the population's support mainly due to the use of extreme violence especially under the leadership of Djamel Zitouni and his successor Antar Zouabri. In 1998, members of the GIA with at their head, Hassan Hattab, decided to form the Salafist Group for Preaching and Combat.[5] Their strategy was to win back local support by focusing their attacks only on the security forces and putting an end to endangering the civilian population. Later on, as a form to appeal to a younger generation and inverse the decline of jihadist groups in Algeria given their lack of popularity, the Salafist Group for Preaching and Combat merged with Al Qaeda in 2006. AQIM was born.

AQIM's Impossible victory

In 2007, only a year into its existence, AQIM perpetrated several attacks with the most notable being against the presidential convoy in Batna that killed 22 people and wounded 107 (Akef 2007). However, the group faced severe adversities and eventually lost its historical stronghold in the Kabylia. As a result, it shifted its operations towards the eastern part of the country, near the border with Tunisia. These setbacks and AQIM's impossible victory in Algeria can be explained by (1) the state's repression and conciliatory measures towards jihadists; (2) the group's violent methods; and (3) its organisational deficits.

The state's conciliatory approach

Since the 1990s, the Algerian security forces have always kept a high military pressure on jihadist groups all over the territory as suggested by available figures. For example, 27,000 armed Islamists were believed to be fighting in the country in the 1990s. Among these fighters, 16,930 were estimated to have been killed (Bennadji 2009). Since the end of the civil war in 2001, the security forces killed hundreds of AQIM's fighters including prominent individuals. The numbers suggest that the government was taking immediate action and promoting its counter-terrorism operations. At the beginning of 2018, the AQIM's branch responsible for propaganda, Adel Seghiri, Aka Abu Ruaha Al-Qasantini, and Bekkai Boualem, and Aka Khaled El Mig, AQIM's head of external relations, were killed by the security forces (Anonymous 2012). Between 2013 and 2018, the Algerian security forces eliminated around 600 jihadists (Ismain 2018). Also, hundreds of AQIM's fighters have surrendered, often in groups, and at times with their families (APS 2016).

This strict approach was coupled with conciliatory methods, such as the adoption in 1995 of the Clemency Law by then-President Liamine Zeroual.[6] These efforts continued to be effective under his successor President Abdelaziz Bouteflika, who in 1999 introduced a Civil Concord Law and in 2005 the Charter for Peace and National Reconciliation. Former fighters were eligible for amnesty under certain conditions (i.e., not having been involved in setting off bombs in public spaces, nor having committed rape or massacre). If former fighters committed such crimes, they would be eligible for reduced prison sentences.[7] Also, the charter exempted members of security forces and pro-government militias from prosecution. Lastly, demobilisation and rehabilitation programmes were also adopted, and the charter allowed for the reintegration of some 15,000 former combatants (RFI 2015).

Algerian authorities worked with former jihadists, "repentants" who were given a voice and spoke on national television about their experience in jihadist groups. Many former jihadists, such as Islamic Salvation Army's former emir in the Larbaa region, Mustapha Kertali, endorsed this reconciliation policy. The participation of formers jihadists was crucial for legitimising the peace process. The authorities, with the help of former fighters and their families, made regular calls to those who remained in their hideouts urging them to surrender and return to society. Not only did this raise awareness of the dangers of violent radicalisation and its fatal consequences, but it also prevented potential individuals from joining the ranks of jihadist groups. Moreover, it inspired many to leave and convinced others to renounce violence for good (Ghanem 2017a). Those who chose to quit were offered protection to defend themselves and their families against possible retaliation.

The authorities provided those who were victims of state violence with financial compensation (up to $15,000 according to fieldwork research in 2008). The state, due to the oil windfalls, was able to invest in development, thus further preventing violent extremism. To ease social tensions and reduce youth's recruitment by jihadist groups, the state invested in better infrastructure, housing, jobs, health, etc. Moreover, a recruitment policy was adopted to offer better professional opportunities, especially to the youth. For instance, Wali (prefects) in the 48 wilaya had to set up "a private status multiservice cooperative," required to gather unemployed youth and integrate them into economic activity (security guards, caretakers, plumbers, etc.). In addition to the military, which was absorbed into the workforce, agreements with public companies such as SOTROUJ (road works) or DHW (hydraulic) were put to the benefit of young graduates (Martinez 1998: 275). These efforts contributed to preventing economic hardships and recidivism of former jihadists. It also hindered Jihadi networks by depriving them of potential recruits who were offered not only a way out of jihadism, but instead an alternative.

AQIM's violent methods

A second reason that contributed to AQIM's reversal in Algeria was the group's use of harsh methods and indiscriminate violence against civilians. It is worth noting that when Hassan Hattab, a GIA veteran, established the Salafist Group for Preaching and Combat, its first goal was to continue the jihad without harming civilians to regain their support. Indeed, the extreme violence of the GIA eventually alienated its supporters among the population and led to its decline. However, while AQIM appeared to be less violent than the GIA, the group managed to estrange the local community due to its punitive approach. Even in its last stronghold, in Kabylia, the group failed to balance levels of coercion and co-optation to avoid alienating local communities.

Due to the conflictual relationship between the Berbers and the central authorities, the local population remained passive to AQIM, and a modus vivendi was established between the two. However, this modus vivendi would rupture when AQIM started extracting money, abducting, or killing wealthy entrepreneurs in the region. Since 2005, the jihadist group is believed to have kidnapped more than 80 individuals (Kabylie 2014). The constant fear of insecurity hindered development and investment projects, thus aggravating an already precarious economic situation. The Chamber of Commerce and

Industry of Tizi Ouzou Province reported in 2014 that more than 71 companies had left Kabylia because of the security situation and the numerous kidnappings (Anonymous 2014). Moreover, the disapproval of the local population escalated, and the relations between the locals and AQIM changed, and this turned the tide of the battle.

Serious organisational woes

Another reason that contributed to AQIM's retreat in Algeria was its organisational malfunctions. AQIM's national emir, Abdel Malek Droudkel, also known as Abu Mosab Abdelwadud, had been leading the group since 2004. However, in practice, Droudkel only offers guidance, since the multiple brigades that compose AQIM are autonomous and independent in conducting their operations. Unable to communicate with each other or even provide their men with a minimum of equipment, AQIM's brigades became weaker throughout the years, and their military potential remains inconsistent. This obstacle obstructed Droudkel's management and weakened its leadership.

Also, the focus on the southern front, meaning the Sahel, has pitted the northern front. Indeed, while the group kept a northern front in Algeria, it decided in 2009 to shift from local to regional jihadism and started a Sahelisation strategy. The choice was as opportunistic as it was pragmatic. On the one hand, the counter-terrorism operations of the Algerian security forces pushed the AQIM outside of the northern regions making it far from the capital and its vicinities. On the other hand, the vast ungoverned lands and loosely patrolled borders in the Sahel proved to be a significant opportunity for the group to extend its scope of action. AQIM's pragmatic leadership was skilful at exploiting the Sahel's extreme poverty, political, social and economic marginalisation, bad governance, lack of opportunities, and the incapacity of the central Sahelian states to provide their disadvantaged local communities with basic needs, security, and protection. The group expanded in the Sahel. However, its northern front suffered from this expansion because the organisational structure hindered Droudkel's leadership. The increasing independence of Belmokhtar is a case in point. Belmokhtar eventually defected in 2012 and established its group, El Murabitun. The latter exploited the Arab Spring and the chaos that followed to deepen its presence in neighbouring Libya and conduct the spectacular attack against the gas facility of Ain Amenas on January 16, 2013. Not only did Droudkel face competition from other groups in the south, but he was also unable to retain a hold on his men.

AQIM lost ground in Algeria due to a combination of continuous counter-terrorism operations coupled with conciliatory measures, harsh punishments, and its organisational woes. Despite the spectacular attack of Ain Amenas in 2013, the group has been unable to carry out any large-scale attack in Algeria since then. Isolated and almost decimated in Algeria, the group tried to find shelter in the east (i.e., Khenchla, Tebessa, Jijel, Skikda), closer to the Tunisian borders where its leadership believed they could get some support and unite their battalions to restructure the already dying *Okba Ibn Nafaa* brigade. It seems that this tactic had a limited impact because the Algerian security forces have been cooperating with their Tunisian counterparts in reinforcing border security (Ghanem 2017c). As a result, several successful operations were recorded with the most recent being in February 2018 that led to the death of eight AQIM leaders in Khenchla ("Algérie: le plan d'infiltration d'al-Qaïda capoté" 2018).

Given the group's limited manpower and organisational incapacity to conduct effective and devastating attacks, the prospects of AQIM's rise in Algeria are limited. Furthermore, the group has been unable to achieve any of its goals. The government in Algiers continues to function, and those deemed *tawaghit* [impious] are still running the country. The prospects of a dawla Islamiyah [Islamic state] in Algeria remain grotesque. While AQIM's end in Algeria may not be close, it might not have been so farfetched an idea either given the circumstances at hand. The organisation might engage in a signalling exercise to remind the government of its presence. Nevertheless, AQIM's peril is manageable. The group remains a nuisance, but not an existential threat for Algeria.

A new Jihadist threat: the Islamic State

With the Arab uprisings and the advent of the Islamic State (IS) in Syria and Iraq, IS tried to gain a foothold in Algeria, and a local branch was created, called *Jund El Khilafa*. Given Algeria's long history with jihadism and its position as a US/EU ally in the fight against terror, it was a natural target. For IS leadership, Algeria was going to be an easy access and recruitment base. However, reality proved to be different, since the only noticeable action that the group was able to carry out was the kidnapping and the killing of French national Hervé Gourdel in September 2014 (Johnston & Willsher 2014). Except for this action, the group has been incapable of conducting any substantial attack or recruiting locally. *Jund El Khilafa* does not have the manpower or resources to present a serious threat to Algeria. To cover its evident shortcomings, the group has published an extensive array of propaganda videos, in which they continue to exaggerate their capacities.

It is beyond argument that one of the main reasons for IS's obstacles in Algeria is the mass trauma of the black decade with a young generation that seems harder to attract than the previous. With the experience of a bloody civil war in mind, the population appears less likely to support groups, such as IS as it did with the GIA in the 1990s. Additionally, the makeup of the Algerian population with its 99% of Sunni, makes it hard for IS to play on the sensitive area of the Sunni-Shia divide (Ghanem 2016).

More importantly, a key reason for IS failing to make progress in Algeria is that Algeria's army has acquired substantial counterterrorism capabilities during their decade-long fight against jihadist groups. In 2018, the Algerian military ranked 23 out of 136 troops in the world (Global Fire Power 2018). The National Popular Army (ANP) is the second most powerful army in Africa after Egypt with total military personnel reaching 792,350, an active force of 520,000, and a reserve of 272,350 (Global Fire Power 2018). That same year, the defence budget represented 6.24% of the Gross Domestic Product (Hodgson 2017). According to SIPRI, in 2017 Algeria was the most significant arms importer in the African continent with 46% of all imports to the region (2017). Also, the PNA has been investing in quality training for the use of sophisticated equipment and counter-terrorism methods. Finally, in order to ensure professionalisation, the PNA has reduced the conscription time from 18 to 12 to 9 months (Belhocine 2014), moved to the employment of contracted personnel, and legally allowed for women's status in the army to be made equal to that of their male counterparts (Ghanem 2015). It is this modern, well-trained, and experienced army that has kept tight control over the jihadist groups, threatened IS, and prevented it from spreading in the country. The successive executions of *Jund El Khilafa* leaders and fighters prove the point above. The Algerian military killed the emir of the group, Abdelmalek Gouri, and two of his lieutenants 2 months after they executed Gourdel. Less than 5 months later, Gouri's successor, Bachir Kherza, was killed with 25 of his men in a military operation in Bouira.

In addition to the fact that Algerian security forces have been able to keep the number of Algerians travelling to Iraq and Syria relatively low, the government also works to confine local jihadists—that are believed to number around 1,000—in specific regions, such as areas bordering Libya and Mali. Given the recent setbacks IS has experienced in Libya, Algerian authorities have intensified their operations along their eastern borders. Some 25,000 troops were sent to the borders with Tunisia (African Manager 2015) and 5,000 along the borders with Libya (Tahir 2014). The army installed new checkpoints as well as trenches to fight the trafficking, especially in the south (Ain Amenas and Djanet) and in the east and southeast (Tébessa and El Oued), an essential source for jihadist movements in the region. The PNA has also brought closer the command of some operational units as is the case with the Border Guard Group that has been moved from Constantine to Ain El Aouinet in Tebessa. The PNA has been able to thwart dozens of attacks and arrest hundreds of jihadists in the region.

What's next?

AQIM's setbacks and IS's incapacity to gain a foothold in Algeria are hardly insignificant, given the fundamental and lethal threat that the jihadists posed to the Algerian state not too long ago. Since the end of the civil war, the state has been using a plethora of tools—ranging from the hard approach to soft ones with conciliatory and rehabilitation measures, development projects, as well as tighter control of the religious sphere (Ghanem 2018)—to neutralise the jihadist threat. The latter remains manageable and is no longer as fatal as it used to be. Today, the threat is highly localised and sporadic, and Algerians feel safer than ever. In the 2017 Gallup's rankings of the world's safest countries, Algeria ranked seventh. The country scored 90 out of 100 and is among the top ten countries where the population feels safe (Gallup Institute 2017). Nonetheless, zero risk does not exist.

On the external level, AQIM and the plethora of jihadist groups such as *Jama'at Nusrat El Islam wa El Muslimin* [Group for the Victory of Islam and Muslims] operating in the Sahel-Sahara belt remain a threat for Algeria that sees this region rightfully as its "soft underbelly" [le ventre mou] (Zoubir 2018: 72). The security situation in neighbouring countries (Tunisia, Libya, Mali) is worrisome as violence shows no signs of receding. Threats coming from these states are various and manifold and range from jihadism to weapon trafficking and human smuggling. The Algerian government has made considerable efforts to mitigate these external threats through border deployment and diplomacy. However, this strategy has its limits. The attack of Ain Amenas in 2013 showed that instability next door has a direct impact internally.

On the internal level, Algerian authorities will have to deal with the mounting and widespread social discontent that has reached even its southern regions. The many clashes that have shaken the oasis city of Ghardaia are a case in point.[8] In this region, the main issue—beyond the animosity between Mozabits and Arabs—remains the incapacity of the government to translate financial wealth into inclusive growth. With the ongoing decrease in oil prices and the erosion of oil revenues, the authorities are losing their power to appease citizens by providing social benefits such as housing, jobs, as well as generous subsidies. As a result, radicalisation, especially among disenchanted youth, might be on the rise. As long as issues such as social exclusion, political marginalisation, economic disparities, lack of prospects, oppression, and indiscriminate violence persist, there will always be people who would yield to the temptation of jihadism. Indeed, jihadism "offers easy, 'grab-and-go' solutions to complex problems; it is an equal employer that provides a friendly community, a glorious cause, and a thrilling adventure" (Ghanem 2017b).

Notes

1 The author of these lines chose to use the word jihadism and not jihad. The amalgam of the two terms is frequent. Jihad was initially an offensive (624–750) to Islamise new territories, then defensive (1086–1492) to protect against the enemy, and finally anticolonial (1798–1880) to defend Muslim lands and regain independence. As for jihadism, it was born in the late 1970s, following three major events that took place in 1979: the Iranian revolution, the Soviet invasion of Afghanistan, and the signing of the Israeli-Palestinian peace treaty. These three events upset the strategic and geostrategic balance of power. It is in Egypt first that the Islamist movement went underground and took up weapons with the group El takfir wa el Hijra (excommunication and exile). The group launched, under the pen of Mohamed Abdel Salam Faraj, his famous book "Al faridha al-ghâ'iba" [the absent obligation] which made the war against the Arab regimes—deemed as "renegades" and "apostates"—an obligation for every Muslim. As written in Faraj's pamphlet "War must be waged only under a Muslim flag and under Muslim command ... wanting to start a warfare against

Imperialism is a useless and worthless action; pure waste of time. We must focus on our Muslim problem, namely, the establishment of God's law in our own country, and subordinate everything to the cause of God. There is no doubt that the first field of jihad is the overthrow of these godless regimes and their replacement by an all-Islamic order. This alone will serve as a starting point for the war outside." Although the writings of Ibn Taymiyya largely inspired the young Faraj, he is at odds with the Islamic tradition since he dissolves jihad in the notion of *qital* [combat]; and makes jihad an individual obligation for all without exception and gives primacy to internal jihad over external jihad. The pamphlet "Al faridha al-ghâ'iba" had immediate repercussions: in Egypt, President Sadat was assassinated on October 6, 1981; in Syria, an Islamist revolt exploded in February 1982 and was heavily repressed, and in Algeria, Bouyali's group was born and took action on November 7 and 8, 1982. At that time, there were two configurations of jihadism: one was internal, centred on the state order perceived as renegade and therefore condemned to excommunication (Algeria, Egypt, Syria); the other was centred on a foreign occupation against which every believer had the duty to fight (Lebanese Hezbollah against Israel and the Mujahideen in Afghanistan against the USSR) Boukra (2009).

2 The MIA was created by Mustapha Bouyali, a former mujahid, and an FLN militant. In the late 1970s, Bouyali set up a mosque committee in the region of El Achour [southwest of Algiers]. It is at this moment that he was approached by Doudi Mohamed, a young imam preaching at the Al Achour mosque. Bouyali was attracted by the Islamist discourse of Doudi and his criticism of the regime. After the departure of Doudi for France in 1980, Bouyali became the imam of the mosque of El Achour. First, Bouyali with a few of his followers established a group whose main objective was to organise punitive missions against liquor stores and "places of debauchery." Bouyali was the object of a first arrest in 1981 and the second one in 1982, following which he would go underground. With the help of his acolytes, Bouyali established the MIA that took action on November 7 and 8, 1982, with the theft of nearly 160 kilos of explosives in the Cap Djanet quarry. On November 17, 1982, Bouyali and his group attacked a gendarmerie roadblock in Moncada [Ben-Aknoun in Algiers]. After the death of Bouyali's brother by the security forces, the MIA would multiply its attacks till the death of Bouyali in 1987. His brothers in arms would die or be put in jail such as is the case of Mansouri Meliani and Abderrahmane Hattab who, after having benefited from the general amnesty of July 31, 1990, would become, a few years later, the founders of armed groups such as the Armed Islamic Group (GIA).

3 The FIS secured 853 out of 1,551 communes in major cities'; 31 wilaya [district] out of the 48 that the country encompasses were under the FIS.

4 The violence and repression of the security apparatuses—from the elections' cancellation in January 1992 onwards—contributed greatly to the violent radicalisation of thousands of people. The state opened *El Muhtashadat* (prisons) in the south of the country where some 40,000 FIS supporters, sympathisers, and many others who were not even involved with the Islamist movement were detained. Extrajudicial killings, arrests, and disappearances were also practiced.

5 Hassan Hattab the emir of the Zone 2, decided in 1996 to leave the GIA, which he described as "deviationist and takfiri," and to establish his own armed organisation. Hattab was followed in his endeavour by GIA's veterans such as Mokhtar Belmokhtar, Amari Saïfi, Abderrezak El Para, Djamel Okacha, and Nabil Saharawi. Back then, Hattab and Okacha were the emirs of the centre, Sahraoui, and Para of the east, and Belmokhtar of south.

6 It is worth noting that the same year, the country returned to the constitutional process and allowed for the reintegration of all political parties (except the FIS) into political life. This permitted to Islamists to have a peaceful opening to express their views and hence an alternative to violence. It is beyond argument that this allowed

non-violent Islamists to reclaim the FIS electorate as well as all those disgusted by the extreme violence of jihadist groups during the bloody decade.

7 It should be noted that, in practice, due to the lack of evidence, the high number of involved fighters and the difficulty of conducting investigations, the law pardoned all jihadists who voluntarily surrendered and who simply denied having participated in the prohibited acts. The state did not conduct any investigation to authenticate such claims.

8 The latest clashes that broke out in the region in 2015 led to the death of 23 people and dozens were injured. The authorities had to deploy 8,000 troops to calm down the situation and re-establish peace.

References

African Manager. 2015, "L'Algérie déploie 25 000 militaires sur ses frontières avec la Tunisie," *African Manager*, June 28, accessed June 15, 2018, https://africanmanager. com/tunis-lalgerie-deploie-25-000-militaires-sur-ses-frontieres-avec-la-tunisie/.

Akef, A. 2007, "Al-Qaida revendique deux attentats-suicides en Algérie," *Le Monde Afrique*, October 9, accessed June 28, 2018, https://www.lemonde.fr/afrique/article/2007/09/10/ al-qaida-revendique-deux-attentats-suicides-en-algerie_953307_3212.html.

"Algérie: Dix ans après la Charte, où en est la réconciliation." 2015, *FranceInter*, podcast, accessed May 28, 2018, https://www.franceinter.fr/emissions/un-jour-dans-le-monde/ un-jour-dans-le-monde-05-octobre-2015.

"Algérie: le plan d'infiltration d'al-Qaïda capoté." 2018, *Presstv*, January 30, accessed June 15, 2018, http://www.presstv.com/DetailFr/2018/01/30/550714/Algrie-alQada-Tunisie-terrorisme.

Anonymous. 2012, "Terrorisme: un chef d'Al Qaïda abattu à Yakourène (Tizi Ouzou)," *Le Matin d'Algérie*, October 13, accessed May 28, 2018, http://www.lematindz.net/ news/9878-terrorisme-un-chef-dal-qaida-abattu-a-yakourene-tizi-ouzou.html.

APS. 2016, "Les familles de deux terroristes se rendent à Jijel," *Liberté*, July 1, accessed June 13, 2018, https://www.liberte-algerie.com/actualite/les-familles-de-deux-terroristes-se-rendent-a-jijel-250469.

Belhocine, S. 2014, "Le service national réduit à 9 mois!," *Jazairess*, January 11, accessed June 15, 2018, https://www.djazairess.com/fr/lemidi/1401110104.

Bennadji, C. 2009, "Révision de la Constitution: vers une présidence à vie pour Abdelaziz Bouteflika?," *L'Année du Maghreb*, vol. 3, pp. 225–261, accessed June 12, 2018, https:// journals.openedition.org/anneemaghreb/367.

Boukra, L. 2009, *Le djihadisme. L'islam à l'épreuve de l'Histoire* [Jihadism. Islam Facing History], Apic, Algeirs, p. 208.

Daoud, K. 2015, "The Algerian exception," *The New York Times*, May 30, accessed May 26, 2018, https://www.nytimes.com/2015/05/30/opinion/the-algerian-exception.html.

Gallup Institute. 2017, "Crime: Algeria among world's safest countries, according to Gallup Institute," *APS*, August 5, accessed June 16, 2018, http://www.aps.dz/en/algeria/19696-crime-algeria-among-world-s-safest-countries-according-to-gallup-institute.

Ghanem, D. 2014, "IS in Algeria: Serious threat or publicity stunt?," *Carnegie Middle East Center*, October 4, accessed June 14, 2018, http://carnegie-mec.org/2014/10/04/ is-in-algeria-serious-threat-or-publicity-stunt-pub-56858.

Ghanem, D. 2015, "Women in the Men's house: The road to equality in the Algerian military," *Carnegie Middle East Center*, November 4, accessed June 20, 2018, http:// carnegie-mec.org/2015/11/04/women-in-men-s-house-road-to-equality-in-algerian-military-pub-61463.

Ghanem, D. 2016, "Obstacles to ISIS expansion," *The Cipher Brief*, September 1, accessed June 16, 2018, https://www.thecipherbrief.com/article/africa/obstacles-to-isis-expansion#.V8fEyP9AEgM.

Ghanem, D. 2017a, "A life after Jihadism," *Carnegie Middle East Center*, November 17, accessed June 23, 2018, https://carnegie-mec.org/diwan/74708.

Ghanem, D. 2017b, "Conditions in the Sahel Benefit Al Qaeda," *The Cipher Brief*, January 29, accessed June 20, 2018, https://www.thecipherbrief.com/article/africa/conditions-in-the-sahel-benefit-al-qaeda.

Ghanem, D. 2017c, "The Algerian army: Cooperation, not intervention," *Carnegie Middle East Center*, December 7, accessed June 16, 2018, http://carnegie-mec.org/2017/12/07/algerian-army-cooperation-not-intervention-pub-74970.

Ghanem, D. 2018, "State-owned Islam in Algeria faces stiff competition," *Carnegie Middle East Center*, March 13, accessed June 16, 2018, http://carnegie-mec.org/2018/03/13/state-owned-islam-in-algeria-faces-stiff-competition-pub-75770.

Global Fire Power. 2018, *Algeria Military Strength*, accessed June 15, 2018, https://www.globalfirepower.com/country-military-strength-detail.asp?country_id=algeria.

Hodgson, C. 2017, "The 12 countries that spend the highest proportion of GDP on their military," *Business Insider*, July 7, accessed June 16, 2018, http://www.businessinsider.com/12-countries-highest-military-budgets-percentage-of-gdp-2017-7/#12-jordan-431-of-gdp-1.

Institute for Economics and Peace. 2017, *Global Terrorism Index, Measuring and Understanding the Impact of Terrorism*, accessed June 15, 2018, http://visionofhumanity.org/app/uploads/2017/11/Global-Terrorism-Index-2017.pdf.

Ismain. 2018, "600 terroristes abattus en 3 ans: La défaite d'Aqmi en Algérie," *Réflexion*, April 21, accessed May 28, 2018, https://www.reflexiondz.net/600-TERRORISTES-ABATTUS-EN-3-ANS-La-defaite-d-Aqmi-en-Algerie_a51232.html.

Johnston, W. & Willsher, K. 2014, "French tourist beheaded in Algeria by jihadis linked to Islamic State," *The Guardian*, 24 September, accessed June 15, 2018, https://www.theguardian.com/world/2014/sep/24/french-tourist-beheaded-algeria-isis-linked-jihadis.

"Anonymous: Quelle lutte antiterroriste?" 2014, *Liberté*, September 24, accessed June 11, 2018, https://www.liberte-algerie.com/actualite/kabylie-quelle-lutte-antiterroriste-210782.

Martinez. 1998, *La guerre civile en Algérie*, Karthala edition, Paris, p. 275.

RFI. 2015, "Algérie: Dix ans après la Charte, où en est la réconciliation," *RFI Afrique*, September 29, accessed June 13, 2018, http://www.rfi.fr/afrique/20150929-dix-ans-charte-reconciliation-algerie-disparus-paix-victimes.

SIPRI. 2017, *Increase in Arms Transfers Driven by Demand in the Middle East and Asia*, February 20, accessed June 15, 2018, https://www.sipri.org/media/press-release/2017/increase-arms-transfers-driven-demand-middle-east-and-asia-says-sipri.

Tahir, M. 2014, "Algérie déploie 5000 soldats et gendarmes de plus à la frontière avec la Libye," *HuffPost Maghreb*, May 29, accessed June 15, 2018, https://www.huffpostmaghreb.com/2014/05/29/armee-algerienne-frontiere-libye_n_5408559.html.

Zoubir, Y. H. 2018, "Algeria and the Sahelian quandary: The limits of containment security policy," in D. Ghanem-Yazbeck (ed.), *EuroMeSCO Joint Policy*, p. 72.

8

GENDER EQUALITY FOR ALGERIAN WOMEN

Fatma Oussedik

Algeria's history has been marked by a succession of violent events that accompanied and led to deep breakdowns. The recent memory of every Algerian man and woman is fed by references to the colonial situation that existed during the nineteenth century and the first half of the twentieth century, as well as the conflict between Algerians themselves that has marked recent history. Since Algeria belongs to the world, its population is steeped in multifaceted globalisation. These are the elements with which Algerian men and women have had to live, build, and create relationships with each other and with the outside world. On each occasion, it has meant redefining the identities of everyone involved. "He" and "she" have faced challenging questions such as the construction of the national state in a post-colonial context, and access to citizenship, values that are today considered almost universal across the globe.

Post-colonial origins of conditions experienced by Algerian women

During the first part of the twentieth century, as large numbers of men were engaged on the battlefield,[1] had been killed in action, disabled through conflict, or even emigrated to France, increasing numbers of women found themselves at the head of the family. They left their homes to take their place in the outside world while caring for children and elders. Yet during these conflicts, women did more than just stand in the background. These events influenced and transformed women's mobility; some moved away from the family home, others moved across the country, and even abroad to support the cause that they had embraced and became part of a new community, that of the fighters. As a result, for these women, family was no longer die only option. Their commitment was personal and put them in touch with others in prisons and in the mountains, regardless of whether they were men, women, or foreigners. Algerian women participated in the war of independence with the revolutionary ideals of the first part of the century (socialism, republicanism, people's rights, equality). Some even took part in the Spanish Civil War alongside the Republicans, trade unionists, communists, and liberals. For these women, a Civil Code was to be imposed after independence; some would from the earliest years of independence rally against the draft bill of the Algerian Family Code.

These struggles, which were part of a broader fight for secularisation, were also due to the fact that through the Plan of Constantine in 1958, the French colonial powers attempted to create a category of mediators for indigenous populations. This attempt was based primarily on the belated and certainly limited educational expansion programme whose content distanced itself from religious texts and was devoted mainly to global scientific revolutions. One of the consequences of this approach was that Algerians gained access, in very small numbers, to the school of law. This access was to expand rapidly after independence and many young women would benefit from it. In addition, emigrant workers discovered trade union activities, and Algerians who were mobilised during the Second World War discovered Europe, women and men approached the second part of the twentieth century with new ways of thinking and living and with new points of reference. When faced with French culture in a colonial context and anti-colonial struggle, Algerians had to redefine their own relationships; this is how collective history is gradually replaced by individual stories.

This building of diverse individuals, removed from a purely family or religious context, which occurred in particular during the struggle for independence, remains a source of conflict within society. It was to be a central issue during the violent clashes that took place between Algerians during what is known as the "Black Decade," i.e., the 1990s, the impact of which is still felt today. Broadly speaking, the violence observed in Muslim societies is an indicator of profound change.

Women were, and continue to be, parties to this conflict: some were murdered while others carried arms, whether they were members of the security forces or of terrorist networks (Gasmi 1998). This study is not designed merely to list these horrors, but is rather intended to demonstrate the violence to which women were exposed during the 1990s. The figures concerning this violence vary from one source to another, so we will focus mainly on the descriptions of situations:

- Women witnessed the massacres of their family members (children, parents, spouses) before being abducted and placed in the service of their torturers;
- Around 1,000–3,000 women were reported to have been raped, and these rapes allegedly occurred in the presence of family members, particularly male family members. It is important to note the desire to humiliate men by taking their wives.

In addition, they witnessed the rape of some of their children (6);

• A large number were subjected to Zaouedj el moutâa, a temporary marriage, which allows the kidnapper to contract a religious marriage with the victim to "legitimise" his rape.

Society did not allow these women to describe what their bodies had suffered, as was possible in Bosnia, for example, during the same time period. Algerian society refused to label them clearly as victims of a category of aggression that is also closely tied to the performance of masculinity in Algeria. This was the reaction of a society that sought to maintain a social order in which stable communities function according to an authoritarian patriarchal logic. Yet these family communities have failed to protect these women. The best example is that of the High Islamic Council in 1998, in a statement that said: "women raped by terrorists are pure, abortion in these circumstances is forbidden. Any resulting children will be cared for by the authorities." Restoring the innocence of those who were first and foremost victims, simultaneously allows the crime against their body and their sexuality to be erased.

Firstly, it is necessary to recognise the uselessness of a community-based approach. As the writer Amine Zaoui said: "the harem has been toppled!" (Zaoui 2009, 13). Many works are still haunted by the revival of an "inside" community, or a closed space. Such approaches find expression in analyses stating that there is an Arab-Muslim world which, using a false and simplistic framework because it is Muslim, is characterised by established communities that function according to debates, readings, and interpretations of the holy book, namely, the Koran. In this social order, women are only goods in the sense that they are exchanged on a matrimonial market between communities and according to the strict rules of this market. This can be defined as an ideal designed to impose a world order, even by force.

However, by denying the breach in social order that public rape represents, and since men have not been able to assume their role as protectors of the community, this means that, more widely, the use of violence is a moment of decay. Shedding blood is no longer clearly part of an exchange between stable social groups. Abderrahmane Moussaoui writes: "Killing becomes secondary when set against the humiliation that is suffered by the body before this ultimate act, and by the corpse after it. The more 'significant' the victim from the perspective of sending a message, the more suitable they are as a means of expression" (Moussaoui 2009: 166).

However, from our point of view, the subject matters confront one another according to a social logic that evolves over the length of the conflict. The figure of the Other is diluted and with each iteration only partial readings are possible. Yet women are not the Other since they are also terrorists and patriots.[2] Nevertheless, in both categories, they remain women. They only have the right to express themselves with regard to politics because of the blood debts that are owed to them, according to kinship rules. We can record the crime, its perpetrators, and its victims, but when the victims are female, they are frequently designated only through family ties. In naming this tie, we name the man who makes it possible for the female subject to exist.[3] Thus, there is a social logic that refers to the relationship between the genders. In the context of Algeria, we assume that communities have not protected women's bodies as required by community law. But in the worst examples, the family foundation does exist. It is the common thread and leads us to the following question: What is this social order that requires so many family ties, while offering nothing in return to women and where victims and murderers avoid speaking about times of war?

In Algeria, the conditions that would allow communitarianism to thrive no longer exist. These commonplace ideas do not reflect the political, social, and economic issues and conditions facing this part of the world. The way that Algerian society is organised is not based on stable communities: land dispossessions, regroupment centres for indigenous populations, migrations, the agrarian revolution, and the speed... transformed Algerian life for both men and women. They did not allow for the emergence of a large number of autonomous subjects because family solidarity remains a necessity in light of high unemployment rates, difficult access to housing, and the weight of social capital, in order to face what is a difficult daily life for many. From the point of view of Algerian women, the history of the concept of community as it applies to them seems to us to signify a dual relationship of subordination which, in Algeria, bears little relation to reality:

- The dominance of a theory of otherness in which the community explains and defines the forbidden; it is, therefore, the theoretical figure of a social group that rejects itself;
- The externality of subjects that resist a context. According to these analyses, Arab feminists belong to the Westernised class;
- This difficulty in formulating a demand for equality, in such a context, explains the emergence of trends such as Islamist feminism. Confronted with their contextual requirements, women have also used readings of the Holy Book to substantiate their claim. The objective here is to distance the self from the former coloniser as a means of reassuring, even legitimising, their belonging to the original group: Algerians, mostly Sunni Muslims, Maliki.

This requirement of belonging to a group is based on the imperative of protecting the group and women even at the cost of alienation. This is precisely what feeds the analysis of local writers who consider feminist views as a Trojan horse of the oppressive West, of an imperialism whose role is to shatter established communities which would resist it. It also forms the substance of the arguments by politicians who advocate for a status quo or paltry amendments to the legal situation of Algerian women. There is, both internally and externally, an obvious difficulty in talking about historically defined societies and their difficulties on a global scale.

If the notion of imperialism remains the conceptual vector around which most contemporary Arab thinking is articulated, there is also a clear desire to render the notion of community more politically efficient even while it is has little actual substance. The concepts of community and imperialism feed into each other and delineate a narrow political space within which Algerian women may move. Being an Algerian woman today means aspiring, for some, to become an autonomous subject in her own country; but who are these women?

The history of the women's movement is the social and political history of Algeria

In a society that long held the fight for liberation against French colonialism as its only point of reference, women remember and remind us that they participated in this struggle with weapons in hand. They are therefore also heirs to this foundational narrative. There is a quest to legitimise the Algerian women's movement with heroic figures who have inscribed their destinies in the struggles for independence against any occupation. Thus, figures like La Kahena, who fought against troops who were Islamising the Maghreb, remains a heroine in the collective consciousness for refusing this occupation. This idea, indeed this principle, feeds the fertile ideological soils of this country more broadly: we must resist the invader. Lala Fadhma N'Soumer was one of those heroines, and more recently, the *Mujahidat* women who fought against French colonisation. These struggles granted Algerian women the legitimacy to fight for equality. They have proved this by forming associations, often with protests against the Family Code and others and were the pioneers in creating an organisational framework for these struggles. Even before the outbreak of the fight for liberation, in 1947 Mamia Chentouf, surrounded by companions such as Nafissa Hamoud, created the first organisation of Algerian women. Like many nameless others, these women see their memory regularly honoured and fill the pages of Algerian women's resistance movement against the colonial yoke. Later, supporting them in the 1990s, Katia Bengana, Nacera Kheddar, and Nabila Djahnine were murdered by the Islamists for refusing to wear the veil, fighting for secularism, and for continuing to work.

The common thread between these two moments of Algerian struggle is the desire to have access to more rights, but also to defend the country. The word country (Patrie in French), comes from the Latin *pater*, meaning father. One might be surprised to find a women's movement staking their claim on such a word. This makes sense only in regard to the dual subordination presented in the introduction, as the women's movement is still largely made of a generation born during or after the war, but who had access to schooling and employment because of the nationalistic ideology of benevolent fathers, fed by an ideology of liberation that Frantz Fanon had largely contributed to defining. These women staked their claim on their country, but also on the struggle to liberate that country, carried by those who from the outset tied their struggles for the motherland to a demand for rights as Algerian women.

However, on Saturday, March 17, 2012, at the 11th congress of the National Organization of the Mujahideen, former *mudjahidat* (National Liberation women's fighters) did not hide their anger following the announcement of the formation of the office of the National Organization of Mujahideen from which they were excluded. Meriem Belmihoub-Zerdani declared, "It is unfortunate that fifty years after independence, women are still underrepresented." Similarly, Toumya Laribi, usually known by her *nom de guerre* Baya, and a member of the famous Ali Khodja commando of the armed struggle, did not hide her bitterness at this congress. "I am one of those who gave their youth for the independence of Algeria. But I must admit that I am somewhat disappointed today when I see the result. They stole our fight." They were all just 18 or 20 years old when they left the family home to join the front. With this distance introduced, as a subject matter, with the protection of the family, is a founding moment in the struggles of Algerian women. "Militants were tortured to death," said Baya. "None of them denounced anyone. The best day of my life was the proclamation of independence." "Mazal' (in Arabic: not yet), we are not yet independent," she says again, in a reference to the post-colonial context.

From the point of view of the permissive social conditions of access to equality, the weakness of female employment weighs heavily on the status of Algerian women

The logic of the so-called Algerian women's movement is part of a traditional, middle class logic: the struggle surrounding family and school issues. The schooling of Algerian women was the decisive factor that allowed their aspirations to be redefined. It accompanied, if not created, significant and unexpected changes in Algeria. The great quiet victory of women during this period is their mass schooling. As Zahia Ouadah-Bedidi (2016) put it: "the differential has been reversed" since "once the threshold for compulsory schooling is passed, surprise, girls continue to study in greater numbers and with more success. Today, more than 60% of graduates and more than 60% of students are girls, all disciplines combined."

After the commitment of large numbers in the country's fight for liberation, the second big break for the Algerian women after independence was the process of questioning women in the private space, and men in the public space. What remains of this binary world can still be seen in the architecture, the urban layout of the medinas, but also in political sciences and history. With or without veils, there are many Algerian women who move in mixed public spaces: the market, the workplace, Mosques, and universities where they are more numerous than men. They drive and travel alone. The elements which formed the basis of a sexual morality comprising methods of enculturation and learning about femininity as a bent 'ayla (girl of a good family) worked for generations, but are today in crisis.

However, since independence, the economy has limited access for women in employment. They were mainly recruited for public services such as medicine, teaching, and administration. Oil revenues have allowed the Algerian government to be the primary employment provider. At the same time, state policy was opposed to family planning and housing construction. In 2016, 82.4% men and 17.6% women were employed, according to official data from the National Office of Statistics. Algeria's unemployment rate is 20% for women compared with 8% for men, a rise that has clearly affected women and graduates of higher education. This unemployment rate for women last September was the highest in the last 10 years.

These are people in the unemployment halo, i.e., people of working age (16–59 years old), who declare that they are available to work yet did not look for a job during the month preceding the Office National des Statistiques (ONS) survey, because they think there is nothing available or they have not been able to find a job in the past, or that they have already taken steps to find a job. This category reached 797,000 people in September 2016, of which, 54.6% are women. In 2017, women filed only 18.5% of investment project requests received by l'Agence Nationale de l'Emploi (ANEM). However, currently, many of them are employed in the informal sector (workshops, food production) for which no figures are available, and there is a small number of private entrepreneurs among them. Taking the unemployment rate into account, they have chosen to be entrepreneurs or to work in the informal sector.

Therefore, while the absolute number of working women has increased during the last 20 years in Algeria,[4] this rate remains low. According to the ONS data, business requests remain low. As in many countries, economically active women face what is known as the glass ceiling, meaning that although women are numerous in many sectors such as health care, education, and justice, they do not occupy public office positions reserved for men. Similarly, their career progression faces many obstacles.

We wish nonetheless to highlight the gap between trained women and employed women. Only an economy based on productivity and work can absorb a female workforce, which is already qualified since 60% of students enrolled at the university are girls. This is also true for young male graduates.

Even becoming a wife presents a challenge in contemporary Algeria. In 2018, there were 42.4 million Algerians according to the Director General of Population and Hospital Reforms of the Ministry of Health. According to the National Office of Statistics in 2017, women of childbearing age are estimated at 10.8 million and the volume of marriages is decreasing. In 2008, the average age when first married rose to 33 years for men and 29.3 years of age for women. Meanwhile, the age gap between husbands and wives, which has been around 6 for about 2 decades, stayed the same. The age when first married has increased for all classes, but this increase is more obvious among women with a higher level of education, who are 3 years older than the age when first married of the other two classes. While there is little difference between women who have been to school and those who have not, they behave the same way. A fourth indicator is the decline of endogamy.

The main conclusions of these indicators are that the average age at marriage is increasing. Polygamy is still, present but affects only 3% of unions. The number of polygamists (essentially bigamists) would be less than 100,000.

A Muslim society characterised by a contrasting legal framework

In Algeria, a limited access of natives to rights was made possible via two parallel sources of law that emerged during French colonial rule. In France, the Republic proclaimed its attachment to secularism, whereas the patriarchal family in Algeria is based on religious law, with regard to the rights of persons and women and substance law, which specifically deals with the economic life of the country. This combination was at work during the colonial period. Its purpose was to block their access to full citizenship.

The Napoleonic Code, which played a major role in the modernisation of many legal systems in the Mediterranean, took into account the religious standards and customs of the natives when it was introduced into the former French colonies. Thus, there were up to five codes at the same time in Algeria: Kabyle, Mozabite, Maliki, Jewish, and Civil Code. The balance of power between these texts caused conflict and negotiations on each occasion between groups. Although property laws were quickly unified for the benefit of settlers or owners, in general, the natives were respected in their private lives, which simultaneously legitimised their native status. Family laws were constructed according to the rules of the Muslim and Jewish faith, to doctrine for the Ibadite Muslims, and to customs for the populations of Kabylia. The European or settler community was subject to the Civil Code. This respect for manners and customs, for the faith of each, allowed for natives to be differentiated.

We can thus make the following observations:

- An anecdotal observation for our article: French secularism did not exist in the colonies;
- More significantly, Islam has been established as the foundation of an Algerian identity in opposition to obtaining French citizenship;
- At the same time, this legal system is the point of departure for Algerians to question their religious status. In our opinion, it marks the beginning of a process of societal secularisation, when a distinction is made between groups.

For 22 years, until 1984, no special provision existed relating to family law, and there was no Family Code. At the beginning of independence, the legislative apparatus of the colonial state and references to Islamic law were renewed. However, the question of the creation of legal texts soon arose, as did the question of the new state's use of legislative power.

It was the legal framework which endorsed the colonial oppression that the independent Algerian state chose to renew in 1984 with the Personal Status Code, which Algerians called the Family Code, and this consists of secular economic rights and legislation based on Islam, relating to the rights of individuals. How could one imagine that an independent state could be satisfied with an arrangement that had its origins in the Code of Indigenous Status?

Firstly, while the law took a long time to be introduced, it was preceded by other similar legislation:

- The 1963 Constitution tied the idea of being Algerian to being Muslim. Some of the same women who would go on to oppose the promulgation of the Family Code would, from 1963, leave the Assembly to protest against this measure that augured the coming of the Family Code;
- From 1963, women rejected a first draft of the Personal Status Code. They were activists of the war of liberation, gathered within the first Union Nationale des Femmes Algériennes (UNFA), and therefore had a strong relationship with the new powers in Algiers, who managed to postpone this text. They were mostly city-dwellers, some were doctors, other midwives, lawyers, and teachers. Few have gained notoriety, their participation in the war of liberation made them emblems and solidified their legitimacy (as for men) to represent all Algerian women;
- In 1975, a clause in ordinance n° 58–75 of September 26, bearing the civil code, filled the perceived legal vacuum, serving only to reconfirm previous provisions:

  > The law governs all matters to which the letter or the spirit of one of these provisions relates. In the absence of a legal provision, the judge decides according to the principles of Islamic law and, failing that, according to custom.

During these first years of independence, political life operated according to the same logic regarding the legal situation of women: state institutions manage the economic space by welcoming heads of families for the distribution of oil revenues through free medicine, the democratisation of education, and industrialising industry. These are all job and service offers proposed as investments in a future that justifies the repression of individual desires or self-concern. Adult men gave up their rights to citizenship in return for managing gender relations, relationships between men, women, and children based on a hierarchy created from religious ideology. All this took place during both the colonial period and after independence.

But society changes and, in 2005, amendments were introduced to the text of the Family Code, passed in 1984. According to lawyer Nadia Aït Zaï (2009: 22): "Without bringing too much upheaval in the traditional architecture of the family,[5] the legislator has entrusted the management of the family to the spouses. Thus, the new text removes the notion of head of the family and the duty of obedience of the wife. These changes will allow the rebuilding of equal relationships between men and women provided that mechanisms are put in place by public authorities to achieve this task. The legal instruments exist" (Aït Zaï 2009: 22).

In addition, a revision of electoral law was carried out. Articles 80 and 102 were amended. The law stipulates that electoral lists must include at least 30% women. On May 17, 2007, only the Workers' Party observed this rule.

In March 2017, the Algerian Parliament passed a bill to amend and supplement the penal code, which penalises violence against women. Women's associations welcomed the fact that the legislator had drawn up measures against violence in the private arena, but deplored the inclusion of a forgiveness clause that allows for prosecution to be dropped. The state does not file a separate civil suit, and given the material conditions of a large number of women as well as family pressures, many victims will give up pursuing their aggressor at the risk of their life.

There are, however, a number of women who concur with this idea of the family on which the legal texts in force are based. In many cases, their position is based on social and economic reasons. Many of them are either unemployed or belong to categories whose income come from the informal sector of the economy. In this sector, performance often depends on the quality of the networks to which the subjects belong. Similarly, it is easy to see that the majority of women claiming the repeal of the Personal Status Code have been educated and are civil servants or are professionals.

In its quest for equality, the women's movement aims to fight against current family legislation

It took two decades for the enactment of this law to become possible.

During the occupation, it was not possible to weaken one's belonging group, the main content of women's struggles, immediately after the country's independence, was to deny to religious dogma the ability to legislate while ignoring their living conditions. In 1984, they lost out with regard to the promulgation of the text of the law, but won with others (and perhaps even Islamists) in creating a debate on the foundations of the Algerian state. The question of the struggle for a secular right or an Ijtihad (jurisprudence) that will be fairer for women's lives has since been raised.

For the purposes of this article, the intrusion of substantive law in a society that previously recognised only beings from Ahl el Kitab, the people of the Book, is a major event.

Women therefore formulated their aspirations because it seemed that the legal approach remained the only way to speak without physical violence about a wider reality that the text masks, while pretending to support it. Legal text makes it possible to clarify more general social stakes posed by the status of women in Algerian society. What is at stake in law is always the text *and* its application; it highlights the balance of domination in relationships. Similarly, rapid urbanisation has weakened social control and provided greater visibility for women's quest for space.

This is why women's legal struggles are an important moment for our society. Revealing the nature of social alliances, they help to understand established social arbitration, with a view to a status quo, through gender relations organised at the legislative level. The method of resolving these issues or leaving them unresolved represents a balance of power and makes it possible to define the social actors of a society in violent transformation. We are confronted with a dominated world in which the family is the reference point for social order to be maintained.

And what of the social bonds that women might build in such a context? They are presented as actresses, almost iconic, a defence of democratic values in the West, but cease to be so in Algeria because the real protection and true freedom of women may be found in the defence of a state resistant to the imperialism of the West even if it oppresses them. These speeches are two sides of the same coin, which assign women to a life oriented towards the constant affirmation of identity both in the kitchen and in the street. How can Algerian women tackle this question? What areas of reference should they use for their struggle: a renewed reading of the text or an immediate claim of secularisation?

The existence of such polarising options supposes that it is not possible for them to speak from the position of who they are and what they have experienced:

- They would have been of no particular interest because women, in peacetime as in times of war, could not be understood in isolation from group strategies or the group's expectations of them;
- We believe that fighting the legal ground, for subjects, namely, women, delivers them as citizens. Their movement is part of a wider quest for another form of integration within globalisation and we propose to consider the violence observed in this part of the world as a demand for change at the national and international level, by a large number of social actors, both women and men.

Conclusion

The signs of religious affiliation that we observe today in Algiers do not include gender separation, any more so than a construction of masculinity and femininity around the idea of a separation between inside/outside. On the contrary, these are often signs that allow female subject matters to widen their space. The strictest of religious costumes is visible in the street, and it even allows some women to be out late in the evening after prayers at the Mosque during the nights of Ramadan. Time, dress code, street harassment: these are all elements that govern women's access to public space, but the issue is no longer access to space. There are profound changes revealed by the figures on schooling, employment, women's political participation, and observing people in the street, which point to new issues for society as a whole, removed from a simple reading of secular/ religious issues, Islamists/Democrats.

At present, many girls remain in school, but the economic crisis and the increase in security concerns have led to a decrease in the number of school children in rural areas in recent years. The establishment of a market economy has given a new impetus to new sectors: traders, speculators, and all those who, seeing the market bloom, are excluded from the fruits of consumerism. However, the increased access of women to the university and the nuclearisation of families that accompanies their rapid urbanisation have contributed to creating a debate surrounding the struggles on the foundations of Algerian family law. On each occasion, it is the women and men of the urban *petite bourgeoisie* (educated and with a life beyond the home) who became involved in the struggle against the promulgation of this law. They (men and women) introduced the idea of *self-interest*, or the emergence of individual rights, to political and community life. The 1989 Constitution authorised multipartism, and women set up commissions, then collectives, and finally associations. Other associations came into existence, including religious associations demanding the full application of religious law.

These demands for change were expressed at the same time as the economic crisis took place due to Algeria's dependence on oil revenue, but the oil price slump is not enough to justify it. The fallout from the oil windfall has led Algerians (men and women) who are increasingly educated, informed, and urbanised, claiming the right to political representation.

The approach and reflections undertaken demonstrate how women's institutions and the space in which they move are, together, an issue in the current context. It seems to us that the nature of the clashes relating to the place of women in Algeria allows us to define the status of women in the quest for social change. Because no communitarian logic has succeeded to protect women's institutions during the conflicts of the 1990s, we feel that this allows us to speak of a centrality of the status of female bodies in the quest for change. Attacks are perpetrated on women's bodies, they are not just "about" them. The legal struggles of women represent an important moment in the social struggles underway in Algeria. The nature of political alliances makes it possible to understand the social trade-offs brought about through gender relations at the legislative level.

The method of resolving these issues or leaving them unresolved represents a balance of power and makes it possible to define the social actors of a society in violent transformation. What then, are the fundamental demands of Algerian women for this society since independence? Feminist struggles in Algeria have constantly sought to question the social order around the question of law.

It is these demands, carried by an entire population, that fed the protest movements that have shaken the country throughout February and March 2019.

On March 8, 2019, during the historic marches throughout the country (at the time of writing still underway), an elderly lady took up the microphone of the El Bilad television channel to sing the hymn of *Etoile Nord Africaine* to the young Algerians around her. The appreciation that they showed her in exchange, as they kissed her on the head, demonstrated the extent to which they considered this legacy to be precious.

Indeed, while the past did not weigh heavy on these demonstrations of dignity, while the martyrs of Algeria's history were kept at a certain distance by the demonstrators participating in the building of a unified and democratic Algeria, a rule of law that would do justice to women, the route they traced was scattered with symbols:

• The women chanted "chkoun h'na: bent Hassiba," "Who are we? The daughters of Hassiba." And they were proud to welcome the sister of Larbi Ben Mhidi.

Similarly, they were proud to have Djamila Bouhired amongst them as the ultimate icon, a woman symbolising integrity, who has gone through life without ever reneging on the image of that young girl laughing at the judges of the colonial state. She proves that it is possible to live for all these years and to stay honest, it is possible not to sell one's history for a bowl of soup. Paying tribute to her was another way of demonstrating respect to all of the Moudjahida, Annie Steiner, Beya Hocine, Zhor Zerrari, and so many others who did not want trucks, shops, and cars in exchange for blood spilled for their homeland.

The movement also remembered that it was North African. That's what this elderly lady came to remind these youngsters. The women's movement in Algeria has always remembered this. It uses this to project itself into the future. Throughout these long decades, the women of the Maghreb have remained in harmony, conscious of the unity of their aspirations. Because whether we call it the Maghreb or North Africa, this space is our horizon. It makes sense of all of our demands.

That is how the movement of March 8, 2019, is part of the longer term, how it wanted the river to rediscover its course. By carving through stone, we have rid ourselves of the scorched earth of history, to rediscover the essence of our soul, and pour it into this river.

These demands also represent a fight for legal recognition of the places acquired by women as well as the transformations suffered by everyone.

Notes

1 During the First and Second World Wars, then the fight for liberation in 1954.
2 During the Bentalha massacre, on the night of September 22–23, 1997, a witness report, according to the daily *Al-Khabbar* and *La Tribune* of October 7, 1997: "Women and children accompanied the aggressors."
3 Still in Bentalha: "The murderers leave first, covered by their acolytes and guided by two women, one dressed in black and the other in red. The latter is called Ould Hamrane Zohra (aka Nacéra) and is the sister of a former GIA emir called 'Djeha,' killed by the security services in 1995."
4 According to the results of a survey conducted by Emploitic, an employment website, published March 6, 2018.
5 Indeed, in this text: The mandatory presence of a wali (marital guardian) for a woman to be allowed to marry has not been removed. The future wife can choose the guardian. Polygamy, certainly more restrictive, is maintained there. Parental authority for the mother is granted to the divorced wife, but not to the married woman. The right to divorce for women, extended to three additional grounds, is always conditional. Divorce can always be pronounced by the sole will of the husband. A woman, for

her part, must invoke seven valid reasons, among which domestic violence does not appear. Inequality with regard to inheritance remains. The most notable advance in the eyes of activists is the abolition of the duty of obedience and the obligation for the husband, who keeps the marital home, to provide the divorced woman who obtains custody of her children, decent housing.

References

Aït Zaï, Nadia (2009). "Overview on the status of women." In *La Longue March of Algerian Women towards Modernity*, Cahiers de Liberté/SAEC, No. 2, Algiers, March–April, p. 22.

Gasmi, Baya (1998). *Me, Nadia, Wife of a GIA Emir*, Paris, Seuil.

Moussaoui, Abderrahmane (1999). "The politics of insult in Algeria: A deadly decade in Algeria." In *The Muslim Worlds and the Mediterranean Magazine*, Nos. 103–104: 165–179.

Ouadah-Bedidi, Zahia (2016). "Inequalities of male-female education in Algeria: When differences are reversed." *Labor Documents*. Paris, Ined.

Zaoui, Amine (2009). "Arab writers transgress taboos in the kingdoms of taboos." In *La Longue Algerian March towards Modernity*. Cahiers de Liberté/SAEC No. 2.

9

POWER, MEDIA, AND HUMAN RIGHTS IN ALGERIA

Chérif Dris

Algeria was the first Arab country which in 1990 granted journalists the right to create their own newspapers. After more than 25 years of authoritarian regime, a new constitution was released, thus paving the way for political and media pluralism. It was the first political liberalisation ever taken in the Arab world.

The new media order that emerged in the aftermath of the 1988 uprising resulted in the mushrooming of hundreds of newspapers while the obstacles that limited the free movement of journalists were also lifted. In this respect, the new Information Code issued in 1990 (Journal Officiel de la République Algérienne Démocratique et Populaire, herafter JORADP, 014 1990) reinforced press freedom; the Ministry of Information, the watchdog which had hitherto limited the flow of information, was dissolved. In the 1990s, during the apex of the period of terrorism, freedom of movement for journalists was somewhat reduced, due to restrictions on access to information on security issues. However, most of the media persisted and resisted. With the adoption of the Law on Information in January 2012, freedom of the press took on another dimension, including the decriminalisation of the written press. Furthermore, the new law opened the broadcasting media to private actors, hitherto monopolised by the government. Thanks to this new legal framework, dozens of privately owned television channels have been created, offering a variety of media content and enhancing freedom of speech for citizens. With this new media configuration, promoting human rights is becoming a crucial issue. The private media, TV channels, and online media are at the forefront of this fight for the promotion of human rights in Algeria. The media aspire to position themselves as a counter-power by denouncing abuses of the fundamental rights of citizens. However, aspiring to fulfil this role has not been welcomed by political authorities less inclined to see the media gaining more power and influencing public opinion in a difficult economic and political context.

This chapter reviews the conflicting relationship between the media and the ruling elite and how the issue of promoting human rights shapes this relationship. It analyses the official laws issued by the government and the way the media interacts with political power. The theoretical basis of this chapter will be the systemic approach in order to explain the interaction between the different actors, the complexity of the Algerian system, and how the human rights issue could play the role of an independent variable determining the relation between both sides of the equation, i.e., media and the political power.

Media and political power during the single-party era

During the single party era, Algerian media were not granted much room tomanoeuvre because the one-party system exerted a tight control over political, social, and cultural life. The ideology of the ruling party, the National Liberation Front, rested on the assumption that plurality could harm national unity.

In line with the political philosophy of the regime, cultural institutions were assigned a role to promote political and social unity, as the ruling elite were very aware that the post-colonial state should be one in which media, especially those reflecting cultural and social diversity, are banned.

The media under the single-party system

Within this ideological framework, Algerian media were assigned the role of protecting national identity. Contending voices were not granted the right to express their opinion in this media as long as the government was the sole shareholder. Besides this, the state-party imposed tight control over the recruitment of journalists and the appointment of editors in chief (Mostefaoui 2013: 27).

This tendency to exercise tight control over the press is one of the legacies of the liberation war, which heavily weighed on the perception of information nationalist leaders had. The cult of secrecy cast its shadow over the way journalists should exercise their profession. Access to information was restricted and the governmental press agency (Algeria Press Service) monopolised the collection and broadcasting of information throughout the Algerian territory (Mostefaoui 2013: 25). In this general context, any journalist who dares to publish an article without referring to the ideological line of the state party could be fired.

The culture of suspicion dominated the media landscape during this era, and in some cases, freedom of information was considered as intelligence with the enemy (Gafaiti 1999: 51). The criticism was allowed as long as the journalist respected the limits imposed by the political authorities and the party. In fact, journalists had to move between two zones: the authorised zone and the restricted zone (Ferchiche 2012: 151–152). Hence, as historian Mohammed Harbi notes, "free discussion, referring to the Tripoli Charter and free criticism in the framework of party organizations are a fundamental right of any activist. Freedom is therefore reserved only for activists. It is limited to internal debates of the party" (Brahimi 2012: 32).

These few lines express without any ambiguity the general mindset within a party whose only concern is to control the Algerian society.

However, from 1962 to 1982, there were no laws to regulate the media in Algeria. The promulgation in 1982 of the Information Code was a turning point as it gave journalists a legal framework to organise their profession.

In October 1988, the situation changed. The restrictions imposed on journalists were gradually lifted. The uprising of the population as a result of the deterioration of living conditions, a direct consequence of the shrinking of oil revenues, led to the first political reforms. This new political context led to a new media era. After 26 years of censorship, journalists regained their freedom of speech and began to organise themselves.

October 1988: human rights issues for journalists

In many respects, the events of October 5, 1988, could be considered a founding moment for human rights issues in Algeria. For the first time, Algerian journalists dared to write on sensitive issues such as the repression of young people who went out to protest in the streets. Standing at the frontline of this media action to promote human rights, Algerian journalists strived to get the right to have more access to sources of information and be able to inform citizens without any restriction. For the first time, torture was reported by some public newspapers as mentioned in the black book on the repression that followed the outbreak of October 5.

Although no trial was organised of those responsible for those abuses, the October 1988 riots brought with them a new political order. The main outline of this new order was unveiled in the first pluralistic constitution endorsed by the general referendum of February 23, 1989.

Multiparty system and media pluralism

The new constitution passed on February 23, 1989, instituted the multiparty system and announced the end of socialism and the advent of a market economy. Whether this openness was imposed by the international community or granted by the regime as a consequence of the struggle within the decision-making structures, the multiparty system opened a new chapter for the Algerian media. The latter had to be in concordance with a new context in which the National Liberation Front (FLN) was no longer the only actor on the political scene (Gafaiti 1999:54).

Against this background, new relations between ruling elites and the media were established. President Chadli Bendje did, with the support of the group of reformers inside the FLN, strive to limit the influence of the conservative wing in the party. The opening up of the media sector to journalists who wanted to create their own newspaper was the first step in this strategy (Dris 2017: 265). They went further by lifting any restriction to the freedom of speech in public media, especially in television and radio.

The information law of 1990: freedom of expression with some limits

One of the main reasons behind the reform group initiative in encouraging journalists to create their own newspapers was the necessity of containing the influence of the old guards in the party. They intended to use this media opening as a leverage for their economic and political reforms, while the conservative wing strived to maintain the status quo as their interests were at stake (Dris 2014: 68). Within this struggle to impose a liberal order, reformers took the bold decision to dissolve the Ministry of Information and put an end to the monopoly over the means of production of information (printing, broadcasting, and access to information). More importantly, a new Law of Information was issued which granted journalists more freedom.

As revolutionary as this seems—the first ever to take place in the Arab world—the reform government imposed some limits. The first was maintaining the monopoly of the state over the broadcasting sector. Secondly, the new Law of Information contained some provisions hindering journalists from publishing all information they accessed. As mentioned in Article 36, access to information doesn't imply the right of journalists to publish any article that could harm national security and national defence, economic and diplomatic interests of Algeria, or the constitutional rights of citizens (JORADP 014 1990).

What sounds problematic with these provisions is the interpretation that may be given to them. How do we define the notion of secrecy when it deals with "national defence," "national security," and "economic strategic interest"? The ambiguities surrounding these notions compel journalists to restrain from dealing with topics in which security actors, Algerian army, or national police are involved. In many cases, newspaper managers impose red lines on their journalists to avoid judicial and security quagmires. It should also be noticed that these lines limit access to information. They offer governmental institutions such as the Ministry of Defence, of Foreign Affairs, and other security services, the justification for their refusal to provide journalists with information. As explained in the following section, with the deterioration of the security situation in the 1990s, the task of Algerian journalists, especially investigating and reporting news, was more difficult while some were sentenced to jail after publishing reports criticising the way the anti-terrorist strategy was handled.

Freedom of the press during the state of emergency

In order to guarantee success for the strategy of terrorism eradication, the political and military leadership enacted a state of emergency on February 19, 1992. Under the provisions of that law, all elected institutions were suspended and constitutional life frozen.

In that security context, freedom of speech was pushed into the background. Decision makers were not really keen to put the security and the stability of Algeria in balances. As long as terrorism threatened Algerian security, any action or discourse that could jeopardise that security was not tolerated. Alongside civil society actors, such as political parties, the Algerian media suffered from the state of emergency as access to information was subject to strict control. But the assassination of journalists was to a large extent the greatest danger to which journalists were exposed. From 1993 to 1996, 55 journalists were killed by terrorist groups (Brahimi 2012: 132–133), while others chose to go into exile in European and Gulf countries.

Besides being a target of terrorist groups, Algerian journalists found great difficulties doing their job as the law relating to the state of emergency gave military authorities the right to tighten access to information. The security strategy adopted at that time gave priority to the management of news related to security issues, which implied control of the media. Two main decisions made that control more feasible. The first was the dissolution of the High Council of Information and the re-establishment of the Ministry of Information. The second was the imposition of a circular on security information.

The draft on security information passed in 1994 seriously affected the ability of journalists to report on issues related to terrorism and human rights abuses. However, the pressure on journalists started before the release of that restriction. Hence, on January 22, 1992, *El Khabar* newspaper published a communiqué signed by the leader of the Islamic Salvation Front, Abdelkader Hachani, assassinated in August 1999. In that communiqué, the leader of the Islamist party called for the neutrality of the Algerian army while many political parties from the opposition and civil society who defended secularism and backed the interruption of the electoral process were not opposed to army interference in political life. The *El Khabar* case was not the only one. In March of the same year, the weekly *Hebdo Libéré* published an investigation that revealed how some judges cheated by presenting a false document to prove their participation in the liberation war. The issues unleashed massive pressure from the government and editor-in-chief Abdelkader Mahmoudi was jailed for 2 weeks (Labter 1995: 40–41).

During the period of Sid Ahmed Ghozali's government, journalist harassment and newspaper seizures became common practice. We mention some of these seizures here: at the end of February 1992, newspaper *El Massar El Magharibi*; at the end of March, issue 29 of newspaper *El Djazair El Yaoum*; and on April 26, 1992, newspaper *El Fourkan* (a weekly French language of Islamist party Islamic Salvation Front). The campaign against journalists continued with the arrest of Saad Bouakba and Ali Fodhil of *Echourouk El Arabi* newspaper for offenses against "security forces" and "incitement, through media, to commit acts that could harm security and national unity" (Djaballah 2005: 142–143). Those few cases were clear indications of the tense relations existing between the ruling elite and the press. The relations between the two sides became even more strained when Belaid Abdeslam was appointed head of the government, Belaid Abdeslam became famous when he referred to some businessmen using the word "mafia" and to some journalists as "mercenaries of the pen." During his era, harassment against journalists continued as was the case of Abdelhamid Benzine, editor-in-chief of *Alger Républicain*, a left-wing newspaper. For having criticised the government of Belaid Abdeslam, Abdelhamid Benzine, member of the Algerian communist party (Partid'Avant Garde Socialiste) and founder of the daily *Alger Républicain*, was sent to jail (Labter 1995: 63).

In drawing an assessment of what happened during the 1990s, it is no exaggeration to conclude that the shrinking of spaces of freedom for the security situation greatly deteriorated. However, with the return to peace in the early 2000s, following the implementation of the Law on Civil Concord and the referendum on National Reconciliation Charter in September 2005, violations of rights of journalists decreased. Assassination is no longer a threat to the life of journalists, but intimidation and different kinds of pressures have not stopped.

With the election of Abdelaziz Bouteflika after the resignation of Liamine Zeroual, the perception of media by the ruling elite did not improve. As he developed a negative perception of Algerian media, Abdelaziz Bouteflika went further by using the words "Tayabat El Hamam" (women who gossip all day long in the hot baths), to portray Algerian journalists and their work. Relations were very tense with the private press, which became more heated during the 2004 presidential campaign as some newspapers had publicly sided with candidate Ali Benflis, a prime minister fired in 2003 by President Bouteflika after he had expressed his desire to run for the presidency. For those who showed defiance towards Abdelaziz Bouteflika, the cost was very high. Pressure from government-owned printing companies intensified as many newspapers were indebted to those companies. Another way to punish those newspapers was to reduce advertising and use that as an economic tool instead of using judicial and political ones.

During the years following the re-election of Abdelaziz Bouteflika for a second term, the number of journalists arrested increased though it remained lower than the number of those arrested during the 1990s, or being killed. However, the Algerian president's perception of the media has never been as bad as that of President Abdelaziz Bouteflika. He never admitted to be subject of the critics in the media. As explained earlier, not only did he refuse to give any interview to Algerian media, he adamantly opposed any reforms of the broadcasting sector leading to the creation of private TV channels. Perhaps the Arab Spring changed that perception and accordingly the nature of relation between media and Algerian political power.

The Arab Spring and the changing Algerian media landscape

At the end of 2010 and the beginning of 2011, many Arab countries experienced social revolts ending in political turmoil and regime change. Fearing the spread of those political revolts to Algeria, Abdelaziz Bouteflika announced some social and political measures in his speech on April 15. Bouteflika's promises led to lifting the ban on the creation of political parties and civil society organisation spawned. The scope of those measures had an impact on the media and accordingly on human rights issues.

We will shed light on this evolution by examining the new Information Code in the Organic Law issued on January 12, 2012, and the provisions it contains, especially those related to the freedom of the press and the limits imposed on journalists. We will also analyse the broadcasting landscape as new private television channels saw the light despite the absence of legal provisions regulating the broadcasting sector.

Organic Law on Information of 2012: the illusion of a democratic media order

The new Information Law was worked out in order to break through the 1990 Information Code (JORADP, Number 014 1990), considered by Algerian journalists as a second Penal Code. It was considered as such because it entails a provision allowing judicial authorities to sentence a journalist to jail for their writings.

The new legal framework decriminalises press offences. Hence, the penalty of imprisonment was abrogated, but payment of fines was maintained. The new law reflects the new strategy of Algerian authorities to provide facilities for journalists to access information (Dris 2012: 317). As stated in Article 83 of the 2012 draft law, "*all authorities, administrations and institutions should provide a journalist with all the information and data they request in order to guarantee citizens the right to information within the framework of this organic law and the current legislation*" (JORADP, Number 12-05 2012). To what extent did the new legal framework reinforce the ability of journalists to have free access to information?

It is widely admitted that pressures on journalists have become less acute. Since the promulgation of this law, the investigation of issues related to human right abuses has increased. Besides, the last Constitution, passed in February 2016, confirmed this principle, stating in its Article 50 that "*freedom of the written, audio-visual and information networks is guaranteed. It is not restricted by any form of prior censorship,*" and that, "*the crime of the press cannot be punished by a jail sentence*" (Algerian Constitution of 1996. JORADP n° 76; amended in 2002 JORADP n° 25, April, 14, 2008; JORADP n° 63, November 16; and 2016 JORADP n° 14, March 7). However, this access to information is limited and journalists cannot have a free hand if they want to investigate sensitive issues such as human rights abuses or corruption scandals. The Algerian legislator deliberately set up safeguards in order to limit the free movement of journalists. Article 84 of the above-mentioned draft law is explicit: "*The right of access to sources of information is recognized to professional journalists except when: the information concerns national defence secret, as defined by the applicable legislation; information undermines the security of the State and / or national sovereignty; the information concerns the secrecy of the investigation and the judicial investigation; the information concerns strategic economic secrets; the information is likely to undermine foreign policy and the country's economic interests*" (JORADP 2012).

As shown by these off-limit areas the ruling elites never allowed journalists to report on topics that could be considered embarrassing to them. Certainly, some journalists were bold enough to investigate issues such as the corruption scandal of Sonatrach, the East-West highway, and Al Khalifa Bank. Other social and political issues such as Ghardaïa riots in 2014 and the arrest of some human right activists, the unemployed movement in Ouargla, and the protest movement against the exploitation of shale gas in In Salah caught the attention of private Algerian media. However, in many cases, journalists found that they were obliged to conduct self-censorship or were prevented by institutional actors in furthering their investigations. If the Organic Law of 2012 and the new Constitution of 2016 provide the guarantees needed by journalists to do their work, they are by no means sufficient to protect this profession from any kind of pressure. The strategy of political authorities to limit the free movement of journalists consists of using the Penal Code. Hence, from 2014 to 2016, "the long arm of justice was used against some journalists for insulting state constituent bodies" (the case of Hassan Bouras (released in May 2018) in 2015 and 2016), "inciting riots and non-armed gathering" (the case of Rachid Aouinein 2015), "publication of photos and videos prejudicial to national interests (case of Youssef Ould Dadain 2014), or "infringement upon the President of the Republic" (ongoing case of Tahar Djehiche) (Reporters without Borders 2017:12).

However, the case of Mohamed Tamalt, an Algerian-British freelance journalist based in London, is without doubt the best example of the clear exploitation of the judicial apparatus to stifle the freedom of expression. On June 27, 2016, Mohamed Tamalt was arrested at the Algiers Airport by the police and imprisoned. On July 4, the Sidi M'Hamed Court sentenced him to 2 years of imprisonment and a fine of 200,000 dinars (1,674 US dollars) based on Articles 144 repeated and 146 of the Criminal Code for «attacking government institutions» and «attack on the person of the President» (Reporters without Borders 2017). During his stay in Koléa prison, 35 km away from the capital city Algiers, Mohamed Tamalt began a hunger strike to protest again his imprisonment despite being diabetic. On December 11, he died after his health deteriorated. Another journalist arrested and taken into custody was Said Chitour. On June 6, 2017, freelance journalist and translator Said Chitour was arrested at the Algiers Airport while returning from Spain and placed in custody. According to Article 65 of the Criminal Code, Chitour may face life imprisonment, "for gathering, with the intention of delivering to a foreign power, information, objects or documents the exploitation of which could harm national defence or the national economy." Said Chitour was released on November 11, 2018.

These cases illustrate how fragile the freedom of writing is for journalists. But as social media, private TV channels, and online media are spawning, it is not useless to question whether the freedom of expression and especially the freedom of writing are consolidated.

Human rights on the screen: the role of private TV channels

Until the mid-1980s, broadcasting space was dominated by public TV channels that offer a content reflecting the dominant ideology. French satellite channels (TF1, A2, M, Canal +, etc.) made their appearance into Algerian households, offering new content, but most importantly a perspective on French and Western culture in general. During the 1990s, when terrorism was at its peak, French and Arab channels competed with Algerian national TV as a provider of national and international news. The restriction on information related to the security situation prevented Algerian viewers from becoming informed about the ongoing situation, not only for news, but even for entertainment as there was no competition in Algeria during that period (Sarnelli & Kobibi 2017: 6).

The situation remained unchanged until 2011, when private TV channels made their appearance, offering Algerian viewers new content both in terms of news and entertainment. The Algerian authorities had never intended to open the broadcasting sector to private capital for fear that opening that sector would allow more freedom to civil society and hence lessen government control. It could hardly be otherwise given Abdelaziz Bouteflika's perception of the role of the press. This breach into the broadcasting landscape would not have happened without the Arab revolts that swept across some neighbouring countries.

The de-monopolisation of the broadcasting sector was strengthened with the release of a new law in March 2014, followed by terms of reference (in August 2016) that contain some guidelines explaining the rights and red lines that should not be crossed by private channels. Those two documents state that owners of TV or radio channels should not have links to any political party and the content broadcast should deal with specific topics and not encompass all issues (Art. 5) (JORADP 2014). Other restrictions were enacted, but the most restrictive one remains the person of the president. Indeed, as stated in terms of specifications (terms of reference) of August 2016, TV and radio channels should avoid offense, defamatory writing, or outrageous discourse against the president (Art. 7) (JORADP 2016).

In order to regulate this sector and organise the process of creating private channels, the new legal framework institutes a regulatory authority, an independent body with the mission to oversee the process of granting licenses and supervising content.

The audiovisual landscape is currently dominated by more than 40 private channels, but only five have a one-year authorisation to operate: Ennahar TV, Echourouk TV, Dzair TV, Dzair News, El Djazairia, Samira TV (cooking), and El Hogar.

While public TV channels refuse to tackle issues concerning human rights abuses, the new private TV stations broke the taboo by broadcasting some sensitive topics like social injustice, inequality between men and women, and the role of the army and security services in political life. Whether reported in the news or debated during television programmes by experts, political and social actors, the discourse adopted concerning human right issues is characterised by boldness. An illustration of the change in media discourse regarding this issue is *HounaEl Djazair* (*This Is Algeria*) in Echourouk TV, presented by Kada Ben Amar. The journalist violated some prohibitions by inviting politicians from opposition parties and human right activists to discuss topics such as the people who disappeared during the 1990s, abortion of the electoral process in 1991, women's rights, corruption, social unrest in the south of Algeria (In Salah and the opposition to the development of shale gas, Ghardaïa, and Ouargla with the movement of the jobless), to mention just few. Another example of change in media discourses regarding the human right issue is El Khabar Broadcasting Channel, before its shutting down. This private TV station dared to report on some human right abuses like violence against women, inequality to access jobs (the jobless movement of Salahedine Belabes in Ouargla). Its famous satirical Talk Show *Nass Stah* (*Roof People*) depicted the problems Algerians are facing such as corruption, dirty money in politics, and the relation between the president and the intelligence services. Other TV channels like Ennahar and Dzair TV, though less critical than Echourouk and El Khabar Broadcasting Channel, opened their studios to opponents of the regime, particularly during electoral campaigns in 2014 and 2017.

As considerable as it may seem, the appropriation of the human right issue by private TV should be considered relatively minor. The political authority still maintains the upper hand on the content private channels should broadcast. As previously explained, some legal provisions contained in the 2014 law and the 2016 specifications are designed to allow the government via the media regulatory authority to tighten control over these private TV stations. Thus, in 2014 and 2015, two TV channels were closed: El Atlas and El Watan. The first one was the target of the presidential circle who accused the media of backing Ali Benflis; but the pretext given to justify that shut down was the absence of authorisation allowing that TV channel to legally operate. The second paid for an interview with former Armée Islamique du Salut (Islamic Salvation Army) leader, Madani Mezrag, who dared challenge President Abdelaziz Bouteflika. On June 24, 2016, a court ordered the pretrial detention of Mahdi Benaïssa, the manager of El Khabar Broadcasting Channel TV, and Ryadh Hartouf, head of production for another talk show, citing irregularities in the station's permits. The order came 5 days after security forces shut down operations at the studio producing talk shows, *Ness Stah* (*Roof People*) and *Ki Hna Ki Ness* (*Just Like Everybody Else*) and confiscated production materials (Human Rights Watch 2016).

As the above examples show, television could not resist the tight control exerted by political power over the media. The situation may not be very different for online and social media.

Online and social media: the new arena for social and political protest

The start of online editions in Algeria was with the electronic version of the printed version. In 1998, some newspapers like *El Watan, El Khabar, le Soir d'Algérie*, and *Liberté* initiated the digitalisation process of their printed version by opening web pages so that readers could get the news they needed. With the development of technological platforms, the number of online versions of printed newspapers increased, and that evolution paved the way for the emergence of pure players that offer a variety of contents. The most prominent are: *Tout Sur l'Algérie, Maghreb-Emergent, Algérie Part, Algérie Patriotique*, and *Sabq Press*.

The situation of these pure players is somewhat particular. Following the example of private TV channels, the pure players operated without any legal basis. However, the Organic Law of 2012 filled this gap by stating in Article 66 that, "*the exercise of the online information activity is free.*" In Article 68, the content of this press is defined as follows, "*the online print media activity consists of the production of an original content, of general interest, regularly renewed, composed of information related to news and subject of journalistic processing*" (Organic Law N°12-05 of 2012). Since the release of this law, online media multiplied, and their number currently exceeds 40. But what about the content they broadcast and especially the question related to freedom of expression and respect of human rights?

The particularity of online press is their ability to bypass the censorship the Algerian authorities could exert. Thus, the Algerian pure players find less difficulties to report on some sensitive issues like the situation of human rights in Algeria, violence inflicted to women (sexual harassment in particular) (Hamadi 2017), sub-Saharan migrants (Nour 2018), corruption (Sadia 2018a), and jailing of some bloggers (Sadia 2018b). These examples shed light on the gap between print press and online media in terms of their capacity to tackle such sensitive issues. Undoubtedly, online media gained much more freedom in reporting on human right issues. As they evolve in virtual space, political authorities find many difficulties in censoring them. There was an attempt in 2017 with *Tout Sur l'Algérie* when the Ministry of Telecommunication tried to block the broadcast of this newspaper, on technical grounds. It took 2 months for the newspaper to reappear after making a great concession by firing their cartoonist Ghilas Aïnouch, as the cartoons he used to publish in this online journal were considered insulting.

However, if freedom of expression is more considerable in those outlets, there is more room to manoeuvre in social media. As the Internet access in Algeria increased at a comfortable pace, the number of Algerians who created a Facebook or twitter account rose at an unprecedented rate. In 2016, 17 million Algerians had Facebook accounts, which represent 43% of the total population (65% men and 35% women) (*Algérie1* 2017). Due to efforts made in order to develop the Internet infrastructure, the use of social media by Algerian people, youth in particular, accelerated at a considerable rate during the last years. Accordingly, the blue space became a tribune for free expression and then an arena for social and political protests. Whether for the opposition movement against the re-election of Abdelaziz Bouteflika for a fourth term in 2014, for some social protests as was the case in Ghardaia, In Salah, Ouargla (2013, 2014, 2015), or even the strike of hospital interns (2018), social networks are the only platform used by protesters to bypass censorship of public media. Videos taken live by cellphone and broadcast on YouTube, Facebook, or Tweeter give visibility to those movements. As explained by Ratiba Hadjmousa (2013: 52), the visible makes the event intelligible. It shows subjectivities: that of the "videographer," but also those of the subjects filmed and interviewed and whose videographer often shares the experience. This visibility is also palpable through the pages created by some youth Algerian like Amir Dz, Anas Tina, and Chemsou Dzjoker.

Conclusion

This chapter addressed the complex relationship between three key variables: media, political power, and human rights. In this vein, Algeria is no exception, and the relation between the ruling elite and the media has never been linear, especially with regard to human rights. In spite of the granted reforms that allowed the emergence of private channels and the intensive use of social networks, political power continues to look at the media with mistrust. The few cases of pressure and harassment suffered by some journalists are a clear illustration of this mindset.

However, unlike other Arab regimes, the political regime in Algeria avoids repression that could have counterproductive effects, especially in term of international visibility. Instead, it prefers more subtle methods such as blackmail by withdrawing advertising or encouraging the creation of media relays (private TV channels or newspapers or even online news sites) to limit the impact some recalcitrant media could have on society.

References

Ahcene-Djaballah, B. 2005. *Chronique d'une démocratie Mal Traitée. Octobre 1988-décembre 1992*. Alger: Editions Dar El GHrab.
Algérie1. 2017. 17 millions d'utilisateurs Facebook en Algérie, January 14. https://www.algerie1.com/tech/17-millions-dutilisateurs-facebook-en-algerie.
Brahimi, B. 2012. *Le pouvoir, la presse et les droits de l'Homme en Algérie*. Alger: Editions Enag.
Décret exécutif n° 16-222 du 8 Dhou El Ka,da 1437 correspondant au 11 aout 2016 portant cahier des charges générales fixant les règles imposables à tout service de diffusion télévisuelle ou de diffusion sonore. *JORADP* N° 48. https://www.joradp.dz/FTP/JO-FRANCAIS/2016/F2016048.pdf.
Dris, C. 2012. "La nouvelle loi organique sur l'information de 2012 en Algérie: vers un ordre médiatique néo-autoritaire?" *l'Année du Maghreb VIII*. Paris: CNRS Editions, pp. 303–320.
Dris, C. 2014. "Les médias en Algérie: un espace en mutation". In *Maghreb-Machrek*. pp. 65–75.
Dris, C. 2017. "La presse algérienne: une dérégulation sous contraintes. Les nouvelles formes de contrôle ou la 'main invisible' de l'Etat". *Questions de Communication*, n° 32, pp. 261–286.
Ferchiche, N. 2012. *La Liberté de la presse écrite dans l'ordre juridique algérien*. Paris: LGDJ.

Gafaiti, H. 1999. "Power, censorship and the press: The case of post-colonial Algeria". *Research in African Literatures* 30(3), pp. 51–62.

Hadj-Moussa, R. 2013. "Les émeutes au Maghreb: Le Web et la révolte sans qualité". *L'Homme et la société* 2013/1—n° 187–188, pp. 39–62.

Hamadi, R. 2017. "Droits de l'Homme: Les autorités doivent lever toutes les restrictions". *TSA*, December 9. https://www.tsa-algerie.com/droits-de-lhomme-les-autorites-doivent-lever-toutes-les-restrictions/ (Accessed July 15, 2018).

Human Rights Watch. 2016. Algeria: TV Executives Jailed Satirical Talk Show Shut Down. https://www.hrw.org/news/2016/07/01/algeria-tv-executives-jailed/.

JORADP. 1990. *Loi n° 90-07 du 3 avril 1990 relative à l'information.*

JORADP. 1996. Loi n° 76, December 8. *Journal Officiel de la République Algérienne Démocratique et Populaire (JORADP).* https://www.joradp.dz/hfr/.

JORADP. 2002. Loi n° 25, April 14. https://www.joradp.dz/hfr/.

JORADP. 2008. Loi n° 63, November 16. https://www.joradp.dz/FTP/jo-francais/2008/F2008063.pdf.

JORADP. 2012. Loi n° 2, January 15. Loi organique n° 12-05 du 18 Safar 1433 correspondant au 12 janvier 2012 relative à l'information. https://www.joradp.dz/FTP/JO-FRANCAIS/2012/F2012002.pdf.

JORADP. 2014. Loi n° 16, March 23. https://www.joradp.dz/FTP/JO-FRANCAIS/2014/F2014016.pdf.

JORADP. 2016. Loi n° 14, March 7. Loi n° 16-01 du 26 Joumada El Oula 1437 correspondant au 6 mars 2016 portant révision constitutionnelle. https://www.joradp.dz/FTP/JO-FRANCAIS/2016/F2016014.pdf.

Labter, L. 1995. *Journalistes algériens: entre le bâillon et les balles.* Paris: Editions Harmattan.

Mostefaoui, B. 2013. *Médias et Liberté d'Expression en Algérie. Repères d'évolution et éléments d'analyse critique.* Algiers: Ed. Dar El Othmania.

Nour, E. 2018. "Annaba/L'auteur de l'agression contre un enfant subsaharien arrêté". *Algérie Focus.* https://www.algerie-focus.com/2018/07/annaba-lauteur-de-lagression-contre-un-enfant-subsaharien-arrete/.

Reporters without Borders. 2017. "Algeria: The Invisible Hand of Power over the Media". https://rsf.org/sites/default/files/rapport_algerie_en_web.pdf.

Sadia, S. 2018a (July 14). "Cocaïne, trafics de tout genre: ces affaires qui gangrènent l'Etat algérien". *Algériepart.* https://algeriepart.com/2018/07/14/cocaine-trafics-de-genres-affaires-gangrenent-letat-algerien/.

Sadia, S. 2018b (July 15). "Droits de l'homme: large solidarité avec le blogueur Merzouk Touati". *Algérie part.* https://algeriepart.com/2018/07/15/droits-de-lhomme-large-solidarite-blogueur-merzoug-touati/.

Sarnelli, V. and Kobibi, H. 2017. "National, regional, global TV in Algeria: University students and television audience after the 2012 Algerian media law". *Global Media and Communication*, March, pp. 1–27.

10

LANGUAGE AND IDENTITY IN ALGERIA

Deconstructing the myth of oneness

Mohand Tilmatine

Introduction

Independent Algeria suffers from similar poor governance, social injustice, and socio-economic and political problems to those of its southern Mediterranean neighbours. The issue of identity and language has plagued Algerian society since the colonial era, and its effects were felt even more acutely after independence, subjecting it to regular and recurring tensions. The struggles of the Algerian National Movement and the particularity of its political parties required a tightening of the ranks by imposing an implacable policy of national unity. Although the National Movement supported the political and cultural vision of the reformist and Salafist movement of the Algerian Ulema (Courrey, 2014), they opposed (while denying it) any diversity, be it political, regional, and/or ethnic.

This discourse of unity will serve as a decisive reference in the ideological orientation of the post-independence nation state and its orientation, articulated around language, religion, and government. These stemmed from fundamental principles of the revolution of November 1, 1954, becoming the so-called "national constants."

Resistance strategies against the policy of *unanimism* of the National Liberation Front (FLN) are considered, using as examples the Kabylie and Mzab regions. The conclusion covers the country's institutional blockage and the deadlock in which it is entangled.

The myth of oneness to serve the national movement

Much has been written about the uncompromising role of France in the formation and then the radical evolution of Algerian nationalism, but the colonial power also attributed to Islam the ability to have united the "vanquished" in order to overturn assimilation (Douzon 1981). What we know for sure is that on their arrival, the French found populations whom they describe as divided "into distinct communities by origin, customs, language, institutions, way of life, religious conceptions" (Isnard 1949: 469), which gave rise to debates about whether or not an Algerian nation really existed.

It is in this context that the Ulema, in the person of Sheikh Ibn Badis, played a role in 1936 in developing the concept of an Algerian personality (šakḥsiyya al-ğazā'iriyya), in a movement aiming at defending an Algerian specificity, defined exclusively as Arab-Muslim and opposing the deculturating phenomena. In doing so, he responded to Ferhat Abbas, who in his 1936 article denied the existence of an Algerian nation (Scagnetti 2003: 40). These attacks targeted his political movement, the Democratic Union of the Algerian Manifesto. This demanded the drafting of a constitution guaranteeing the freedom and equality of the inhabitants without distinction based on race and religion and ensuring the freedom of religion in light of the principle of the separation of church and state (Rahal 2004: 163; Abbas 1984). Because of this stand, the Democratic Union of the Algerian Manifesto was perceived as a "majority French-speaking party, which questions the definition of the Algerian, Arab and Muslim nation" (Rahal 2004: 162). The Algerian reformist thinker Malek Bennabi even saw in it a policy of colonial assimilation, a "de-Algerianisation" instrument, resulting in a clash of the Algerian elite which was divided between French and Arabic speakers:

> First at the top of the ladder, the appearance of two clans in the elite circle: the one who will speak Arabic and will try with Ben Badis to find Islamic references [...] and the one who will speak French and wear all the masks— Kemalism, Messalism, anti-Messalism, Berberism, Progressivism, pseudo-existentialism, fake Marxism—to serve or support under each of these labels the timely gods of the mascots or event in fact to serve oneself- Even under all these masks. (Bennabi 1990: 117)

"The country," says Bennabi (1990: 118), "did not count just two 'elites' but two superimposed 'societies'. One represented the traditional and historical country and the other wanted to make history from scratch." From the beginning, the Berberists were classified within this text as part of "de-Algerianisation" camp and would very soon be in the centre of the debates on an Algerian identity, which would recharge and find its feet in a republican, Islamic, and nationalist model at the same time.

Much as the revolution that gave birth to the French state initiated a campaign against the regional patois of France, the emerging Algerian state declared its war against forms of religious expression such as maraboutism or Ibadism (Tuomo 1983). Also the "Berberists," a group of activists of the National Movement, were protagonists of a conflict that would pit the supporters of an "Algerian Algeria" in 1949 against those of an exclusively "Arab and Islamic" Algeria (Harbi 1980; Ouerdane 1987; Ali-Yahya 2013). Among the reasons for this conflict was an unpublished manuscript entitled *Call to the United Nations* launched in 1948 by the nationalist leader Messali Hadj in which he traced the history of Algeria to the Arab conquest and maintained that it was "an integral part of the western Arab world known as the Arab Maghreb" (Ouerdane 1987: 41). This text would be subject, in 1949, to an ideological tract of under 30 pages, drafted by Idir el Wattani and entitled "*Algeria will live.*" It included the statement that "the nation does not necessarily presuppose a community of race, religion or language" (p. 5) and demonstrates that this group of activists has been "wrongly" qualified as "Berberist," because despite the Kabyle origin of this group, their "claim was primarily democratic and encompassed the entire national movement" (Hadjerès 1998; Aït Benali 2015). Nonetheless, the so called "Berber-materialists" or "Berber-Marxists," mostly Kabyles, would not escape the bloody repression ordered by the leadership of the FLN, including senior officials from Kabylie.[1] Far from being solely the fault of the FLN leadership, the hostility to the Berberist trend came from all the political movements (Harbi 1992: 51). Thus, in addition to the degrading positions of the Ulema vis-à-vis the Kabyle language (Tilmatine 1997), Messali described the "Berberists" as a "virus" and a "colonialist creation to destroy Arabism" (McDougall 2017: 191).

The myth of unity would also be imposed on the Mzab, another case of diversity, but this time a religious one which holds a special place in the Algerian context. Indeed, the confederation of the cities of the region had always been self-sufficient, a condition it maintained even during the colonial era. This was thanks, in particular, to the signing in 1853 of a treaty which guaranteed the autonomy of the region, before opposing harsh resistance thereafter, and finally losing it with the annexation of the Mzab in 1882 (Holsinger 1986).

The postcolonial state: change with continuity

Being the sole, direct, and exclusive heir to the National Movement, the FLN has taken the government's lead in building an authoritarian regime based for decades on the one-party system. Its absolute power rested on a legal-ideological instrument that allowed the repression of any specific, regional, religious, or language claim and thus established a "government's constitutional system through the party" (Borella 1964). FLN's unanimity would exploit history and make this wedge a common practice (Harbi 2012). The FLN wanted to build a collective memory around oneness, while avoiding a people's division and legitimising the role of leader attributed to the generation of the November Revolution. To reach this objective, rereading history was essential. It was necessary to act on the present and the future by referring to this glorious past in order to offer a radiant future. The *mujahidin* cult (former veterans) would then be sanctified and a slogan "One hero, the people," would erase any distinctions that could overshadow the power of the single party.

The rewriting of cultural and political memory was taking place in all areas. Anything that could recall colonial France was banned and countless names of *mujahidins*, completely unknown, replaced the names of streets, neighbourhoods, buildings, schools, institutions, and cities or villages. One of the most curious examples of this recovery of the national personality consisted in getting rid of colonialism's symbols and remnants, even if they were great artistic works. Thus, it was decided, for example, to cover the 1914–1918 Algiers memorial monument designed by the artist Paul Landowski, who was also the creator of the famous Christ redeemer of Rio de Janeiro (Meddi 2012).

Islamic radicalism and Arabisation

Post-independence Algeria would soon be part of a radical Arab nationalism. A policy of militarising power would be implemented upon the arrival of Ben Bella and Boumediene (Addi 2017) with an identity and language policy based on the recovery of the national personality as a measure of independence while maintaining unity. Muzzling political parties would be the result of adopting legislation prohibiting the establishment of political parties based on regional, language, or religious beliefs (Ordinance 1997).

As Islam and Arabic became, respectively, the state's religion and language, an intense policy of Arabisation was launched and the role of Islam in Algerian society was strengthened. One of the most important figures in defending the policy of Arabisation was former President Boumedienne for whom "without the recovery of this essential and important element which is the national language [i.e., the Arabic language], our efforts will remain vain, our personality incomplete and our unity a body without soul" (Tilmatine 2015: 7). The reign of Boumedienne would soon see the establishment of a true "doctrine for Arabic teaching and Arabisation" (Baghli 1977: 17). The place of the Arabic language would rest on two constants and criteria: Islam and the war of national liberation. These choices are included in all the founding documents of the future Algerian nation.

Islam and Arabisation mainly affected the education system. This reality has even been acknowledged by the current Minister of Education who justifies the crisis of the Algerian school system by the historical constraints related to the Jacobin tradition. This was imposed by the colonial republican school model, as well as by social-political challenges that led the leaders of Algeria to seek legitimacy in the generalisation of education and the development of a national sentiment that aimed to minimise cultural particularities. A policy document that shows the texts setting policy for education and training in Algeria revolve around an ideological construct aiming at securing the socio-political choices of independent Algeria such as democratisation, Arabisation, and socialism. These values rest on "the Algerian community cornerstone, that is Islam" (Benghabrit-Remaoun 2001). Indeed, the Algerian government in the line of the Ulema considered the education system as the most strategic instrument for the "recovery of the personality and the Algerian identity." The National Education Orientation Act of 2008 once again emphasised that Islam was the foundation on which Algerian identity was based (Tilmatine 2015: 11–12).

The imposition of Arabic as the only national language in all areas of society would be swiftly reflected in laws and decrees that sometimes looked surreal. They were designed to combat the colonial language French, and especially Berber, often presented as the Trojan horse of *Hizb Fransa* (party proponent of France) in Algeria. This designation itself sends us back to Bennabi's "two elite clans," which to date still reflects two divergent social and civilisational representations, articulated around two opposing reference systems. On the one hand that of an Arab world, of Umma *"Arabiyya,"* to which independent Algeria belongs, and on the other hand, the modern "Western" world embodied by "colonial" France, which would use French speakers to serve its "neocolonial" aims in Algeria.

These divergences are even more evident since the eruption of political Islamism and its deaths and attacks. These two societies are described as "the family that moves forward and the family that moves back" by journalist T. Djaout, murdered in 1993 by Islamists just after the publication of his column. The confrontation touches all areas: language, status of women, family, sources of political power, governance types, and overall the form of civilisation Algerian society preferred.

Successive FLN governments have from the outset counted in their ranks members of the Association of Ulema who have shaped the foundations of Algerian statehood—a gesture that clearly indicates a desire to endorse Arab-Muslim cultural options. It is important to note that the Ulema, which today constitutes the official religious position of the Algerian government, were granted positions in the "structuring" ministries of the FLN ideology, such as education, justice, and religious affairs. The Ulema founder, Sheikh Ibn Badis, was presented as a cohesive figure of national unity combining the Islamic, cultural, and identity values of the Algerian nation. Today, he has a particularly prominent place in the official history of the National Movement and in the pantheon of heroes of independent Algeria. The date of his death, April 16, 1940, is regularly celebrated as Science Day, *Youm el Ilm* in Algeria. Islam is a state religion and everything is measured in terms of religion. With Islam and the Arabic language there is no recognition for authors, however brilliant as they might be. They would only be Christians, *kuffar*, or Westernised lay Francophones. How to justify then the silence on Latin authors like Saint Augustine, Apuleius of Madaurus, and the other Maxime of Madaurus or Maximilian the grammarian, or closer to us, Jean and Marguerite Taos Amrouche, Mouloud Mammeri, Kateb Yacine, and others, all geniuses from Algeria, acknowledged elsewhere while completely ignored in their home country? How to justify their complete omission from the official collective memory and of a revolutionary memorial tailored only to fit Arabist and Islamist dimensions and pretensions, acknowledged only for being impious names. Or should Algeria be cut off from the world of philosophers, of the Cartesian and Mediterranean Greco-Latin heritage, just to be exclusively annexed forever to Salafism and to the prophets of Islam?

The dominant place of Islam is obvious in comparison with the treatment given to other religions, which, while representing a tiny minority, do exist in Algeria. The most publicised presence is the phenomenon of conversions to neo-evangelism, which is gaining ground all over the country. The government has tried to curb this trend and to control it by promulgating an ordinance in 2006 that subjects non-Muslim cults to severe conditions while setting up a legal solution to abusive behaviour. In a climate of growing Islamisation, this can take on the appearance of true persecution. The pressure does not only affect Christians, but also other Muslim religious branches qualified by the President of the Republic himself as "new ideas that are strange to the Algerian people" likely to affect the "stability of Algeria, spread hellish terrorism and recollect national tragedy scourge" (APS 2018). With hundreds of arrests, Ahmadis are most affected by this repression which has been condemned by international non-governmental organisations.

Even though Mozabites are not officially treated as foreign sects, Ghardaia and the region have been sinking for about 10 years in a wave of violence with clashes between Muslims of the Maliki rite and Ibadi. The media mentions, for the first time, "tribal, ethnic, even confessional" clashes that are justified for several reasons. These include large-scale demographic changes due in particular to the sedentarisation of nomadic Arab populations from neighbouring areas who settled in the region while looking for jobs (Dris-Aït Hamadouche & Zoubir 2009; Hadj-Moussa & Wahnich 2013; Belakhdar 2015).

These events return the scourge of the control of religious diversity adopted since the independence of the country. This new policy never really convinced Mozabites who feared from the start that it was based on socialism and democratic centralism as well as the great nations concept (Arab or Islamic) which might be unfavourable to minorities and erase religious and cultural differences. Proof of this was the Ibadite experience in Libya after the advent of the Qaddafi regime in 1969 and its attempts to coerce the Ibadites into Maliki Sunni, or even in Djerba in Tunisia, where the authorities prohibited them from organising and expressing themselves as a community (Boudi 1995: 99). These factual examples illustrate the role of the Mozabite reformists and their institutions. Through negotiation and compromise with the new masters in Algiers, they managed to maintain a discrete, relative autonomy of decision in the region despite the introduction of laws and decrees on the unification of law in Algeria (Jomier 2015: 620–624).

In the context of Berber identity and language claims, these demographic changes are perceived as a threat by the Mozabite community. It should be recalled that according to numerous laws adopted by the *Jamāɛa* (lay council of the Mzab communities) since the 16th century, the Mozabites strictly limit or prohibit the settlement of nomadic populations in Ghardaia (Chérifi 2015: 182–192). On their side, the Arab populations, of mainly nomadic origin, blame the Mozabites for creating problems with integration. It is obvious that their centuries-old inhabitation of a territory largely dominated by the

Mozabite community triggers different and opposite discourses regarding the legitimacy of this or that group and, inevitably, feelings of exclusion and injustice on both sides.

Identity and language

From the viewpoint of identity and language, the Mzab, although Berber-speakers, are confined to their own confessionalism (Cuperly 1984). The vast majority of Mozabites are proud of their command of literary Arabic because it is "the language of the Koran and paradise." Some Mozabite reformists such as Sheikh Mohammed Ali Dabbûz are trying to link the Mozabite identity to Arab nationalism and especially to the Islam of the Ulemas and even to the Algerian nation" (Ghazal 2010, 2005; Jomier 2012). Thus, for him, the Mozabites are "culturally and ethnically Arab" and their Arabic fluency would be "a proof of their Arabity." For Sheikh Dabbûz, the Ibadites, through the Rustumide kingdom of Tahart, would even be at the birth of the Algerian national state (Jomier 2012: 46–49). However, the Mozabites refuse to accept this trend of Islamist militants which even wanted to exclude their mother tongue, which would be a survival of the *Jahiliyya* (Boudi 1995: 97). Nevertheless, unlike the Kabyles who use, cultivate, and insist on Latin script for the transcription of Berber, the Mozabites more frequently opt for Arabic. It may seem paradoxical that it is precisely the national character of the Amazigh demand—defended by the state in order to counter any regionalisation/kabylisation of Berber—which will bring it to the Mzab by suddenly giving it a dual minority character in its religious and language identity.

Another means of resistance broadens the outlook for the Mzab: minority rights, based on human rights, starting with an inalienable concept and protected by international law. The anchoring of Mozabite demands in Berber national demands gives them access to international forums through the Amazigh World Congress. This space provides international visibility to the Mozabite question and the repression of its activists; it also has a transnational dimension through the contact made with other groups with whom they already share their Ibadity and to which is now added Amazighity (Djebel Nefoussa in Libya and Djerba in Tunisia).

More recently, with the emergence of the Movement for the Autonomy of Kabylie and its anchoring in the Kabyle political landscape, the process of intermingling with Kabylie was manifested by the creation of an Autonomist Movement of the Mzab. Perceived as extremely dangerous, the authorities imprisoned a large number of its activists, followed by extreme tension in the region which was already explosive because of numerous inter-communal clashes.

De-escalation, repression, and resistance

These events are a reminder that a long-running conflict has never been seriously addressed by the relevant parties. Social and identity movements experienced by the country since the 1980s favour the development of an identity discourse on both sides (Berber against Arabs) with aspects that are at once religious, territorial, and socio-economic (Dufresne-Aubertin 2017: 209–222). On the Mozabite side, these tensions highlight the traditionally difficult and ambiguous relations with the central power. However, they also underscore the contradictory discourse of the Ibadite community between, on the one hand, requests for recognition of its Algerian identity and its real inclusion in national projects, and, on the other hand, a need for autonomy due to its religion and culture. These are needs which, moreover, provoke criticism of separatist tendencies juxtaposed with speeches proposing autonomy, even independence, by certain sectors of the Berber claim in Kabylie. The sentencing of many Mozabite militants accused of separatism, and the systematic repression of all opposition and protests, aggravate the already dire situation and further widen the gap between different population groups, in particular Berber speakers, from government.

Berber claims

Since the establishment of Amazigh as an official language in 2016, the institutionalising of Berber grievances became a "new Berber policy" of the nation-state (Chaker 2017). In the absence of a final settlement or a lessening of resistance and demands through repression and violence, the authorities pretended to adopt these demands in order to better channel them, possibly even by stifling them through bureaucratic inertia. The regime, taking the moral high ground, began to announce its intention to repair errors. For the former minister, Taleb Ibrahimi, the mistake was to "perpetuate the nationalist discourse based on the pair Arabity/Islamity instead of returning to our three-dimensional identity [Arabity, Islam, Amazighity]." Prime Minister A. Ouyahia acknowledges, for his part, "the historical error of the single party" and his management of the events of the Berber Spring of 1980 in Tizi Ouzou. He even stated that President Bouteflika was opposed to banning the Mammeri Conference of April 1980 (*Le Matin* January 2018). To these are added actions towards the Berber culture and the Kabylie: recognition of *Yennayer* (Berber New Year) as a national and public holiday, its teaching in school, the opening of a National Research Centre in Amazigh Language and Culture, the establishment of an Amazigh Academy, and rehabilitation of Kabyle personalities and intellectuals like Mouloud Mammeri to whom a whole year of tributes is devoted, including issuing a stamp commemorating him. In addition, the great rebel of the Kabyle Protest, musician Matoub Lounès, has been venerated by the state since 2014. He was even described as a *Chahid* (martyr) on June 28, 2018, by the Algerian Minister of Culture, who went to visit his grave to commemorate the 20th anniversary of his assassination (*Le Matin* June 2018). The recapture of former enemies of the nation goes even further with the inauguration of a statue in memory of Mohamed Haroun, one of the famous bombers, who went from being called a terrorist to national hero.

But the most noteworthy move by the state and its representatives made is undoubtedly the recognition in 2016 of Amazigh as an official language in the Algerian Constitution. Suddenly, the Algerians who were all Arabs in previous versions of the Constitution all became "Amazigh" or, at least for some, "Berbers more or less Arabised or Arabised by Islam." Yet the preamble to the Constitution makes it clear that Algeria is an "Arab" land. If Arabic is the official language of the state, what would Amazigh be—or even worse, which state?

Peoples' resistance: memory and the creation of heritage

The innate relationship between memory and territory is a very important aspect of the studies carried out by the historian Pierre Nora, who developed the concept of "Realms of Memory" for this purpose. For the author, a site of memory "in every way goes from the most material and substantive objects, like war memorials and National Archives, to the most abstract and intellectually built elements like the notion of lineage, generation, or even region and 'human-memory'" (Nora 1984: Presentation). It can be a monument, an important person, a museum, an archive, just as much as a symbol, a motto, an event or an institution, the memory of the group, collective imagination and memory "vested with a symbolic aura" (ibid. XXXIV). A historical memory is "what remains of the past per the experience of the groups, or what these groups made of the past [...]. The historical memory that is globalising, borderless, blurred and telescoping, stems from the belief to assimilate only what strengthens it" (Nora 2011: 300).

In the Mzab, the work on memory appears in various ways such as religious festivals, carpet fairs, community assistance to individual and group projects, major private libraries, oral history associations, and of course, the transmission of Ibadi religious traditions (Chérifi 2015: 296–336). Since 1991, state-certified associations strengthened the old unofficial network of associations responsible for renewing this work of historical memory. The focus was, however, on locations of the Ibadi minority (Aillet & Gillot 2012) while taking advantage of the fact that heritage ownership often takes a hybrid form in which state and community ownerships come together. This hybridisation very often reflects the government's attempts to assume control of a debate on identity that it had previously condemned, but has since accepted Algeria's Amazighity component. This claim's institutionalisation is recurrent in recent years (Le Saout 2017).

The patrimonialisation process is another factor in this work on memory. According to Di Méo, it reflects an act of "collective sense-making" which derives from "a principle of convention," which in turn translates into an "implicit social agreement [...] on collectively accepted values of a shared identity vis-à-vis an item, a territory, an idea, or a practice that acquire a certain timelessness" (2008: 2). In this regard, patrimonialisation becomes a form of identity claim, as for the Mzab, without this being explicitly stated; a form of people's re-appropriation of its past, its culture, and also its territory. Patrimonialisation comes in various forms. It is mainly the function of civil society and affects practically all socio-cultural, legal, or political areas that allow the recovery, conservation, or restoration of a space, property, or practices related to culture and language. Identity awareness has gradually favoured various initiatives to rebuild or update local heritage.

In Kabylie, music was the essential vehicle of the Berber claim. The success of some committed singers such as Idir, Aït-Menguellet, Ferhat Mehenni, and Matoub Lounès has strongly contributed to the grievances and especially to the construction of Kabyle advocacy action. This generation of singers, who have made their greatest mark on the Kabyle scene since the 1970s, is paving the way for a new wave of young singers. They in turn draw on the musical heritage of the 1950s and 1960s, enabling the audience to rediscover them thanks to their modernisation or fusion with other genres, such as jazz, hard rock, rap/hip hop, or slam.

In everyday life, a number of local festivals that disappeared as a result of the policies of homogenisation and Arabisation are reappearing. Kabyle associations favour the reactivation of old festive traditions such as *tafsut ijeɣɣigen* (flowers or spring festivals) or the development and institutionalising of specific days for a particular local product: Prickly pear day (*tamaɣra ikarmusen*), day of the fig (*n tbexsisin*), etc.

The emergence of Kabyle autonomists (Movement for the Autonomy of Kabylie) reinforces this trend. Their involvement in constructing and repairing some memorials covers many symbolic areas, which shape the Republic. These are, according to Nora (1984): the creation of new national/public holidays: National day, day of Kabyle Nation, the Kabyle student, creation of new national symbols: a flag, ID card, Kabyle national anthem, or even, lately a "Kabyle national team" who participated in the last CONIFA Football World Cup (31 May–9 June 2018), broadcast by a new Kabyle television channel (Tq5tv).[2]

Much more obvious and more general in this process is the recovery of the toponymic heritage of the Kabyle region. This involves the "re-Berberization" of street and place names now visible everywhere in Kabylie, despite the formal prohibition of these practices by Algerian legislation. This tendency is expressed even more clearly by the use of Berber (in Latin and Tifinagh) on road signs and neighbourhoods of towns and villages where Arabic transcription is often blocked or erased to make room for Berber and Latin transcriptions. This practice also extends to the windows and signs of retail stores as well as national institutions.

The occupation of these increasingly numerous spaces in Kabylie aims to restore a sense of common belonging, to structure and build a national consciousness, and to contribute to the patrimonialisation of events, historical dates, symbolic, or ideal reality into national assets (Di Méo 2008: 2).

New technologies, such as the Internet and social media, have played a fundamental role in this reconstruction of identity through cultural heritage. In addition to creating numerous pages that support and disseminate these dates and events, many Kabyle animators are working towards the use and construction of a digital heritage whose contingency measure was recognised by UNESCO in 2003.[3] The best example in this regard is the existence of a Kabyle localisation team.[4] Its contributions in the framework of the Unicode Common Location Data Reposition) now gives visibility to Kabyle, as a language used in many applications,[5] considered in social media as an important and modern form of the Kabyle heritage without forgetting the symbolic impact of such a presence in new technologies.

Conclusion

Created to free Algeria, the FLN was to disappear once the goal of liberation had been achieved. However, once the country became independent, the FLN came to power with a policy that reproduced the ideological patterns and choices of the National Movement. By adopting the Ulama's thinking and slogan, "Islam is our religion, Algeria our homeland and Arabic our language," the FLN re-imposed the myth of oneness. In so doing, they made a clean sweep of all the linguistic, religious, and regional diversities which existed during the colonial period. A myth and an exclusion policy that will clearly emerge in the founding texts of the country. Since Arabic and Islam were established as the language and state religion, this excluded or at least established a de facto legal imbalance in dealing with diversity. This status and its subsequent supportive measures would have important repercussions in Kabylie, where resistance to the policy of Arabisation gave rise to a chain of demands. These claims were faced with the inflexibility and repression of the state which gradually led to authoritarian and sovereign aspirations. Public institutions are deteriorating due to systematic corruption, as well as an economy suffering from the oil windfall. This cocktail has fed a climate of permanent tension and social conflict. Riots have become a form of social protest affecting all regions, including the Mzab. The Mzab was doubly affected, not only as a religious minority, but with additional identity and social grievances.

Faced with the emergence of the Movement for the Autonomy of Kabylie and the magnitude of this movement, the government seems to opt simultaneously for carrots and sticks. A process of relaxation and the recognition of Berber identity and language, with the recovery of Kabyle symbols and icons, was achieved while maintaining a constant watch over militants. This led to the adoption of a policy of repression and absolute restriction of individual and collective rights. It would seem that the "November generation" is caught in a chronic incapacity to embrace the country's national identities, the diversity of its languages, its cultures, and its religions. It is also unable to give up the myth of unity and the intangibility of its "national constants," which keep the country in a state of regression in which it sinks even further in the meanders of the Islamist path.

Following the riots of 1988 and the introduction of political pluralism in 1989, the FLN was dismissed as the governing party (Hubert 1967). As a result, the de-constitutionalising of Islam as a state religion seemed to be a prerequisite to curbing the harmful influences of the Islamist hydra in all the public spaces of Algerian society and which have already brought the country to the very brink of the abyss. It is difficult, nevertheless, to imagine today changes of this scale without a deep questioning of the current system of governance. Will Algeria ever go beyond the model of the hyper-centralised nation-state? Could Algeria face the multiplicity of autonomist and sovereign movements with rational political arguments, instead of demonising these ideas? Why be afraid of a debate conducted under euphemisms as "national re-foundation" or "modular regionalisation" so as to avoid clearly naming federal or similar models? Even solutions of asymmetric management as in Spain, for example, embrace a modern perspective of post-nationalism (Heller 2011) and achieve regional integration.

Notes

1 In a letter signed by Ben M'hidi, Abbane, Krim, Ouamrane, Zirout, Bentobal, and Si Cherif, dated August 20, 1956, sent to the leaders of the federation of France, the authors assure the FLN officials in France of their total support in their "killings of Berberists, Messalists and other counter-revolutionaries." http://www.kabyles. com/wp-content/uploads/2007/02/fln-demande-liquidation-berb%C3%A9ristes. jpg (consulted on the 30/03/2018). No longer available.
2 https://tq5tv.com/.
3 http://portal.unesco.org/fr/ev.php-RL_ID=17721&URL_DO=DO_TOPIC& URL_SECTION=201.html, (accessed 22/03/2019). No longer accessible.
4 https://pontoon.mozilla.org/kab/ (accessed 21/05/2017).
5 http://cldr.unicode.org/ (accessed 21/05/2017).

References

Abbas, F., 1984, *L'indépendance confisquée (1962–1978)*, Flammarion, Paris.
Addi, L., 2017, *Le nationalisme arabe radical et l'islam politique. Produits contradictoires de la modernité*, Barzakh, Alger.
Aillet, C. & Gilotte, S., 2012, "Sedrata, l'élaboration d'un lieu de mémoire," *Revue des mondes musulmans et de la Méditerranée* 132, 91–114.
Aït Benali, B., 2015 (November 26). Mémorandum de Messali versus le document d'Idir El Wattani: Comment définir la nation algérienne? *Huffpost*, https://www. huffpostmaghreb.com/ait-benali-boubekeur/memorandum-de-messali-versus-le-document-didir-el-wattani--comment-definir-la-nation-algerienne-_b_8626888.html.
Algérie Presse Service (APS), 2018 (April 16). Le Président Bouteflika appelle à faire face "avec clairvoyance" aux idées "étrangères." http://www.aps.dz/algerie/72707-le-president-bouteflika-appelle-a-faire-face-avec-clairvoyance-aux-idees-etrangeres.
Ali-Yahya, A., 2013, *La crise berbère de 1949. Portrait de deux militants: Ouali Bennaï et Amar Ould-Hamouda. Quelle identité pour l'Algérie ?* Barzakh, Alger.
Baghli, S.-A., 1977, *Aspects de la politique culturelle de l'Algérie*, UNESCO, Paris.
Belakhdar, N., 2015, "L'éveil du Sud" ou quand la contestation vient de la marge. Une analyse du mouvement des chômeurs algériens, *Politique africaine* 1(137), 27–48.

Benghabrit-Remaoun, N., 2001, 13, "École et religion," in Mahiou, A., & Henry, J. (Eds.), *Où va l'Algérie?* Institut de recherches et d'études sur les mondes arabes et musulmans. doi:10.4000/books.iremam.417 (accessed May 26, 2018).

Bennabi, M., 1990, *Le problème des idées dans le monde musulman*, El Bay'yinate, Alger.

Borella, F., 1964, "La constitution algérienne: un régime constitutionnel de gouvernement par le parti," *Revue algérienne des Sciences Juridiques* 1, 51–98.

Boudi, S., 1995, "Les Mozabites face à la crise algérienne," *Hérodote* 77, 93–102.

Chaker, S., 2017, "Berbérité/Amazighité (Algérie/Maroc): 'Lanouvelle politique berbère", *Studi Magrebini*, Università degli studi du Napoli'L'Orientale, 129–153.

Chérifi, B., 2015, *Le M'zab. Études d'anthropologie historique et culturelle*, Éditions Sédia, Alger.

Courreye, C., 2014, "L'école musulmane algérienne de Ibn Bâdîs dans les années 1930, de l'alphabétisation de tous comme enjeu politique," *Revue des mondes musulmans et de la Méditerranée* [Online], 136|(accessed April 28, 2018).

Cuperly, P., 1984, *Introduction à l'étude de l'Ibādisme et de sa théologie*, OPU, Alger.

Di Méo, G., 2008, "Processus de Patrimonialisation et construction des territoires" Colloque *Patrimoine et industrie en Poitou-Charentes: connaître pour valoriser*, September 2007, Poitiers- Châtellerault, France, 87–109, Geste éditions, La Crèche. <halshs-00281934 (accessed June 25, 2018).

Douzon, H., 1981, "Les occasions perdues," in H. Alleg (dir.), *La Guerre d'Algérie*, t. 1, *L'Algérie des origines à l'insurrection*, pp. 514–515, Paris, temps Actuels.

Dris-Aït Hamadouche, L., Zoubir Y., 2009, "Pouvoir et opposition en Algérie: Vers une transition prolongée ?," *L'Année du Maghreb*, V, 111–127.

Dufresne-Aubertin, L., 2017, "Revendications morales et politiques d'une révolte. Les émeutes du Mzab en Algérie (2013–2015)," *L'Année du Maghreb* 16, 209–222.

Ghazal, A., 2005, "Seeking common Ground: Salafism and Islamic Reform in modern Ibādī Thought," *Bulletin of the Royal Institute for Inter-Faith Studies* 7 (1), 119–141.

Ghazal, A. N., 2010, "The other frontiers of Arab Nationalism: Ibadis, Berbers, and the Arabist-Salafi press in the Interwar Period," *International Journal of Middle East Studies* 42, 105–122.

Hadj-Moussa, R., Wahnich, S., 2013, "Les émeutes: Contestation de la marge ou la marge de la contestation ?," *L'Homme & la société* 1 (187–188), 9–14.

Hadjerès, S., 1998. La Crise du PPA de 1949 et l'actualité algérienne. Extracts for his book. https://www.socialgerie.net/IMG/pdf/1949_crise49.-EW_1998_08_04-2004_02_27.pdf.

Harbi, M., 1980, "Nationalisme algérien et identité berbère," *Peuples Méditerranéens* 11, 31–37.

Harbi, M., 1992, *L'Algérie et son destin. Croyants ou citoyens?*, Arcantère Éditions, Paris.

Harbi, M., 2012, "L'Histoire est instrumentalisée en Algérie," *Jeune Afrique*, July 5, 2012.

Heller, M., 2011, *Paths to Post-Nationalism. A Critical Ethnography of Language and Identity*, Oxford University Press, Oxford.

Holsinger, D.C., 1986, "Muslim Responses to French Imperialism: An Algerian Saharan Case Study," *The International Journal of African Historical Studies*, 19 (1), 1–15, University African Studies Center, Boston, http://www.jstor.org/stable/218692, (accessed April 30, 2018).

Hubert, M., 1967, "L'expérience algérienne du parti unique constitutionnalisé," *Revue de l'Occident musulman et de la Méditerranée*, n°4, 81–97.

Isnard, H., 1949, "Aux origines du nationalisme algérien," *Annales. Economies, sociétés, civilisations* 4, 463–474.

Jomier, A., 2012, "Iṣlâḥ ibâḍite et intégration nationale: Vers une communauté mozabite ? (1925–1964)," in C. Aillet (dir.), *L'ibadisme, une minorité au cœur de l'islam, Revue des mondes musulmans et de la Méditerrannée* 132, 175–195.

Jomier, A., 2015, *Un réformisme islamique dans l'Algérie coloniale: oulémas ibadites et société du Mzab (c. 1880—c.1970)*, PhD thesis, Department of Modern and Contemporary History (Histoire moderne et contemporaine), INALCO, Paris.

Le Matin, 2018 (June 30). "Azzedine Mihoubi s'est recueilli sur la tombe de Matoub Lounes et le qualifie de 'Chahid'!" https://www.lematindalgerie.com/azzedine-mihoubi-sest-recueilli-sur-la-tombe-de-matoub-lounes-et-le-qualifie-de-chahid.

Le Matin, 2018 (January 18). "Bouteflika était contre l'interdiction de la conférence de Mammeri en 1980!" https://www.lematindalgerie.com/bouteflika-etait-contre-linterdiction-de-la-conference-de-mammeri-en-1980/.

Le Saout, D., 2017, "Les associations amazighes au défi de l'institutionnalisation au Maroc et en Algérie. Entre logique consensuelle et logique protestataire," in M. Tilmatine & T. Desrues (eds.), *Les revendications amazighes dans la tourmente des « printemps arabes»*, pp. 161–193, Centre Jacques-Berque, Rabat.

McDougall, J., 2017, *A History of Algeria*, Cambridge University Press, Cambridge.

Meddi, A., 2012 (October 25). "Patrimoine: le Pavois d'Alger se dévoile," Elwatan2. https://elwatanlafabrique.wordpress.com/2012/10/25/patrimoine-le-pavois-dalger-se-devoile/.

Nora, P., 1984, "Entre mémoire et histoire: La problématique des lieux," in P. Nora (ed.), *Les lieux de mémoire*, Tome 1, La République, Galimard, Paris.

Nora, P., 2011, *Présent, Nation, Mémoire*, Gallimard, Paris.

Ordinance n° 97/09 of 06 March 1997 organic law on political parties having repealed and replaced Law 89/11 of 05 July 1989 on associations of a political nature. http://lexalgeria.free.fr/politiq.htm.

Ouerdane, A., 1987, "La «crise berbériste» de 1949, un conflit à plusieurs faces," *Revue de l'Occident musulman et de la Méditerrannée*, 44, 35 47.

Rahal, M., 2004, "La place des réformistes dans le mouvement national Algérien: Vingtième Siècle," *Revue d'histoire* 83, 161–171.

Scagnetti, J.-Ch., 2003, "Identité ou personnalité algérienne ? L'édification d'une algérianité (1962–1988)," *Cahiers de la Méditerranée* 66, 367–384.

Tilmatine, M., 1997, "Les Oulémas algériens et la question berbère: Un document de 1948," *Awal.* 77–90.

Tilmatine, M., 2015, "Arabization and Linguistic Domination: Berber and Arabic in the North of Africa," in *Language Empires in Comparative Perspective*, Christel Stolz (Eds.), 1–16, Walter de Gruyter, Berlin/München/Boston.

Tuomo, M., 1983, "Les mouvements politiques et la question culturelle en Algérie avant la guerre de libération," *Cahiers de la Méditerranée* 26 (1), 3–14.

11

THE LANGUAGE SITUATION OF TWENTY-FIRST-CENTURY ALGERIA

Navigating the ideology

Hayat Messekher and Mohamed Miliani

Introduction

Language policies in Algeria have transformed the linguistic phenomena of assimilation, acquisition, and cultural cross-fertilisation; they have become increasingly intricate, leaving the construction of education in total shambles. Very often, decisions about language planning and policy ignore the sociocultural parameters rooted in the daily reality of the country. Mainstreaming, i.e., the eradication of the most distinctive and diverse traits characteristic of the Algerian society, has been at the core of the political agenda of some lobbies in government that were pushing for a monolithic view of Algeria. All decisions concerning the planning of national and foreign languages have given priority to the Arab–Islamic dimension of the country. In addition, a number of political and educational decisions have attempted to limit the scope and importance of French. That meant putting English high on the government priority list as the language for development. This begs the question of whether the government might bring to the fore the role of a totally new "alien" language that does not yet belong to anyone. School has thus become the laboratory where the language problems are posed, but where highly disputable answers are brought, providing instead makeshift solutions to lasting problems. With such a background, it is difficult to assess the possible introduction of English as the first foreign language in education as a replacement of French, raising questions as to whether this process responds to a social demand; whether it is a means to do away with the "language of the former colonizer"; or whether it is the exigencies of the more extreme fringe of the population that clings to the largely proclaimed "language for development" for a hidden agenda.

Language ideology and language planning

Worldwide, languages are natural, social, and linguistic phenomena that become systematically politicised and thus divide more than unite people. The situation is not any different in other post-colonial countries with policies of reconstruction that met diverse obstacles, not least of which is the definition of national and official languages. In Algeria, the function, role, and acquisition of all languages, whether national (two mother tongues), supranational (classical Arabic, a.k.a. Modern Standard Arabic),[1] or foreign (mainly French and English) have systematically been subjected to ideological filters that have rendered the overall sociolinguistic environment more complex if not more entangled to deal with. Although there is no one single definition of ideology, Woolard (1998: 3) defines language ideology as, "representations, whether explicit or implicit, that construe the intersection of language and human beings in social world." In a way, language ideology describes and at times constrains social belief systems, positioning, and performance of social identity; and with time, language ideology becomes inherent in linguistic practices, and in narratives about language, but ends up transforming reality. In Algeria, successive governments and institutions have since independence been agents in the production and exercise of specific language ideologies, the most important of which is the standard language ideology. In fact, the latter goes back to pre-independence as it was meant, "to create a sense of national unity and resistance to the French colonial power" (Messekher 2015: 261). Furthermore, it is important to note that such standard language ideology defined by Lippi-Green (1997: 64) as, "a bias toward an abstracted, idealized, homogeneous spoken language which is imposed and maintained by dominant bloc institutions and which names as its model the written language...[and which promotes] the language subordination process" will ultimately lead to valuing and mystifying the standard language and the mainstream culture while devaluing and delegitimising the non-standard languages and dialects and their cultures. For decades, government planning has opted for top-down actions in favour of classical[2] or Modern Standard Arabic, labelled as the official language and medium of instruction. This has shown more political manipulation than serene and matter-of-fact procedures to help the nation regain its once stable language dynamic. Thus, since independence, the linguistic pluralism of Algeria has been eroded by convergent visions, making room for policies of depleting assimilation. The processes of vernacularisation (of Berber/Tamazight[3]) and internationalisation of the education system have not received proper attention from the political and cultural authorities in undertaking in-depth research to make well-informed decisions. Only recently have makeshift attempts such as the formalisation of the Berber language been pushed forward to alleviate political tensions around this issue. However, the Jacobin policies (creation of the Academy of the Arabic language in 1986, banning the use of foreign languages—the 1991 Law on Generalization of Arabic—, overbid of Arabic-only decisions: e.g., in the 1990s change of city names into Arabic: Oran became Wahran, Tlemcen became Tilimsen, etc., restored less than a year later) that have led to some kind of social anomie are still being pursued through a constant overbid of nationalism where even religion serves as a determinant factor in the overall linguistic landscape.

We aim in the present chapter to unveil the intricacies of the language policies Algeria has tried to promote since independence in 1962, in particular, recent attempts regarding the English language that is praised by Algerians from all walks of life, but for different reasons and concerns. Against such a background, the status of all languages involved remain undeclared, if not left to ideological interference. This affects in particular the Algerian dialects and Amazigh varieties resisting stigmatisation and rejection, and the French and English language racing for the position of second language. The position of English is privileged by all political, cultural, and scientific authorities. Nevertheless, this seemingly united view poses problems because of the hidden motives of large sections of the population. Ideology is not far from these progressive views: "[s]ince independence, language has been a huge political, social and ideological issue in Algeria" (the Permanent Committee on Geographical Names 2003: 2). This is confirmed internally by decision-makers who view language as ideology and power because it has become, "a point of convergence of all fantasies, fears and identity expectations of social and ideological actors who clash on the Algerian scene" (Dourari 1997: 20). This has rendered the overall language market hostage to very different views and stances verging very often on discourses of exclusion.

Algeria, a crucible of linguistic phenomena

Algeria is a multilingual country that has witnessed the establishment, cross-influencing, and mixing of different world languages, whether they were Semitic, Indo-European, Nordic, and/or Asian. The various invasions and settlements Algeria has known have brought an undeniable richness to the spoken languages and communities that have established themselves in North Africa. Berber is the only native language while Algerian Arabic was established during the return of the Arabs from Andalucía in Spain, thus forming the Maghrebi variety of Arabic (Elimam 1997), not to mention the southern variety of Hassaniya Arabic spoken in Mauritania. The more formal or classical type of Arabic, el-fus'ha, often associated with the Quran, was given official status in the Constitution of 1963. However, even if, "... the official discourse... persists in its pretentions to 'promote the national culture'... the state substitutes to the actual language, active and creative, an exterior language, fetishized and purportedly superior" (Elimam 2004: 35). Despite its general use, the Algerian dialect has received no attention whatsoever on the part of officials regardless of the fact that its role was recognised in the nineteenth-century history of Algeria during the time of Emir Abdelkader. As for Berber and its regional varieties, it has only recently been recognised (in 2002 and 2016, respectively) after half a century as a national and official language of the country, and after years of social contestations and political manoeuvring. Is this not a case of politicking?

Against these unnatural interventions from the polity, the contact of languages has dictated its own rules allowing the development of bi/trilingualism, assimilation, and cultural cross-fertilisation. These living languages have influenced each other in ways that the politicians ignored. Instead of a thriving dynamic of language, they were preoccupied with a concern for monolingualism: classical Arabic being first. Yet, while French has more users than in post-independence Algeria, the Algerian dialect has responded more to natural language exchanges to dictate its own rules in energetic and creative ways. Furthermore, when considering the Arabic language, there has been no deliberate language reform through changes of certain aspects such as grammar or orthography, despite the presence of the Academy of Arabic. Thus, Arabic rests on a stable base, which makes it difficult to adjust to time variation and lexical modernisation, or neologisms. In addition, language spread has seen an increase in the number of classical Arabic users through schooling with little impact on interlingual communication of the whole speech community. Notwithstanding the more ideological validation by the 1991 Law on the Generalisation of Arabic that totally ignores the Algerian dialect by stating: "the Arabic language is a component of the 'authentic' national personality and a standard feature of the nation" (Art. 2), stability is far from characterising the Algerian language panorama. Moreover, "Algerianity, as specific nationality and culture... is fought against to the sole profit of an Arab supranationality... but where only the Arab feature is underlined" (Dourari 1997: 29). National identity is then the ultimate victim of all these manoeuvrings. Politically speaking, nothing is yet finished, witness the language maintenance of Tamazight. This is another hotly debated issue that makes the protection of its corpus necessary for preserving it, primarily, as a first language/mother tongue, just like Algerian Arabic, but also as an official language against all types of pressures, political or social, that endanger its status. This is why the overall linguistic phenomena need to be managed in the most coherent way possible to avoid a partisanship that might threaten the social and linguistic equilibrium pre-colonial Algeria experienced.

Language dynamism vs language planning

Native and foreign languages in the sociolinguistic milieu do not necessarily coexist well, partly because of the users' contradictory perceptions and ambiguous attitudes, but also due to the politicians' partisan ideological views. Ambivalence is thus a constant attitude with the unspoken, the undeclared, because of very subjective stances expressed vis-à-vis used languages, but also because of the politicians' depreciation (of the mother tongues[4]: Berber or Algerian dialect) or overrating languages (classical Arabic, English) against mere logic. Languages used in the natural social milieu seem to develop differently in institutional environmental. All languages, " see their development seriously handicapped by the tensions born from over/ideologization of attitudes towards them and to contrary decisions which result from it" (Chachou 2013: 31). What seems to stand out is the sometimes antagonistic nature of the citizens' language practices compared to their social representations. Several students chose to study French, which they still qualify as the language of the colonisers. Even the purists do not refrain from using borrowings from other languages.

Today's linguistic context is very often opposed to the previously prevailing situation where an admitted equilibrium existed, even if the dichotomy between dominating and dominated languages was clear to all: the language of the coloniser vs the native vernaculars of Arabic and Berber that had been marginalised by the colonising power. This inequality between languages is undoubtedly accepted by a majority, but contested by a minority that sees it as a conflict to be settled in a democratic way: a minority language needs all the attention of the politicians. The hierarchy of languages is effected through both normal language practices (mostly innovations) and state institutions (administrations, schools) establishing norms and sub-norms: "in the domain of languages more than anywhere else it happens that the ideology underlies the vision and orientates it" (Taleb Ibrahimi 1995: 12). Hence, regardless of language practices, "Arabic remains, in spite of the quest for modernity officially proclaimed in the fundamental texts of the country, prisoner of its theological references" (Rouadjia 1991: 120). Not only does the official status of Arabic impose a hierarchy that does not do justice to all vernaculars, but caught between the sacred (the language of the Quran) and the secular (its dialect), the Algerian language community has more problems defining a position for its own identity that needs to be stable and serene. The dialect is the most popular linguistic means for the creative fields (popular arts: poetry Melhun) and innovation (neologisms, jargons, and regional dialects), which the formal institutional language does not bring because of the still embryonic competences in classical Arabic. Foreign language policy has not followed clear pathways to building overall coherence. The proof of such a statement is the introduction of the English language at the primary level as a replacement of French in 1993. That was sheer intellectual suicide[5] when considering long-term visions and not conjectures.

Sociocultural parameters

The characterisation of any society is central to defining individuals living in a given sociolinguistic milieu. Indeed, people's customs, lifestyles, and values help characterise a social group. Furthermore, these sociocultural parameters are so complex that they need the largest and most exhaustive view possible, including education, language, religion, culture, values, and attitudes. Therefore, citizens' language development can be explained in various ways by referring to certain multifaceted factors (social interactions) that directly and indirectly shape and affect people's thoughts and behaviours, particularly linguistic ones. This is no less the case in Algeria where factors like cultural identity (sometimes in the narrow form of regionalism) and deprivation (of the Berber ethnic group), attitudes, family, and kinship structures mould mindsets. These are difficult to unveil because of their intricacies in making individuals who are today influenced by their religious beliefs, social practices, cultural sensitivity, and educational background. Social sources of individual development, according to the Vygotskian philosophy, appear in cultural contexts, where language and symbol systems govern human cultural, linguistic, and communication activities. This is why explanations about individual progress towards citizenship must be based on all sociocultural factors (including lifestyles, perceptions, and values). These too depend on people's belief systems, habits, and customs that in turn affect language development and learning in positive (cultural cohesion) or negative ways, such as stereotyping and rejection. This does not mean that individuals have no responsibility when learning or participating in activities that involve the other, their interlocutor. Individual choices still prevail.

Languages in education

In Algeria, ideology is at its height in the domain of education where language policies seem to follow a very bumpy trajectory depending on the decision-makers' political colours. Whether in a top-down or bottom-up process, the vitality of a language helps its status to evolve, even against the manipulations of the decision-makers. The contrary is also true, but with a different outcome. This characteristic has been fought against by successive governments that have tried, not always for the better and not in an expert manner, to coordinate with national stakeholders to pursue the objectives of what rarely looked like a serene and shared language strategy. What has been missing over the years is a clearer and more adequate strategy to improve language acquisition of the mother tongues, mostly the Algerian dialect seen by a minority as an unworthy language in teaching and learning, if only for the building of a more coherent system within schools and colleges. This has not taken place because the embedding of foreign languages in education has not been stable enough within a system that is still being destabilised by makeshift language policies. The two official languages, Arabic and Tamazight, have taken diverging routes reflecting policies that have emphasised the policy of convergence: one state, one territory, one language, and one religion. Berber has only recently been included in the government's agenda indicating firstly, that too much time has been lost because of politicking; and secondly, amateurish manoeuvrings are creating more problems for the teaching of Tamazight. This, we hypothesise, may end up like the failed policy of Arabisation where too much interference by monolingual politicians has led to a cultural dead-end. Moreover, political sloganeering is still the name of the game, and thus, too limited to solve real educational issues on the ground.

Planning national and foreign languages

Officially, foreign languages have no real social place despite all the speeches by politicians. Thus, the law on Arabic states clearly that: "... use *may be made* of a foreign language and as *complementary support*" (Art. 22). Primacy of classical Arabic is systematically underlined as if there was an alternative to such a situation. Ambivalence is thus a recurrent characteristic of political narratives. Arabic (classical/school or modern standard) was established immediately after independence as the official language in the 1963 and 1976 (and subsequent) Constitutions. Berber remained outside the system for political reasons. The Algerian dialect, the vernacular language, exists in different varieties in the language market, which itself comes from the more generic Maghrebi Arabic (Elimam 1997) that is shared with countries such as Morocco, Tunisia, Mauritania, Senegal, Western Sahara, and Niger. Thus, to speak about status planning, one has to draw a typology of juridical statuses that are likely to apply to the Algerian context between joint official languages, promoted, or partner languages. This is the case for French and English whereby English is being given priority over French for partisan considerations. In the case of French, the allocation or reallocation of a status has responded more to political intervention than to its real functions within society. In social terms, inconsistency of views continued when a fringe of the population devalued Algerian Arabic and Tamazight, i.e., their own mother tongues, to the point to report school Arabic as the first language instead of their mother tongues that are the actual first language. On the other front, Algeria had to wait until 2002 and 2016 to see Berber be given its long overdue status of national and official language of Algeria.

Berber and its varieties (vernacular dialects) have been ostracised for decades by highly centralised bureaucratic administrations, despite pre-independence negotiations between politicians originating from the two ethnic groups, Arabs and Berbers. This policy has been followed along with the reduction of the scope and importance of the French language that was systematically rejected as the language of the coloniser. Worse still, in the 1990s, the Ministry of National Education has, despite the wish to develop foreign languages, decided to limit the list of foreign languages to be taught to only the most prestigious French and English. This turned out to be a red flag as German, Spanish, and Italian became optional subjects along with drawing and music in secondary schools. This decision affected their teaching at the university level. The unfortunate outcome is that the last three languages continued to be taught, accepting the utter aberration that would-be BA students have had no secondary school background in their chosen language. Thus the BA degree became a two-tier academic course depending on the choice to study either English/French or German/Spanish/Italian.

The policies of defrancisation

Here also, ideology is at the forefront in making decisions to fight against the French language at school and university levels, despite the fact that, "in reality, French is the lingua franca of Algeria" (The Permanent Committee on Geographical Names 2003: 2). This statement comes as a complete contradiction to what decades of quasi-blind policies towards coexisting languages reveal. Regardless of the fact that French is the language of administration, school, and media, these policies have often used slogans instead of concrete and realistic measures to encourage and promote certain foreign languages in a more progressive way. Despite the presence of a majority of unbalanced French-Arabic (spoken and/or written) bilingualisms in favour of the latter language, inflexible plans to do away with French have been more like incantations hoping its status will change overnight after 132 years of inculcation in favour of this "war booty" as described by the Algerian writer, Kateb Yacine. Nevertheless, "the cultural development by negation put forward by the proponents of Arabisation as a 'rebirth' can hardly be explained" (Miliani 2003: 57). Indeed, and contrary to pure common sense, language planning has been carried through decrees and laws that have had recourse to coercive sanctions (e.g., the 1991 Law on Arabisation). The sanctions have been highly criticised by the population not recognising this linguistic dictatorship that was bound to generate opposition and resistance from wide swathes of the population. We hypothesise that the younger generations have suffered from language schizophrenia because of the exclusion of their mother tongues from school. A number of sociolinguists shared this view because the language situation is ambiguous, since: "it is tacitly admitted that French has not regressed in Algeria since the establishment of the policy of Arabization and its disappearance from the large media... one is struck by the quasi-presence in the communication of the young" (Mekkaoui 2002: 167).

The many policies of hidden eradication of French cannot always be explained logically. The sentiments of the proponents of this policy are a mixture of social, political, religious, and personal likes and dislikes that rarely hold against logical arguments. Indeed, "the French language appears, until now, as a historical legacy, difficult to internalize but also as a part of linguistic consciousness impossible to repress" (Sebaa 2002: 17). Here lies the dilemma of the country and the Algerian individual, inferring that any solution is nothing more than a biased and incomplete attempt to respond to real language problems.

English as the "language for development": myth and reality

Positing that English is an international language, a *lingua franca* or the language for development, is an absolute tautology in today's world.[6] In fact, when looking at the relationship between language and development, Appleby et al. (2002: 327–328) consider four different possible relationships:

- Language *in* development, where English plays and will continue to play a significant role in socioeconomic development;
- Language *as* development, i.e., English taught as an end in itself;

- Language *for* development, as a tool for other domains of development; and finally
- Language *of* development, or the discourses that construct the ways in which development happens.

However, what is worrying about the dominant discourse of English *for* development in Algeria is that English-only measures or policies will not yield positive results in the long-term for any given world language. Miliani (2001: 22) posits that:

> This argument, to explain some educational choices, seems rather like an alibi when one knows that it needs more than a simple incantation to introduce technology and develop a scientific mentality with the sole presence of the English language.

What is regrettable is that politicians as well as lay people seem to lean towards a policy that accommodates only English, thus discarding the existing languages that have different functions, not least that of identity. It is true that worldwide English has gained more than any other international language in scope, visibility, usefulness, prestige, and interest. In Algeria, putting aside the important role English has in education, it is also important to gauge its importance by the tuition fees for private language schools which may amount to thousands, thus making of English a language of the well-off. According to Bruthiaux (2002: 290–291):

> In most markets, the consumers of English language education are the relatively well-off, already far beyond the stage of mere survival. To the extent that the severely poor are aware of it at all, the global spread of English is a sideshow compared with the issue of basic economic development and poverty reduction... In practice, far less English is used in most cultures than many observers in the rich English-speaking world imagine.

In light of the above, it is important then to raise the issue of English as a language for development within the Algerian context. Here, it is important to note that many English-speaking countries are not developed, even though English has undoubtedly helped many of these countries achieve some development. This is why culture cannot be separated from the overall growth of countries. Nevertheless, English as the language of development has been the motto for a certain category of Algerians who associate French with either colonialism or past history. This feeling is strongly ingrained in people, as even the youngest generations that have not experienced this terrible ordeal express their rejection of French because of stereotyped negative views. Besides, it is also necessary to consider the important Islamic political groups that fight everything that is French and who are obsessed with authenticity (*sic*) as central to the identity of Algerians. The consequence of this obsession is that, "education will always suffer from a primary monolithism of the decision-makers, which is the expression of the fear of the alien, the other..." (Miliani 1996: 9). One example of this is all the attacks against the former Minister of National Education who is systematically accused of being Francophile, simply because she wishes to change the system that has become obsolete.

The failed 1993 introduction of English at primary level

Unstable intentions behind the reforms undertaken in the process of nation-building have characterised the political sphere for the past 5 decades since independence. Modern Standard Arabic has had the lion's share, and policies like the domination of one language and imposition through schooling are quintessential. Thus, the introduction of English in primary schools in 1993, announced in 1990, has generated opposed views: either partisan enthusiasm from Islamists (do away with French) or measured doubt from the other extreme of the spectrum embodied by more scientific and less ideological people. In fact, the first group aimed at that as a continuation of the struggle against French, rebuffing very objective considerations. The introduction of English in the fourth grade of primary school was not a social demand though English is a fantasised and popular language among the young generation.

Big money was put in the hands of the administration to invest in the project, without the consent of the population. The reform started hastily, but faded away without an official evaluation of what did not work. The real debate was between the practical application of language for knowledge/research and language as a medium of instruction. The gap between the pedagogical development (that is, the use of Arabic as a medium of instruction) and its actual scientific limits, expressed in other languages, French in particular, has continued to grow. Drying out the paths to the French language has not been replaced by substantial responses.

Where do we go from here?

Can one predict the future of languages in contact when politics and partisanship lead the way to tomorrow's Algeria? There could be a debate only if democracy is promoted and the entrenched one-party system disappears, which is a long way if ever from the state of affairs today. However, things seem to be less entangled than they were before Berber was awarded the status of official language by the former President of the Republic. Today, there are two mother tongues, Tamazight and Algerian Arabic that try to avoid clashing with the main official language, namely, Modern Standard Arabic. Modern Standard Arabic was selected as the main medium of instruction even if it is not the language of communication. Co-existing with them and in a live-or-die battle, are French and English. French is currently dominant, but in the next 20 years English will probably overtake it.[7] As for the Maghrebi Arabic, it will refer to a mythical past even if today's reality (language for communication) is contested by politicians with a known educational and political background. Besides, the policies towards foreign languages should be coherent in order to avoid creating an individual who behaves, "less as a citizen, is often critical about Westernization of the State, but develops an attraction-rejection relation towards these countries and their languages" (Miliani 2003: 70), but leading inevitably to students' semi-lingualism, i.e., their incompetence in either language. One can push this idea a bit further by suggesting that the hypothesis of a change towards destabilising Arabic monolinguism is not a null hypothesis. The country may become one with a couple of linguistic prostheses. Indeed, "there are currently no reliable surveys of the language repertoires of Algerian speakers, surveys which show the complexity of these repertoires, which describe how and what repertoires are established, at what stage, what relations develop between the different components of these directories" (Morsly 2005: 55). Everyday struggles show opposing groups or lobbies that want their political agenda to be applied. The language market seems to be the prisoner of an education system that has become a real battlefield of individual interests or groups with a very narrow-minded perspective and an international agenda. The dangers Algeria finds in her way to development are too many. Extremism is a reality expressed in the polity of the country, and independence through languages is not just an ideological slogan; citizens of all walks of life are adamant that the use of English and the rejection of French will open the doors to development.

Globally, people learn an additional foreign language for a variety of purposes that range from political, purely individual, or economic reasons. Decision-makers need to reconsider the language planning and policy of the country. Although language ideology will never cease to dominate the linguistic landscape, pragmatism needs to be advocated. The real question is not whether English or French should be the first foreign language in Algeria, but what the main drives are to teach X or Y language. Are we choosing a specific additional foreign language for global politics, international relations, or for diplomacy? Algeria's strategic position in Africa and proximity to Europe and the Middle East, certainly makes Arabic, French, and English necessary functional languages. Equally important is openness to South–East Asia and to Latin America which is also tied to the leadership role that countries in these regions play in preventing and managing conflicts. Hence, Mandarin, Malay, or Spanish could eventually be needed. Again, are we choosing a specific additional language because of economics, considering issues around international trade, and competitiveness on the global market? In such a case, we should consider the current and future markets for goods and services for Algeria as well as the economic imperatives in the next two or three decades, especially when under a pressing need for economic diversification. Will Algeria's major trade partners be in Francophone or Anglophone Africa, in Asia, or in North or Latin America? The following anecdote illustrates some of these complexities: The former Algerian Minister of Youth and Sports learned a hard lesson during a visit to the construction site of a stadium under the responsibility of a Chinese company. Showing his dissatisfaction with the delay in completion, after speaking in Modern Standard Arabic in a press conference and adding a brief remark in French, the minister addressed the Chinese manager in charge of the project in an intermediate English level maybe thinking to impress the whole audience. However, after listening diligently to the minister, the Chinese manager responded in perfect Modern Standard Arabic. Regardless of the assumptions made by both parties—the Algerian minister taking it for granted that the Chinese manager would speak English, and the Chinese manager believing the Algerian minister would use Modern Standard Arabic—this reveals the strategic vision of the Chinese. Knowing that Algeria is an important market for their goods and services, they learned Modern Standard Arabic, probably assuming that because it is the official language of the country, it would automatically be used by the minister. So, in a sense they learned the language of the target market in much the same way other Chinese sales persons learn Algerian Arabic in order to sell their goods in markets.

Finally, additional foreign languages can be learned for personal reasons (intrinsic motivation). However, the aggressive policies by the diplomatic representations (in particular the French) towards the marketing of their languages should not be underestimated. This phenomenon has undoubtedly triggered some interest in foreign language learning by the young fringes of the population.

No matter the reason for learning an additional foreign language or deciding to teach it, the benefits are numerous: economic, political, personal, and even cognitive. Such learning enhances the cognitive skills of children and opens their minds to new cultures, new worlds, new literatures, and histories, boosting their personal growth. Regardless, we should opt for an additive multilingualism and not for a subtractive one.

Notes

1 Modern Standard Arabic is a simplified form of classical Arabic and is currently used in education, media, and publications. It is considered a lingua franca in Arabic speaking countries.
2 Certain linguists have developed a critical view stating that: "the leaders have preferred to import the 'ready to consume' under the pretext of an 'Arabo-Muslim' label. This has resulted in a profound marginalisation of young and old individuals. This process refers to the notion of 'de-substantialisation of the individual'. In short, the individual has been gradually deprived of what his ancestors have patiently worked out over the centuries" (Elimam 2004: 15).
3 Berber and Tamazight are used interchangeably. Tamazight is a generic term used to encompass varieties of Berber: Kabyle, Tachawit, or Chaouia (Aurès Mountains), Tumzabt (M'zab oasis), Chenoua (northwest of Algeria), Tamahaq (in the south), Tagargrent (northern Sahara), Taznatit (Timimoun, Touat and southwest M'zab).

1 "We try to replace the mother tongue with another language, 'pure,' whose learning modalities would only be 'technical.' But in doing so, we put the instance 'subject' (I), in a situation of repression and, consequently, we stir up a natural mechanism (survival of the species?) of constancy" (Elimam 2004: 38) [Author's translation].

5 "We are moving—with what has just been decided (introduction of English in the fourth year of the Foundation School) and with the system (education) in place— towards a linguistic imbroglio, an exacerbation of social tensions, more acute identity crises, a loss of cohesion" insists Mr. Miliani who expresses his fear of a 'creolization and pidginisation of languages'" (Miliani quoted in the newspaper El Watan, October 5, 1993) [Authors' translation].

6 Total users in all countries, 2018: 1121,806,280 (as L1:378,250,540; as L2: 746,555,740). http://ethnologue.com/language/eng.

7 The very recent startling announcement in favour of English, by the current Minister of Higher Education and Scientific Research, does not spell good news to the French language.

References

Appleby, R., Copley, K., Sithirajvongsa, S., & Pennycook, A., 2002, Language in development constrained: Three contexts, *TESOL Quarterly*, 39(3), 323–346.

Bruthiaux, P., 2002, Hold your courses: Language education, language choice, and economic development, *TESOL Quarterly*, 39(3), 323–346.

Chachou, I., 2013, *La Situation sociolinguistique de l'Algérie* [The sociolinguistic situation of Algeria], L'Harmattan, Paris.

Dourari, A., 1997, *Malaises linguistiques et identitaires en Algérie* [Linguistic and identity discomfort in Algeria], *Anadi, Revue d'Etudes Amazighes,* (2), 17–41.

Elimam, A., 1997, *Le Maghribi, langue trois fois miilénaire* [Maghribi, A three thousand year old language], ANEP, Algiers.

Elimam, A., 2004, *Langues maternelles et citoyenneté en Algérie* [Mother tongues and citizenship in Algeria], Dar El Gharb, Oran.

Lippi-Green, R., 1997, *English with an Accent: Language, Ideology, and Discrimination in the United States*, Routledge, London.

Mekkaoui, F.Z., 2002, *Les stratégies discussives des étudiants et l'utilisation du français,* [Students' discussive strategies and the use of French], *Insaniyat,* 17–18, 167–186.

Messekher, H., 2015, A linguistic landscape analysis of the sociopolitical demonstrations of Algiers: A politicized landscape, in S. Bensaid & R. Rubdy (eds.), *Conflict, exclusion and dissent in the linguistic landscape*, pp. 260–279.

Miliani, M., 1996, The circulation of European educational theories and practices: The Algerian case, *Mediterranean Journal of Educational Studies*, 1(1), 1–12.

Miliani, M., 2001, Teaching English in a multilingual context: The Algerian case, *Mediterranean Journal of Educational Studies*, 6(1), 13–29.

Miliani, M., 2003, Arabization in higher education in Algeria: Linguistic centralism vs. democratization, *International Journal of Contemporary Sociology*, 40(1), 55–74.

Morsly, D., 2005, Madame, est-ce qu'on peut avoir deux langues maternelles? [Madam, can we have two mother tongues?], in M. Rispail (dir.), *Langues maternelles: Contacts, variations et enseignement, Le cas de la langue Amazighe* [Mother tongues: Contacts, variations and teaching, the case of the Amazigh language], pp. 49–62, L'Harmattan, Paris.

Permanent Committee on Geographical Names, 2003, *ALGERIA Language & Toponymy: How Politically Driven Language Policies have Impeded Toponymic Progress.* Crown Copyright.

Rouadjia, A., 1991, *Les frères et la mosquée: Enquête sur le mouvement Islamiste en Algérie* [The brothers and the mosque: Investigation of the Islamist movement in Algeria], Bouchène, Algiers.

Sebaa, R., 2002, *L'Algérie et la langue française: L'altérité partagée* [Algeria and the French language: Shared otherness], Editions Dar El Gharb, Oran.

Taleb Ibrahimi, K., 1995, *Les algériens et leur(s) langue(s), Eléments pour une approche sociolinguistique de la société algérienne* [Algerians and their language(s), elements for a sociolinguistic approach of the Algerian society], Dar El Hikma, Algiers.

Woolard, K.A., 1998, Introduction: Language ideology as a field of inquiry, in B. B. Schieffelin, K. A. Woolard, & P. V. Kroskrity (eds.), *Language Ideologies* (pp. 3–47), Oxford University Press, New York.

PART II
International relations

12

ALGERIA IN THE MEDITERRANEAN

Ahmed Mahiou

Algeria is the largest African country by land area, and its location and size together make it one of the most important countries bordering the Mediterranean. It has a central place in the western part of the Mediterranean with a coastline of about 1,200 km and faces Europe, its main partner. This is firstly, at the economic level, as a destination for most of its oil and gas exports and conversely, as a source for the bulk of its imported equipment and consumer goods, and secondly, at the political level, to define its position in stabilising this critical and dangerously turbulent region.

Given its geographical position, Algeria finds itself essentially involved in inter-Mediterranean relations, particularly with Europe, as it was under Roman domination for nearly 500 hundred years, from −40 BC to 430 AD, then under the Vandals for 1 century (430–533), and finally under the French for over a century (1830–1962).

During the French colonial era, Algeria was temporarily integrated in the European Economic Community between 1957 and 1962 as a French department. After independence, a de facto affiliation continued until the first agreement of April 26, 1976, which formalised the association status. This was replaced by that of April 22, 2002, thus defining bilateral relations that also fall within the framework of Euro-Mediterranean relations.

These result from different accords regarding protection or cooperation in the Mediterranean region, above all from the Barcelona Declaration of November 28, 1995, then from the new accord signed in Paris on July 13, 2008, which launched the Union for the Mediterranean, though this Union is currently dormant due to conflict in the Mediterranean basin.

Algeria is also included in a regional network related to the League of Arab States, the Arab Maghreb Union, and the African Union (Mahiou 1982a: 127–145), regional relations that obviously affect Algeria's Mediterranean policy.

Moreover, important bilateral relations with its neighbouring countries, especially France and Morocco, are always highly complex

Therefore, this contribution is about better understanding the role of Algeria in the Mediterranean, attempting to highlight its most important aspects. The following background locates the position of the country to establish if there is a Mediterranean policy in Algeria in its relations both with Europe and in more general international relations.

Algeria's position in the Mediterranean

With an area of 2.4 million square kilometres, that is nearly five times the size of France and eight times that of Italy, Algeria is the largest of all Mediterranean countries and, indeed, in Africa since Sudan split. However, the extent this territorial area should be put into perspective as 80% of it lies in the Sahara, which limits agricultural self-sufficiency and leads to the country's food dependency, as will be shown in this paper.

With a population of over 42 million inhabitants, Algeria quadrupled its population between independence in 1962 and 2018. After a slowdown in which population growth appeared to have entered a demographic transition phase, it has increased again. This poses new issues especially as over half of the population is under 20, raising serious concerns around education, employment, and the need to limit social unrest and illegal immigration.

The overall Gross Domestic Product is about $100 billion, far lower than that of developed Mediterranean countries (France $2,200, Italy $1,750, Spain $1,000), but ranking third behind Turkey ($400) and Israel ($200). The annual GDP per capita is $4,000; this places Algeria in a medium position, far behind European countries (France $35,800, Italy $30,000, Spain $25,000), but fourth among other countries of the southern and eastern Mediterranean, with Israel $31,800, Turkey $2,000, and Libya $5,500. The number of Algerians living below the poverty threshold of less than $2 per day varies from simple to double according to information sources; but according to the World Bank about 6% of the population falls in this category, that is about 2,600,000 people.

The main resources are hydrocarbons (oil and gas with a production of 150 million tons, half of which is gas); annual export brings in about $50 billion with considerable fluctuations depending on the price of a barrel of oil, but the resultant $100 billion dollars in foreign reserves provides some financial comfort to the country. Nevertheless, the size of these revenues should not conceal the excessive imbalance this represents for the economy: profits from hydrocarbons constitute 97% of exports and will decline in future decades (estimated at about 10 years for oil and about 40 years for gas).[1] Such dependency on a non-renewable resource has grave implications for the country's future. Tourism, which could be a lucrative sector considering the country's potential, is blocked because Algeria has delayed investing in this field, and security concerns discourage tourists. Algeria was a major producer and exporter of wine before independence (15 million hl);

but after the closure of European, particularly French, markets and the uprooting of vines during the 1970s (reduced from more than 350,000 ha to less than 50,000), it reduced to less than 500,000 hl today. Foreign direct investments remain modest at 1.5–2 billion compared to Egypt (11–12 billion in normal periods) or even Morocco (2.5–3 billion) and, moreover, they focus on hydrocarbons.

At the industrial level, Algeria missed the opportunity to become an emerging economy (Ahmed 2004). After independence in 1962, Algeria was in almost the same position as South Korea, and both countries benefitted from international economic aid. At the beginning of the 1960s, Korea still employed nearly 80% of its active population in agriculture, representing three quarters of its national revenue; in 1962, it inaugurated the first of its five-yearly development plans. Today, it draws only 10% of its GDP from agriculture and has become the world's eighth industrial economy, holding the top rank in certain fields like electronic consumer goods, steel industry, automotive, and naval construction. Algeria indeed launched plans during the 1960s and 1970s (Benachenhou 1980), particularly with its strategy of industrialising industries (Destanne de Bernis 1971; Bouyacoub 2001). However, this remains in its infancy with only a few assembling industries, obliging it to import large quantities of products from abroad, including from South Korea, particularly cars and electronic equipment.

In spite of its large surface area as indicated above, water shortage in Algeria is such that it has less than 10 million cultivable hectares, barely 5% of its area. This includes 1.5 million hectares of land fit for intensive production, located on the coast and threatened by urbanisation in the north and desertification in the south. In comparison, France has more than half of its area in cultivable lands (30 million out of 55 million hectares) and Italy has 40% (12 million hectares). In addition, low productivity explains Algeria's dependence on imported food, especially grains,[2] milk, sugar, and corn, with the annual food import bill running into billions of dollars. To compensate for the water shortage and meet the needs of major cities, there has been considerable investment in seawater desalination and projects are planned to use the Sahara's enormous subsoil resources (like those in Libya) knowing that they are not renewable since it is about two subsoil water resources coming from the Albian table.[3]

A medium military power at the international level with an army of around 280,000 men, Algeria takes second place in Africa behind Egypt, with 400,000 men and ahead of Morocco, with 200,000. Russia sells it most of its weapons; however, since rapprochement with North Atlantic Treaty Organisation (NATO), equipment procurement took place from France (combat helicopters), Germany (frigates), and the USA (night combat weapons). The military budget is around $10 billion as per the 2018 budget. The army has played an important role since the country's independence, and its influence in political life is maintained due (Benchikh 2003; Nemar 2010), on the one hand, to the Islamist terrorism it faced, particularly during, the "black decade" between 1990 and 2000[4] and border threats due to armed conflicts in Libya and Mali.

Without being a strategic crossroad, Algeria is at the heart of the Europe/Africa axis, making it the only Mediterranean country with neighbours in ten other countries (seven in Africa, including Western Sahara, and three in Europe). Such proximity facilitates economic exchanges, especially for the export of hydrocarbons (it supplies 25% of European consumption, thus ranking second after Russia) and the import of equipment and consumer goods.

Algeria's Mediterranean policy

The day after its independence, Algeria had not yet developed a Mediterranean policy, apart from the broad sentiment that the Mediterranean belonged to Mediterraneans and that warships belonging to non-neighbouring countries (especially those of the USA and of the Soviet Union) should withdraw from the region (Grimaud 1989).[5]

Algeria positioned itself from the outset towards two other regions, the Arab world and Africa, which it considered to be priorities. Moreover, Algeria became the spokesman for third-world demands, militating within the non-aligned group which became an important player in the international arena. During that period, Mediterranean relations were perceived as a network of bilateral relations. This also applied to relations with the two Maghreb neighbours (Morocco and Tunisia) and with France.

Algerian-French relations were complicated and sometimes conflicting; they constantly need tuning to find compromises between Algeria's wish to control its economic development through nationalisation that would harm French interests, and the need for cooperation between both countries. Even during a seemingly normal period, tension is never far away, as shown by the continuing differences regarding memory and history, since colonial occupation and the war for independence easily result in divergences and arguments. From the Algerian perspective, France is blamed for retaining a neo-colonial attitude and not sufficiently engaging in direct investments, not improving conditions for the considerable Algerian community (the largest abroad, between 2 and 4 million people including an estimated 1.5 million with dual citizenship) (Meynier and Khalfoune 2012, 682),[6] and a restrictive visa policy. On the Algerian side, Algeria is blamed for restricting the use of French and distancing itself from French-speaking countries despite having been the second largest French-speaking country after France; discouraging investors with multiple legal and practical obstacles to business initiatives, and inadequate control of its borders to contain illegal immigration.

Regarding other international issues, Algeria considered that cooperation in the Mediterranean was blocked by the Arab-Israeli conflict and more precisely the Palestinian issue; it feared that an overall Mediterranean project had become a way to impose the presence of Israel on Arab states in diplomatic meetings and the region's cooperative bodies. However, Algeria does not reject any form of cooperation and in particular has participated in the 5 + 5 dialogue on migration in the Western Mediterranean, officially launched in the Rome Declaration of October 10, 1990 (Algeria, Libya, Morocco, Mauritania, Tunisia, Spain, France, Italy, Malta, and Portugal). After some hesitation, Algeria decided to actively engage in this dialogue by participating in the Tunis summit (December 5–6, 2003) and hosting several ministerial conferences. It considers this political dialogue could contribute to a better approach of the European Union's Mediterranean policy regarding Algeria.

As previously indicated, Algeria maintained that the Mediterranean belonged to Mediterraneans, and in particular militated for the departure of foreign fleets from the region, as expressed in January 1970 in a statement by the head of state. During the third conference of the United Nations on the Law of the Sea, Algeria defended the concept of a semi-locked sea that applies to certain maritime spaces in order to better protect the interests of neighbours and restrict military activities of non-neighbours. In the same vein, it proposed a conference on the Mediterranean on July 1972, but the attempt was short-lived, failing to agree on participants. These could not include all neighbours as Israel was then not recognised by any Arab State; it could not limit itself to non-aligned nations as that excluded too many participants; it could have included those that did not belong to a military bloc—which is a more relevant criterion—but that excluded the countries of southern Europe, members of NATO. Finally, failing an interstate conference in 1982, Algeria instead hosted a meeting of progressive parties of the region, during which it adopted a document calling for the dismantling of foreign bases in neighbouring countries and for the retreat of foreign fleets from the region.

Algeria has always maintained its interests as a neighbour in a semi-locked sea by referring to equitable principles and special circumstances in terms of maritime space management and delineation during the conference on the Law of the Sea. Its main concern was to avoid being unduly disadvantaged during the demarcation of the Mediterranean's business areas, particularly the main Balearic Islands 300 km off the Algerian coast (Benchikh 1980: 284–297). The narrow constraints of the Mediterranean mean that there is no high sea and that the delimitation of spaces would mean setting the limits of exclusive economic zones and territorial waters, which assumes agreements between neighbouring countries as set forth in the Convention of December 10, 1982, on the Law of the Sea. At present, only one such accord has been signed by Algeria with Tunisia, ratified by the Algerian Parliament on January 9, 2013, and it still needs to discuss its maritime space with four other neighbours (Morocco, Spain, France, and Italy).

Finally, at the environmental level (Gacemi 2009: 687–701), Algeria has not taken all the necessary measures to suppress or limit sea-polluting discharges such as waste water, industrial waste, degassing, and pesticides. This is despite having ratified the Barcelona Convention for the protection of the Mediterranean

Sea on February 16, 1976, and whilst expressing its concern over maritime pollution. Algeria has considerable impact on the Mediterranean:

- It has 1,280 km of coastline;
- 95% of its international trade is by sea;
- 11 commercial ports including three for hydrocarbons export;
- A fleet of 12,600 leisure ships;
- A merchant fleet of 34 ships including 14 tankers for shipping oil products, liquefied gas, and chemicals;
- Hydrocarbons exports of 90 million tons/year by sea;
- 1,300 tankers reach the Algerian ports every year;
- And finally, a fishing fleet of about 3,500 small units.

Algeria and Europe

Algeria as always been interested in Europe in the broad sense and more particularly in the process of the 1973 Conference on Security and Cooperation in Europe. Subsequent to the launch of the conference, Algeria indicated that the security issues raised ignored the Mediterranean, and consequently led other Maghreb countries, as well as Egypt and Syria, in representing the interests of the southern shore in these issues. However, the idea of a conference on security and cooperation in the Mediterranean only was advanced in 1990 at the initiative of Spain and Italy; this translated into an inter-parliamentary conference in June 1992, and Algeria remained because the Palestinian issue and Israel's policy in the occupied Arab territories still constituted difficult obstacles. Algeria therefore privileged relations with Europe in the European Community (EC) and European Union over the Barcelona Process and the Union for the Mediterranean.

Algeria and the EC

Algeria has had special relations with the European Community compared to other countries of the Mediterranean, as it was part of a French department from 1957 to 1962. In fact, the Rome Treaty that attaches it to Europe was signed in 1957, which was paradoxically the year when the liberation struggle for independence from France and therefore from Europe intensified. After its independence, Algeria did not opt to sever links with France because its economy was too closely related to that of the northern shore of the Mediterranean (France in particular), for both imports and exports. It also continued to be part of the EC in implementing certain regulations and tacitly benefiting from advantages acquired through its former membership, although it had not yet concluded an association agreement. Thus, there was an ambiguous legal situation that lasted until the European Economic Community (EEC)-Algeria Agreement on April 26, 1976 (Tavernier 1972: 1; Mahiou 1982b: 22) which implemented an almost identical scheme to those of the EEC. The 1976 Agreement was replaced on April 22, 2002. That this new agreement took longer to conclude compared to agreements signed by other Mediterranean partners is partly explained by Algeria's domestic concerns, Islamist terrorist violence during the 1990s, but above all by divergences in terms of democracy and human rights, freedom of movement, as well as commercial considerations such as energy, agricultural products, and investment finance.

These divergent points appeared in other ways during the Barcelona Conference in 1995. Algeria was one of the southern shore countries most criticised in the Barcelona process, with the following concerns:

• The political aspect (democracy and human rights) leading to interference in the government's internal affairs;
• The economic aspect was inadequate because the European Union did not engage as it had with countries in eastern Europe, highlighting the fact that the EU received more benefit each year from its exchanges with all Mediterranean countries than the aid it granted them over 5 years;
• The humanitarian aspect was objected to as the EU not only limits freedom of movement, but also requests southern countries to police illegal immigration.

Although Algeria adopted certain obligations that engage it in specific fields, it considers that these issues still remain open for debate within the framework of the Union for the Mediterranean (UfM) and formed the basis of its hesitation to participate in the 2008 Paris Summit.

Algeria and the Union for the Mediterranean

The UfM was founded during the Paris Summit on July 13, 2008, gathering 43 states adjacent to the Mediterranean, or members of the EU, under French-Egyptian co-chairmanship. The UFM does not exactly match the initial project of President Sarkozy who wanted to limit it to Mediterranean neighbours; it was amended to include all EU countries due to objections from other EU members, particularly Germany. The name itself changed to add the Barcelona Process to the UFM and thus demonstrate that the new institution is a continuation of the previous organisation.

Although the content of the new institution remains undefined, it currently concentrates on certain projects: the depollution of the Mediterranean, maritime and land ways, civil defence in response to natural disasters, a Euro-Mediterranean university, and solar energy. If Algeria deems the retained projects interesting, it then requests clarification of the following points:

• Project financing, since Europe undertook no commitment, referring instead to the policy of each state and in the hope of petrodollars investment, especially from Gulf states;
• The role of the UFM in the Middle East peace process, expressing the hope that Europe should not limit itself to including only Israel in such Union

without attempting to find a solution to the Palestinian issue. The Paris Summit has offered an opportunity to the Syrian and Lebanese presidents to normalise their diplomatic relations; but the Israeli and Palestinian presidents announced no new element in the lengthy peace process;

- The institutional aspect still remains ambiguous; this includes issues such as the organogram, headquarters, and designation of the Union's Secretary General. Algeria attaches paramount importance to this aspect and indicated that this had been forgotten by the project's initiator, President Sarkozy. Indeed, President Sarkozy privileged Egypt to co-chair the UFM and indicated that the organisation's headquarters could be in Tunis and that the Secretary General could be Moroccan. During the ministerial meeting in Marseille in November 2008, a consensus was reached that the UFM's headquarters would be in Barcelona, a northern country; that the Secretariat General would be from a southern country, but with the assistance of five deputies, three Europeans and two from the south, including one from Israel and another from Palestine; and finally, that the Arab League become a full member of the UFM. However, Algeria expressed reservations on such consensus, particularly on the creation of five deputies for non-compliance, which was decided during the Paris Summit.

Regardless, Algeria knows that it is not only closely related to Europe, but is largely dependent on it for its foreign exchange, whereas, inversely, European dependence on Algeria is minor (1% of its exchanges). Even in the sensitive field of hydrocarbons, and more precisely gas, European imports (40–50 billion m^3) currently represent less than 10% of the total, Russia being the first supplier (more than 160 billion m^3). Algeria can therefore exercise pressure in this field only if it has the cooperation of the Organisation of Petroleum Exporting Countries and Russia. Another more recent problem with international migration will be covered below.

Algeria and the Mediterranean

Non-alignment is still the major axis of Algeria's international policy, and this explains its embarrassment when the network of alliances with other states, particularly the various regional organisations to which it belongs, interfere with its Mediterranean policy.

Algeria and the Maghreb

The Maghreb countries—especially those of the central Maghreb (Algeria, Morocco, and Tunisia)—have many similarities: a common history, similar population, the same languages (Arabic and Berber), and colonial occupation which left a common legal administrative legacy and significant influence of the French language in education and daily life, although this has declined considerably with the policy of Arabisation. All these elements are unifying factors in the region, and yet the unity of the Maghreb has broken down.

The first difficulty appears to be that boundaries were not fixed for the Saharan regions. This led to land claims in the aftermath of Algeria's independence, particularly from Morocco, which demanded the annexation of a significant portion of Algerian territory. This even led to the brief Sand War in 1963 as well as continuing tension and mistrust, despite the conclusion of a border agreement dated July 15, 1972.[7]

The second difficulty was that of the political neighbourhood, especially at a time when the political options of the Maghreb countries were very divergent and where, during the 1970s, the socialist option of Algeria worried its neighbours. The National Charter of 1976[8] specified a Maghreb of the peoples, as opposed to the Maghreb of the states which was the preference until then, considering that there would be regional integration only when the actors in charge of such a project effectively emanate from their respective peoples. This was opposed by both the revolutionary regimes that had chosen socialist development, with the support of the communist countries, and the moderate or conservative regimes that had preferred a liberal choice with the support of the Western countries.

The third difficulty is the leadership conflict between Algeria and Morocco focused on Western Sahara, which has blocked the process of a union started in 1989. The Marrakesh Agreement that founded the Arab Maghreb Union had been applied for only a few years, as the Algerian-Moroccan disagreement over Western Sahara resurfaced in 1996, and the process of a union has been frozen ever since. It is true that every member of the Arab-Moroccan Union hopes to revive the regional construction process and it has the support of Europe, which encourages integration in this region in order to have a larger unified market. But in practice, no credible initiative has been launched,[9] and, as things stand, there is no indication of how or when the integration process could be restarted.

Algeria and the Arab World

The League of Arab States was similarly stymied when Algeria tried to encourage reform to promote and deepen cooperation or integration between members (Mahiou 2011). The League is primarily a political institution designed to bring Arab countries closer or facilitate their path to independence, as most were still under colonial rule. Thus, Algeria benefited from important diplomatic and financial assistance during its war of national liberation (1954–962). In return, and after independence, it tried to contribute to a better functioning of the institution, in particular by suggesting or supporting institutional reforms likely to make the actions of the League more effective.

Drawing inspiration from the United Nations, Algeria has established various bodies to cover economic, social, cultural, and technical cooperation in the Arab world. While the political action of the League has encountered tension or blockages, the organisations attached to it have functioned fairly regularly without encountering any major difficulties. In many respects, Arab states have tried to avoid shifting their political disagreements to more technical forums, thus enabling them to establish and/or strengthen links between members.

The Arab world has devoted much time to a project of economic integration. In August 1964, the first Arab common market initiative was launched which faced serious obstacles. The initiative was relaunched after the Amman Economic Summit in 1980 and the adoption of resolutions on the Charter for Arab Economic Action, the Arab Economic Action Strategy, and the Arab Development Contract, respectively. It was not until the Cairo Convention of February 19, 1997, that the Great Arab Free Trade Area was finally created and laid the foundation for this regional economic unit involving all Arab countries. Algeria continues to have doubts about its implementation because of the weakness of economic exchanges between Arab countries; these represent barely 10% of their international trade,[10] and as long as such a strong extraversion continues to prevail, the interest of a common market is hardly obvious and the chances of an economic union are even more random, including at the subregional level.[11]

Algeria and Africa

Algeria's relations with Africa are based on anti-colonial solidarity, aid to liberation movements, and bilateral or multilateral economic aid, especially when the price of oil rises. Algeria has been heavily engaged in providing financial assistance to south Saharan countries by acting within the United Nations and various international economic organisations. This includes advocating for a new international economic order to facilitate the development of Third World countries and to introduce more equity in international economic relations.

Algeria's support for the unity of the continent is evident in symbolic, but concrete actions, launching the road to African unity in the 1970s that it now wishes to transform into a highway towards West Africa, and supporting the ambitious project of a trans-Saharan gas pipeline connecting West Africa to the Mediterranean coast to supply Europe. It maintains a comprehensive diplomatic network in Africa in order to influence the foreign policy of the members of the Organization of African Unity, which has become the African Union.

Algeria and NATO

In 2000, Algeria accepted the offer to join NATO. There were two reasons for this delay in joining this military alliance which plays an important role in the Mediterranean: on the one hand, NATO supported France during the liberation struggle; on the other hand, Algeria was one of the leaders of the Non-Aligned Movement whose policy is to avoid the clash between East and West.

Thus, it did not start to establish contacts with NATO until the day after the collapse of the communist bloc. Overtures were at first timid, but became more committed once Algeria was seriously affected by Islamist terrorism. Since the 2000s, Algeria has participated in civil and military meetings with NATO and occasionally in joint military exercises in the Mediterranean, as did her two Maghreb neighbours, Morocco and Tunisia. On the other hand, Algeria remains firm on two principles regarding the use of its armed forces:

- It opposes any deployment of foreign forces or any military base on its territory;
- It refuses any engagement of its armed forces outside the national territory.

There are, however, three exceptions: first, there was support for the Arab countries (specifically Egypt) in their clashes with Israel, especially during the 3rd Arab-Israeli War of 1967 (commonly known as the Six Day War), and the 4th Arab-Israeli War of 1973 (known as the Yom Kippur War). These two wars are directly related to the Palestinian issue and the defence agreement of the League of Arab States.

Secondly, the direct or indirect aid given to the five countries of the Sahel in their clashes with Islamist terrorism. According to a declaration by the Algerian Prime Minister in November 2017, more than $100 million was mobilised for this purpose. In addition, Algeria has joined forces with the Sahel countries to coordinate security efforts, particularly in the fight against terrorism and organised crime. To this end, it hosts a Joint Operational Staff Committee headquartered in Tamanrasset (southern Algeria) and an intelligence-sharing mechanism, the Fusion and Liaison Unit whose headquarters are in Algiers.

Finally, aid was given to France to facilitate its armed interventions in the Sahel. Indeed, Algeria was already involved in the multilateral strategy of securing the western Mediterranean because of its participation in the 5 + 5 group. Established in 1990 after a meeting of foreign ministers held in Rome, this group aims to initiate a process of regional cooperation between five countries of the north coast (Italy, France, Spain, Portugal, and Malta) and the five countries of the Arab Maghreb Union (Algeria, Libya, Morocco, Mauritania, and Mauritania) in the south. Inevitably, as terrorism escalates, cooperation has expanded to include security aspects, including military cooperation, especially during regular meetings of defence ministers (Benantar 2013: 57–75; Henry 2013: 39–56).

For many observers, the French fight against terrorism in the Sahel and particularly Wolverine and Barkhane operations would not have been successful without the logistical support of the Algerian army, whose security skills are widely recognised. This includes exchange of information, overflight of the territory by military aircrafts, and, apparently, fuelling facilities. However, Algiers refuses to participate in the G5 Sahel force for two reasons: legally, the constitution prohibits the engagement of military forces outside the national territory[12]; politically, the decision to create this force is a French initiative with which Algeria has not been associated; and the presence of American advisers is unacceptable.

Algeria and international migration

Since 2000, the phenomenon of international migration has taken on an unforeseen and worrying dimension in the Mediterranean basin, which now attracts the various refugees (political, economic, environmental) who are trying to reach Europe. After being a predominantly transit area, Algeria is now a destination for immigrants, especially African nationals from south of the Sahara as well as those of the Middle East (in particular Syrians, since the destabilisation of their country) and also of illegal migration of their own nationals. The management of sub-Saharan migrants poses problems in its international relations with Europe and its Maghreb neighbours, and at the national level, dealing with the acceptance of immigrants by respecting international commitments.

Europe has gradually imposed on the countries of the Mediterranean south coast a number of obligations previously announced at the Barcelona Conference of 1995. These were reaffirmed by the agreement on the UFM in 2008 and, prior to that, in the 2002 Association Agreement, with regard to Algeria.

Firstly, south countries should accept the commitment to readmit those nationals who have entered European territory irregularly. This concession does not result from the Association Agreement, but was obtained in 2017 in an Algerian-European compromise, whereby the two parties agreed on an exchange at an appropriate level for readmission in parallel with an exchange on visa facilitation. However, the debate is not closed, because the European Union accuses Algeria of accepting only about a quarter of the expelled migrants while it claims major difficulties in identifying persons without identity cards, and the issuance of new identity documents for expellees.[13]

Secondly, they should work together to prevent or reduce the flow of illegal migrants, whether from the Maghreb or elsewhere. To this end, the European Union has adopted a programme to set up platforms for drones in coastal islands and cities in western Mediterranean countries. Thus, the EU wanted to establish a base in the coastal town Ain Temouchent, in western Algeria, to fight migrant smuggling in the Mediterranean. Algeria, however, refused the request both as a matter of principle (the refusal to have bases on its territory) and for fear that these drones would be used as a surveillance system for spying.

In brief, Algeria's Mediterranean policy has certain basic principles which attempt to incorporate the following new regional developments:

- The persistence of Islamist terrorism, which has now spread from the Maghreb to the east and south of the Sahara, and into Europe, as shown by attacks on both Mediterranean countries (France and Spain), as well as the United Kingdom and Germany;
- The flow of illegal migration of both political and economic refugees has grown to such an extent that the initiatives of the Maghrebi and European initiatives to deal with them have been futile.

Notes

1 According to some estimates, Algeria could become an oil importer in the next 10 years if domestic consumption continues to increase at the current rate, and if new deposits are not discovered and exploited.

2 Depending on rainfall, the grain harvest can vary from one to two (20–40 million quintals), and in a drought year, the amount of grain imports exceeds $2 billion.

3 The Albian aquifer is the largest freshwater reserve in the world, straddling three countries: Algeria (70%), Libya (20%), and Tunisia (10%). It reportedly contains more than 50 trillion cubic meters of freshwater, resulting from the accumulation that has occurred during the wet periods that have followed each other over the past 1 million years. In April 2005, as part a Sahel and Sahara Observatory project, Algeria, Tunisia, and Libya implemented a mechanism for concerted management of their deep-water resources that are part of the aquifer, and entrusted this mission to Sahel and Sahara Observatory.

4 The black decade corresponds to the 1990–2000 period during which there were violent confrontations between security services and Islamist groups. These resulted in significant material destruction in addition to casualties of between 100,000 and 200,000.

5 The Algerian head of state said, "We are for the departure of fleets of all countries that are not part of the Mediterranean region. What we need is a real cooperation between the two sides of the Mediterranean, 'a lake of peace'" (quoted by N. Grimaud, "Algerian policy in the Mediterranean" in Awraq, *Estudios sobre el mundo árabe Contemporary Islam*, Vol X, 1989, p. 196).

6 The figures for foreigners are approximate, since French statistics do not provide for origin or nationality. Nevertheless, the French Statistics Institute, l'Institut national de la statistique et des études économiques, evaluated the number of Algerian immigrants and their children (at least one parent born in Algeria) to 1,713,000 in 2008. However, according to Gilbert Meynier, specialist in the history of Algeria and Tahar Khalfoune, the number of residents of Algerian origin in France in 2012 can be estimated at four million, including two million dual nationals (see Meynier and Khalfoune, in Bouchène et al., 2012).

7 The Convention was ratified quite quickly by Algeria (Ordinance No. 73–20 of May 17, 1973, JORA No. 15 of June 1973, pp. 546–550), while on the Moroccan side, the final ratification took place belatedly. To consolidate this cooperation, at the African Summit in Rabat, the parties concluded the long-awaited agreement on July 15, 1972, under which the parties agreed to jointly exploit the Gara-Djebilet iron deposit, in exchange for the abandonment by Morocco of its claims on Tindouf and Bechar which remain Algerian territory. This agreement, signed by the King, has still not been ratified by the Moroccan parliament since such ratification implies, directly or indirectly, the recognition by Morocco of the principle of "uti possidetis" and the respect for the borders inherited from the colonial era that had delayed Morocco's membership of the Organisation of African Unity.

8 The National Charter was discussed and adopted by referendum in 1976, setting out the project of building a socialist society; the text that has a constitutional value, was published in the *Official Journal of the People's Democratic Republic of Algeria* of July 30, 1976 (No. 61, pp. 714–777).

9 Former Tunisian President Moncef Marzouki, tried after his election, at the beginning of 2012, to revive the Union du Maghreb Arabe, but he had to give up because of the two main concerned countries' reluctance; Algeria and the Morocco.

10 In comparison, these exchanges reached 40% within the Association of Southeast Asian States and 70% within the European Union.

11 For example, in the Arab Maghreb Union three-quarters of the five members' economic exchanges are with the European Union, while trade between them is less than 5%.

12 The Constitution of 1989—which provisions were taken as such by the subsequent Constitutions of 1996 and 2008—indicates that "the National People's Army has for

permanent mission the safeguarding of independence and the defence of national sovereignty" (Article 24), and especially that "Algeria will not resort to war to undermine the legitimate sovereignty and freedom of other peoples" (Article 25). It is this last provision that is invoked by the Algerian authorities to refuse any operation outside the national territory.

13 Europe claims that more than half a million Algerians (530,000) obtained Schengen visas in 2015, while Algeria agreed to readmit only 24.2% of Algerians expelled from the EU, only 3,900 Algerians of the 16,065 expected to be expelled from the EU during the same period.

References

Ahmed, A.S. (2004). Asian Development: What Lessons for Arab Economies? Elements of development strategy: The case of Algeria, Paris, Editions ISPROM-PUBLISUD.

Benachenhou, A. (1980). *Planning and Development in Algeria (1962–1980)*, Algiers, Algeria, Commercial Printing House, 1980.

Benantar, A. (2013). Complexe de sécurité ouest-méditerranéen: externalisation et sécurisation de la migration, *L'Année du Maghreb IX*. https://journals.openedition.org/anneemaghreb/1843

Benchikh, M. (1980). 'The Mediterranean Sea, a Semi-enclosed Sea', Revue générale de droit international public, No. 1, pp. 284–297.

Benchikh, M. (2003). Algeria: A militarized political system, Paris, L'Harmattan.

Bouyacoub, A. (2001). 'Industrial policy: State of Play and Perspectives', in A. Mahiou and J.-R. Henry (dir.), *Where Is Algeria Going?* Paris, France, IREMAM, pp. 185–205.

Destanne de Bernis, G. (1971). 'Industrializing Industries and the Algerian Options', *Revue Tiers Monde*, pp. 545–563.

Gacemi, M. (2009). 'Coastal protection in Algeria between management and legislation. The case of Arzew's industrial division', *Law and Society*, 2009/3 (No. 73), pp. 687–701.

Grimaud, N. (1989). 'Algerian policy in the Mediterranean' in Awraq, Estudios sobre el mundo árabe Contemporary Islam, Vol X, 1989, p. 196.

Henry, J.R. (2013). Les nouveaux modes de gestion de la proximité euromaghrébine. *L'Année du Maghreb IX*. https://journals.openedition.org/anneemaghreb/1831

Mahiou, A. (1982a). 'Algeria and International Organizations', *French Directory of International Law*, pp. 127–145.

Mahiou, A. (1982b). 'Note on Algeria/EEC Relations. Ambiguities and paradoxes', in J. Touscoz (ed.), *The Enlarged European Community and the Mediterranean—What Cooperation?* Paris, France, PUF, p. 220.

Mahiou, A. (2011). 'The League of Arab States between Inertia and Change' in Mélanges en l'honneur du Doyen M. Benchikh, Paris, Pedone.

Meynier, G. and Khalfoune, T. (2012). *Après l'indépendance: les relation tumultueuses entre l'Algérie et la France, in Histoire de l'Algérie à la période coloniale, 1830–1962*. Edited by Jean-Pierre Peyroulou, Abderrahmane Bouchène, Ouanassa Siari Tengour, Sylvie Thénault. Paris: La Découverte.

Nemar, R. (2010). 'Beyond Barracks: The Role of the Army in Algeria', *The Notebooks of The Orient*, 2010/4, no. 100, pp. 19–32.

Tavernier, P. (1972). 'Legal Aspects of Economic Relations between the EEC and Algeria', Quarterly Review of European Law, 1972, p. 1 and A. Mahiou, 'Note on Algeria/EEC Relations. Ambiguities and paradoxes', in J. Touscoz (ed.), *The Enlarged European Community and the Mediterranean—What Cooperation?* Paris, France, PUF, 1982, p. 220.

13

ALGERIA–FRANCE

Permanent normalisation

Aomar Baghzouz

Relations between Algeria and France seem doomed to an endless search for true normalisation. Still prisoners of a conflictive past illustrated by persistent commemorative litigation, and a present in the hands of influential lobbies on both shores of the Mediterranean who are hostile to any reconciliation, these relations remain heavily symbolic despite close and multidimensional bilateral cooperation.

Indeed, 132 years of colonisation plus 57 years of post-independence coopera-tion (1962–2019) and migration that have punctuated this shared history have given rise to a complex relationship between Algeria and France. The Evian Accord was signed in 1962 to end hostilities and facilitate cooperation between the two countries, but these have since ground to a halt.

Since Bouteflika came to power in 1999, there have been four French heads of state in the Elysée Palace, but attempts at reconciliation made with Chirac, Sarkozy, and Hollande failed and the friendship treaty has not materialised. France has struggled to build a relationship with Algeria similar to the French-German reconciliation model. For its part, Algeria hesitates to embark on an in-depth partnership and face a France that remains nostalgic for its former colony.

The arrival of Emmanuel Macron in 2017 as a friend of Algeria at the Elysée Palace augurs well for a new era of cooperation and reconciliation. When he was a candidate in the presidential elections, Macron had declared in Algiers that French colonisation was "a crime against humanity" (Liberation 2017). This statement still resonates as an implicit promise to Algerians to work to overcome the past. However, after the initial jubilation, expectations still need to be met.

Even culture and the economy fail to elude the burden of history and current misunderstandings. In recent years, there has been renewed interest in Algeria by French investors despite an undesirable business climate. Nevertheless, in a field where Chinese competition is particularly tough, relations have overall declined.

Culture continues to be a means of drawing together, despite the persistence of mutual prejudices about Islam and the West.

What follows is a review of Algerian–French relations in President Bouteflika's era, from 1999 to 2019. This will investigate obstructions to a normalisation between Algeria and France, from Chirac to Macron, while questioning the prospects of a common future in the context of the economic and political crisis affecting Algeria, and multiple challenges in the Mediterranean.

Past identities and representations

Post-colonial Algerian–French relations are based on a common history that united them for over a century, both in cooperation and dispute. The paradox is that since Algerian independence in 1962, both countries remain closely inter-twined and yet constantly tense. Successive heads of state of different generations and different political opinions have not helped bilateral relations move from the conflict and pain of the colonial period and to glimpse the future in a spirit of lasting appeasement and mutually beneficial partnership. "An impossible break and an improbable normalization," summarises Frédéric Charillon (2016: 98), given a status quo maintained by both objective factors relating to the real events that marked the colonial period and subjective representations inherent in images and often distorted perceptions of history.

The wounds of 132 years of colonisation still seem alive after 57 years of independence and mutual attempts at reconciliation. Post-colonial France has certainly wanted a cooperative relationship with Algeria, but "the end of the roller coaster" (Daguzan 2015: 34) remains elusive. While independence has led to a strong interdependence between the two countries, opposing post-colonial national identities have been forged (Naylor 2001: 286). Gaullist France attempted a conversion from colonialism to Third Worldism, taking care not to appear to be pursuing neo-colonial objectives in North Africa. For its part, Algeria con-tinued for a few years with its revolutionary commitment, focusing on economic independence in the framework of a socialist policy. Independent Algeria has done everything to separate from French hegemony, even if during "the time of cooperation (1962–1980)," as Henry and Vatin claimed in their eponymous article (2012), it gave the impression of wanting to build an exceptional relation-ship with its former coloniser. More broadly, "France and Algeria have manufac-tured extroverted identities that have become increasingly incompatible with the evolution of international political, social, and economic realities" (Naylor 2001: 287). The ensuing clash of identities contributed to the emergence of numerous disputes that marked a turning point in bilateral relations. These include the Algerian wine crisis in 1967, the nationalisation of hydrocarbons and French oil interests in 1971, and the suspension of emigration to France in 1973.

According to Meynier (2016: 37), "An Algerian national feeling was built against the French settler" as evidenced by the inclusion in the national anthem of a whole couplet addressed to France.[1] This antipathy towards France continued after independence, an othering that justifies in hindsight certain official errors which "capitalize on the legacy of the revolution by deriving its legitimacy from it" (Vermeren 2016: 16) and by waving the spectre of *Hizb* França[2] (Party of France). At the same time, official French perceptions of Algeria remain coloured by a post-colonial bitterness mingled with nostalgic memories of French Algeria. In a general way, France is reluctant to accept its colonial past. "France decol-onized without self-decolonizing," remarked Cameroonian political scientist Achille Mbembe (2010).

Algiers-Paris: the tumultuous history of a couple

If each French president had "his own Algeria" as claimed by Nicole Grimaud (2008), Abdelaziz Bouteflika, who has been in power for two decades (from 1999 to 2019), keeps regular contact with France, as did most of his predecessors. The Algerian policy towards France has less to do with the longevity of its lead-ers than a foreign policy shaped by the hardships of the war of national liberation. In 1999, Bouteflika's mission was to reconcile Algeria with itself while boosting its image on the international scene after the dark decade of terrorism and internal instability. Regarding France, he has challenged the taboos and built individual partnerships with successive residents of the Elysée.

Bouteflika-Chirac (1999–2007): friendship without a treaty

After an eclipse in bilateral relations after the black decade, in particular the cancellation of the 1992 election, the Bouteflika-Chirac partnership tried to imbue the Algerian–French relationship with a new dynamic. Despite the Quai d'Orsay's critical attitude towards Bouteflika's election in 1999, the two presi-dents agreed on the need to make up for lost time. Their respective high-profile visits to Paris in June 2000 and Algiers in March 2003 presaged a resurgence of bilateral relations whose culmination would be a friendship treaty. Jacques Chirac's decision to stay out of the war in Iraq was well received in Algiers when he made his triumphal visit. And in view of the major initiatives taken dur-ing his presidency (recognition of the Algerian war of independence, opening the military archives, the year of Algeria in France in 2003, resumption of Air France flights, reopening the consulate and the French cultural centre of Algiers, etc.), and Bouteflika's willingness to work towards deepening cooperation with France, there were hopes that a treaty would seal a redefined relationship. The draft, developed in 2003, was to be signed in 2005, but it was torpedoed by the memory litigation revived by the French law no. 2005-158 of February 23, 2005, which defended colonialism. Specifically, the controversial clause 4 asked teachers and textbooks to "acknowledge and recognize in particular the positive role of the French presence abroad, especially in North Africa."

As a result, the two countries settled for friendship without a treaty, as Chirac's successor, Nicolas Sarkozy, had wished.

Bouteflika-Sarkozy (2007–2012): a difficult relationship

The Bouteflika-Sarkozy partnership defeated the ambitions of both countries to raise the level of their relationship, despite some attempts at reconciliation and a constant diplomatic dance between Algiers and Paris. Both were opposed on several issues and particularly that of memory. Although Sarkozy has no colonial past and played a role in the amendment of the law of February 23, 2005, he rejected the idea of repentance when he came to power in 2007. For his part, Bouteflika insisted on an apology from France. The two heads of state also differed on how to normalise relations between the two countries. While Bouteflika prioritised the legacy of history, Sarkozy's focus was on real and immediate bilateral cooperation projects; in brief high politics versus bottom-up economic normalisation. Moreover, Sarkozy advocated the same approach at the regional level by launching the Mediterranean Union project, to become the Union for the Mediterranean. Sarkozy even invited his Algerian counterpart to "build the Mediterranean Union based on the French-Algerian friendship (...) just as France once invited Germany to build the Union of Europe based on the French-Germanic friendship" (Sarkozy 2007). This approach to Bouteflika would fail, especially since March 2011 marks "the French military intervention in Libya that was perceived in Algeria as a strategic disaster" (Daguzan 2015: 35), whose subsequent developments reinforced Algeria's concerns.

Bouteflika-Hollande (2012–2017): allies in the Sahel

The honeymoon of Bouteflika-Hollande culminated on January 11, 2013, when clearance was granted to the French air force to overfly Algerian airspace to reach Mali, and refuelling facilities for ground forces. At the risk of transgressing Algeria's security policy, Bouteflika wanted to show he was willing in an exceptional partnership with the former coloniser. By breaking this taboo, Bouteflika has been accused by the opposition of double standards in the crises in Mali and Libya, but he argued that such a decision did not contradict the security and geostrategic objectives of Algeria. These two countries are understandably opposed to terrorism and Bouteflika's gesture has the same response as Hollande's support to Algeria during the hostage-taking in the gas complex of In Amenas on January 16, 2013. Regardless, the Bouteflika-Hollande duo strengthened economic and security cooperation. Thus, the first Algerian-French economic forum was held in June 2013, and in the Sahel, Algeria has become an important ally of France since Operation Serval in 2013. But the upturn that characterised this relationship did not overcome their disputed memory; like his predecessors Hollande confined himself to acknowledging them without apologising. In December 2012, he addressed the Algerian National Assembly on "the suffering inflicted on the Algerian People," and criticised the colonial system as "deeply unjust and brutal," nothing more. His visit to Algiers was nonetheless symbolically crowned by a declaration of friendship and cooperation between France and Algeria.

Bouteflika-Macron since 2017: two generations, two styles

With the arrival of Emmanuel Macron at the Elysée Palace, a new Algerian–French partnership was formed with the obdurate Bouteflika. At the start of each mandate, the persistent question surfaces: will Algerian-French relations overcome its constraints and achieve a true normalisation? A subsidiary question is "what would differentiate Macron from his predecessors to boost bilateral relations to the so desired and expected level of excellence" (Zoubir 2017: 41). While President Macron condemned colonisation when calling for a renewal of these relations, the first year of his mandate brought nothing original or tangible. It is true that he undertook to restore to Algeria the skulls of its martyrs killed in 1849 and kept in the Musée de l'Homme in Paris, but the Algerians expect more than that. In reality, the unique Bouteflika-Macron relationship is a double-edged sword that may either succeed in expurgating the historical burden or keep it in a perpetual status quo. On the one hand, 80-year-old Bouteflika has known all the leaders of the Fifth Republic since General De Gaulle, with the exception of François Mitterrand; and on the other hand, 40-year-old Macron begins his first term in office at the head of the French state: a veteran of the Algerian revolution facing a young wolf of French politics, born 15 years after independence and described as a friend of Algeria. "Two heads of State with diametrically opposed paths, two generations of politicians, two lives, two different styles," according to Alilat (2018: 34). Bouteflika is militant, firm, but conciliatory, while Macron is direct, audacious, and transgressive, and it is not clear whether this generational gap and difference in style represents a handicap to the much sought-after reconciliation. Regardless, Macron wants to open a new page with the generation that has not known French colonisation, and which feels detached from the ideological stakes of his elders.

Repentance at the core of Algerian-French misunderstandings

Beyond the personal momentum and trajectories taken by successive presidential tandems, as described by (Zoubir 2008), Algerian-French relations remain marked by differences in perception and historical misunderstandings. The main difficulty in extracting bilateral relations from the weight of history stems from the violence of memory, not so much in the physical sense, but the sense of shock induced by the partition and the communitisation of memory (of the colonial past) both in France and in Algeria.

In the French perception, an approach towards repentance would humiliate not only France, but also returnees, veterans, and *Harkis*.[3] In addition, "it would expose the French State to international sanctions for crimes against humanity with the obligation to compensate the victims" (Baghzouz 2010: 516). Admittedly, it has been suggested that these crimes would be judged by French courts, but the possibility of repentance gives the French the impression of an unconditional capitulation similar to the one imposed on the Nazi

Germany in 1945 (Perville 2006; 8), In Algeria's view, on the other hand, the question of memory has become a prerequisite for any deepening of the bilateral relationship. For many Algerians, colonial crimes are imprescriptible and cannot be amnestied despite the Evian Accords of 1962. But "while France wants to shelve the most painful episodes of colonization preferring to focus on the future, Algeria opposes any form of amnesia in the name of the duty of knowledge and rewrite common history" (Baghzouz 2010: 517). Everything happens as if it were a systemic misunderstanding whose resilience is opposed to any effort of normalisation. This explains the fact that when the treaty of friendship was being concluded, on February 23, 2005, the French National Assembly adopted a law which acknowledges the positive role of colonisation. Despite its amendments, this law was highly controversial due to certain questionable provisions and has definitely led to new tension in Algerian–French relations. Elysée's diplomats attempted to promote reconciliation, and the 2005 compromise proposed by Chirac himself (later accepted by Sarkozy) described the events of May 8, 1945, as "inexcusable tragedy," a euphemism repeated on February 27, 2005, in Sétif by the French Ambassador Hubert Colin de Vedrière, and again on May 8 of the same year in Algiers by the French Minister of Foreign Affairs, Michel Barnier. Nevertheless, this does not sit very well with those in Algeria who demand the completion of the recognition process, based on copious jurisprudence[4] in the matter of repentance.

Memory is not the only problem that plagues relations between Algiers and Paris. Their recent history is punctuated with disputes and misunderstandings around topics as diverse as the French nuclear tests in Algeria (1960–1966), the murder of the Tibehirine monks, restitution of the archives, French support of Morocco over Western Sahara, or yet again the *Panama Paper* in the French daily *Le Monde* that questioned President Bouteflika. Much has been said and written about these conflicting issues, and while they remain unsettled, they will inevitably lead to future problems.

Difficult normalisation through the economy

Because the economy does not collide head-on with government sovereignty and historical memory, it constitutes a privileged ground to progress with normalisation. According to this neo-functionalist vision, real achievements are primary while developing cooperation in key economic sectors would create a merger of interests, a de facto solidarity that would spill over onto other sectors and reinforce inter-dependency. This method has allowed France and Germany to lead European regional integration; but can it be applied to the Algerian–French relationship to create an exemplary north–south partnership? Relations between Algeria and France are not that simple.

Once Algeria gained political independence, "the colonial relationship was brutally converted into cooperation" (Henry 2003: 40) with an economic dependence on the former metropolitan power. Algeria sought to free itself from

France in 1971 by nationalising hydrocarbons, to the dismay of oil companies such as Total and Elf. This decision caused a diplomatic crisis with France, which boycotted Algerian oil and threatened to stop buying Algerian wine, then the second source of foreign currency. But unlike the 1967 wine crisis that culminated in grubbing-up and converting thousands of hectares of vineyards by order of President Houari Boumediene, the dispute over oil soon found a settlement, particularly through compensation (Grimaud 1972: 1303).

Forty-eight years later, Algerian-French economic cooperation cannot discard the stigma of history to the point that Algeria's economic sovereignty has a particular association with France. Although Algeria made a diversification of economic partners a principle in its foreign policy, "in France, the idea is still strongly rooted that Algeria still needs France" (Santelli 2010). The French participated in the initial development of the newly independent Algeria through, among others, the Constantine Plan of 1958 for economic development and contributed to the budget until 1965 (Henry 2012: 13).

However, France is learning the hard way that if we cannot consider in an economy, "Algeria without France" (Bachaga 1964), we cannot consider Algeria's future only with France. In 1999, France remained Algeria's top economic partner, according to Algerian trade figures. This position gradually eroded in favour of China which became the largest supplier in 2013, while Spain became the top customer in the same year. In January 2018, France takes second place behind China as a supplier, but this time Italy has risen to top spot. France's reduced position in Algeria's foreign trade is due to both the stiff competition exerted by the Asian, Gulf, and southern Europe countries and the low attraction of the Algerian market combined with the tangled relations between Algiers and Paris.

Apart from hydrocarbons, France still ranks first for foreign investment in Algeria, other than hydrocarbons, despite a noticeable preference for Morocco. Indeed, in 2015, Foreign Direct Investments net stock from France to the Kingdom was 9,278 million euros versus only 1,750 million euros for Algeria. The reluctance of French investors for the Algerian market can be explained by the many drastic trading conditions imposed by the Algerian government, and listed above. Added to this is the constantly negative perception of Algerian risk by the French Foreign Trade Assurance Company. In the same vein, the French complain about the rule of 51%–49% and the general investment framework in Algeria which, according to Macron, remains closed and offers scant protection to both domestic and foreign businessmen.

Despite these difficulties, French investment in Algeria cannot be ignored. Between 2002 and 2016, a total of 158 French investment projects were declared to the National Agency for Investment Development for 340 billion dinars (about US$ 3 billion) to generate 22,316 jobs. Moreover, according to its embassy in Algiers, France remains the most important foreign employer in Algeria, generating 40,000 direct jobs and 100,000 indirect jobs for about 500 companies. In addition, French investments are widely diversified, encompassing the financial, pharmaceutical, automotive, and food processing industries. France also intends to strengthen its presence in the oil sector, particularly through partnership agreements between Total and the Algerian Group Sonatrach.

A climate of confidence needs to be established between both authorities and entrepreneurs to boost cross-investments that strengthen the economic partnership. France is convinced that Algeria is a major economic partner with great potential, while Algeria has made it clear that France can bring significant development. Structuring projects have emerged such as Renault's industrial clusters in Oran, Alstom in Annaba, and Sanofi in Algiers. At the institutional level, major structures have been created to oversee an ambitious economic partnership. This is the case of the High Level Intergovernmental Committee and the French-Algerian Economic Committee set up in 2012, coordination frameworks through which all business partnerships are negotiated and concluded between the two countries. To give more visibility to this partnership, a road map is foreseen for the current five-year period (2018–2022).

Cooperation to address regional security challenges

One of the most important aspects of this exceptional partnership is the launch in May 2015 of a strategic dialogue between Algiers and Paris to address common security challenges. Under the presidencies of Bouteflika and Hollande, this was an informal framework for dialogue on regional and international political and security issues of common interest. Recurring issues related to terrorism and its financing, organised crime and counter-radicalisation, as well as the burning topic of illegal migration. Despite its informal nature, this mechanism makes it possible to coordinate the positions and actions of the two countries both bilaterally and at the level of the United Nations on vital issues such as regional peace and stability. For this reason and because of its strategic nature, Bouteflika and Macron wish to protect this high-level forum. After the dark decade (1992–2002) which engulfed Algeria in chaos, Algiers' role has become pivotal for France. Its expertise in the fight against terrorism is now appreciated within "a new security deal that is more Sahelian than Mediterranean" (Charillon 2016: 101).

Nevertheless, the political and security cooperation between Algeria and France is often thwarted by disagreements on annoying issues. When the Armed Islamic Group slaughtered Algerians in the 1990s, the theory of "Who Kills Who?," overused by some French media circles, angered the Algerian authorities whose responsibility had been rejected. The controversy reached its climax in 2009 when the former defence attaché in Algiers, General Buchwalter, labelled responsibility for the murder of the Tibehirine monks in 1996 a blunder by the Algerian Army (Daguzan 2009: 95). Yet within French society, the hardships experienced in Algeria during the dark decade aroused great compassion and sympathy.

It was some time before the French authorities could accept that terrorism attacks on their territory and elsewhere in Europe are the same as those in Algerian society. It is a transnational threat that is currently a matter of concern for both Algiers and Paris who have agreed to join forces in a new environment marked by the proliferation of armed groups such as Al Qaeda in the Islamic Maghreb, Boko Haram, and the Islamic State of Iraq and Syria (ISIS). The Arab uprisings triggered since 2011 have aggravated the terrorist risk in countries such as Libya, Mali, and Tunisia and made international cooperation more necessary than ever. In this context, the French operation Wolverine took place in Mali in January 2013, with the invaluable collaboration of Algeria. Both countries feel they have a heavy responsibility to secure an area plagued by instability. The result is a political–military cooperation involving the security forces of both countries in order to face common challenges.

Another sensitive point between the two capitals involves the creation of the G5-Sahel under the leadership of France. Formed in 2014 and launched in July 2017, the G5-Sahel is a regional force composed of troops from Mauritania, Mali, Burkina Faso, Nigeria, and Chad whose objective is to counter the terrorist threat. In spite of repeated prodding by Paris, Algeria shows no interest in the G5-Sahel because the cardinal principle in its foreign policy is not to deploy its troops outside its borders. It also considers that the French initiative duplicates that of the Joint Operational Chief of Staff Committee created in 2010 and which brings together under its aegis the armed forces of the Sahelian countries. Macron intends to make the G5-Sahel a coalition serving its strategic goals, where Algeria intends to play a major role. From a geopolitical point of view, Algiers sees Paris's unilateral activism as an obstacle to its ambition in this area.

Culture as a means of reconciliation

Culture can be a means of bringing people together. The close cultural ties that exist between Algerian and French societies have been shaped by a long-shared history and geographical proximity that perpetuates this legacy. As a result, "few societies experience such a degree of interweaving and cultural harmony" (Henry 2003: 42). In the aftermath of independence, Algeria's priorities were perhaps not those of cultural cooperation, but this did in fact manifest itself in strong academic and university cooperation for nearly two decades (1962–1980). Thousands of French nationals remained in Algeria, contributing to the reconstruction of this country and the francisation of generations born in the 1950s and 1960s (Henry & Vatin 2012). The francisation was a result of a process initiated by the Constantine Plan and affected mainly the first elites of Algeria before the Arabisation initiated in the late 1970s. This decision of the young Algerian state represented a major identity issue and a means to fully recover its Arab-Muslim personality. But it was not devoid of ulterior political motives as the conservative circles wanted to use it to gain political power. The language of the coloniser was also that of many stakeholders in the independent state and Arabisation then became a political issue replacing the French-speaking elite in the machinery of state.

Since the accession of Bouteflika to power in 1999, cultural cooperation between Algeria and France has experienced a new momentum and the French language has recovered, maintaining its status as first foreign language despite competition from English. Today, after 56 years of independence, Algeria remains the main French-speaking country in the Mediterranean after France, with nearly 12 million French speakers including the Algerians of France. Without being an official member of the International Francophone Organization, and despite the decline observed in the use and teaching of French, Algeria seems to want to jealously guard this "spoils of war" to quote Kateb Yacine. Algerian society is reincorporating French for its own benefit: its press has many titles in French and its literary production in the language of Molière remains vigorous and well received in France (Vermeren 2016: 18). Conversely, French television channels are keenly watched in Algeria to keep an eye on the political, sporting, and cultural news of the European neighbour. In view of this interest, President Macron has even mentioned, during his visit to Algiers in February 2016, the possibility of creating a French-Algerian cultural channel based on the model of the French-German channel *Arte*. This shows that the reconciliation between Algiers and Paris must also be done through culture. In addition, French and other foreign language learning centres flourish in all the universities and cities of Algeria and students show an exceptional enthusiasm for studying in France. The French Institute network in Algeria is planning to open "France services/ areas" in small and medium-sized cities, at a time when the Algerian cultural centre in Paris is very active. Cultural exchanges are multiplying, culminating with the organisation of Algeria's year in 2003 in France, which was the most striking demonstration of the deep interpenetration between the two societies. In a clear sign of this cultural porosity, the singer Idir or comedian Fellag can fill a theatre in Paris much as their French counterparts Lavoine or Dussolier can do in Algiers. Artists from both shores have their audiences that are good arguments for promoting intercultural dialogue.

Interfaith dialogue is another factor; since Islam has become a reality in France; Algeria can play a role in its structuring. The presence since 1992 of the Algerian Dalil Boubakeur at the head of the Grand Mosque of Paris, the most iconic Muslim institution in France, testifies to the importance of Algeria as a key player in rebuilding Islam, as desired by Emmanuel Macron and his predecessors. But Algiers' stranglehold seems to have diminished since France decided to end foreign influences. This is perhaps the message that the Elysée wanted to pass when the rector of the Grand Mosque of Paris was not among the religious leaders invited to Emmanuel Macron's new year reception in January 2018, or when the Algerian Salafi Imam of the Sunna mosque of Marseille was expelled to Algeria that April. Nevertheless, while seeking to control the religious space in France, Macron advocates the Islamic-Christian dialogue as an integral part of the overall cultural dialogue. For his part, Bouteflika, whose country gave birth to St. Augustine, also advocates inter-religious and intercultural dialogue. At a time when the United Nations is celebrating the International Decade for the Rapprochement of Cultures (2013–2022), the two heads of state can therefore focus on culture as the foundation for the rebuilding of the Algerian-French relationship.

People: the borders and bridges between the two shores

To speak of reconciliation through culture leads us inevitably to evoke those men and women who serve as bridges between the two shores of the Mediterranean and who maintain constructive links, succeeding where politics and even the economy fail. These are the cross-border movements analysed by Robert-Henry[5] (1991), who once crossed the sea to settle or resettle on the other side of the Mediterranean, feeding an imaginary relationship with his country of origin. Living together quite harmoniously in this liminal zone are migrants, dual nationals, returnees, Harkis and their children, and the Jews of Algeria who represent "the interface of the French-Algerian society between the two countries" (Henry 2004: 17). In addition to this multitude of cross-border migrants are the nationals who came between 1962 and 1980 and all those cultural leaders such as writers, historians, and filmmakers from both shores, who have worked for reconciliation and mutual understanding. Many of those who crossed the border have disappeared, like Albert Camus, Gilbert Meynier, or Mouloud Feraoun; but their legacy is invaluable work, witness to the overlapping of the two societies, and a true anthem for peace. Jean Pélégri (1989), through the evocative title of his novel *My Mother Algeria*, sums up the feeling of these thousands of hybrid French-Algerians who have a dual background. Gilbert Meynier (2017) for his part synthesises in his latest book *Algeria and France: Two Centuries of Crossed History* the singular relationship of love, passion, and hatred that the long period of colonisation and decolonisation has shaped. In the wake of the controversy aroused by the law of 2005, Meynier, together with several academics and politicians from both sides of the Mediterranean—including Benjamin Stora, Edgar Morin, Hocine Aït Ahmed, and Abdelhamid Mehri—praised the "positive effects" of colonisation, calling for reason to prevail (Aït Ahmed et al. 2007).

French Algerians share this mixed identity either through their mothers, like the politician Arnaud Montebourg, or their fathers, like actress Isabelle Adjani and actors Daniel Prévost and Jacques Villeret. These personalities who embrace rather than deny their origins defend the idea of a peaceful multicultural society and constitute a link in the Algerian-French relationship. They include football players of Algerian descendant who delighted France during the World Cup and at the Euro, like Zinedine Zidane and Karim Benzema, not to mention talented francophone authors such as Assia Djebar, Kamel Daoud, Yasmina Khadra, Boualem Sansal, and Rachid Boudjedra. These and many other intellectuals represent a diversified society on which to build a renewed Algerian-French relationship, likely to serve as a model for Europe and its south.

This idyllic picture is, however, nuanced. Admittedly, the Algerian-French society is a fact that imposes itself on all the protagonists and constitutes a bulwark against attempts at rupture. But the recurring problems experienced by certain segments of this society often lead to new tensions in bilateral relations. This is the case, for example, of the mobility between the two countries of Algerian nationals or Harkis and their children, which suffers from divergent perceptions. Other cross-border cultural movements continue to arouse controversy in Algeria. Enrico Macias, for example, the French singer born in Algeria, was prevented from returning there because of pressure brought to bear by a revolutionary family; and the writer Albert Camus, also born in Algeria, suffered the same fate when the authorities refused to allow the Camus cultural caravan (readings in seven Algerian cities) to cross Algeria in 2010, 50 years after his death. The war may have been over for 57 years, but some in both Algeria and France continue to stoke the flame of memory.

Conclusion

Algerian-French relations have improved significantly over the past two decades without reaching a mature phase. President Bouteflika has tried to take bilateral cooperation with his French counterparts from Chirac to Macron to an exceptional partnership level. The process of normalisation between the two countries proceeds one small step at a time. But at each advance the old demons resurface, preventing this relationship from being permanently reconciled. After periods of reconciliation and relaxation come periods of cold and even tension. The irony of these relations is that at the height of crises, hybrid Algerian-French society ensures the perpetuation of these particularly dense and complex historical links. The relationship between Algeria and France is solid because it is cemented by an exceptional mixed society and mutual interests. Each country remains for the other a privileged otherness in the regional and international context of economic crisis and dismantled transnational security perils.

While Algiers and Paris are aware that they have everything to gain from a peaceful and expurgated relationship, they have not managed to break the glass ceiling despite declarations of intent. Macron recommended in 2017 that "with Algeria, France must build a strong line around the Mediterranean that extends to Africa." But 1 year after coming to power, "everything remains to be done" (Tahchi 2017), while France, as the former colonial power, must make the greatest step towards reconciliation. The Bouteflika-Macron duo does not seem to depart from the tradition unveiled since independence: promises with much fanfare at the beginning of each mandate followed by disillusionment. It is an Algerian-French story in an eternal circle failing to dispel the old suspicions and create a climate of trust.

On both sides of the Mediterranean, we scrutinise the slightest sign of change in the hope of an inflection in the other side. On the French side, we wonder about Algeria after Bouteflika who resigned after his fourth term in April 2019, and hope for a new generation in power. On the Algerian side, there is no longer any illusion about Macron's ability to reconcile the two countries, but hope remains that France will end up accepting its past. In sum, uncertainty still weighs on the future of a bilateral relationship whose main characteristic remains the perpetual quest for an improbable normalisation.

Acknowledgements

The author would like to thank professors Ahmed Mahiou and Jean-Robert Henry for having kindly reviewed the text. Thanks also to Yahia Zoubir for his editing and supervision and to anonymous reviewers for comments.

Notes

1 The third couplet of the Algerian national anthem is addressed to France in these terms:
O France, the time of reproach has passed
And we have closed like a book;
O France, the day of reckoning is at hand
So prepare to receive from us our answer!
In our revolution is the end of empty talk;
and we have resolved that Algeria shall live –
So bear witness, bear witness, bear witness! (Kassaman)
2 Hizb França, literally "party of France" in Arabic, is a movement with a strong pejorative connotation that dates back to the early years of independence to designate alleged pressure groups of French-speaking Algerians supposed to "play the game of France" and considered to be enemies of Algeria. Expressed with the hints of a narrow nationalism, it is still used today to discredit particularly the partisans of the opening on France.
3 The term Harkis refers to Algerians who enlisted alongside the French Army during the war of independence from 1954 to 1962, and whose number was then estimated at 263,000. Fearing reprisals from the National Liberation Front after the signing of the Evian Agreements in March 1962, they massively left Algeria to settle in the South of France. But many of them were abandoned after the ceasefire and were imprisoned or killed. However, the Harkis are not a homogeneous community. Alongside conscripts and enlisted soldiers, the French Army had auxiliaries on monthly contracts without military status. Some were paid modest salaries such as "moghaznis" (police officers) and "mobile security groups" (assimilated to les Compagnies Républicaines de Sécurité), while others were volunteers, such as men from self-defence groups formed in villages. The engagement of the Harkis, mostly illiterate peasants, was motivated by multiple factors: pressure from the notables and the French Army, National Liberation Front threats, village rivalries, and a desire for revenge, food needs or political options. If we include the descendants of the Harkis, this population now exceeds 400,000 people (https://histoirecoloniale.net/les-harkis-qui-etaient-ils.html).

1 Jurisprudence on repentance is justified by the fact that countries like France, Italy, Germany, Japan, South Africa, and even Australia have already repented for the suffering they inflicted on the Malagasy, Libyan, Namibian, South Korean, South African, and Australian Aborigines.
5 Jean Robert-Henry uses the title *Border Movements*, an Algerian novel written in 1956 by André Rosefelder, to expand the analysis to "border workers of the French-Maghreb relations and especially French-Algerian."

References

Aït Ahmed, H., Harbi, M., Mehri, A., Meynier, G., Morin, E., Stora, B., et al., "Algeria–France: Let's get over historical disputes," Le Monde, November 30, 2007, viewed April 19, 2017, https://www.fr/idées/article/2007/11/30/france-algérie-depassons-le-contentieux-historique_984515_32.32.html.

Alilat, F., 2018, "Algeria: Singularity and transgression," Jeune Afrique, No. 2979, p. 34.

Bachaga, B., 1964, *Algeria without France*, Broché, Paris.

Baghzouz, A., 2010, "Algerian–French relations since 2000 or a quest for an improbable refoundation," *L'Année du Maghreb*, VI, 507–526.

Charillon, F., 2016, "The French-Algerian relationship with regard to foreign policy analysis," *Questions Internationales*, No. 81, September–October, 97–104.

Daguzan, J.F., 2009, "French-Algerian relations or the perpetual tango lesson," *Maghreb-Mashrek*, No. 200, Summer 2009, 91–99.

Daguzan, J.F., 2015, "Algeria's foreign policy: Time for adventure?" *Politique Etrangère* 3/2015, 31–42.

Grimaud, N., 1972, "The French-Algerian oil dispute," *Revue française de science politique*, Paris, 1276–1307.

Grimaud, N., 2008, "Elements for the interpretation of the relations between France–Algeria where each President has its own Algeria," *Maghreb-Mashrek*, No. 197, Autumn 2008, 61–66.

Henry, J.R., 1991, "Border workers of the French-Maghrebian space," Annuaire de l'Afrique du Nord 1991, Paris: CNRS Editions, 301–311.

Henry, J.R., (ed.), 2003, Algeria and France: Crossed destinies and imaginations, Centre des Archives d 'Outre-Mer – Mémoires méditerranéennes, Aix-en-Provence.

Henry, J.R., 2004, La Méditerranée occidentale en quête d'un 'destin commun'," *L'Année du Maghreb*, I, 5–26.

Henry, J.R., & Vatin, J.C., (eds), 2012, *Time for Cooperation: Social Sciences and Decolonization in the Maghreb*, Karthala, Paris.

Libération, 2017, In Algeria Emmanuel Macron calls French colonization "a crime against Humanity," viewed April 1, 2019, from: https://www.liberation.fr/politiques/2017/02/15/en-algerie-emmanuel-macron-qualifie-la-colonisation-francaise-de-crime-contre-l-humanite_1548723.

Mbembe, A., 2010, *Out of the Dark Night: Essay on Decolonization*, La Découverte, Paris.

Meynier, G., 2016, "Algeria and the weight of the past," Questions Internationales No. 81, September–October, 32–41.

Meynier, G., 2017, *Algeria and France: Two Centuries with Crossed History*, L'Harmattan, Paris.

Naylor, P.C., 2001, "France and Algeria: A history of decolonization and transformation," *Middle East Quarterly*, Spring 2001, 8(2), 464 pages.

Pélégri, J., 1989, *My Mother Algeria*, Laphomic, Algiers.

Pervillé, G., 2006, "The immediate history of the French-Algerian relationship: Towards a French-Algerian friendship treaty?," Communication given at the colloquium "Assessment and Prospects of the Immediate History," GRHI, Toulouse, 5–6 April. Viewed on March 24, 2010 from http//www.communautarisme.net/L-histoire-immediate-de-la-relation-franco-algerienne.

Santelli, E., 2010, Appendix 1. French-Algerian exchanges, the new deal, *Sociology* 3, volume 1, viewed on March 30, 2018, from URL: http://journals.openedition.org/sociologie/466.

Sarkozy, N., 2007, Speech of December 4 in Constantine, viewed on April 17, 2018 from http://www.afrik.com/article13087.html.

Tahchi, B., 2017, "Macron and Algeria, everything remains to be done," *Outre-Terre, French Review of Geopolitics*, No. 51, 2017/2, 303–307.

Vermeren, P., 2016, "A short history of Algeria since independence," International issues, No. 81, September–October, 11–18.

Zoubir, Y., 2008, "Errements dans les relations algéro-françaises," *Maghreb-Machrek*, 2008/3, No. 197, 31–38.

Zoubir, Y., 2017, "Emmanuel Macron et l'Algérie: Amorce d'une véritable réconciliation?" *Cahiers de l'Orient,?*", *Les Cahiers de l'Orient*, 4/, No. 128, 37–46.

14

UNDERSTANDING ALGERIA'S FOREIGN POLICY IN THE SAHEL

Abdelkader Abderrahmane*

Introduction

The Arab Spring, ongoing crises in Libya and Mali, and the dramatic 2013 hostage-taking at the BP Statoil gas plant in In Amenas turned the spotlight on Algeria. World media interest led to an avalanche of analyses and comments on its foreign policy. Even during the Cold War and the era of the Non-Aligned Movement, in which Algiers played a leading role, Algeria did not face as much scrutiny nor find itself the focus of as much media interest as it has since these events.

Different adjectives such as lax, indolent, and nonchalant have been employed to describe Algeria's position and its refusal to engage its army in fighting terrorism outside its own territory. However, as the pivotal state in the region, Algeria has spared no effort to bring peace to its Malian, Libyan, and Tunisian neighbours. It is undoubtedly a force for stability in the broader region of North Africa and the Sahel, and its influence and peace-searching diplomacy make this African giant an indispensable regional interlocutor for the African Union, the USA, Russia, France and, more broadly, the European Union.

This chapter will therefore analyse some of the core fundamentals of Algeria's foreign policy such as non-interference in the domestic affairs of other states, and the non-intervention of the Algerian army beyond Algeria's national borders. This analysis will also argue that

Algeria's foreign policy is shaped by its own history and that despite its policy of non-interference in other States' internal affairs, Algiers has nonetheless demonstrated thorough leadership away from the spotlight of discussions on military intervention.

---

* This chapter is dedicated to my love, Luqmâne & Ilyês.

Algeria's legacy

Any analysis of Algeria's regional and foreign policy would be incomplete without a review of its past, and particularly the nationalism and pan-Africanism which provide an insight into what drives Algerian policy, its motives, and what is often perceived externally as its singularity and specificity. For "understanding Algerian politics requires taking a step back to contemplate what [is] happening around it" (Malley 1996, 9).

Once described by Amílcar Cabral[1] as the Mecca of revolutionaries, Algeria has since its independence in 1962 played a leading political role in Africa. Its doctrinal principles are anchored in the national consciousness and have their roots in its own history which was marked by profound violence and attacks (Julien 1994; McDougall 2017). In this regard, the brutal and violent imposition of French colonialism in Algeria over 132 years is unrivalled (Brower 2011). Likewise, for Horne (1984), Algeria's terrible eight-year long war of independence, from 1954 to 1962, is comparable only with the Vietnam War of 1956–1975.

Diplomatic relations in Algeria have from independence been based on their own history and the principles they consider to be intangible. As one of the founding members of the Organization of African Unity, Algeria initially adopted an anti-imperialist position, leading the Non-Aligned Movement. Until the 1980s, Algeria also played an active role in the liberation of other African states and movements such as South Africa's African National Congress, Angola's Movimento Popular de Libertação de Angola, and Zimbabwe's Zimbabwe African National Union, often providing them with financial, political, and military support.

This solidarity with national liberation movements together with Algeria's active role in the emerging Non-Aligned Movement and the nationalisation of the oil industry in 1971, pointed to an aspiration to become the "best, the most progressive, in a word, the Third World's guide [*aiguillon*]" (Malley 1996, 141).[2] As a result, Algeria's political activism undeniably gave the state international leadership status. As Malley writes, "it was under Boumedienne's rule (1965–1978) that Algeria came to be considered a '*montreur de conduite*,' or catalyst, for the Third World" (ibid.).[3] The climax of Algeria's political activism is probably the Algiers Summit of the Non-Aligned in 1973 and the special session of the United Nations (UN) General Assembly on the "New Economic International Order" and for a system of international relations that will guarantee the right of the then "Third World States" (ibid., 91). Badie (2014, 200) commented that after having accumulated the twin humiliations of both the colonisation and the decolonisation processes, it is not surprising that Algeria had a leading [political] role.[4]

Foreign policy and Algeria's non-intervention doctrine

Algeria's foreign policy of neutrality and its reluctance to send the Algerian army (the Popular National Army) to fight terrorism outside Algerian territory have led to derogatory adjectives such as lax, indolent, and nonchalant. "A giant afraid of its own shadow" (Daragahi 2013), a "prickly, paranoid strategic partner" (Boukhras 2012), "Algiers' pivotal ambivalence" (Ammour 2012), and even "sponsoring regional terrorism in the Sahel and Mali" (Keenan 2012) are some of the terms used to describe Algeria's role in the Malian crisis and the hostage-taking crisis of In Amenas. Zounmenou even argued in 2012 that "Algiers transformed the northern part of Mali into its own dustbin."[5]

In this regard, Article 29 of the Algerian Constitution stipulates: "Algeria shall not resort to war to attack the legitimate sovereignty and the liberty of other peoples. It shall endeavour to settle international differences by peaceful means" (Constitution of the People's Democratic Republic of Algeria, Edition 2016); Article 28 states that "[...] The National People's Army shall have the permanent mission to safeguard national independence and the defense of national sovereignty. It is charged to ensure the defense of the unity and territorial integrity of the country, as well as the protection of the territory, its air space and the different zones of its maritime zone" (ibid.).[6]

Since its independence, Algeria has had a clear policy with the role of its army well defined within its national borders limited to guaranteeing the republican order and safeguarding the territorial integrity of the country. Algiers has steadfastly refused to send any of its troops abroad, with only two exceptions: when they participated in the 1967 and 1973 Arab-Israeli wars.

Algeria's foreign policy had been defined under President Houari Boumedienne; these principles are the defence of national independence, the refusal of any form of foreign intervention, the absence of any foreign military base, and the refusal of any regional or military alliance (Benantar 2016, 88). Forty years since the death of Boumedienne, these principles remain in force. In a press interview in 2017, the former Algerian Prime Minister Ahmed Ouyahia reiterated Algiers' position, stressing that "Algeria would never send its soldiers to be killed in a war beyond its national borders" (Cridem 2017). This refusal to allow any foreign intervention is also found in both government policy and amongst the Algerian population, profoundly jealous of their national sovereignty. Following the massive street protests which started in Algeria on February 22, 2019, and which led to the stepping down of the former President, Abdelaziz Bouteflika, who was in power since 1999, there were slogans such as "This is a family business. No foreign intervention please." Similarly, amidst these protests the then Deputy Prime Minister and Minister of Foreign Affairs Ramtane Lamamra had engaged in an international shuttle to explain to different chancelleries and the foreign press that what [was] happening in Algeria was a "moment of family issues," diplomatically warning that Algeria would never accept any interference in its domestic affairs (L'Expression 2019).

Algeria's international political activism

Algeria remains committed to fighting international terrorism and all related activities such as arms and drug trafficking, despite their policy of non-intervention. In this regard, Algeria has forged strong security ties with Washington which sees

Algiers as a key actor in the fight against international terrorism. In January 2010, the then United States (US) Ambassador in Algiers, David D. Pierce, acknowledged that no country is more important than Algeria in the fight against terrorism and Al Qaeda in the Islamic Maghreb in the Sahel and North Africa (Hamel 2014). According to him, Algeria undertakes 60% of the burden in the fight against terrorism in the region while Morocco, Mali, Niger, and Mauritania cover the remaining 40% all together (ibid.).

The 9/11 attacks are widely acknowledged as being the linchpin behind the United States' decision to work closer with Algeria in its Global War on Terrorism (GWOT). As a result, Algeria managed to return to the international political arena after years of ostracism due to the internal political and security crisis the country was undergoing. The USA in particular realised how important Algeria could be in their fight against international terrorism. As a result, in August 2015, former US Secretary of State John Kerry confirmed Algeria's key constructive role in the fight against GWOT, expressing the US' readiness to work with Algeria to achieve this aim (Boulter 2015).[7]

Algeria has also become an integral player in the GWOT through its inclusion in the newly negotiated Trans-Sahara Counterterrorism Initiative (Bedjaoui 2006) and is a founding member of the Global Counterterrorism Forum and co-chair of Global Counterterrorism Forum's Sahel Region Capacity Building Working Group.[8] Algeria uses this forum to champion the Algiers Memorandum on Good Practices on Preventing and Denying the Benefits of Kidnapping for Ransom by Terrorists. As a result, in October 2014, Algeria, Canada, and the United States co-sponsored the first in a series of Global Counterterrorism Forum Kidnapping for Ransom technical workshops at the International Institute for Justice and Rule of Law (Country reports on terrorism 2016).

Similarly, Algiers has attempted to convince both the international community and the UN to follow the African Union which has endorsed the principle that "terrorism is a threat to human rights" and "cannot be justified under any circumstances" (United Nations 2009). Algeria has also lobbied for the UN to explicitly ban ransom payments for kidnapped individuals which it considers may nurture terrorism and terrorist activities (Rezag 2010). In 2013, Algiers also put drug trafficking in northwest Africa as its top national security threat linked to militancy in the region and has consequently charged its army with fighting this scourge (Chikhi 2013). Similarly, when the United Nations Security Council adopted Resolution 2178 condemning foreign terrorist fighters, Algeria publicly expressed its support for and commitment to the UN's Global Counterterrorism Strategy. Algeria recalled its prior experience with returning foreign fighters from Afghanistan in the 1990s and the need to address the phenomenon comprehensively (United States Department of State 2015).

On the African continent, Algeria is also the main backer of the Nouakchott Process, launched by the African Union (AU) in March 2013, which brings together 11 Maghreb, Sahel, and west African countries to promote regional security cooperation (International Crisis Group 2015, 12). In addition, Algeria has supported efforts to strengthen the Northern Standby Brigade of the African Standby Force, the African Union Peace, and Security Council's enforcement arm intended for rapid intervention as well as peace support and humanitarian operations (Nickels 2014). Last, but not least, after having been a strong advocate for the implementation of such a continental institution, Algiers has since 2015 hosted the headquarters of the African Police Cooperation Mechanism (AFRIPOL) a pan-African organisation that fosters police training and cooperation in response to security threats such as terrorism, drug trafficking, and cyber-criminality, under a harmonised African strategy (Africa Research Bulletin 2016). Also, housing this key logistic base reflects Algeria's strong commitment before the AU Peace and Security Council that enables the AU to play its role in managing peace and security (Ramzi 2011).

On the regional front, and in line with its international commitment, Algiers has also constantly demonstrated thorough leadership away from the spotlight of discussions on military intervention. For instance, in order to be more efficient in the Sahel, Algeria has sought to marshal a coordinated regional response to cross-border terrorism, smuggling, and other armed group activity in the Sahel's vast and under-policed border regions (Blyth 2013). The Field Country Process which translated into the setting up of the "Tamanrasset Plan" agreed to in 2009 by Algeria, Niger, Mali, and Mauritania, which led to the establishment, in 2010, of a joint military operations centre, the Common Operational Joint-Chiefs of Staff Committee located in Tamanrasset (southern Algeria) and of a joint intelligence cell Fusion and Liaison Unit in Algiers is a concrete example of this regional security cooperation. While progress has yet to be widely demonstrated, cooperation between the countries in conducting operations, analysing security threats, and sharing border responsibilities is a laudable model, and the initiative demonstrates Algeria's willingness to instigate collaboration.

Regarding regional cooperation, it is, however, important to underline that despite the Tamanrasset framework, the Sahel states (Mauritania, Mali, and Niger) have constantly maintained and sought to expand their security cooperation directly with external powers such as France, the United States, and have on occasion even worked with each other in joint military operations instead of coordinating through and with Algeria. Furthermore, since its military intervention in Mali in 2013, France has, in order to facilitate rapid deployments in Africa, reviewed with Chad, Mali, Niger, and other African countries, its military positioning on the continent.[9] In Niger, for instance, Paris has reinforced its military cooperation with Niamey by extending its military base in Niau Sahel (Abderrahmane 2014).

On several different occasions, Algeria has faced external initiatives emanating from France and its African allies that to some extent duplicate Algiers' own. For instance, it was no coincidence that the French-backed G5 Sahel framework for promoting peace and security coordination between Mauritania, Mali, Burkina Faso, Chad, and Niger convened an extraordinary summit in Nouakchott just 1 day after the Nouakchott Process was launched (International Crisis Group 2015, 12). Similarly, in 2014, France launched a Regional Intelligence Fusion Unit which bears striking similarities to the Algiers-based Fusion and Liaison Unit (ibid.). In 2016, France attempted to convene a summit on Libya in Paris without inviting any official from Algeria, which may indicate that "Paris would like to torpedo the efforts of Algiers and the UN in bringing a lasting peace solution in Libya" (Oukazi 2016).

This ambivalent regional cooperation explains why "Algerian officials argue that the intelligence officers of many Sahelian countries are unreliable and too close to France. This is perceived by Algiers as a constant attempt to thwart Algeria's influence and policy in the Sahel, and thus a major impediment to CEMOC full efficiency" (Zoubir 2018, 86).

Algeria's regional policy

From a geo-strategic and security angle, the Sahel is of tremendous importance for Algeria which perceives this region as highly vulnerable for its own security and stability. The Sahel is an increasingly important strategic zone for all its neighbouring countries, including Algeria and the European Union (EU). The region has important assets such as natural resources, but is at the same time confronted with titanic challenges including demographic growth, poverty, terrorism, and organised crime.

With this in mind, Algiers has spared no effort to bring peace and stability to its Malian, Libyan, and Tunisian neighbours and to secure the Sahel region through bilateral relations with its neighbours, especially through military and security coordination (Benantar 2016).[10] To do so, Algeria advocates an approach encouraging the involved countries to take charge of their own issues, helping to strengthen and organise regional security through strengthening its borders, and improving that of its neighbours, which imposes a heavy financial and human burden.[11]

For instance, Algeria has been playing an important role in terms of training and logistical aid to its neighbours (Abdelmoumen 2017). In this regard, Algeria has over the past 10 years or so, spent more than US$ 100 million on Mali, Chad, Niger, Libya, and Mauritania, to form and train special forces squads as well as provide them with adequate equipment (TSA—Algérie 2017).[12] Algeria has also trained Niger's elite forces and provided the country with technical advice and aid. For Niamey, security is a successful field of cooperation between Niger and Algeria (*Africa Time* 2016). Algeria also provides regular financial aid to its neighbours and beyond. For instance, in 2012, Algeria wrote off US$ 3 billion debt of ten poor African States (Titouche 2012), while in 2013, Algeria annulled an extra US$ 902 million debt of 14 other African countries (Boumazza 2013).[13]

In Mali, Algeria has been the chief mediator of the Inter-Malian dialogue which eventually brought all together the main Malian protagonists to sign an agreement leading to the Bamako Agreement signed in April 2015. These peace accords were first signed in May 2015 and then in June of the same year and were the result of five rounds which had started in July 2014 under the auspices of Algiers. In this respect, in January 2018, the former Malian Minister of Foreign Affairs, Soumeylou Boubèye Maïga, stressed Algeria's availability to help Mali draw a new law of national agreement [loi d'entente nationale] (*Africa Time* 2016). For Maïga, Algeria has always played a major and essential role in the stability of Mali, and the *pierre angulaire* (the foundation) of Mali's national and foreign affairs politics is the Algiers' Peace Accords (Algérie Presse Service January 13, 2018).

In fact, Algiers has always been eager to broker peace agreements between Bamako and different opposition groups such as the Tuaregs. For instance, Bamako called for Algeria to be the mediator between the Malian capital and the Tuareg opposition in 2006 and in the 1990s (Zoubir 2018, 76). Algerian authorities are constantly wary that a spill-over effect from Mali could destabilise their country (ibid.). Since its independence in 1962, Algeria has so far managed to integrate its large Tuareg population in a common national identity. Nonetheless, for Algiers, the issue of Tuareg in Mali and their possible attempt at secession or independence is of high importance for its own national security (ibid.).

Following the disastrous North Atlantic Treaty Organisation military intervention in Libya in 2011 which led to the collapse of the Libyan state, Algeria's diplomatic relations with Libya have been focused on finding a final and lasting solution to the current dangerous Libyan political stalemate. In this regard, Algeria has advocated national reconciliation through an inclusive process bringing together rivals, including Islamists and Qaddafi-era officials. In order to do so, Algiers has been pushing a consensual, democratic solution, culminating in elections and a new constitution (Balmasov 2016) and has also had a special role in rebuilding a united Libya, working closely with consecutive UN special representatives and heads of the UN Support Mission in Libya (International Crisis Group 2015, pp. 14–15). Algiers' efforts have, however, been hindered by the ongoing political crisis in Libya and the incapacity of the Government of National Accord to control the plethora of militias in the frontiers (Ghanem-Yazbeck 2017). Yet, despite all these difficulties, Algiers has pursued its efforts for a solution to the Libyan quagmire through peaceful and political means which would preserve the territorial unity and integrity of Libya. One such example is through building up strong national institutions such as a united Libyan army (Métaoui 2018). In order to secure its borders and thus strengthen regional security, the Algerian authorities have also prevented the transit of Moroccan and other foreign citizens who are known to supply the local Islamic State (Abderrahmane 2016).

In nascent democratic Tunisia, Algeria has also played a key behind-the-scenes role in stabilising the post-Ben Ali political transition as well as fostering strong and close cooperation on counter-terrorism and cross border security. In this regard, in May 2014, Algiers provided financial assistance with a US$ 200 million in loans and deposits (International Crisis Group 2015, 19–21). Both Algeria and Tunisia have also strengthened their cooperation with multiple bilateral meetings between the structures in charge of border security by coordinating actions and exchanging information as well as experiences in both border security and the control of smuggling activities (Zoubir 2018).

Algeria also helped train Tunisia's untrained and inexperienced security forces in counter-terrorism tactics, teaching them strategies of the Gendarmerie Elite Rapid Intervention Units as well as of criminology and forensics laboratories. The two countries have exchanged several high-level delegations with Tunisia sending, for instance, several delegations from its army, its intelligence branch, and its air force to Algiers (ibid.). Facing the common threat of Al Qaeda in the Islamic Maghreb terrorism, in 2012, both countries signed a border security agreement facilitating joint patrols and operations to fight Al Qaeda in the Islamic Maghreb linked groups in Jebel Chaambi as well as organised crime and smuggling groups. In 2013, Algiers and Tunis established a Joint Intelligence Unit (ibid.).

Synthesis

The Sahel is of paramount importance for Algeria, and historically its role in the Sahel has been key. Algeria has always prioritised the stability of this area which it considers its security belt. In this regard, Algeria's action has been multiform and based on dialogue regarded as a fundamental instrument for the settlement of the conflicts undermining this zone. Importantly, "Algeria's code of conduct in the Sahel is driven by its sense of solidarity duty with its neighbours of the Sahel, the objective need to invest in the collective security and the strategic necessity to participate in their economic development."[14]

Consequently, for Algiers, ensuring the security of Algeria as well as the stability of the whole region is based on two fundamental axes. The first is safety, which is based on the deployment of military units and security forces equipped with all the means and equipment necessary to secure borders with neighbouring countries and prevent any infiltration of terrorists or circulation of arms, particularly in this context of security degradation in the region. The second axis, diplomatic, is reflected through the initiatives of mediation and rapprochement of the points of view between the belligerent parts, led by Algeria with a view to achieving national reconciliation in those countries as well as coordinating and cooperating with them in the field of counterterrorism, with an emphasis on the timely exchange of information.

Furthermore, any attempt to analyse Algiers' foreign [and regional] policy through the lenses of neighbouring conflicts hinders a clear transparent assessment of Algeria's position shaped by its own legacy of revolt, independence, and civil war. Also, to assess Algiers' diplomacy without looking at its own internal nation-state building and historical regional alliances and affiliations is deemed to fail. Importantly, the ongoing regional crises should not overshadow Algeria's long standing investments in regional security, promoting at key moments dialogue and state-building for their neighbours' respective internal crisis. Indeed, Algeria's image is paradoxically one that does little for regional security, while it is on the contrary the most engaged state to secure its own borders and therefore the one of its neighbours (Benantar 2016, 94). This may be explained by the fact that the growing militarisation of the world's politics too often overshadows the role of other efficient instruments of actions (Abdelmoumen 2017). Moreover, it is paramount to remember that the refusal from Algeria to send its army beyond its national borders is part of a politics adapted to the context, objectives, and means of Algeria (ibid.). Importantly, "Algeria's action in the Sahel is far from carrying any intention to play a policeman's [regional] role. Such intention stands totally against Algeria's doctrinal position with respect for states' sovereignty and non-interference in their domestic matters that is lying at the heart of its foreign policy and national defence."[15]

Having said that, the Algerian authorities bear their own responsibility in this confusing situation due to a rather poor communication on their part. Although Algeria is the pivotal state in the region (Chase et al. 1996), they do little to publicise their country's numerous political endeavours and successes. Indeed, rather than controlling communication, the Algerian authorities prefer letting rumours spread, which to some extent, nurtures the state's risk of destabilisation (Abderrahim 2013).[16] As a result, and in a cynical Goebbels style whereby if you tell a lie big enough and keep repeating it, people will eventually believe it, this poor communication from Algiers has allowed countless outsiders to nurture all kinds of rumours about Algeria and its people. With time, these have become the norm, not to say the "truth."[17] Yet, as Malley (1996) indicates concerning the analysis of Islam which may be transposed to a general perception of Algeria, "Western observers are so entranced [with Algeria], that they tend to confuse reality with their phantasms" (Malley 60; Corm 2015, 42).

Conclusion

Two hundred years ago, Georges Washington (1732–1799) made the following puzzling comment to John Adams (1735–1826): "Don't you think Sir, that Central Barbarian[18] State is rather particular...I do not understand...It works well with Tunis, Tripoli and the Sultan of Fez but when it comes to Algiers, it gets complicated" (in Essedratti 2012). More than two centuries since Washington's perplexing question to Adams, there is little doubt that Algeria remains an enigma to many across the world. As a result, this has often led to an incomplete portrayal of this African giant which does little to help understand this complex country and its foreign policy.

However, and as has been underlined in this study, it is only through the historical lenses that one may get any closer to understanding Algeria's regional policy. History bears a heavy responsibility for the construction of a nation, its doctrine, and principles, and Algerians do not escape this reality. This is undoubtedly why

Malley argues that "present and likely future developments make an understanding of [Algeria's] past all the more necessary" (Malley op. cit., 116).

Having said that, there is no doubt that Algeria is a stabilising force in the broader region of North Africa and the Sahel. Its influence and peace-searching diplomacy make it an indispensable regional interlocutor for the AU, the USA, Russia, France, and more broadly, the EU. Algeria has increasing involvement in regional, but also international negotiations, particularly in the ongoing Malian and Libyan crises. Taken together with its eagerness to secure its borders, Algeria has positioned itself as the essential regional power in the fight against terrorism and regional insecurity, contradicting the image of an insular Algeria uncomfortable with regional and international cooperation.

Notes

1 Amílcar Lopes da Costa Cabral (1924–1973) was a Bissau-Guinean and Cape Verdean intellectual, nationalist, and diplomat who was known as one of Africa's foremost anti-colonial leaders.

2 It is also from this perspective that the former Algerian President, Abdelaziz Bouteflika, vigorously denounced foreign interventions such as NATO's military actions in Kosovo, during his term at the United-Nations General Assembly in September 1999.

3 Houari Boumedienne, who was 13 years old in 1945, once declared that the massacres of Sétif and Guelma, Algeria, perpetrated by the French forces that year and which he had personally witnessed, had irremediably shaped his view of the world. For Boumedienne to declare, "that day, the teenage I was became a man," cited in Achiari (2013).

4 Lebanese writer and novelist Amin Maalouf similarly commented that "you could read ten large tomes on the history of Islam from its very beginnings and yet, you would still not understand what is going on in Algeria." Read 30 pages on colonialism and decolonisation, and you will then better understand" (Maalouf 2011, 77).

5 Commentary from David Zounmenou, workshop on Mali, Clingendael, The Hague (the Netherlands); German Institute for International and Security Affairs, Berlin (Germany), September 2012.

6 It is paramount to underline that Articles 28 and 29 do not mention any banning of sending Algerian troops abroad. Algeria's refusal to send its troops abroad is therefore a matter of doctrinal position. According to an Algerian diplomat, "it is crystal clear that this position has no legal ground whatsoever and is mere political stance. That is the reason why some of Algeria's foreign partners, such as France, have been regularly challenging this position, but, to no avail, so far. However, Algeria's position [...] will eventually and inevitably be adjusted, especially with a view to peace and security issues in the Sahel. Algeria seems to be in a situation that cannot be corrected in a brutal manner. It will therefore be moving and adapting progressively" (Interview held in Algiers on December 9, 2018, with an Algerian senior diplomat on condition of anonymity).

7 According to an Algerian senior diplomat, "Algeria and the United States maintain solid relations, and Algeria's constructive role in promoting regional stability is quite appealing to Washington. The bilateral cooperation in fighting terrorism and bolstering the security has been growing significantly and it has proven to be productive" (Interview held in Algiers on December 8, 2018, conducted on condition of anonymity).

8 https://www.thegctf.org/Working-Groups/Sahel-Region-Capacity-Building

9 For a general view on France's foreign policy and intervention in its former West African colonies, see (Pigeaud December 2017).
10 Similarly, Algeria transported both African troops to the war-torn Central African Republic to support the African Mission to the Central African Republic and the African Union Mission to Somalia troops to Somalia in 2009.
11 Email interview with an Algerian senior diplomat on condition of anonymity (June 2018).
12 In comparison, by January 2018, the 28 member states of the EU had pledged US$ 134 million to the G5 Sahel all together.
13 According to an Algerian senior diplomat, "it is undeniable that Algeria is engaged in Africa in more than a way and in no small way. Its help to African countries is, by all means, far from being small. It however goes unnoticed" (Interview held in Algiers on December 8, 2018, conducted on condition of anonymity).
14 Email interview with an Algerian senior diplomat on condition of anonymity (Algiers, June 2018).
15 Email interview with an Algerian senior diplomat on condition of anonymity (Algiers, June 2018).
16 According to an Algerian senior diplomat, "communication is Algeria's Achilles heel. For them, 'Algeria and communication are absolutely contradictory. Algeria does not really know about communication and is [therefore] not communicating in an effective and productive manner. "Algeria keeps reacting to things happening around it, without it or against it. Therefore, it finds itself in a strange and jeopardising situation, a sort of quagmire, where it devotes all of its energy to handling emergencies whereas fundamental matters are neglected'" (Interview held on condition of anonymity in Algiers in June 2018).
17 The 40-year long Western Sahara conflict which opposes the Frente Popular de Liberación de Saguía el Hamra y Río de Oro, POLISARIO and Sahrawi nationalists to Morocco is a perfect example. Indeed, Algeria's position over the Western Sahara conflict has been one of the most contested yet little understood aspects of this 4 decades old dispute. This confusion stems, in part, from Algiers' lack of communication, but also from numerous hypotheses that have been put forward to explain Algeria's motivations. However, as Mundy writes, "Algeria did not create Western Saharan nationalism generally nor Polisario specifically." See J. Mundy (2010, 3).
18 The term "barbarian," from the Greek Barbaros (βάρβαρος) literally means "whoever is not Greek is a barbarian." In ancient times, Greeks used it mostly for people of different cultures. In the Roman Empire, Romans used the word barbarian for many people, such as the Berbers, the first inhabitants of North Africa.

References

Abdelmoumen, Mohsen. 2017. "Terrorism risks to become unmanageable in the near future." *American Herald Tribune*. July 3. Retrieved from https://ahtribune.com/politics/1759-tewfik-hamel-terrorism.html (accessed December 15, 2017).
Abderrahim, Kader. 2013. "Plutôt que de maîtriser cette communication, le régime préfère laisser courir les rumeurs et, d'une certaine manière, alimente la déstabilisation de l'Etat," *El Watan*. June 13. Retrieved from http://elwatan.com/actualite/plutot-que-de-maitriser-la-communication-le-regime-prefere-laisser-courir-les-rumeurs-13-06-2013-217286_109.php (accessed July 15, 2014).
Abderrahmane, Abdelkader. 2014. "Françafrique and Africa's security." *open Democracy*. February 14. Retrieved from https://www.opendemocracy.net/opensecurity/abdelkader-abderrahmane/françafrique-and-africa's-security (accessed February 10, 2016).

Abderrahmane, Abdelkader. 2016. "The dangers of a new Libyan intervention." *IRIN*. March 28. Retrieved from http://www.irinnews.org/opinion/2016/03/28/dangers-new-libyan-intervention (accessed March 16, 2017).

Achiari, André. 2013. "Les massacres de Guelma." March 28. Retrieved from http://dakerscomerle.blogspot.fr/search/label/a%2027%20-%20LES%20MASSACRES%20DE%20GUELMA (accessed April 14, 2014).

Africa Research Bulletin, Vol. 52, 2. January 2016. Retrieved from https://onlinelibrary.wiley.com/doi/pdf/10.1111/j.1467-825X.2016.06752.x (accessed April 16, 2018).

Africa Time. 2016. "Le MAE nigérien salue la qualité de la coopération avec l'Algérie dans le domaine de la sécurité." July 28. Retrieved from http://fr.africatime.com/niger/db/le-mae-nigerien-salue-la-qualite-de-la-cooperation-avec-lalgerie-dans-le-domaine-de-la-securite (accessed March 7, 2018).

Algérie Presse Service. 2018. "Le premier ministre malien loue le rôle de l'Algérie dans la stabilité de son pays." January 13. Retrieved from http://www.huffpostmaghreb.com/2018/01/13/en-visite-en-algerie-le-premier-ministre-malien-loue-le-role-de-lalgerie-dans-la-stabilisation-de-la-region_n_18993140.html?ncid=tweetlnkfrhpmg00000009 (accessed January 13, 2018).

Algérie Presse Service. 2018. "Le MAE malien salue la disponibilité de l'Algérie à aider son pays pour l'élaboration d'une loi d'entente nationale." *Huffpost Maghreb*. January 14. Retrieved from http://www.huffpostmaghreb.com/2018/01/14/le-mae-malien-salue-la-disponibilite-de-lalgerie-a-aider-son-pays-pour-lelaboration-dune-loi-dentente-nationale_n_19001490.html?ncid=tweetlnkfrhpmg00000009 (accessed January 15, 2018).

Ammour, Laurence Aïda. 2012. "Regional security cooperation in the Maghreb and Sahel: algeria's pivotal ambivalence." *Africa Security Brief* (18). Retrieved from http://africacenter.org/wp-content/uploads/2012/02/ASB18.pdf (accessed February 6, 2018).

Badie, Bertrand. 2014. *Le Temps des HUMILIES. Pathologie des relations Internationales* (Paris: Odile Jacob).

Balmasov, Sergey. 2016. "Algeria: Russia's crisis-proof partner in the Arab World." *Russian International Affairs Council*. June 1. Retrieved from http://russiancouncil.ru/en/inncr/?id_4 = 7727#top-content (accessed February 6, 2018).

Bedjaoui, Mohammed. 2006. "Algeria and the global war on terror: A conversation with Mohammed Bedjaoui." *Council on Foreign Relations*. April 13. Retrieved from http://www.cfr.org/algeria/algeria-global-war-terror-conversation-mohammed-bedjaoui/p34047 (accessed April 9, 2018).

Benantar, Abdennour. 2016. "Les principes de la politique étrangère et de sécurité de l'Algérie mis à l'épreuve." *Questions Internationales*, 81 (September–October), 86–96.

Blyth, Fiona. 2013. "Perilous Desert" Finds interconnected threats and solutions in the Sahara." *Global Observatory*. May 2. Retrieved from http://www.theglobalobservatory.org/reports/490-perilous-desert-insecurity-in-the-sahara-edited-by-frederic-wehrey-and-anouar-boukhars.html (accessed March 9, 2015).

Boukhras, Anouar. 2012. "The paranoid neighbor: Algeria and the conflict in Mali." *The Carnegie Papers*. Retrieved from http://carnegieendowment.org/files/paranoid_neighbor.pdf (accessed September 6, 2014).

Boulter, Emily. 2015. "An awkward alliance: US–Algeria security cooperation." *Global Risk Insights*. September 21. Retrieved from http://globalriskinsights.com/2015/09/an-awkward-alliance-us-algeria-security-cooperation/ (accessed November 11, 2017).

Boumazza, Amina. 2013. "L'Algérie annule la dette de 14 pays africains." *Algérie-Focus*. May 29. Retrieved from http://www.algerie-focus.com/2013/05/lalgerie-annule-la-dette-de-plusieurs-pays-africains-dun-montant-de-902-millions-de-dollars/ (accessed May 29, 2018).

Brower, Benjamin, Claude. 2011. *A Desert Named Peace, The Violence of France's Empire in the Algerian Sahara*, 1844–1902 (New York: Columbia University Press).
Chase, Robert, Hill, Emily, & Kennedy, Paul. 1996. "Pivotal states and U.S. strategy." *Foreign Affairs*, 75 (1), 33–51.
Chikhi, Lamine. 2013. "Algeria puts army in charge of fighting drug trafficking." *Reuters.* July 25. Retrieved from http://www.reuters.com/article/2013/07/25/us-algeria-drugs-trafficking-idUSBRE96O0ZX20130725 (accessed March 6, 2016).
Constitution of the People's Democratic Republic of Algeria, Edition 2016. Algerian Constitutional Council. http://www.conseil-constitutionnel.dz/pdf/Constitutioneng.pdf.
Corm, Georges. 2015. *Pour une lecture profane des Conflits* (Paris: La Découverte).
Country Reports on Terrorism. 2016. United States Department of State Publication. Retrieved from https://www.state.gov/wp-content/uploads/2019/04/crt_2016.pdf.
Cridem. 2017. "L'Algérie ne rejoindra pas le 'G5 Sahel' car le soldat algérien ne meurt pas dans une guerre hors des frontières de son pays." December 8. Retrieved from http://www.cridem.org/C_Info.php?article=705510 (accessed December 9, 2017).
Daragahi, Borzou. 2013. "Algeria: A giant afraid of its own shadow." *Financial Times.* April 3. Retrieved from http://www.ft.com/intl/cms/s/0/5e3b9414-9b84-11e2-a820-00144feabdc0.html#axzz2RMrTrTN5 (accessed September 6, 2014).
Essedratti, Zeineb. 2012. "Bouteflika, Jefferson et la particularité algérienne." *Djazairnews.* September 6. Retrieved from http://www.djazairnews.info/pdf_fr/fr-06-09-2012.pdf (accessed September 9, 2012). No More Accessible.
Ghanem-Yazbeck, Dalia. 2017. "The Algerian Army: Cooperation, not intervention." *Carnegie Middle East Center.* December 7. Retrieved from http://carnegie-mec.org/2017/12/07/algerian-army-cooperation-not-intervention-pub-74970 (accessed January 5, 2018).
Global Counterterrorism Forum. 2016. "Capacity-building in the West Africa Region Working Group." Retrieved from https://www.thegctf.org/Working-Groups/Sahel-Region-Capacity-Building (accessed March 29, 2018).
Hamel, Tewfik. 2014. "Le dilemme de l'activisme algérien dans le Sahel-Maghreb." *Le Quotidien d'Oran.* August 28. Retrieved from http://www.lequotidien-oran.com/?archive_date=2014-08-29&news=5202309 (accessed March 17, 2018).
Horne, Alistair. 1984. *A Savage War of Peace: Algeria*, 1954–1962 (London: Macmillan).
International Crisis Group. 2015. "Algeria and its neighbours." *Crisis Group.* October. Retrieved from http://www.crisisgroup.org/~/media/Files/Middle%20East%20North%20Africa/North%20Africa/Algeria/164-algeria-and-its-neighbours.pdf (accessed April 6, 2016).
Julien, Charles, André. 1994. *Histoire de l'Afrique du nord. Des origines à 1830* (Paris: Grande Bibliothèque Payot).
Keenan, Jeremy. 2012. "Algerian 'state terrorism' and atrocities in northern Mali." *openDemocracy.* September 25. Retrieved from http://www.opendemocracy.net/jeremy-h-keenan/algerian-%E2%80%98state-terrorism%E2%80%99-and-atrocities-in-northern-mali (accessed July 16, 2013).
L'Expression. 2019. "L'homme qui sait parler au monde." March 21. Retrieved from http://www.lexpressiondz.com/actualite/312335-l-homme-qui-sait-parler-au-monde.html (accessed March 22, 2019). No More Accessible.
Maalouf, Amin. 2001. *Les Identités Meurtrières* Paris: Le Livre de Poche.
Malley, Robert. 1996. *The Call from Algeria. Third Worldism, Revolution, and the Turn to Islam* (London: University of California Press).
McDougall, James. 2017. *A History of Algeria* (Cambridge: Cambridge University Press).

Métaoui, Faiçal. 2018. "Frontières: Messahel défend l'isolement positif de l'Algérie." *TSA: Algérie*. January 22. Retrieved from https://www.tsa-algerie.com/frontieres-messahel-defend-lisolement-positif-de-lalgerie/ (accessed January 22, 2018).

Mundy, Jacob. (2010). "Algeria and the Western Sahara Dispute," *The Maghreb Center Journal*, Issue 1. Retrieved from http://maghrebcenter.files.wordpress.com/2011/07/maghrebcenter-journal-mundy_algeria-w-sahara.pdf (accessed October 9, 2016).

Nickels, Benjamin. 2014. "Algeria's role in African security." *Sada*. April 3. Retrieved from http://carnegieendowment.org/sada/55239 (accessed April 5, 2014).

Oukazi, Ghania. 2016. "Réunion de "parrains" à Paris, Esseradj à Alger: La Libye, entre parasitages et tuteurs autoproclamés." *Le Quotidien d'Oran*. October 4. Retrieved from http://www.lequotidien-oran.com/index.php?news=5234228&archive_date=2016-10-04 (accessed October 5, 2016).

Pigeaud, Fanny. 2017. "Débâcle de l'accusation contre M. Gbagbo." *Le Monde diplomatique*.

Ramzi, Walid. 2011. "Algeria to host rapid reaction force." *Magharebia*. January 27. Retrieved from http://magharebia.com/en_GB/articles/awi/features/2011/01/27/feature-01 (accessed February 6, 2018).

Rezag, Kamel. 2010. "Contribution of Algeria to the panel on the ransoms payment issue as a source of financing terrorism." *Permanent Mission of Algeria to the United Nations*, New York. September 7. Retrieved from http://jean-charles-brisard.com/docs/Kamel%20Rezag%20Bara%20Key%20Notes%20Remarks.pdf (accessed July 7, 2015).

Strachan, Anna-Louise. 2014. "Conflict Analysis of Algeria." *Governance, Social Development, Humanitarian, Conflict (GSDRC)*. Retrieved from http://www.gsdrc.org/docs/open/GSDRC_ConflAnal_Algeria.pdf (accessed February 6, 2014).

Titouche, Ali. 2012. "L'ardoise est de 3 milliards de dollars: l'Algérie efface la dette de dix pays africains." *El Watan*. July 31. Retrieved from http://elwatan.com/economie/l-ardoise-est-de-3-milliards-de-dollars-l-algerie-efface-la-dette-de-dix-pays-africains-31-07-2012-18078_111.php (accessed March 12, 2018).

TSA Algérie. 2017. "Ouyahia condamne l'esclavagisme en Libye, révèle le montant de l'aide de l'Algérie aux pays du Sahel." November 30. Retrieved from https://www.tsa-algerie.com/ouyahia-condamne-lesclavagisme-en-libye-revele-le-montant-de-laide-de-lalgerie-aux-pays-du-sahel/ (accessed December 8, 2017).

United Nations Security Council. 2009. "Security Council amends United Nations Al-Qaida/Taliban sanctions regime, authorizes appointment of ombudsperson to handle delisting issues." December 17. Retrieved from https://www.un.org/press/en/2009/sc9825.doc.htm (accessed November 18, 2017).

United States Department of State. 2015. Country Reports on Terrorism 2014: Algeria. June 19. Retrieved from https://www.refworld.org/docid/5587c75c28.html (accessed March 8, 2019).

Vince, Natalya. 2013. "In Amenas: A history of silence, not a history of violence, *Textures du temps*. January 20. Retrieved from http://texturesdutemps.hypotheses.org/576 (accessed February 10, 2015).

Zoubir, Yahia, H. 2018. "Algeria and the Sahelian quandary: The limits of containment security policy," *EuroMeSCo Joint Policy Study*. April. Retrieved from https://www.euromesco.net/wp-content/uploads/2018/03/EuroMeSCo-Joint-Policy-Study-8_The_Sahel_Europe_African_Border.pdf (accessed May 1, 2018).

15

CHINA'S RELATIONS WITH ALGERIA

A strategic partnership?

Yahia H. Zoubir and Youcef Hamitouche

Introduction

Of all the Maghreb countries, Algeria has the strongest political, diplomatic, economic, and trade relations with China. Through this chapter, we will show how relationships with multiple interests have been built that allow China to establish itself in this country by questioning what underlies them, their real weight, and their prospects. Answering these questions requires us to look back at how these relations were established in the 1950s and how the transition from solidarity to an ideological foundation to business relations became possible. As part of its global strategy of presence in the Mediterranean, its presence in Algeria cannot be limited to simple commercial opportunities. There is every reason to believe that China is seeking to increase its political and economic influence through its bilateral relations, which it promotes and prefers, and by developing relations with the other countries of the southern Mediterranean.

Algeria's relations with the People's Republic of China date back to the 1950s when Algeria was fighting French colonialism. Two events marked the establishment of strong ties between the two countries: the Afro-Asian Bandung Conference in April 1955 and China's establishment, 4 years before the country's independence, of diplomatic relations with the Provisional Government of the Algerian Republic proclaimed in September 1958. China was the first non–Arab state to extend such recognition on December 20, 1958. In the last decade, the two countries have developed sustained cooperation and partnership at all levels. Such a strategy allows China to counterbalance French and American interests in Algeria and North Africa on the one hand (Belhadj et al. 2016, 329); and on the other hand, Algeria's policy of maintaining an independent foreign policy, which rests on the diversification of its relations with the outside world. For China, as for the European Union and the US, Algeria is an important regional power not only because of its size, geographical location, and geopolitical position, but also because of its rich mineral resources, such as zinc, iron-ore, uranium, oil, and gas resources. Also, because of its military might, Algeria might fit in the category of middle powers (Zoubir forthcoming).

For China, Algeria's assets and potential are attractive for reasons other than economics. Indeed, Algeria is also important politically at various levels, for instance, its influence and role in the Mediterranean, sub-Saharan Africa, and in the African Union. Thus, both economically and politically, Algeria fits into China's policy in the Mediterranean and in sub-Saharan Africa, as well as in the Belt and Road Initiative (land and maritime). Having Algeria as a reliable strategic partner on the continent is a significant asset for China, which continues to view Africa as a strategic hub for its own modernisation.

The chapter will focus on the development of the historical, political, economic, military, and cultural ties between the two countries at various periods, with focus on the last two decades.

China and revolutionary Algeria

During China's ideological stage of foreign policy (1950s–1970s), the Chinese Communist Party paid great attention to the struggle of the Middle East against Western colonialism (Li Anshan 2007). This was the period when political relations between Algeria and China intensified due to the revolutionary ideology the two shared, and to the role of Algerian diplomacy in the United Nations, the Non-Aligned Movement, the Organisation of African Unity, and the Arab League. Both countries cooperated and exchanged views on international issues, particularly on liberation movements.

Following Algeria's independence, China provided political and military support to the Algerian National Liberation Front and National Popular Army, the ALN (Shinn & Eisenman 2012, 233). China's foreign principles have in some ways inspired Algeria's own foreign policy to this day. In the 1950s, China opposed the North Atlantic Treaty Organisation's political, economic, and military support for France against Algerians in their struggle against France (Deshpande 1973, 81–82).

China supported the Algerian National Liberation Front not only politically, but also its military force, the ALN. Peking hosted ALN delegations in spring 1959 and in 1960, respectively; China provided arms, military training (guerrilla tactics like those the Chinese provided to the Vietnamese), and financial aid estimated at $10 million (Copper 1975, 135).

China's policy towards post-independent Algeria

In the 1960s and 1970s, China and Algeria closely coordinated their efforts at the United Nations on liberation movements such as the Palestinian Liberation Organisation and the African National Congress (Calabrese 2017). Following its "opening up" policy, China pursued a pragmatic foreign policy, gradually ending the radical, confrontational foreign policy of the 1950–1970s, focusing instead on its modernisation drive. Thus, trade relations, not ideology, have dominated relations with developing countries, including Algeria. China now engaged in economic and cultural cooperation, while upholding the principle of non-interference in others' internal affairs. To modernise the country, China searched for new suppliers of energy and raw materials, such as hydrocarbons, which are strategic for its economy, regardless of those suppliers' ideological and political inclinations. Thus, China has pursued an oil diplomacy based on strengthening political partnerships and trade relations with other countries as well as on increasing direct foreign investments. This is precisely the vision that determined its relations with developing countries.

In this context, relations with Algeria developed at a faster pace because of the long-standing relationship and because of Algeria's own needs (diversification of economic partners). Both sought to serve their mutual interests through the strengthening of economic relations and trade links. Algeria's geopolitical location provided an opportunity for China to spread its influence on Europe and in sub-Saharan Africa through the expansion of Chinese companies exporting low-cost products. Algeria's location did and does present an advantage for Chinese investors about transportation costs, particularly with the availability of air, sea, and land transport routes that link Algeria to Africa and Europe (Kab 2015).

Political relations

During the Cold War, closer ties with China faced challenges and constraints due to Algeria's good political relations with both the Soviet Union and Western countries (Zoubir 2019). Even after its independence, Algeria was still linked to France politically, culturally, and economically, based on the pre-independence Franco-Algerian Evian Accords. Furthermore, following the Sand War (1963) between Algeria and pro-Western Morocco, Algeria intensified military and political cooperation with the Soviet Union (Zoubir 1990–1991).

Obviously, the development and improvement of Algeria's relations with the Soviet Union, engaged then in a bitter ideological conflict with China, complicated ties between Algeria and China. The Chinese argued that Communist China, not the USSR, showed closer solidarity with the Third World than the Soviets, who were seeking détente with Western countries. They also asserted that China's support for the Algerian revolution was more important than the support the Soviet Union provided (Zoubir 1995). Notwithstanding these difficulties, Algeria and China shared the revolutionary culture and were active members of the Non-Aligned Movement (Lincot 2017).

At the political level, the Chinese believed that Algeria could influence other countries in the Middle East and North Africa to recognise the People's Republic of China (Copper 1975, 135) and restore China's "legal and legitimate seat in the Security Council of the United Nations Organization."

This proved successful when China replaced Taiwan in the Security Council in 1971, owing partly to Algeria's diplomacy and lobbying. Relations between the two countries increased in 1982 with the establishment of the mixed commission for economic, trade, and technical cooperation, which later included agriculture, energy, scientific research (Ying & Xin 2008), and nuclear power.

During the Islamist armed insurgency in Algeria in the 1990s, the two countries signed in 1997 an agreement on holding regular political consultations (Chinese Foreign Ministry 2004; Xu 2004), while Western countries maintained a tacit diplomatic embargo on Algeria (Zoubir & Darbouche 2009). In that difficult context, Algeria sought to reinforce its cooperation and relations with China whose objective was to find an alternative to the partnership with Western countries. In February 2004, Chinese President Hu Jintao visited Algeria, where he held discussions with President Abdelaziz Bouteflika, raising the possibility of establishing a new economic and political international order (Xinhuanet 2004). During his visit to China in November 2006, Bouteflika declared that: "Our relations intensified during the last years, they have been consecrated by a declaration about a strategic partnership initiated during my visit in 2004" (Xinhuanet 2014).

The two countries signed the Declaration on Strategic Partnership and Cooperation in 2006, during the Forum for China-Africa Cooperation held in Beijing (Ying & Xin 2008). In April 2015, during the Algerian-Chinese Trade and Investment Forum that China held in Beijing, China and Algeria signed 15 draft agreements, two agreements, and a memorandum of understanding on industry, mining, agriculture, and tourism (Ministry of Industry and Mines April 2015). Henceforth, the intensification of political relations between the two countries witnessed frequent high-level official visits while economic ties saw the establishment of air links between Beijing and Algiers, the presence of 50,000 Chinese workers in the construction sector, and the flow of Algerian business people to Yiwu (Zhejiang Province) in search of cheap Chinese consumer goods. This cooperation between the two countries has expanded since the establishment of a Joint Committee for Economic, Commercial, and Technical Cooperation in 1982, which encompassed almost all fields: energy, agriculture, construction, scientific research, culture, military, and nuclear sector, as well as animal production, irrigation, and combating desertification (Xinhuanet 2014).

China and the Western Sahara issue

Despite the close relations with Algeria, China has not supported the Algerian stance on the independence of Western Sahara. China has adopted a neutral position, but seems inclined at times to favour Morocco's offer of a "large autonomy" to the Sahrawis because it sees it falsely as falling within one of its five principles, i.e., respect of sovereignty and territorial integrity of states. China favours a political resolution to the conflict, encouraging the POLISARIO Front (the Frente Popular de Liberación de Saguia el Hamra et du Rio de Oro) and

Morocco to engage in negotiations-based resolutions of the Security Council to reach a just, lasting, and acceptable settlement, as inscribed in United Nations documents. Algerian officials are quite disappointed with China's ambivalent attitude. In an interview (Zoubir [interview in Beijing] 2016), a high-level official declared that, "we have supported China on many issues, including the PRC's gaining a seat at the UN Security Council. We told our Chinese partners that Western Sahara is a different question from Tibet or Xinjiang, to no avail." Clearly, China's position derives from Morocco's threat that should China recognise the Sahrawi Arab Democratic Republic, Morocco would establish diplomatic relations with Taiwan or raise the issue of Tibet (Zoubir [interview in Shanghai] 2018; Hammond 2017). In exchange for China's neutrality, Morocco would abstain not only from recognising Taiwan, but also avoid raising concerns about China's policy towards Muslims in Xinjiang. Of course, China's position on Western Sahara derives also from its economic interests in Morocco (for example, the meta-project in Tangier). Indeed, between 2011 and 2015, Chinese Foreign Direct Investment in Morocco increased 195%, with a 93% increase between 2014 and 2015 alone (Luedi 2017). China appreciates Morocco's geopolitical position and Morocco's privileged economic partnership with European countries, particularly France and Spain, and its friendship with most French-speaking sub-Saharan countries (Maury & Rabbaa 2015). Therefore, these and other factors work in favour of Morocco (Hafti 2017) and thus represent opportunities for China to access the European and West African zones, while keeping its strong ties with Algeria. However, a former Chinese ambassador asserted that China's relations with Morocco are in no way commensurate with China's relations with Algeria (Zoubir 2018, interview).

Sino-Algeria military cooperation

Until the last two decades, Algeria had imported 90 percent of its weapons from the Soviet Union/Russia (Zoubir 2011). For quite some time, Algeria did not import much military hardware from China, except for Chinese-made Soviet AK-47s. However, political, economic, and cultural transformations in Algeria in the 1990s and 2000s led Algerian authorities to diversify sources of arms and military training, including with the United States, Western countries, and China. In the mid-1990s, Algeria bought arms from China worth merely $100 million (Calabrese 2017). However, with the rise of oil revenues until 2014, Algeria decided to replace its obsolete military hardware with modern weaponry. The National Popular Army (ANP) began to equip its different forces with modern Chinese weapons, making Algeria one of the nine African emergent customers for Chinese military exports (Cowburn 2016). There was a large increase of Chinese arms exports to Algeria in the period 2013–2017 (Mediterranean Dialogue [MD] Staff 2018), making Algeria one of the primary customers of China's arms in Africa (Calabrese 2017). Algeria acquired various types of weapons from China, such as the LZ45 155 mm self-propelled howitzers, delivered in 2014, which the armed forces use in tactical exercises, the 50 C-802/CSS-N-8 anti-ship missiles, and 50 FM90 surface-to-air missile systems. In July 2017, the Algerian Navy acquired the third and final C28A corvette ordered from China in March 2012 (Calabrese 2017). Chinese sales to Algeria included three frigates (Alden et al. 2018, 337) and the Chinese Hainan patrol boats, armed with mines and rockets for anti-submarine missions, products of Chinese shipyards (Badis 2018). Moreover, the military partnership between China and Algeria took on a new dimension with the launching of the Algerian satellite into space (Badis 2018). In view of the modernisation and professionalisation of the ANP, the military does not seek cheap and low-quality weapons or to acquire arms and military equipment surplus that the Chinese army wishes to discard. On the contrary, the ANP purchases high-tech and modern military equipment to transform the ANP into one of the most modern in Africa (Pairault 2015, 11). In sum, China has gradually become an important military partner, thus reducing dependence on Russia, Algeria's traditional supplier (Pairault 2015, 11). However, Russia remains Algeria's main supplier; Russia's arms sales to Algeria increased by 4.7% in 2012–2016, compared to 2007–2011. Today, Russia accounts for 66% of Algerian arms imports, whereas imports from China and Germany account for 15% and 12%, respectively (Fleurant 2017, 34).

The military cooperation with China also involves military training; about 500 Algerian officers visit China annually to train in two or three Chinese academies (Zoubir 2016, interview). The two countries also cooperate on security issues to fight international terrorism, especially since Chinese multinational oil companies, such as Sinopec, are present in the Algerian oil extraction of hydrocarbons in the Sahara where terrorist groups have remained active (Lincot 2017). This explains why the two countries have strengthened their cooperation in the fight against terrorism (China's Ministry of Foreign Affairs 2016).

Because of the insecurity on its borders, resulting from the collapse of regimes following the Arab uprisings, Algeria has increased its defence budget and developed even closer military cooperation with China, including the naval sector (Zhao 2016). Nonetheless, Algeria is diversifying its military hardware and China cannot at this stage provide Algeria with the same type of equipment that it can get from other developed countries. Algeria is interested in purchasing advanced military equipment, even asking Washington to re-examine its restrictions on Algeria's military imports from the United States (Ybarra 2019).

Economic cooperation, investments, and trade

Bilateral economic and trade cooperation between China and Algeria increased rapidly in the early 1980s. The cooperation in construction building projects, agriculture, and water reservoirs had begun in 1980 (Chinese Foreign Ministry 2004), at a time when economic and trade relations and cooperation between the two countries had been limited, due to Algeria's weighty commercial relations with Europe, particularly France. The trade volume totalled only

US$ 170 million in 1982; it rose to US$ 199 million in 2000, and to US$ 292 million in 2001 (Chinese Foreign Ministry 2004). Since the 2000s, commercial relations have grown exponentially. Algeria became a sizeable market for Chinese companies; indeed, between 2005 to June 2016 alone, Chinese corporations secured $22.2 billion contracts (African Daily Voice 2018), mostly in housing construction, roads, highway, rail, and hydrocarbons and the trade volume has reached more than $8 billion in recent years.

The Algerian authorities chose to rely on China to help fulfil the promise that the president had made to provide housing for the population; indeed, until China's involvement, Algeria had a severe housing shortage. Given that the housing crisis had reached dire proportions which could have triggered social unrest, only China was able to deliver housing rapidly and at relatively low cost. China's involvement in building many civilian infrastructures was due to the booming financial resources that Algeria earned from the rapid and huge increase of oil prices in the world energy market.

In addition to housing, China obtained a contract worth over $7 billion for the construction of half of the 1,200 kilometre-long highway from the border with Morocco to the frontier with Tunisia. The construction projects took on strategic importance for Bouteflika's regime, whose legitimacy rested on its promises to improve the welfare of its citizens, create new jobs, and stimulate economic growth.

Other examples of cooperation include the 3,000 kilometre North-South Trans-Saharan Highway linking Algeria to Nigeria, the most difficult portion of which was built by the China State Construction Engineering Corporation (Xinhuanet 2017). The Chinese have also worked on extending the railroad network and telecommunications. The Chinese obtained a $3.5 billion contract for the development of a railway won by the Chinese Civil Engineering Construction Corporation (CCECC) (Souiha 2010).

In the telecommunications sector, companies such as Huawei and Zhongxing Telecom Equipment represent an example of China's direct investment in Algeria. China also opened a telecommunications training centre in Oran (Lafargue 2008, 68). The China State Construction Engineering Corporation has built tens of thousands of dwellings in different towns, as well as edifices such as the Sheraton-run Hotel, and a huge shopping mall.

In view of the Belt and Maritime Silk Roads, coupled with the aspiration to penetrate the Mediterranean, China signed an agreement with Algeria worth $3.3 billion to build a huge new port of El Hamdania, in Cherchell, 100 km west of Algiers: the transport and merchandise routes to European ports and beyond (TBP & Agencies 2016). The China State Construction Engineering Corporation, the China Harbour Engineering Company, and the Public Algerian Port Services Group, will carry out this project under the 51/49% rule (*Jeune Afrique* 18 Janvier 2016). Algerian law requires that Algerians own 51% of any industrial joint ventures with foreign companies. The port in Cherchell is a mega port with 23 docks capable of processing 26 million tonnes of goods per year. The port, which will rank among the 30 most important ports in the world, will have a processing capacity of 6.5 million containers and 25.7 million tonnes/year of cargo. It will also be a pole of industrial development (*Huffpost Algérie* 2018). Chinese banks will finance this project, while the Shanghai Ports Group will manage it.

This port will benefit not only Algeria, but also Africa as it will allow for the transportation of goods and merchandise to African countries (Sahel-Saharan countries, central Africa, etc.) through the trans-Saharan road in 15 instead of 45 days. Algeria seems willing to face this challenge, for Chinese funding represents the first opportunity for Algeria to seek external financing for such a type of project.

In terms of investments, Algeria has received roughly 7.3% of China's investments in Africa, the third after South Africa and the Democratic Republic of Congo (Pairault 2016). Algeria is quite interested in partaking in China's silk road (Boukhelfa 2017) and has signed an agreement with China to join (March 2018) and was admitted to the Asian Infrastructure Investment Bank (December 2018).

After the collapse of oil prices in 2014–2015, Algeria turned to China to finance several infrastructure projects (Chikhi 2016).

For the first time in history, in 2013, China became Algeria's largest trading partner outside of hydrocarbons, supplanting France, the traditional partner hitherto (Sun & Zoubir 2015).

France is the European country whose position in North Africa in general, and Algeria in particular, has declined the most because of fierce competition from China. The strengthening of cooperation between Algeria and China increased to such a level that they signed a Comprehensive Strategic Partnership in 2014 (Rabhi 2014), the first of its kind between China and a MENA country (Zoubir 2016, interview). This partnership resulted in direct Chinese investments in all of Algeria's priority sectors in the 2015–2019 five-year plan, an investment of $60 billion (Djazairess 2017; del Panta 2018); these investments were to expand cooperation within the framework of the Comprehensive Strategic Partnership, which would lead to a greater involvement of China in Algeria in industry, science, and technology (Paris 2014).

By 2017, China remained the largest exporter to Algeria with $8.396 billion (World Integrated Trade Solutions 2019). The Chinese Renminbi has become an accepted mode of payment in exchanges between the two countries (Zoubir 2016, interview; Chikhi 2016); for Algeria, this aims at reducing dependence on the US dollar. Overall, Chinese companies have realised $60–90 worth of projects between 1999 and 2016 (Zoubir 2016, interview). The private and public companies of the two countries established joint ventures in Algeria on the principle of the 51/49 rule, which, even if resented, has not deterred Chinese companies from coming to do business in Algeria (Zoubir 2016, interview).

Algeria in China's energy strategy

Although China does not import much oil from North Africa, Sino-Algerian relations have witnessed a new period of cooperation in the field of energy. Oil supplies from Algeria and Libya represented only 2% of Chinese oil imports. The long geographic distance between the two countries accounted for China's apparent lack of interest in North African oil (Lafargue 2008, 70) and to the heavy presence of American oil companies in Algeria and Libya. However, the MENA remains the principal source of natural gas for China as China's energy imports from these two regions have witnessed a steady increase in recent years due to China's growing, substantial consumer needs (Zhao 2011). In addition, China's interest in North African oil aims at reducing the heavy reliance on Middle Eastern oil and diversifying its energy supplies as much as possible.

Algeria has oil reserves amounting to 12.2 billion barrels (Export.gov 2019); it also boasts "20 trillion cubic meters of technically recoverable shale gas, representing 707 Tcf of technically recoverable shale gas, the third-largest quantity of untapped shale gas resources in the world" (Export.gov 2019). In 2017, Algeria possessed 4,504 billion cubic metres of proven natural gas reserves (Organisation of Oil Exporting Countries 2019). This might provide China with an alternative source of hydrocarbons. Chinese oil companies, such as China National Petroleum Corporation, China Petroleum, Chemical Corporation, and China Petroleum Engineering and Construction Corporation have all launched large investments in exploring oil and gas in Algeria (Pecoraro 2010, 12). In addition, Algeria boasts other raw materials, like uranium, iron, and gold, which are essential for China's modernisation.

China National Petroleum Corporation has obtained a contract with the Algerian state-owned company Sonatrach. China's Sinopec inked a contract worth 420 million euros to develop gas reserves in Zarzaitine, a region situated near the border with Libya (Diaby 2014, 79). The China National Oil and Gas Exploration Company signed an agreement with Algeria on October 8, 2016, and the China Petroleum and Chemical Corporation (Sinopec) announced the completion of the Toual 3D seismic acquisition project located in the Saharan swathes of Algeria (Benabdallah 2016). Yet, the relationship between China and Algeria in the energy sector remains quite limited, although this might change in the future due to the US export of shale oil to Europe. This in turn may mean the reduction of Algerian gas supplies to Europe, a traditional market for Algerian hydrocarbons, and would compel Algeria to seek other markets for its energy outputs in countries like China and India.

Clearly, China's growing and stronger presence in Algeria's oil sector resulted from the withdrawal of some Western companies (BP and Norway's Statoil in particular) following the terrorist attack in January 2013 against the gas plant in Tiguentourine, near In Amenas (Gallucci 2016). In addition, China expanded its interests to the mining and raw materials sectors; Algeria has an estimated 2 billion tonnes of phosphates, making it one of the most important fertiliser producers in the Mediterranean basin. This explains why Chinese companies, like CITIC Group and Wengfu (one of the world's leaders in phosphates and fertiliser), began production of the phosphate mine in Tebessa, with 2 million tonnes per year, which will rise to nearly 10 million tonnes after the establishment of partnership with Chinese companies (APS 2018).

China is also cooperating with the Algerian public industrial group, Manadjim El-Djazair, to develop and exploit marble and granite mines (Kenzi 2018).

Furthermore, China is present in the construction of dams and irrigation systems, such as the water dam in Draa Eddis, in the highlands around Sétif. This gigantic dam is entrusted to the Chinese company CWE that will allow Algeria to develop its hydroelectric energy and to reduce its dependence on hydrocarbons (L.B. 2009). Chinese companies like CGC Overseas Construction and Geo Engineering Mining Company Shaolin secured contracts to begin prospecting in the Hoggar, in the deep south (Lafargue 2008, 65).

China's comparative economic advantages offer many opportunities for Algeria, such as access to new technologies, development of nuclear power (e.g., in Ain Oussara), infrastructure, and direct investment (Li & Yuwen 2016). The existence of the nuclear site worried the United States and the United Kingdom about a possible collaboration between China and Algeria to develop nuclear weapons (Sciolino & Schmitt 1991). To alleviate such concerns, Algeria signed the Nuclear Non-Proliferation Treaty in 1993, and cooperated with the International Atomic Energy Agency (Burr 2007). Nuclear cooperation with China increased following the signing of a contract in March 2008 for the construction of a civilian nuclear power plant (Pairault 2015, 11).

Cultural and scientific cooperation

China and Algeria signed nearly 20 exchange and cooperation agreements on culture, education, sports, and media (Chinese Foreign Ministry 2004). However, China's cultural presence is very modest and limited, except for the organisation of some cultural events. Surprisingly, unlike most African countries, Algeria does not host a Confucius Institute. The teaching of the Chinese language is available only in the form of intensive courses at the universities of Algiers, Constantine, Annaba, and Oran; only seven Chinese teachers are present in the country (Lifa 2010). According to Tsui Xiaobzi, cultural advisor at the Chinese embassy in Algiers, the absence of Chinese cultural centres is due to limited space at the embassy. It is also due to the refusal of the Algerian Ministry of Foreign Affairs, the Ministry of Culture, and the Algerian Ministry of Higher Education to open Chinese cultural centres or Chinese Language Institutes in the universities (Lifa 2010; Oul 2019). Even some Algerian officials do not comprehend why the Algerian authorities refuse the establishment of Confucius Institutes in the country (Zoubir 2016, interview). According to an anonymous Algerian official, opposition to the establishment of a Confucius Institute in the country comes from religious figures. A Chinese professor confirmed this mistaken identification of Confucius with a religious figure when he stated that, "We were told that Confucius was referring to our religion. But in China, Confucius is the nation's first educator" (Li Linghong, cited in Azzoug 2014a). What is peculiar is that, on the one hand, Algerian officials wish to consolidate the country's relations with China; on the other hand, they do little to encourage the teaching of Chinese. The explanation may also lie in the fact that French remains the dominant foreign language in the country. There is evidence that Algerians are keen to learn the

Chinese language in private schools when available and in Language Institutes in Algerian universities. (Azzoug 2014b). In addition, hundreds of Algerians study in China some of them through Chinese scholarships (Oul 2019). Although China has sought to enhance its commercial interests through cultural roots in Algeria, the French-speaking lobby in Algeria obviously constitutes a challenge to China's cultural presence and expansion. The Chinese Xinhuanet and China Central Television, CCTV (now China Global Television Network) are available in Algeria, but it is not known how many Algerians read the Chinese press or watch CGTN, both available in French.

In the scientific fields, China signed a contract on space cooperation with Algeria (Paris 2014). In 2013, the two countries signed a bilateral cooperation agreement covering space science, technology, and other agreements with the Algerian Space Agency (Xinhuanet 2014). China has provided necessary assistance to Algeria for the completion of the Alcomsat-1 Algerian space telecommunications satellite, an exceptional achievement (Badis 2018). With the success of the satellite programme, Algeria and China have continued developing satellite programmes for earth observation focused on the environment, regional planning, mining and agricultural resources, urban planning, transport, prevention and management of major risks, as well as the field of communication (Badis 2018).

Conclusion

Sino–Algerian relations have witnessed an exponential growth since the early 2000s. This has allowed Algeria to lessen its economic and trade dependence on France, which used to account for more than 50% of Algeria's trade. This has changed to the point where the president of the European Parliament Antonio Tajani considered the extension of China's influence in the continent, including Algeria, as a threat to European interests, stating that, "Africa is now risking becoming a Chinese colony, but the Chinese want only raw materials. Stability does not interest them" (*Jeune Afrique* 2017). Despite France's attempts to regain its share of the Algerian market, Chinese firms continue to secure most of the projects and China has remained Algeria's main trading partner. The Sino-Algerian ties have worried the French as could be seen in France's Senate report (Allizard & Jourda 2018), which expressed concern about China's commercial, economic and even space ambitions in Algeria, as well Algeria's participation in the Belt and Road (Ouramdane 2018). It remains to be seen whether the close ties between Algeria and China will continue their growth and whether their partnership is truly strategic (Zoubir 2019).

References

Alden, Chris, Alao, Abiodun, Chun, Zhang & Laura Barber. (2018). *China and Africa: Building Peace and Security Cooperation on the Continent*. New York: Palgrave Macmillan.
African Daily Voice (Newsroom). 2018 (December 29). China remains the leading supplier of Algeria. https://africandailyvoice.com/en/2018/12/29/china-remains-the-leading-supplier-of-algeria/ (accessed January 5, 2019).

Algerian Ministry of Industry and Mines. (2015). "Algeria, China ink several agreements, Mo Us." *APS*, April 28. Retrieved from http://www.andi.dz/index.php/en/presse/1212-algeria-china-ink-several-agreements-mous (accessed September 11, 2018).

Allizard, Pascal & Jourda, Gisèle. (2018). *Sénat français, 520. Session Ordinaire de 2017-2018: Rapport d'information de la commission des affaires étrangères, de la défense et des forces armées (1), le groupe de travail sur les nouvelles routes de la soie (2)*. 30 May 2018. Retrieved from https://www.senat.fr/rap/r17-520/r17-5201.pdf (accessed October 24, 2018).

APS. (2018). "Transformation de phosphate: Partenariat conclu prochainement avec la Chine." Retrieved from http://www.aps.dz/economie/69534-transformation-de-phosphate-partenariat-conclu-prochainement-avec-la-chine (accessed May 20, 2018).

Azzoug, Samir. (2014a) "Le chinois la langue du futur." *DjaZairess* (from ElWatan). 5 February. https://www.djazairess.com/fr/elwatan/444711. Retrieved September 5, 2019.

Azzoug, Samir. (2014b). "Pour l'installation de l'institut Confucius en Algérie." *El Watan*, 5 February. https://www.elwatan.com/pages-hebdo/etudiant/pour-linstallation-de-linstitut-confucius-en-algerie-05-02-2014. Retrieved May 7, 2014.

Badis, Adlène. (2018). "Chine-Algérie: L'éloge d'un partenariat prometteur." Retrieved from http://www.reporters.dz/index.php/item/90644-chine-algerie-l-eloge-d-un-partenariat-prometteur (accessed May 25, 2018).

Belhadj, Imen, Sun, Degang & Yahia H. Zoubir. (2016). "China in North Africa: A strategic partnership." In Zoubir, Y. H. & White, Gregory. (Eds.), *North African Politics. Change and Continuity*. London & New York: Routledge.

Benabdallah, Lina. (2016). "Algiers and Beijing have improved their economic ties, but Algeria can certainly benefit more." *Carnegie Middle East Centre*. Retrieved from http://carnegie-mec.org/diwan/66145 (accessed February 10, 2017).

Boukhelfa, Ahcene. (2017). "Ceinture et Route. La chaine CGTN in French (Interview of Ambassador Boukhelfa) May 15, 2017. Retrieved from https://www.youtube.com/watch?v=VSYE8otDkeY (August 15, 2019).

Burr, William. (2007). "The Algerian nuclear problem, 1991: Controversy over the Es Salam nuclear reactor." U.S. Department of State. National Security Archive. Retrieved from https://nsarchive2.gwu.edu/nukevault/ebb228/index.htm (accessed November 3, 2016).

Calabrese, John. (2017). "Sino-Algerian relations: On a path to realizing their full potential?" Middle East Institute. October 31. Retrieved from http://www.mei.edu/content/map/sino-algerian-relations-path-realizing-their-full-potential (10 November 2017).

Chikhi, Lamine. (2016). "Hit by oil price drop, Algeria turns to China for funds." *Reuters*. January 20. Retrieved from https://www.reuters.com/article/algeria-economy-china-idusl8n15223j (accessed January 10, 2017).

China Ministry of Foreign Affairs. (2004). "China-Algeria relations." January 18. Retrieved from http://www.china.org.cn/english/features/phfnt/85069.htm (accessed Mars 15, 2017).

China Ministry of Foreign Affairs. (2016). "China, Algeria vow to boost counter-terrorism cooperation." July 13. Retrieved from https://www.mfa.gov.cn/zflt/eng/jlydh/sjzs/t1380516.htm (accessed February 21, 2017).

Copper, John F. (1975). "China's Foreign aid program an analysis of an instrument of Peking's foreign policy." PhD diss. Political Science, University of South Carolina, International law and Relations.

Cowburn, Ashley. (2016). "Two-thirds of African countries now using Chinese military equipment, report reveals." *The Independent*. Retrieved from https://www.independent.co.uk/news/world/africa/two-thirds-of-african-countries-now-using-chinese-military-equipment-a6905286.html (accessed January 19, 2017).

Del Panta, Gianni. (2018, September 28). China's Growing Economic Role in Algeria." *ResetDOC*, https://www.resetdoc/story/chinas-growing-economic-role-algeria/ (accessed August 20, 2019).

Deshpande, GP. (1973). "China's policy in Africa 1949–64." PhD diss. Jawaharlal Nehru University, School of International Studies, New Delhi.

Diaby, Fodé S. (2014). "Les stratégies des entreprises chinoises en Afrique: quels objectifs, quelle coopération?" Université de Nice Sophia Antipolis: école doctorale 513 Droit et Sciences Politiques, Economiques et de Gestion, p. 79.

Djazairess. (2017). "La Chine, le plus grand investisseur étranger dans le marché Algérien." September 4. Retrieved from https://www.djazairess.com/essalam/64900 (accessed November 10, 2017).

Export. gov. (2019). "Algeria - Oil and Gas – Hydrocarbons." 31 January. https://www.export.gov/article?id=Algeria-Oil-and-Gas-Hydrocarbons. Retrieved March 11, 2019.

Fleurant, Aude & Wezeman, Pieter D., Wezeman, Simon T. & Nan Tian. (2017). "Tendances des transferts internationaux d'armements 2016. In. *Groupe de Recherche et d'information sur la Paix et La Sécurité (GRIP). Dépenses militaires, production et transferts d'armes - Compendium 2017*. P. 34. Retrieved from: https://www.grip.org/sites/grip.org/files/RAPPORTS/2017/Rapport_2017-7.pdf (accessed March 11, 2019).

Gallucci, Maria. (2016). "Terror attack on Algerian gas plant raising security fears for North Africa's oil and gas infrastructure." *International Business Times*. https://www.ibtimes.com/terror-attack-algerian-gas-plant-raising-security-fears-north-africas-oil-gas-2341217.

Hafti, Youssef. (2017). "Moroccan-Chinese relationship: The interaction of 'Going East'." In Degang, Sun & Zhongmin, Liu. (Eds.), *The New Frontier of the Middle East Politics and Economy*. Beijing: World Affairs Press, pp. 211–244.

Hammond, Joseph. (2017). "Morocco: China's gateway to Africa?" *The Diplomat*. 1 March. Retrieved from https://thediplomat.com/2017/03/morocco-chinas-gateway-to-africa/ (accessed March 25, 2018).

Jeune Afrique. (2016). Algérie: prêt chinois de 3,3 milliards de dollars pour la construction du port d'El Hamdania. January 18. Retrieved from https://www.jeuneafrique.com/294779/economie/algerie-33-milliards-de-dollars-pour-le-port-del-hamdania/ (accessed February 18, 2017).

Jeune Afrique. 2017 (March 29). "L'Afrique risque de devenir une colonie chinoise' selon le président du Parlement européen." https://www.jeuneafrique.com/422521/politique/lafrique-se-trouve-situation-dramatique-selon-president-parlement-europeen/.

Kab, Faiza. (2015). "Les relations Algéro-Chinoises à travers la visite historique du Premier ministre Algérien (in Arabic)." *Arab Information Centre. No: 2015\PRS\4652*. 27 April. Retrieved from http://www.arabsino.com/articles/15-04-27/12348.htm (accessed Mars 10, 2017).

Kenzi, Adam. (2018), "Partenariat Algéro-Chinois: Cinq projets industriels et d'infrastructure Portuaire Retenus." 31 January. Retrieved from https://www.algeri-epatriotique.com/2018/01/31/partenariat-algero-chinois-cinq-projets-industriels-dinfrastructure-portuaire-retenus (accessed May 25, 2018).

Lafargue, François. (2008). "New economic actors in the Mediterranean, China in North Africa." European Institute of the Mediterranean (IEMed), https://www.iemed.org/anuari/2008/aarticles/EN64.pdf.

L.B. (2009). "Barrage Draâ Eddis à Tachouda: 400 000 DA pour 22 nouveaux expropriés." *El Watan*. 12 October. Retrieved from https://www.djazairess.com/fr/elwatan/139848 (accessed January 15, 2017).

"Le grand port d'El Hamdania à Cherchell sera financé par un prêt de l'Etat chinois, selon Raouya." *Huffpost Algérie.* 2 July 2018. https://www.huffpostmaghreb.com/ entry/le-grand-port-del-hamdania-a-cherchell-sera-finance-par-un-pret-de-letat-chinois-selon-raouya_mg_5b3a123ae4b007aa2f81c888. Retrieved March 13, 2019.

Li, Anshan. (2007). "China and Africa." Unpublished paper (Zoubir's personal library).

Li, Xue & Yuwen, Zheng. (2016). "The future of China's diplomacy in the Middle East." *The Diplomat.* 26 July. Retrieved from, https://thediplomat.com/2016/07/the-future-of-chinas-diplomacy-in-the-middle-east/ (accessed July 5, 2017).

Lifa, Abdelkader. (2010). "156 étudiants algériens inscrits dans des universités chinoises. *Elmoustakbal.* Retrieved from https://www.djazairess.com/elmoustakbel/1262 (accessed December 10, 2016).

Lincot, Emmanuel. (2017). "Les relations entre la Chine et l'Algérie." 14 February. Retrieved from https://www.youtube.com/watch?v=FlYR6DxzztE (accessed Avril 20, 2017).

Luedi, Jeremy. (2017). "Under the radar: What's behind China's love affair with Morocco?" *Global Risk Insights.* 26 March. Retrieved from https://globalriskinsights. com/2017/03/chinas-love-affair-with-morocco/ (accessed June 18, 2018).

Maury, Rédéric & Rabbaa, Nadia. (2015). "Le Maroc, un pont d'or pour la Chine. *Jeune Afrique.* 29 December. Retrieved from http://www.jeuneafrique.com/mag/286294/ economic/maroc-pont-dor-chine/ (accessed February 15, 2017).

Mediterranean Dialogue [MD] Staff. (2018). "Asia and the Middle East lead rising trend in US exports grow significantly." *Modern Diplomacy.* 12 March. Retrieved from https:// moderndiplomacy.eu/2018/03/12/asia-and-the-middle-east-lead-rising-trend-in-arms-imports-us-exports-grow-significantly/ (accessed June 6, 2018).

Oul, Ahmed (2019, January 19). Bourses d'études chinoises pour les étudiants algériens. ObservAlgerie. https://www.observalgerie.com/actualite-algerie/immigration-bourses-etudes-chinoises-pour-etudiants-algeriens/ (accessed August 15).

Organisation of Petroleum Countries. (2019). "Algeria facts and figures." Retrieved from https://www.opec.org/opec_web/en/about_us/146.htm (accessed March 11, 2019).

Ouramdane, Mehenni. (2018, June 17). "Algérie-Chine: La France s'inquiète du rapprochement entre les deux pays." 17 June. Retrieved from https://www.algerie-eco. com/2018/06/17/algerie-chine-la-france-sinquiete-du-rapprochement-entre-les-deux-pays/ (accessed October 22, 2018).

Pairault, Thierry. (2015). "China's economic presence in Algeria." Retrieved from https://www.researchgate.net/publication/280793405_China's_economic_presence_in_Algeria (accessed March 11, 2019).

Pairault, Thierry. (2016). "Stock d'investissement direct chinois en Afrique 2015. Communiqué annuel du MOFCOM." December. Retrieved from https://www. pairault.fr/sinaf/index.php/statistiques/958-stock-d-investissement-direct-chinois-en-afrique-2015 (accessed March 7, 2017).

Paris, Robert. (2014). "Quand et pourquoi l'Algérie a basculé de son alliance française vers celle de la Chine ?" *Matière et Révolution.* 26 January. Retrieved from https:// www.matierevolution.fr/spip.php?article3071 (accessed May 4, 2017).

Pecoraro, Eugenia. (2010). "China's strategy in North Africa: New economic challenges for the Mediterranean region." *EUGOV Working Paper* No. 26/2010. https://core. ac.uk/reader/13324492.

Rabhi, Meziane. (2014). "Algérie—Chine: Signature d'un plan de coopération stratégique," *Liberté.* 9 June. Retrieved from https://algeria-watch.org/?p=29054 (accessed July 20, 2018).

Sciolino, Elaine & Schmitt, Eric (1991) "Algerian reactor came from China." *The New York Times*. November 15. Retrieved from https://www.nytimes.com/1991/11/15/world/algerian-reactor-came-from-china.html (accessed September 11, 2018).

Shinn, David H. & Eisenman, Joshua. (2012). *"China and Africa: A Century of Engagement."* Philadelphia, PA: University of Pennsylvania Press.

Souiha, Farida. (2010). "La société algérienne au miroir des migrations chinoises." *Moyen-Orient*. 7 August–September, pp. 15–52. https://www.pairault.fr/sinaf/doc_importes/fs2010.pdf.

Sun, D. & Zoubir, Yahia H. (2015). "China's economic diplomacy towards the Arab countries: Challenges ahead." *Journal of Contemporary China*, Vol. 24, No. 95, pp. 93–921.

TBP and Agencies (2016). "Algeria, China ink $3.3 billion mega port deal." *The BRICS Post*. 18 January. Retrieved from http://thebricspost.com/algeria-china-ink-3-3-bn-mega-port-deal/#.W4RGObo6_ak (accessed January 10, 2017).

World Integrated Trade Solutions (2019). "Algeria Import in thousand US$ China between 2013 and 2017." Retrieved from https://wits.worldbank.org/CountryProfile/en/Country/DZA/StartYear/2013/EndYear/2017/TradeFlow/Import/Partner/CHN/Indicator/MPRT-TRD-VL (accessed December 18, 2018).

Xinhuanet. (2004). "Les pays en développement doivent renforcer leur solidarité pour mieux défendre leurs intérêts, déclare le président chinois." 4 February. Retrieved from http://french.china.org.cn/french/100564.htm (accessed Mars 27, 2017).

Xinhuanet (In Arabic). (2014). "L'Algérie et la Chine sont des exemples exemplaires de coopération et d'amitié durable." 26 February. Retrieved from http://arabic.people.com.cn/31660/8547268.html (accessed February 21, 2017).

Xinhuanet. (2017). "Algerian PM lauds efficiency of Chinese company in high-way construction project." 30 April. Retrieved from http://www.xinhuanet.com/english/2017-04/30/c_136246926.htm (accessed January 10, 2018).

Xu W. (2004). (February 4). "Regard rétrospectif sur les relations amicales entre la Chine et l'Algérie." http://french.china.org.cn/french/100579.htm.

Xu, W. China.org. (2004). "Regard rétrospectif sur les relations amicales entre la Chine et l'Algérie." http://french.china.org.cn/french/100579.htm.

Ying, Tang & Wang, Xin. (2008). "Algeria, China strengthen strategic partnership." *China Daily*. 19 December. Retrieved from http://www.chinadaily.com.cn/cndy/2008-12/19/content_7320543.htm (accessed February 10, 2017).

Ybarra, Maggie. (2019). "The Politics of selling weapons to Algeria-Algiers looks to shift away from its dependence on Moscow." *The National Interest*. 7 March. https://nationalinterest.org/print/feature/politics-selling-weapons-algeria-46362 (accessed March 15, 2019).

Zhao, Lei. (2016). "China delivers warship to Algeria." *China Daily*. 20 July. Retrieved from http://www.chinadaily.com.cn/world/2016-07/20/content_26155715.htm (accessed February 10, 2017).

Zhao, Shelly. (2011). "The geopolitics of China-African oil." *China Briefing*. 13 April. Retrieved from http://www.china-briefing.com/news/2011/04/13/the-geopolitics-of-china-african-oil.html (December 18, 2018).

Zoubir, Yahia. H. (1990–91). "The United States, the Soviet Union, and the Maghreb: Prospects for the future." *The Maghreb Review*, Vol. 15, Nos. 3 & 4, Winter. pp. 164–187.

Zoubir, Yahia. H. (1995). "The United States, the Soviet Union and the decolonization of the Maghreb: Algeria, Morocco, Tunisia, 1945–1962." *Middle Eastern Studies*. Vol. 31, No. 1, pp. 58–84.

Zoubir, Yahia H. (2011). "Russia and Algeria: Reconciling contrasting interests." *The Maghreb Review*, 36, 3, 99–126.

Zoubir, Yahia H. (2016). Interview, Beijing (anonymous).

Zoubir, Yahia H. (2018). Interview, Shanghai (anonymous).

Zoubir, Yahia H. (2019). Les Relations de la Chine avec les pays du Maghreb: La place prépondérante de l'Algérie. *Confluences Méditerranée*. 2, N° 109, pp. 91 à 103.

Zoubir, Yahia H. (forthcoming). 'The giant afraid of its shadow': Algeria, the reluctant middle power." In Adham Saouli, (Ed.), *Middle East Powers in the Middle East*, Oxford/ Hurst University Press.

Zoubir, Yahia H. & Darbouche, Hakim. (2009). "The Algerian crisis in European and US foreign policies: A hindsight analysis." In. Cavatorta, Francesco and Vincent, Durac. (Eds.), *The Foreign Policies of the United States the European Union in the Middle East*. London & New York: Routledge. pp. 32–54.

16

TRANSNATIONAL TRADE AND NEW TYPES OF ENTREPRENEURS IN ALGERIA

Saïd Belguidoum

Algeria is emblematic of the reorganised commercial supply networks in the southern Mediterranean. The boom in imported consumer products labelled Made in China has led to a reorganisation of Algerian supply networks and the places in which those goods are sold. In three decades, there has been a shift from "globalization from below" (Portes 1999), limited to a few regions of the world and driven by pioneering migrant entrepreneurs, to a true globalisation of the entire trade structure. This transnational commerce has freed itself from the heritage of post-colonial domination which had previously dominated trade between the global north and south.

Within this global trade framework, supply routes have multiplied. Commercial hubs have sprung up on all continents where transnational entrepreneurs from countries all over the world meet; the business trip to Dubai, Istanbul, or China has become commonplace. At the heart of these new dynamics, new traders have adopted the system of trading posts on transnational routes that they helped to create. In 30 years, three generations and three different kinds of traders have succeeded one another.

This emergence of international routes, and the rapidity and very large scale in which they arose, raise questions about these new entrepreneurs. Breaking with traditional supply circuits, their initiative is remarkable, even more so since these economic actors are often young. While some of them do come from trading families, nothing destined them to become the pioneers of these new routes.

What is equally remarkable is how such a change could have occurred in a country where the private sector has long been marginalised and in which private business still has an ambiguous and controversial identity in an economy caught between the rigours of strict bureaucracy and unrestrained distribution markets.

This chapter focuses on the specific actors in this transnational economy and on "globalization from below." It draws on field research in several sites (Algeria, Dubai, China) and attempts to show how these new kinds of entrepreneurs have come into being in a country that is still in the making.

From managed economy to liberalisation: slow steps towards private enterprise in Algeria

The emergence of a private sector in Algeria must be understood within the general context of this country and the dominant role played by the state in all sectors of society since independence. In the years following independence, a managed economy was chosen for development, whereby the pervasive state was both regulator and main operator of the economy. Through its active and interventionist policies, its regulations, and its bureaucracy, the state played a leading role in stimulating and controlling the major transformations that Algerian society has undergone. As for private enterprise, it has long been confined to the margins of public policy (Addi 1990).

To understand this situation, it is necessary to mention the neo-patrimonial nature of the state. Neo-patrimonialism (Eisenstadt 1973; Médard 1991) results from a combination of a bureaucratic system, which manifests through the institutions that conform with a modern state, and practices of clientelism and allegiance to power that enable one to obtain special privileges, particularly access to economic resources. Such a system maintains permanent confusion between the public and private domains and is based on the permeability of the borders between politics and economics. As a result of this confusion, there is constant suspicion towards the private sector, which has to operate within the clientelism, corruption, and informality generated by this type of governance.

The Boumediene years (1965–1979) saw the triumph of populist ideology inherited from the national liberation movement, which considered that development was the responsibility of the state as conductor and manager of the economy. During this period, the foundations of the neo-patrimonial state were established, based on the redistribution policy made possible by high oil revenues. From 1996 onwards, a period of economic liberalisation began, although the shackles of the administered economy remained. The state transferred its monopoly prerogatives to private groups, assigning them import markets for a number of commodities such as basic food staples (oil, sugar, coffee), pharmaceuticals, construction materials, and industrial equipment (Hachemaoui 2012).

As this bureaucratic and clientelist system was pushed to its limits, the neo-patrimonial state organised and distributed privileges within the economy while allowing entire sections of informality to flourish. Thus, we have the paradox of a society whose economy oscillated between an unbridled laissez-faire attitude in many sectors of economic and social life (particularly wholesale distribution and retail) and an omnipresent bureaucracy.

Since the economic opening of the 1990s, some major private figures have emerged. Large corporations have acquired public recognition: Mehri, Rebrab (CEVITAL), Condor, Hasnaoui (construction and real estate development), Haddad (ETRHB), and BIOPHARM (pharmaceutical industry) to mention some of the best known. The regular public policy statements by the President of the Entrepreneurs' Forum attest to the desire for legitimacy that entrepreneurs wanted. But the Khelifa affair, a consortium that quickly came to dominate the economy before collapsing after bankruptcy and the arrest of its CEO, continues to weigh heavily on public opinion, which suspects the private sector of corruption and of taking public money.

This is the context in which the Algerian private industry is growing. In full expansion since the economic opening (76% of these companies were created between 2000 and 2011), private business accounts for 98% of all economic entities and employs 73.2% of the economically active population (excluding agriculture, administration, and education).[1] However, for the most part, these are small companies with little capitalisation: 98.7% of private companies have fewer than 10 employees and only 932 companies, out of the 915,316 existing, report having more than 250 employees ONS 2012.

Mass consumption and the emergence of trans-national entrepreneurs

In a country that depends largely on the redistribution of gas and oil revenues, the services and trade sector have the most intense business. It is mainly in the tertiary sector that the private sector is growing, with 89% of business, 55.6% of which is for trade in its various forms. As the needs of an ever-increasing population are growing, the state, unable to meet this new demand, is liberalising the economy.

Until 1996, foreign trade was closely controlled by the state through its public companies. The amendment of the Commercial Code has radically transformed this framework, enabling 34,000 private import companies to be set up in less than 10 years. By abandoning a managed economy, which gave the state a monopoly on imports, and by enacting new rules on imports and the foreign currency market (with its often strict and confusing rules which are regularly changed, favouring informed agents), the state left the field partially open for a free market that new agents could access. A multitude of hybrid practices in both imports and distribution in the domestic market occur alongside this shift, playing on the confusion between licit and illicit practices. The porosities and laxity of an inefficient legal system (lack of coordination between agencies for control, trade registers with fake addresses, generalised tolerance of the parallel currency market, etc.), and the interpenetration between the interests of private companies and those of government officials, encouraged the development of the free enterprise while ensuring the large-scale supplying of the Algerian market.

While the vast majority of entrepreneurs specialise in retail (84%), a growing number of wholesalers and importers have been organising a market whose products are mainly imported. The growth of these companies has been rapid, from 21,500 in 2006 to 34,100 in 2010 for import companies and from 41,200 to 66,900 for wholesale companies (CNRC 2011). These new entrepreneurs set up a supply system that flooded the Algerian market with consumer goods. Their rapid rise is generally considered illegitimate and is associated with pariah capitalism (Péraldi 2007). In fact, this refers to a very distinct category of new economic operators. They have taken over a space that is difficult to monopolise and therefore escapes the system of kickbacks of the "protected people" in the neo-patrimonial system: the consumer goods market in personal goods (clothing, cosmetics, sports goods, toys, etc.), household goods (furniture, household articles and linens, light fixtures, cleaning products, computing and mobile telephony), and other small objects of everyday life (small commodities). This new dynamic can only be understood by placing it within the general context of globalisation.

Discreet globalisation and the transnational economy

Since the end of the 1990s, and in the wake of the globalisation of the capitalist economy, a discreet, but effective transnational trade has arisen, bringing to light new kinds of entrepreneurs. This is the result of a double process: first, the growth of a consumer market linked to the emergence of large urban middle and working classes in the countries of the global south that have been neglected by multinational companies; and second, the progressive emancipation of supply chains from their post-colonial framework, allowing for the emergence of new sources of supply of consumer goods supply.

Portes (1999) and Tarrius (2002) were among the first to highlight the specificities of this new form of "globalization from below," a term coined by Portes. In his work on Latin American migrants to the USA, he found that the new dynamics of transnationalism were a response to globalisation by migrant "communities that sit astride political borders... that, in a very real sense, are 'neither here nor there' but in both places simultaneously" (Portes 1999, 16). He showed that: "The economic activities that sustain these communities are grounded precisely on the differentials of advantage created by state boundaries. In this respect, they are no different from the large global corporations, except that these enterprises emerge at the grassroots level and its activities are often informal" (ibid.).

Echoing this sentiment Tarrius describes and analyses "the origins, in the western Mediterranean, of real networks of mobile entrepreneurs...they attest to the fact that *another* globalization does actually exist: a discreet globalization, from the bottom-up, which is rarely studied and yet has weighty consequences for our future" [translation] (Tarrius 2002, 15).

The transnational economy, which was based for a time on immigrant communities, subsequently grew thanks to a new generation of migrants, those travelling entrepreneurs who settled for varying periods in the trading posts of these new places supplying the global economy with consumer goods. These actors have the know-how to "sit astride political borders" (Portes 1999) and "have the ability to be here, there, and here and there at the same time" [translation] (Tarrius 2002).

These discrete, alternative supply spaces were created on the margins of globalisation, enabling networks of transnational traders to play on the advantages created by different practices at different borders (currency exchange, purchasing power, customs taxation).

The establishment of transnational trade routes

The process has been rapid and occurred in two main phases: from transport by bags to containers, in other words, the transition from a resourceful amateur working in an essentially cross-border economy (France, Tunisia, Morocco) to that of a transnational economy with professional networks. Two supply and distribution routes were linked. The first one, transnational, is a network of trading posts. Originally located in Marseille, these trading centres then moved to Istanbul and Dubai, before going further back up the road to the source in China: Hong Kong, Guangzhou, Shenzhen, and primarily, Yiwu. The second route, a national one, supplanted the "souk" network that had been used for distribution. In three decades, new roads and trade centres were built connecting urban spaces linked together by flows of traders and goods. These spaces are discontinuous and discrete, networked, and constantly shifting. More important than the scale of nation-states, it is the scale of places and regions, their influence, and the roads that connect them that make up the defining characteristics and strength of this transnational economy (Belguidoum & Pliez 2015, 2).

Initially, an informal commerce carrying bags of goods, called *trabendo*, ensured the supply for a booming market. Although this kind of trade has not disappeared, it was quickly replaced by trade using containers (Péraldi 2001). The visibility of the bag trade probably explains why today the transnational economy continues to be confused with the informal economy. Of course, informality exists in transnational trade. For example, many traders try to hide part of their revenue to avoid taxation, importers make extensive use of the parallel currency market, and goods are ultimately sold through a very informal retail distribution system. But if we content ourselves with the generic term "informal" to classify a new form of world trade, we are prevented from seeing the nature of this economy. "Informal" is a blanket term and not very useful to describe practices. With strong pejorative connotations in Algeria, it refers to any business that is not regulated by the state, particularly in terms of taxation. This notion confuses the extreme diversity of statuses and situations and puts in the same basket licit and illicit, legal and illegal activities, smuggling, counterfeiting, underdeclaring at customs, sales without officially registering the business, and so on.

Using this term as a yardstick, there would thus be no economy except under the conditions set by the state within the limits of its organisational, normative, and financial scope of action.

The strength of this transnational trade is that it has discreetly taken hold on the margins of the global economy by appropriating untapped areas or creating new areas.

The spaces, trading centres, and routes of this new trade

In Algeria, this Silk Road has materialised in the development of a network of commercial towns combining the experience and skills these new traders have acquired in recent decades. Large urban and suburban marketplaces are emerging, reconfiguring the framework and the internal structure of cities through the creation of shopping streets and commercial districts. Small, medium, and large cities are affected by these distribution networks that supply the numerous weekly markets, boutiques, and stores that proliferate in increasingly special-ised urban neighbourhoods. There is not a city today, large or small, that does not have its own market for imported consumer goods. At the end of 2010, the Algerian government identified some 765 sites of informal commerce, as many as there are towns, in which some 70,000 traders operate. This shows the extent of the phenomenon.

Although peripheral at the beginning, these places have consolidated, special-ised, and professionalised as they have grown. At one end of these routes is China, from where manufactured goods leave for the entire planet. At the other end is an ever-growing mass consumer market, reaching people that had previously been left out. These markets are certainly not linked exclusively to Chinese supply chains as Turkey, the Middle East, Dubai, Malaysia, and recently Indonesia are other sources. There are many emerging regional and local markets (the branches of these new silk routes), numerous trading centres they connect, and actors working in them. This networked economy has the capacity to adapt very quickly to changes in markets and customs regulations.

In Algeria, the network of markets selling imported goods is becoming more hierarchical and specialised as supply routes change. Of the 34,000 officially registered importers, 68% are concentrated in five *wilayas*: Algiers, Oran, Setif, Constantine, and Oum el Bouaghi (CNRC 2011).

It is above all in eastern Algeria that these networks of traders have gained visibility by operating in medium-sized and small towns, which have become real trading centres controlling the distribution market. Medium-sized cities (El Eulma, Aïn M'lila), small towns, and large villages (Aïn Fakroun, Tadjenanet, Bir el-Ater) are becoming commercial hubs, organising the distribution of goods imported by their entrepreneurs. Their concentration in eastern Algeria is partly due to their close proximity to the Tunisian and Libyan borders, but they are not necessarily located on the main traffic routes. They have emerged there more because of the special drive of a category of new actors. El Eulma (furniture, mobile telephony, computing, cleaning products, and hardware), Aïn M'lila (spare parts for cars), and Aïn Fakroun (clothing) are the three towns that have become dominant over the past 10 years in their specific field, extending their distribution network throughout Algeria and even beyond by establishing links with Moroccan, Tunisian, and Libyan traders. Other towns in eastern Algeria have also specialised in less visible goods. This is the case of Belaïba and El Djezar (spare parts for public works machinery and heavy vehicles), small towns located near Barika and Bir el-Ater in the wilaya of Tébessa (second-hand clothing), which was once a hub for products from Libya, and Tadjenanet near El Eulma, very active in importing wood.

El Eulma and Yiwu: essential places of Algerian trade

We cannot understand how the Algerian route works without taking into account the essential role played by two towns: Yiwu and El Eulma, two discreet and emblematic localities of this kind of globalisation.

Yiwu: the starting point for the new silk road

This city of 1.5–2 million people, located 280 km from Shanghai in Zhejiang province, is the largest wholesale market in China and one of the largest in the world, specialising in the sale of small items such as stationery, jewellery, DIY equipment, interior decorations. In the early 2000s, Yiwu became the necessary starting point and location for transnational trade offices for people from countries all over the world. Many Algerian merchants come here to place orders. There are also about 50 registered Algerian freight forwarding offices; many Algerian traders also work unofficially by going through Chinese partners. In 2011, Algeria became the tenth-largest importer of Yiwu products (Belguidoum & Pliez 2015, 1).

El Eulma, the emblem of transnational trade in Algeria

At the same time, El Eulma in Algeria has become established as the main commercial hub for domestic goods (personal goods, furniture, household appliances, computers, drugstore items, hardware, etc.). By 2015, there were nearly 3,300 wholesale and semi-wholesale traders at its huge market, called the Dubai souk.

Organised into large specialised sectors, the El Eulma market is directly connected to marketplaces in China (Yiwu, Guangzhou, Shenzhen), the Middle East, and Europe. Welcoming thousands of buyers daily from throughout the country and, for several years now from Tunisia, this town ensures distribution through transport companies covering all of Algeria, as far as the great south (Belguidoum, Chouadra, & Alikhodja 2017).

Networks and three generations of entrepreneurs

This emergence of a transnational economy, and its speed and scale, raise questions about these new trader-entrepreneurs. Breaking with traditional trade circuits, their spirit of initiative is remarkable, especially since these entrepreneurs are often young. While some of them do come from merchant families, nothing predicted they would become the pioneers of these new routes.

Along with these young people who have a university or secondary education in a wide variety of disciplines, small traders are already integrated into the regional souk network, together with a few large established traders who seized the opportunity of this new trade. The convergence between these various experiences and related skills leads to this collective transformation.

Aïn Fakroun is an illustration of how quickly a trade route can be built thanks to flexible and efficient networks. At first, Aïn Fakroun's commercial activity was quite discreet. In the mid-1980s, local young people took advantage of the region's extensive network of emigrants in France to start bag trading. Others initiated trade with Bir el-Ater, near the Tunisian border, which at that time was a hub for cross-border trade. The goods were sold on the local markets of the region as far as Constantine. Starting in 1992, Aïn Fakroun changed scale. Local traders set up their own networks in Libya and Egypt. The goods were brought by semi-trailer trucks, stored in Aïn Fakroun, and resold in the urban markets of the region. In 1997, the first imports from Dubai arrived and local traders began to specialise in importing cheap clothing. By the early 2000s, the goods were brought directly from China. Flows from Yiwu, Guangzhou, and Shishi (in Fujian) were becoming more numerous—traders had followed the route back to its source.

Starting one's first trade business usually drew on family solidarity (father, brothers, and uncles), or sometimes that of friends, who provided financial assistance and the information essential for this kind of work. Following the first major successes, other imitators arrived, encouraged by the availability of the market. They made it possible to organise networks that were both flexible and hierarchical, based on relationships of trust.

Pioneers on transnational routes

The organisation of this kind of trade requires support in the countries where purchases are made. El Eulma's prosperity, for example, was due to the fact that the first traders to settle in Dubai were primarily from the same town. These pioneers also continued to move towards China and set up the first offices in Yiwu and Guangzhou.

In the mid-1990s, most Algerian importers still went to Istanbul, even though Dubai was an increasingly popular destination because it was considered the source. The majority of goods destined for Algeria arrived in Tunisia, Libya, or

Egypt because there was only one direct container shipping line between Dubai and Algiers. This was the golden age of Dubai for these pioneers. Three agencies run by Algerians had a de facto monopoly in organising transactions with importers and wholesalers who then sold imported goods throughout Algeria.

The import business proved to be sufficiently lucrative that it quickly had emulators among wholesalers and then among their own customers in the early 2000s. The job of importer became commonplace, with multiple consequences. When small importers believed they were at the source in Dubai, those already in place used Dubai as a base for prospecting Asian supply centres in order to precede the small traders and offer them their services. From Dubai, these pioneers had already travelled regularly to Hong Kong, attended the annual Canton fair, and then the wholesale markets of Yiwu. In each of these cities, they opened their own offices between 2001 and 2005 in order to supply an increasing number of customers, mainly from eastern Algeria.

Algerian traders discovered Yiwu in the late 1990s. Pioneering traders from El Eulma and Bir El-Ater opened their trading offices there. The job of trading consists of supporting the importer when dealing with suppliers, acting as a translator, participating in negotiations, handling customs documents, checking the conformity of the goods and containerisation, organising maritime transport, and serving as a guarantor to suppliers for payment delays.

In less than 10 years, these pioneers consolidated their position as intermediaries in all import services along an axis stretching from El Eulma to Yiwu, passing through Dubai and Guangzhou. However, the competition was fierce and required the main players in the market to constantly update their offer. They needed to provide new products, enter new markets, and maintain their reputation and margins because they were quickly followed by others. Dubai and Yiwu were becoming starting points from which pioneers prospected for new buyers in East and Central Africa: fewer demanding markets with less competition among importers.

Following the pioneers, other Eulmis, as well as young people from other towns in the east (Sétif, Bordj Bou Arredj, Constantine) and from Kabyle imitated them. A few hundred work as freight forwarders in Yiwu, Guangzhou, and Shenzhen. After the Egyptians, Syrians, Lebanese, and Turks, Algerians constitute the largest foreign community living in Yiwu, estimated in 2012 at 500 people. There are between 2,000 and 3,000 Algerians living in the whole of China. Two types of actors make up this permanent community: big traders and a myriad of new entrants trying to make a name for themselves. About 50 big trading offices have hung out their shingle. They handle major export business to Algeria and are in contact with a large number of customers. They employ a local workforce (Hui and Uighur translators) as well as young people from Algeria (relatives and friends). Over the past 2 or 3 years, a new generation of small traders has been getting involved, who, while competing with the big offices, have taken advantage of the large amount of trade flows with Algeria to try to squeeze in. Coming directly from Algeria, they are sons or brothers of import traders or have learned the trade from a relative already settled in Guangzhou. Their setting up a business is part of a strategy to enable the family business to have a permanent base in China. Until they have a regular customer base, they operate without officially declaring their business, and thus partner with Chinese freight forwarders or work with larger Algerian traders. A few dozen undeclared traders work in this way. Unlike their predecessors who learned Chinese on the job, these new arrivals take language courses (a 6-month course in private schools for 8,000 CNY). As a sign of their desire to settle in Yiwu long-term, marriages with Chinese women are contracted allowing for better social integration and undoubtedly better anchoring in a society where they have no or few cultural references, unlike France, a traditional country of Algerian emigration. This permanent presence of numerous and available freight forwarders makes it easier for importers to travel back and forth and guarantees faster delivery of orders that can also be placed by telephone. The job of trader also includes that of financial facilitator.

Conclusion: towards a new era of transnational commerce

The future of this economy is still problematic. Part of this market accumulation is expected to be invested in other sectors, such as industry and real estate. In general, trade routes and networks are constantly being restructured, marking their high instability. The ambiguities of Algeria's international trade policy and the government's repeated desire to tighten import conditions create permanent uncertainties for those working in international trade. To this, we must add the constant rise in currency prices (dollar, euro, and revaluation of the Yuan—RMB) against an increasingly devalued dinar.

Competition among trade offices, their need to keep their customers, the opening of Chinese offices sending their own agents to Algeria, prospecting wholesalers by offering attractive credit rates, and China's visa limitations since 2016 are other elements to be considered.

However, over the past 2 years, there has been a trend towards reorganising trade circuits and a degree of professionalisation of transnational trade. The consolidation of regional redistribution marketplaces such as the dynamic El Eulma has occurred alongside the professionalisation of the job of importer. The golden age of discovery in the late 2000s was followed by a period of restructuring driven by large Algerian importers and large offices in China, Yiwu, and Guangzhou. Transnational trade is entering a new era.

Note

1 This census, the first of its kind done in Algeria by the ONS, covered the entire country and counted all the companies conducting business in a fixed place during the reference period from May 8–August 8, 2011. (ONS, 2012).

References

Addi, L., 1990, "Forme néo-patrimoniale de l'Etat et secteur public en Algérie," in Addi, Lahouari, H. El Malki, JC. Santucci (eds.). *Etat et développement dans le monde arabe*, pp. 17–34, Editions du CNRS, Paris.

Belguidoum, S., 2011, "Le dynamisme des nouvelles places marchandes de l'Est algérien: reconfiguration urbaine et nouvelles donnes sociales," paper presented at the seminar *Entre le licite et l'illicite: migrations, travail, marchés*, September 13–17, 2011, Cerisy, France. from <halshs-00936444>.

Belguidoum S. & Pliez O., 2015- 1, "Made in China. Commerce transnational et espaces urbains autour de la Méditerranée," *Les Cahiers d'EMAM, 26*, pp. 7–16. http://emam.revues.org/909.

Belguidoum S. & Pliez O., 2015- 2, "Yiwu: The creation of a global market town in China," *Articulo—Journal of Urban Research*, 12. http://articulo.revues.org/2863.

Belguidoum S., Chouadra S. & Alikhodja N., 2017, "El Eulma (Algérie), anatomie d'une place emblématique du commerce transnational," *Les Carnets de l'IREMAM*, [Online] https://iremam.hypotheses.org/6456.

Centre National du Registre du Commerce (CNRC), 2011, *Les créations d'entreprises en Algérie, Statistiques 2010*, Alger.

Eisenstadt, SN., 1973, *Traditional Patrimonialism and Modern Neo Patrimonialism*, London, Sage Publications Ltd.

Hachemaoui M., 2012, "Institutions autoritaires et corruption politique. L'Algérie et le Maroc en perspective comparée," *Revue internationale de politique comparée*, 2012/2 (Vol. 19), pp. 141–164, Paris, France.

Médard JF., 1991, "L'État néo-patrimonial en Afrique noire," in J.-F. Médard (ed.), *États d'Afrique Noire: Formations, mécanismes et crises*, p. 323, Paris, France.

Office National des Statistiques (ONS), 2012, *Premier recensement économique-- 2011—Résultats définitifs de la première phase*, Collections Statistiques 172/2012, Série E: Statistiques Economiques 69—Alger, p. 228.

Péraldi M., 2001, *Cabas et Containers, Activités marchandes informelles et réseaux migrants transfrontaliers*, Paris, Aix-en-Provence, Maisonneuve & Larose et MMSH.

Péraldi M., 2007, "Les aventuriers du nouveau capitalisme marchand," In F. Adelhad et JF. Bayart, *Voyages du développement*, pp. 73–113, Editions Kartala, Ceri, Paris

Portes, A., 1999, "Globalization from below: The rise of transnational communities," *Actes de la recherche en sciences sociales*, Volume 129-1, pp. 15–25, Paris, Le Seuil.

Tarrius A., 2002, *La mondialisation par le bas: Les nouveaux nomades de l'économie souterraine*, Balland, Paris.

17

ALGERIA'S FOREIGN POLICY IN THE GULF

Iran and the GCC states

Fatiha Dazi-Héni

Introduction

Studies of Algerian foreign policy in the Gulf region have focused mainly on Iraq and Iran rather than the Gulf Cooperation Council states (GCC). This article challenges the perception that Iran is politically close and reliable, and the GCC states hostile to Algeria. Except for the late 1970s, very few academic sources were dedicated to relations between Algeria and the Gulf, notably the six Arab monarchies which were members of the GCC.[1] Those publications related mainly to the mediating became role of Algeria between in the early 1980s the two big northern Persian Gulf states of Iraq and Iran on the Shatt el-Arab border (1975), and subsequently the liberation of US hostages in Tehran (1981) and attempts to mediate in the Iraq–Iran war in the early 1980s.

This article will briefly refer to Algeria's emergence as a leading "small state mediation in International relations" (Touval & Zartman 1985). The article will also discuss the work done by Algeria in multilateral institutions such as the Organization of Petroleum Exporting Countries (OPEC) and the Organization of Islamic Cooperation.

The chapter will put into perspective Algerian diplomacy with Iran and the GCC states during the previous three decades: firstly, with what is referred to as the "black decade" of Algeria's civil war in the 1990s and secondly, President Bouteflika's come-back in 1999 coupled with the re-assertion of Algerian foreign policy. At the time, Algeria was concerned not only with attempts at national reconciliation, but also with finding a manageable equilibrium between its "difficult" Gulf counterparts, namely, Iran, Saudi Arabia, and the other Arab Gulf monarchies, while enduring a domestic tragedy.

Thirdly, this paper considers the decade of Arab uprisings, starting in 2010, and how the foreign policies of some Gulf states became more assertive, notably in North African states. Fourthly, how Algeria took advantage of its neutral positions vis-à-vis the rivalries and tensions between Gulf states, specifically during the Gulf crisis; and finally, how since independence, Algeria's long-standing principle has benefitted the current Algerian regime during a sensitive transitional phase.

The golden age: Algerian foreign relations with the northern Gulf states

Since Algeria's independence, its foreign policy has been based on its continuous support for national liberation causes, an indisputable component of its intrinsic values. Most analysts of Algerian foreign policy consider the period from 1965 to 1981 as a golden era of multilateral activism and international standing (Bruno 1977). Algeria's approach to international politics indeed reflects its decolonisation experience. Then, as a third world country, Algeria became an appropriate paradigm of the "small states" theory in the literature of international relations, and also a model in the theory of international mediation.

Algeria played a decisive role within the Middle East by mediating in conflicts and tensions between the two Yemen (1972), Iraq and Iran on the Shatt el-Arab border issue (1975), between Syrians and Palestinians (1976), Jordanians and Palestinians (1978), between Iraq and Syria (1978), and also between Egyptians and Libyans (1977). Algeria was also directly involved in ending the 1975 Vienna hostage ordeal. Ultimately, in helping to solve the hostage crisis between Iran and the United States in January 1981, Algeria gained its distinction as a skilful "small state" mediator (Slim 1992, 206–231) or "honest broker" (Daguzan 2015, 31–40), in a highly sensitive international crisis.

Algeria's mediation in the US hostage crisis

Algeria was one of the very few countries which had positive relations with the revolutionary regime in Teheran. Iranians had a profound respect for the Algerian Revolution, which they considered to be the precursor of their own revolution. The same feeling of respect, though for other reasons, was also noticeable in the American acceptance of Algiers as the mediator for the hostage crisis. US-Algerian relations were neither warm nor unfriendly and, despite its support for the Iranian Revolution, Algeria was trusted by the United States. Although Syria or Libya were on far better terms with Iran than Algeria, the Islamic Republic chose Algiers as an intermediary between them and the United States in order to find a way to release the 52 US hostages. Iranians were well aware that the relations between US, Syria, and Libya were far from friendly; therefore, of the three, Algeria seemed the most likely to be accepted by Americans. The successful Algerian intervention was facilitated by perceptions on both sides that Algiers had no direct interests at stake.[2]

Difficult Algerian mediation In the Iraq–Iran war

Following a brief period of friction between the two northern Gulf neighbours, Iraq decided to abrogate the 1975 Algiers agreement on September 17, 1980. Five days later, President Saddam Hussein ordered his army to launch a massive military operation on Iranian territory. He portrayed himself as the leader of the Arab world's aspirations. Bagdad constantly stressed the fact that Iraq was leading the battle in defence of Arab honour. In this context, Algeria was unique among Arab states in refraining from taking sides.

Unlike its Arab counterparts, Algeria abstained from public condemnation of either side. Instead, the Algerian government urged both sides to resolve their differences and work towards a peaceful outcome. This neutral position made Algiers the most suitable third party to try to mediate in the raging Iraq–Iran war. The Algerian peace mission was nevertheless ill-fated when the airplane crashed on May 3, 1982, carrying Foreign minister Ben Yahia at about 10 kilometres from the Iranian-Turkish border.

An active diplomatic presence in international forums

Algeria's natural resources, most notably, natural gas, provide it with a degree of economic independence, which is a prerequisite to its success in conducting a non-aligned foreign policy.

The Arab League and Organisation of Islamic Cooperation are international forums where Algeria's foreign policy has distinguished itself, notably on the Palestinian cause. Most recently during the Arab uprisings, Algeria has had to defend opposite statements and decisions during Arab League meetings. These are specifically on Hezbollah and the Syrian regime and contrary to those declared by the GCC states, which were the heavyweights in this forum during this current 2010 decade.

As an active leading member of non-aligned countries and of the Organization of African Unity (Zoubir 2015), Algeria ensured that the sanctity of sovereignty and independence would be preserved.

A corollary of this political orientation found its echo when Algeria became a member of OPEC in July 1969.[3] A few months after its accession to OPEC, Algeria had indirectly participated in a changing balance of power that prevailed between foreign oil companies and host countries. On February 24, 1971, Algeria nationalised its oil industry by up to 51% for oil fields and 100% for gas fields and oil and gas pipelines. Then, in September 1971, the OPEC ministerial conference endorsed the Algerian proposal to commit member states in oil companies present in their territories.

Algeria also played an important role in the decision of Organization of Arab Petroleum Exporting Countries to progressively reduce oil production in order to pressure Israel's Western allies. This took place on October 17, 1973; exactly 1 week after the Egyptian-Israeli war was launched on October 10. It was also during the closing session of an OPEC meeting in Algiers on March 6, 1975, that President Boumedienne announced the signing of the Algiers agreement between Iraq and Iran over the Shatt el-Arab border dispute (Lieb 1985, 67–86). The death of Boumedienne in December 1978 added to the disorder in the ranks of OPEC, resulting in the declining role of Algeria to the benefit of Saudi Arabia, then the leading OPEC exporter.

From the black decade to the Arab Spring

Algerian foreign policy began its decline under Bendjedid's presidency in the 1980s, and experienced a "desert crossing" during the civil war (Martinez 2000). Algeria was severely affected by the sharp drop of oil in the early 1980s when the price of a barrel of oil reached $10. Nevertheless, this moment was instructive and changed the priorities of Algerian foreign policy, particularly with the Gulf region, but also with the rest of the international community.

Abdel-Aziz Bouteflika's comeback in 1999 as the long-lasting foreign minister (1963–1979) contributed to strengthening the Algerian presidency's good relations with the military (Martinez 2016) that had brought him to power (Zoubir 1999, 15–29). He also normalised external relations, notably with Washington in the aftermath of the attacks in the United States on September 11, 2001. Benefiting from its experience in fighting violent radical Islamists, Algeria became a reliable partner in the international community in the fight against terrorism and in the field of intelligence sharing and expertise.

As for the Arab Spring, Algeria's traumatic experience of civil war mixed with its strong non-interventionist belief, advocated since independence, remain its guiding principles particularly with regard to Syria and Libya (Crowley 2017).

Algerian's Gulf policy during the black decade

Algeria used to have cordial relations with Iran thanks to its various mediations on sensitive international and regional issues, as discussed in previous paragraphs. Algiers' common vision with Teheran regarding challenges of Third-Worldism[4] and the need to safeguard shared interests inside OPEC contributed to both countries having a similar geopolitical leaning. But the civil war diminished this trusted relationship when Algeria severed its diplomatic relations with Iran in 1993 because of Teheran's support for the Islamic Salvation Front (FIS).

On the other side of the Persian Gulf, Algeria had never fully trusted the conservative Gulf monarchies due to different geopolitical sensitivities. In addition, Saudi Arabia's obvious financial support to the Algerian Salafi movement and full support for Morocco on the Western Sahara issue were deterrents to good relations. Nevertheless, diplomatic relations with Saudi Arabia, active in exporting its religious soft power, had never been severed.

Iran, not such a friendly partner to Algeria

The second Gulf war and prior to that the Gulf crisis when Iraq invaded Kuwait on August 2, 1990, have more to do with the conservative regimes of the GCC states than with Iran. Nonetheless, this event matched internal problems in Algeria and the growing popularity of the Algerian Islamists. According to Zoubir (1993), "The Islamicists were the most vocal against Iraq's invasion due to their resentment toward Saddam Hussein, a secular ruler who showed no pity to Islamicist movement."

On the other side, Iran was the sole Islamic Revolutionary Republic in the Muslim world and provided political support to the FIS following their victory in the municipal and departmental elections on June 1990. Tensions between Algeria and Iran became critical when Algiers decided to halt the legislative electoral ballot on January 1992 to prevent FIS from realising its electoral victory, and Teheran firmly condemned the annulment of the elections. Through media networks, Algiers accused Teheran of having a hand in the FIS strategy to gain power with the ambition of creating an Algerian Islamic Republic. Algiers severed its diplomatic ties with Teheran on March 1993, when Algerian Prime Minister Redha Malek, previously Algerian ambassador to Washington, accused Teheran of providing military support to the Armed Islamic Groups (GIA) (Khouni 2007, 238–239).

This distrustful atmosphere between Algiers and Teheran was also noticeable when Egyptian and Tunisian policymakers accused Iran, and until 1997–1998, Sudan, of being the main supporters of the local Islamists (Zoubir 1999, 21). Wilfred Buchta, in Who rules Iran? (2000) provides an accurate approach of Iranian influence through the Islamic Revolutionary Guard Corps[5] in their efforts to export the Islamic Revolution internationally, to Arab countries. Within the multipolar power structure of Iran, the Islamic Revolutionary Guard Corps is assumed to be the most powerful supporter of Middle Eastern opposition movements such as the Palestinian Hamas. In addition, it provides training and financing assistance to foreign Islamic movements such as in Sudan with training camps for senior Algerian GIA members.

It was only in the aftermath of the Algerian civil war and once Bouteflika had won the presidency that relations with Teheran started to improve. Bouteflika met Iranian President Khatami during the General Assembly of the United Nations in New York on September 8, 2000. One year later, on October 2001, both countries exchanged their respective ambassadors.

The very dark years of this decade explain why Algeria was keen to reject any external interference in its domestic affairs, specifically with Iran which was actively trying to export its revolutionary Islamic revolutionary ideas to the Arab world at that time.

Saudi Arabia's influence on Algerian Salafi jihadists

Strangely enough, Algeria did not use the same criteria with Saudi Arabia, particularly since most of the financial support for FIS came from Saudi Arabia together with the religious Wahhabi influence. The academic work of Bilel Ainine (2016) is a highly valuable reference source in trying to answer this problematic question. Media, governments, and some academics concur in emphasising the decisive role and influence of the Saudi Wahhabi on radical Sunni Islamists movements, notably during the Algerian civil war.

Ainine supports the view that Wahhabi's role in shaping Algerian Islamism is ambiguous, insufficiently documented, and highly hypothetical. If Wahhabi's influence and financial support from Saudi Arabia are indisputable, their role in radicalisation and their impact in blowing up Algerian armed groups are far from being as decisive as is widely claimed and rooted in global public opinion, specifically in Algeria.

Wahhabi Salafi influence in Algeria began in the early 1980s when Saudi and Algerian governments signed a university agreement allowing Algerian students to study in Saudi's Islamic universities. This Wahhabi Salafi influence is in addition to an already well-established local Salafism dominated by the heritage of Imam Ben Badis.[6] But the more relevant influence is that of the Algerian fighters in Afghanistan who returned to Algeria in the early 1990s. According to Ainine, Algerian fighters in Afghanistan were more persuaded by tactical military commitment than by Wahhabi talks of jihad. Moreover, cultural differences between Afghanis and Pakistanis did not help Algerian fighters in Afghan camps to assimilate. Wahhabi preachers' ideological influence in Afghanistan had a minimal impact according to Ainine's survey of Algerian fighters. Algerian fighters, like their Saudi counterparts, developed their own logic to fight against their own regimes when they returned home.

Kepel (2002) also pointed out that the group of Algerian fighters who created an extremist group called "Al Hijra wa-l-Takfir" (Exile and Redemption) joined GIAs on their return and were far more influenced by Sayyid Qutb's ideas[7] than by Saudi Wahhabism.

These fundamentals could explain why Algerian authorities never felt the need to impose a severe response to Saudi Arabia's religious and financial networks of influence. On the contrary, the Iranian regime was ideologically and logistically active in supporting FIS empowerment and in military training for GIA's influential members.

Bouteflika's effect on Algeria's foreign policy

Since his accession to the presidency in April 1999, Bouteflika skilfully reshaped Algerian relations with France, the United States, and the North Atlantic Treaty Organisation alliance (Mortimer 2006, 155–171). He began as presiding officer of the Organization of African Unity for a year and became one of the main promoters of the New Partnership for Africa's Development. In the Middle East, he normalised relations with Iran in 2000 and hosted the Arab League summit in March 2005.

Bouteflika was also able to capitalise on his "traversée du désert," the years he spent in exile between 1979 and 1998. He was then a consultant to Fahd Al-Oteiba, a close adviser to Sheikh Zayed, President of the United Arab Emirates, and he established a substantial network of ties with Gulf monarchs, especially with the ruling dynasty of Abu Dhabi. Little information filtered through from his exile, but Bouteflika's connections with royals and their business entourage were said to be very useful in maintaining a balanced relationship with Saudi Arabia, the UAE, Qatar, and also Kuwait, despite their several divergences on Middle Eastern and Gulf security issues. This did not prevent the Algerian security apparatus from sharing a close and cordial relationship with the Saudi Ministry of Interior under Nayef (1975–2012) and his son Muhammad (2012–2017) who used to spend time hunting in Algeria. This multidimensional Gulf foreign policy helped Algeria break its isolation in the aftermath of the dark decade.

With the meteoric ascension to power of the new Saudi Crown Prince, Muhammad Ben Salman, since June 2017, this situation has changed. Since June 2017, the Gulf crisis opposing Qatar, on the one hand, and Saudi Arabia, the UAE, Egypt, and Bahrain, on the other hand, has dramatically changed the balance of power inside the GCC region. Nevertheless, Algeria was able to maintain a neutral approach in accordance with its traditional diplomatic policy of non-interference. According to Mortimer (2006, 155), "The former Foreign minister-turned-president exploited his reputation abroad to convert it into political capital at home." As an illustration, he helped to end "the moral embargo imposed on Algeria by the international community and the full incorporation of the country as a strategic partner in the fight against international terrorism in the aftermath of the attacks of September 11, 2001" (Martin 2013, 65–60). Previously, he pushed for a domestic normalisation with the 1999 Civil Concord law, and in 2005, the *Charter for Peace and National Reconciliation*. However, Algeria's shift towards pragmatism—its participation in NATO's Mediterranean dialogue and strategic rapprochement with the United States in the 2000s—did not result in any major changes to the country's guiding ideological imperatives.

Algeria in the context of the Arab Spring

The Algerian regime's attitude towards the Arab uprisings was mainly shaped by domestic considerations. The impact of the still traumatic black decade, security policy, and geostrategic imperatives were far more critical than the fear of potential democratic diffusion. As argued by Anouar Boukhars (2013) in his paper on Algerian policy in the context of the Arab Spring, this consideration was not a decisive factor in explaining Algerian foreign policy.

However, for fear of the Arab Spring spreading at home, and most notably to Saudi Arabia (Dazi-Héni 2018a), panic on the part of the GCC states was the most relevant factor explaining their new interventionist foreign policy.

This reached such a point that they became the most assertive Arab states to combat democratic diffusion, especially after the fall of Egyptian President Mubarak on February 11, 2011. An exception was Oman which shares with Algeria an aversion for external interventionism, and also Kuwait that prefers mediation and appeasement (Dazi-Héni 2018b, 41–46).

This apprehension even led to an unprecedented Saudi-Emirati military intervention in Bahrain in March 2011, and to general military interventions (Young 2013, 2016) from small states such as Qatar and the UAE in Libya or in Yemen, which has had a Saudi-led coalition since March 2015.

The foreign policies of the Gulf oil states reach their golden age when plenty "*tharwa*" takes control over "*thawra*" as theorised in Bahgat Korany's books on the foreign policies of Arab States (Korany and Dessouki 2010). This process would shape the Gulf states' influencing strategies in the Mediterranean region, mainly in Egypt, Libya, and to a lesser extent, Tunisia (Benantar & Chena 2015). Algeria remains immune due to the fact that it combines both components: "*tharwa*" and the heritage of "*thawra*."[8]

Algerian foreign policy puts it at odds with the emerging international human rights norm of the "responsibility to protect." This approach became a major challenge for Algerian foreign policy during the current decade with the Libyan and Syrian crises. Algeria's nervousness also reflects its own fear of seeing Western powers orchestrating regime change in the Arab world, similar to what happened in Iraq on April 2003 with the US military intervention that left it in chaos.

In the Libyan case, Algeria's decision was mainly motivated by strategic and security imperatives. Algeria was also concerned about the effects of regime change on the conflict in Western Sahara and the fear of seeing France, as the major NATO player in the Libyan intervention, disturbing the balance of power in the region to the benefit of its main North African ally, namely Morocco, but at the expense of Algeria. Algeria also feared that an external intervention in Libya would reawaken ethno-tribal demands for sovereign identity all over the sub-Saharan region, as is the case with the Tuareg in Mali, with possible extension to Algeria.

When the Gulf states engaged in Libya with Qatar supporting the government based in Tripoli (western country), and the UAE supporting the one based in Tobruk (eastern country) (Gaube 2017), Algeria opposed the intervention pushed by these Gulf states in 2011 and supported a mediated political solution.

For the same reasons, Algeria also refused to join the Arab Saudi-led coalition in Yemen on March 2015. Morocco actively participated in the military campaign in Yemen with 1,500 troops, six aircraft, intelligence, and logistical support (Gaube 2017). Rabat recalled its troops 1 year later fearing popular pressure considering the lack of Moroccan public support for a military commitment in the Yemen war.

Algeria adopted a low profile over the Syrian conflict, never outspokenly supporting Syrian president Bashar el-Assad. Nonetheless, the Algerian regime, and in particular the military and security apparatus, remained close to the Syrian regime. Assad himself drew a parallel several times between the Syrian civil war and the Algerian black decade, claiming that: "The Algerian people's position on the Syrian conflict is not surprising, considering they had to undergo a challenge that was similar to the Syrian people's, which is currently facing terrorism" (AFP 2013). Fearful of damaging its reputation, Algeria preferred to manage its own public opinion and, more globally, that of the Arab world by keeping a low profile despite its support for the Assad regime.

More than the Libyan conflict, the Syrian crisis has had even more impact in terms of bipolarisation and tensions in the Middle East. This polarisation was a consequence of the Iranian and Hizballah support for the Syrian regime. The Syrian conflict in the Middle East has a huge collateral impact due to sectarian factors and the Iran-Saudi "cold war." These make Algeria's uncompromising position against outside interference difficult to sustain, particularly in the Arab League forum. Considering the Iranian support via their powerful Lebanese proxy, Hizballah, and direct Russian intervention in Syria, Boukhars (2013) warned that "Algeria's foreign policy non-interference principle has deepened its trust and worsened its public image."

Algerian's policy orientations towards Gulf regions: a variable adjustment?

Since the outbreak of the Arab Spring, Algerian foreign policy has faced formidable challenges. Its deep commitment to non-interventionism is likely to pose the risk of marginalising Algeria as a leading power in North Africa and damaging its reputation in the Arab League states regarding Syria.

Political disagreements with Gulf states became increasingly inflexible. These related in particular to the military intervention by Saudi Arabia and the UAE in Yemen, but also to Qatar when Doha intervened in Libya and actively supported Nahda's Tunisian Islamist party during the transition process. Their very different political culture makes them historically not good partners, especially since Gulf states choose to support Morocco in its border claims in the Western Sahara (Partrick 2016, 186–207) while Algeria remained the main supporter of the Frente popular para la Liberación de Saguia el-Hamra y Río de Oro (Polisario Front).

During the Arab Spring and particularly during the Syrian conflict, the Saudi-Iran cold war also impacted on relations with Algeria which had always tried to retain its neutrality with both sides of the Persian Gulf states in order to maintain balanced relations.

In March 2016, during the Cairo summit of the Arab League, Algeria voted against a Gulf initiative declaring Hizballah a terrorist organisation. Algeria also opposed designating Hamas as a terrorist group for the same reasons. Finally, Algeria kept coherent positions in respecting the basic foreign policy principles it had since independence and equally defended their reasons for disagreeing with the GCC states. Thus, Algiers successfully avoided being used by each party in the Saudi-Iranian cold war, choosing instead to follow its own historical priorities in the area of foreign policy.

GCC crisis and its impact on North African states

Gulf states, especially the new hardline axis of Saudi Arabia and Abu Dhabi, followed by Bahrain, have lost considerable international credibility since they provoked a crisis inside the GCC with Qatar on June 5, 2017 (Dazi-Héni 2017). In the meantime, they have embarked on a difficult war in Yemen that is entering its fifth year. Together with Washington and Tel Aviv, they have pushed for a strict Iranian containment since Washington decided to withdraw from the Iranian nuclear deal, the Joint Comprehensive Plan of Action (JCPOA), on May 8, 2018.

These Gulf positions are significantly transforming the GCC, which used to be a peaceful conservative citadel in a very uncertain region. Geopolitics in that region are finally working in favour of Algeria, whose constant position has strengthened its independent manoeuvrability more than any other North African states. The Qatar crisis is a relevant example in this situation.

Algeria shares neither significant stakes nor close-knitted relationships with Iran and the GCC states and has accordingly refused to take sides in the Gulf dispute between Qatar and Saudi Arabia, the UAE, Bahrain, and Egypt since June 5, 2017. Morocco also refused to take part, but was in a much more difficult position in opposing Arab Gulf states, having to choose between friends. Although the UAE and to a lesser extent Saudi Arabia remain among the top investors in Morocco, in recent years, Qatar ranked fifth in terms of net inflows of foreign investment. The UAE is the third ranked investor in Morocco and the first Arab state's investor with $6 billion in the Casablanca Stock Exchange. Close personal relationships bind the Moroccan king, Mohammed VI to the Crown Prince of Abu Dhabi, Mohammed Bin Zayed (MBZ). This relationship is institutionally strengthened by a strong security partnership (a significant number of Moroccans are members of the UAE police forces). Moreover, there are around 500,000 Moroccan expatriates in the GCC divided mainly between the UAE and Qatar, and to a lesser extent in Saudi Arabia. This context explains why Rabat ultimately decided, on May 1, 2018, to sever its diplomatic relations with Iran, thereby sacrificing its limited relation with Teheran in favour of the young Saudi Crown Prince, Mohammad Ben Salman Al Saud. Rabat accused the Iranian embassy in Algiers of serving as a facilitator for Hizballah's support and training of Polisario. This surprising Moroccan decision satisfied its main Gulf allies and allowed Rabat to maintain its links with Doha without angering Riyadh and Abu Dhabi (Fakir 2017).

Nevertheless, the cordial relations between Rabat and Doha that date back to 2013, coinciding with Shaykh Tamim's access to the throne and a new Islamist Moroccan government led by Prime Minister Benkirane from the Islamist

Justice and Development Party, contributed to displease MBS. The Saudi Crown prince's political belief in both domestic and foreign affairs became: "either you are with me or against me." Thus, the Gulf crisis was aggravated by the growing interpersonal rivalries between the main princes involved in this unprecedented crisis: Mohammed Ben Zayed (UAE), Mohammed Ben Salman (Kingdom of Saudi Arabia), and Emir Tamim as the head of Qatar.[9] This crisis then became a tool for each of these new leaders to test their allies' loyalty. Therefore, North African states and also in a far more serious way those in the Horn of Africa have been hugely impacted by this crisis (Dazi-Héni and Le Gouriellec (2019)).

It seems that the cooling relations between Rabat and Riyadh first came from Morocco. This was because Riyadh had lobbied and voted in favour of North America against Morocco to host the football World Cup in 2026. In reverse, Doha campaigned for the Moroccan candidacy. On the Saudi side, Crown Prince Mohammed was annoyed when King Mohammed VI did not welcome him during his North African tour in early December 2018, a few days after the Khashoggi affair and the G20 meeting at Buenos Aires. Morocco also intensified the crisis by announcing through its Foreign Minister on Al-Jazeera's Qatari channel (January 19, 2019) that it would withdraw from the Arab coalition in the Yemen War. This provoked the fury of Riyadh, which responded by broadcasting a documentary on the sensitive Sahraoui issue, contesting the Moroccan narrative.

However, this episode is unlikely to endanger the strong historic bilateral relationship even if it fails to reach the heights it had under kings Fahd and Hassan II. The new Saudi Crown Prince, like many of his peers, does not share the same strong personal links as the previous generation of Saudi royals had with the Moroccan royals or even those from Jordan, not to mention the Lebanese political elite.

As for the Tunisian case, Qatar has displayed growing interest in financially helping this country after the electoral victory of the Islamist al-Nahda party. Besides, the strong relationship its leader Rachid Ghanouchi used to have with Doha led the emirate in trying to strengthen its position in Tunisia. However, the Tunisian people did not accept Qatari interferences in their domestic affairs, and the UAE thus saw an opportunity to play on this Qatari failure, by investing and delivering financial support. There is currently (2019) a thawing of Saudi-Tunisian relations, but it is under popular scrutiny due to the popular anti-Gulf sentiment.

Since February 22, 2019, Algeria has faced a huge pacifist mobilisation all over the country. This movement was initiated through social media networks from the new millennial, globalised generation consisting of youth, football clubs, associations, and student and local citizens' district affiliations that had all refused a fifth presidential mandate for Abdel-Aziz Bouteflika.[10] It soon became intergenerational, with different social and regional origins across the country and has led to an unprecedented regime crisis that will probably need considerable internal compromise, especially from the key institution, the army. These will probably lead to a transition process in order to rejuvenate elites in all fields (politics, the army, economy, administration). Therefore, most of Algeria's main foreign partners

(France, Europe, Russia, United States, China, and the Arab world) remain prudent and wish a peaceful transition process. For the Gulf states, and especially the UAE which aspires to a more assertive policy in the Mediterranean (Dazi-Héni 2019), there is no benefit in interfering in an Algerian regime known for its opacity, despite several visits between the Algerian armed forces Chief of Staff, Gaid Saleh, and the Abu Dhabi Crown Prince (MBZ) during the crisis. Qatar, on the other hand, became more or less a subcontractor of Turkey in trying to monitor the Algerian Muslim brothers' parties even if different Islamist branches (Movement for Society and Peace, al-Rachad) did not contribute to the popular movement (Khelifi 2019).

Conclusion

Few academic studies have been published on Algerian foreign policy with the Gulf region. Our long-standing familiarity with this region, including several scholarly articles on GCC states, and our understanding of the Algerian regime, have helped us to draw a more accurate and contemporary picture of these relations between Algeria, Iran, and the GCC.

In exploring the topic, we first faced a perception made of generalist reports and public opinion trends. In reality, as shown in our section on the "black decade" where Algerian foreign policy was paralysed by the civil war, this period which overlapped with the second Gulf War became a repository of false ideas.

Iran was not a reliable counterpart even though Algiers and Teheran shared the same global vision on a wide range of international issues. Second, Saudi Arabia's religious and financial networks were not as influential and decisive in the radicalisation of Algerian Islamists. Furthermore, official relations mixed with personal and sustainable business contacts through President Bouteflika's connections with Gulf royals and business elites were useful, if not always cordial, in maintaining formal relations.

Algeria's policy of non-interference has limited its strategic options in its immediate neighbourhood since the Arab uprisings. This re-asserted principle in the Gulf region of relations with both sides (GCC and Iran) played in Algeria's favour by preventing it from being used by either side in the Iran-Saudi "cold war," and also in the current Gulf crisis.

Notes

1 GCC states comprise Saudi Arabia, Bahrain, United Arab Emirates, Kuwait, Oman, and Qatar since they held their first opening summit on May 25, 1981, in Abu Dhabi.
2 For a detailed analysis of this case study, see Sick, Gary (1985). "The partial negotiator: Algeria and the US hostages in Iran," in Touval, Saadia Zartman, I. William (eds.), *International Mediation in Theory and Practice*, Boulder, Colorado, Westview Press, pp. 21–53.
3 The difficult negotiations between the newly independent Algeria and France made at that time Algeria's adherence to OPEC inopportune. See for a detailed analysis, H. Malti, "Algeria and OPEC," https://algeria-watch.org, 26 mars 2018.

4 For the concept of "Third-worldism," see Ghettas, Mohammed Lakhdar, (2017), Algiers and the cold war: International relations and the struggle for autonomy, London, IB Tauris.

5 Islamic Revolutionary Guard Corps or Sepah-e Pasdaran has been created on May 5, 1979, see: Buchta Wilfried, (2000). Who rules Iran? The Structure of Power in the Islamic Republic, Washington Institute for near East Policy & Conrad Adenauer Stiftung publications, Washington DC.

6 Imam Abdelhamid Ben Badis (1889–1940) was the founder of Salafism in Algeria. He particularly insisted on critics' vis-à-vis Sufism that he considered carrying a lot of innovations forbidden on the religious level. See Bilal Ainine, chapter 1 for a detailed analysis on Ben Badis heritage in Algeria.

7 Sayyid Qutb (1906–1966) was a leading member of the Egyptian Muslim Brotherhood and author of books where he developed what is believed to be the inspiration of radical Islamism and for violent groups, such as al-Qaida. He was jailed and hanged under President Gamal Abdel Nasser on August 29, 1966.

8 A. Benantar is an assistant professor in Sorbonne University Paris 8, he discussed the conceptual approach tharwa/thawra during the seminar on the Gulf crisis of June 2017 and its impact on Northern African States, Sorbonne University- Paris 8, March 22, 2019.

9 Indeed, the true enemies of MBS and MBZ are mainly the Emir's father, Shaykh Hamad who abdicated in favour of his son on June 25, 2013, and his closest acolyte, Hamad Bin Jasem—HBJ—who was the powerful prime minister and minister of foreign affairs during Shaykh Hamad's reign.

10 See, essential Algerian media websites: www.elwatan.com; www.tsa-algerie.com; www.algeriepart.com. See, also, Ourahmoune, Nacima. (2019). "Algérie: quand les millennials défont le trauma avec humour et imagination," www.theconversation. com, 12 March.

References

Ainine, Bilal (2016). "Islam politique et entrée en radicalité violente: Le cas des salafistes radicaux violents algériens," Thèse de sciences politiques sous la direction du Pr. Xavier Crettiez, université de Versailles St Quentin en Yvelines, Hal. archives-ouvertes.fr, Septembre. Kepel, Gilles, (2002). Jihad: The Trail of Political Islam, Harvard University Press.

"Assad compares Syrian War to Algeria Conflict," Agence France Presse, November 6, 2013.

Benantar, Abdennour, Chena, Salim et al. (2015). La sécurité en Méditerranée occidentale, Paris: L'Harmattan. Boukhars, Anwar (2013). "Algerian Foreign Policy in the Context of Arab Spring," http://carnegieendowment.org, January 14.

Buchta, Wilfried (2000). Who rules Iran? The Structure of Power in the Islamic Republic, Washington Institute for Near East Policy & Conrad Adenauer Stiftung Publications, Washington, DC.

Crowley, Patrick (2017). Algeria: Nation, Culture and Transnationalism, 1988–2015. Liverpool, Liverpool University Press.

Daguzan, Jean-François, (2015). "La politique étrangère de l'Algérie: le temps de l'aventure?" Politique étrangère, 3, pp. 31–40.

Dazi-Héni, Fatiha (2017). "Picking a quarrel with Qatar." www.mondediplomatique. com, July.

Dazi-Héni, Fatiha (2018a). "Question 70 : L'Arabie saoudite est-elle le fer de lance de la réaction aux 'printemps arabes?" L'Arabie saoudite en 100 questions, Paris, Tallandier, Texto, Edition pp. 228–230.

Dazi-Héni, Fatiha (2018b). "Kuwait and Oman mediating Policy traditions in rupture with Gulf crisis protagonists," Current developments in the Gulf region, Berlin, Orient II/ 2018, Deutsches Institute, April, pp. 41–46.

Dazi-Héni, Fatiha (2019). "Les pays du Golfe: Nouveaux acteurs émergents en Méditerranée ?", *Revue de Défense Nationale, La Méditerranée stratégique* (Dir), Pierre Razoux, Juillet.

Dazi-Héni, Fatiha and Le Gouriellec, Sonia (2019). "Red sea: Growing overlapped security issues at stake between Gulf states and the Horn of Africa states." Research Paper, June. https://irsem.fr,.

Etienne, Bruno (1977). *L'Algérie, cultures et révolution,* Paris, Ed du Seuil.

Fakir, Intissar (2017). "As the Qatar crisis worsens, Morocco is struggling to remain neutral," www.al-monitor.com, 10 July.

Gaube, Florence (2017). Both ends of the Spectrum: GCC-Maghreb Relations, The Arab Gulf States Institute in Washington.

Khelifi, Meriem (2019). "Pourquoi l'Algérie ne sera pas islamiste!", www.elwatan.com, 28 March.

Khouni, Rania (2007). "La République islamique et le Monde Arabe depuis 1979: Enjeux politiques, culturel ou économiques?", thèse de 3ème cycle de sciences politiques sous la direction de Bernard Hourcade, Université Paris III Sorbonne Nouvelle, pp. 238–239.

Korany, Bahgat and Dessouki, Hilal Ali E., (2010), *The Foreign policies of Arab States: The Challenge of Globalization*, 3rd edition. Cairo: American University of Cairo.

Lieb, Diane (1985). "Iran and Iraq at Algiers' 1975," in Touval, Saadia, and Zartman, I. William (eds), *International Mediation in Theory and Practice*, Boulder, Colorado, Westview Press, pp. 67–86.

Martin, I. (2013). "Whither Algeria? Two normalizations, three unresolved crises and two crucial unknowns," in Brichs, F.I. (ed.), *Political Regimes in the Arab World. Society and the Exercise of Power*, London, New York, Routledge, pp. 65–69.

Martinez, Luis, (2000). *The Algerian Civil War (1990–1998)*, New York, Columbia University Press.

Martinez, Luis, Boserup, Rasmus Alenius, (ed.), (2016). *Algeria Modern: From Opacity to Complexity*, Oxford, New York, Oxford University Press.

Mortimer, Robert (2006). "State and army in Algeria: The 'Bouteflika Effect'", *The Journal of North African Studies*, Vol. 11, N° 2, pp. 155–171.

Slim, Randa M. (1992). "Small-state mediation in international relations: The Algerian mediation of the Iranian hostage crisis," in Bercovitch, Jacob, and Rubin, Jeffrey Z. (eds), *Mediation in International Relations. Multiple Approaches to Conflict Management*, New York, St. Martin's Press, pp. 206–231.

Touval, Saadia and Zartman, I. William (eds), (1985). *International Mediation in Theory and Practice*, Boulder, CO, Westview Press.

Young, Karen (ed.) (2013). *The New Politics of Intervention of Gulf Arab States*, London: LES Middle East Center.

Young, Karen (ed.) (2016). *The Interventionist Turn in Gulf States' Foreign Policies*, Washington, DC, The Arab Gulf States Institute.

Zoubir, Yahia H. (1993). "Reactions in the Maghreb to the Gulf Crisis War." *Arab Studies Quarterly*, Winter, Vol. 15, N°1, pp. 83–104.

Zoubir, Yahia H. (1999). "The Algerian crisis in world affairs." *The Journal of North African Studies*, Vol. 4, N° 3, pp. 15–29.

Zoubir, Yahia H. (2015). "Algeria's Roles in the OAU/African Union: From National Liberation Promoter to Leader in the Global War on Terrorism." *Mediterranean Politics*, Vol. 21, N° 1, pp. 55–75.

18

ALGERIA AND THE CONFLICT IN WESTERN SAHARA

Principles and geopolitics

Souadou Lagdaf and Nardjes Flici

Introduction

The decolonisation of Western Sahara remains a crucial issue for Algeria, which has been pushing for its resolution since the onset of the conflict between Morocco and the Sahrawi nationalist movement led by the Polisario Front (POLISARIO). This is especially true in the last two decades of the regional instability weighing on Algerian borders, exacerbated by the situation on the other borders with the Sahelian states, leaving Algerian policymakers with the suspicion that Morocco is exploiting these conditions to undermine the country's national security.

Algeria's position in the conflict stems from historical developments and its own anticolonial experience, and from binding international laws. However, behind these positions and policies, a deeper understanding of Algeria's resolute stance on the Western Saharan conflict should be considered by examining the traditional rivalry between the two neighbours (Jacobs 2012; Zoubir 2000).

For Algeria, the status of Western Sahara is unambiguous: all United Nations (UN) resolutions on Western Sahara adopted by both the General Assembly and the Security Council consistently and unequivocally reaffirm the principle of self-determination, and no country recognises Morocco's sovereignty over the territory it has occupied since late 1975. Morocco, however, claims sovereignty over this territory and accuses Algeria of prolonging the conflict to deny Morocco its "historical right" and to garner geopolitical gains. This is why Moroccans affirm that a resolution of the Western Saharan conflict can only be resolved through direct negotiations with Algeria, a view Algeria categorically rejects. It is also necessary to examine Morocco's strategy regarding Western Sahara and the instruments Algeria uses to prevent Morocco from achieving its objectives within international institutions, such as the United Nations (Henache 2018), the African Union) and in their bilateral relations.

The historical and political context

Algeria has long been recognised as having a fundamental role in supporting liberation movements, a position inspired by the values underlying the Algerian Revolution of 1954. However, since the February 2019 Algerian protest movement calling for political change and transition towards a second republic, many have questioned whether this change might affect the future of Algeria's position on Western Sahara.

By 1975, Algeria had already been independent for 13 years when, in the midst of the Cold War, a Spain, weakened by the illness of General Franco, collapsed into political crisis following his death. Spain eventually decided to cede its North African colony to Morocco and Mauritania, a decision the UN has never recognised. The position then taken by various nations on this revision of neo-colonial politics still remains intact at the time of writing (2019). American and French involvement in this conflict continues, and so too does the unequivocal position assumed by Algeria since the beginning of the invasion of the former Spanish colonial territories.

The United States took an interest in the new circumstances in North Africa and consequently in the positions adopted by the various parties. A secret Central Intelligence Agency report dated June 30, 1978, underlined Algeria's clear position regarding the conflict in Western Sahara: "Algeria refuses to recognize the Moroccan-Mauritanian annexations, advocates self-determination for the Sahara, and gives substantial material support to the POLISARIO insurgency" (CIA 1978). In the same document, the CIA even outlined Algeria's policies opposing colonial aggression in its geographical region: "Algeria will continue its support of the POLISARIO and will try to keep the issue before international forums. Algeria will not, however, seek outside help other than diplomatic support as it does not wish to dilute its influence over the POLISARIO" (CIA 1978).

The subsequent evolution of international politics marked by the end of the Cold War, the fall of the Berlin wall, and the eruption of the Gulf wars, has had a considerable impact on this conflict. For Western powers, the political instabilities that characterise the Arab nations impede any solution to the conflict in Western Sahara. This situation, exasperated by the hindrance of the hegemonic powers, has provided observers and scholars with certain insights into the role of the various protagonists, including Algeria, associated with the conflict.

The views of scholars and analysts regarding Algeria's role in the Sahrawi question intersect from different angles, and two orientations in particular emerge as the most prominent and most often cited. The first underscores Algeria's support for the right of peoples to self-determination based on the values and principles for which the Algerian people fought in their long battle against French colonialism. The second emphasises the regional rivalry between Algeria and Morocco, with Morocco accusing Algeria of exploiting the anticolonial struggle of the Sahrawi people in order to reduce Moroccan hegemony in the region. The latter position reflects French administrations, which seek to protect the Rabat monarchy and hinder any solution within the UN Security Council and the European Union that might bring about a definitive outcome of the conflict. The supporters of this position have indeed done little to conceal their desire to push Algiers into a more direct and incisive involvement in the decision-making process surrounding Western Sahara.

In addition to rivalry for regional supremacy, the second analysis also suggests a deliberate Algerian attempt to curb the strengthening of the Moroccan monarchy in the region. As Damis put it, "Algerians fear that the absorption of the Sahara by their neighbours would only encourage Moroccan expansionist tendencies and whet the Moroccans' appetite for pursuing their unfulfilled and frequently articulated irredentist claim to territory in Western Algeria" (cited in Zoubir 2007).

Other scholars, such as Ruiz Miguel, dismiss suggestions that economic and strategic interests (such as opening a path to the Atlantic) spurn Algerian support for the Sahrawi cause. "Algeria already has access to the sea of its products through the Mediterranean and it pretended an outlet to the Atlantic would do it through Agadir, through Morocco, just as currently the gas pipeline through which it exports gas to Europe crosses through Morocco" (Ruiz Miguel 2004).

The studies surrounding the Algerian involvement in the Western Saharan conflict explain much about the relationship between Algiers and Rabat and how Morocco exploited Algerian support for the Polisario Front in the game of alliances during the Cold War era in order to present itself as an anti-communist bulwark in the region. Since then, Algeria's position has been, on the one hand, subject to the contradictory political and economic relations it holds with France and their impact on North African countries. On the other hand, this affected the regional strategies Paris adopted in the Sahel: "The dispute over Western Sahara has become a defining feature of North Africa's international politics and regional relations. Its significance cannot be underestimated" (Mundy 2010). All of these explain how the Western Saharan crisis has become a political and economic tool used to condition the attitude of the great powers towards the parties involved in the conflict.

Algeria's decisive political, social, and economic support for the Sahrawi cause since 1976 is in full compliance with UN resolution 1960, 1514 (XV), and is of particular importance to Algerian foreign policy because it relates to the decolonisation of a neighbouring territory. Recent interpretations of Algeria's position in the North African conflict therefore seem more associated with adverse political propaganda and the political and strategic justification of power games in the international arena, rather than a qualified interpretation of a regional balance of power.

The imprint of Algeria's political identity on the Western Sahara conflict

While many analysts and observers describe the doctrinal principles behind Algeria's foreign policy as being idealistic, retrospective, and irrational, others find them pragmatic and purposeful. The foundations of the Algerian principles are present in the Tripoli Program[1] of June 1962, stipulating Algeria's determination to fight colonialism and support liberation movements (Chikhaoui 2015). Algeria's points of reference for its policies were borne out of the achievements of its own turbulent history; but as honourable and certainly understandable as its fight against colonialism may be, it remains largely in contrast with the pragmatism of international convergence. A general lack of understanding pervades the international community as it struggles to come to terms with Algeria's persistence to support national liberation movements such as the Polisario Front without direct involvement.

Immediately preceding its independence, the soon-to-be Algerian Republic felt the need to protect itself from the dangers and threats to its independence. After 132 years of French colonialism, during which they endured humiliation, pain, and forced servitude, Algerians revolted and wrested their independence through bloodshed (1954–1962). Algerian nationalism emerged within that context. Algerians also found important international support in neighbouring Maghreb and other Arab nations, and in Afro-Asian countries, which supported its war effort and helped plead its cause before the United Nations. It is therefore only natural that the now independent Algeria would want to provide similar support to other oppressed peoples seeking self-determination.

The founding act was the Algerian Revolutionary leaders' Proclamation of November 1, 1954, which asserted the legitimacy of the fight for independence, while the Soummam Congress[2] in 1956 proclaimed that, "The invasion and occupation of a country shall in no way amend the nationality of its inhabitants" (el-mouradia.dz online). Since 1962, Algeria has unequivocally supported various national liberation movements in Africa, the Middle East (especially Palestinian movements), North and South America, Europe (Canary Islands), and Asia, earning titles such as the "Mecca of the revolutionaries" and the "capital of liberation movements" (Byrne 2016). The preamble of the first Constitution of independent Algeria of 1963 states the nation's commitment to apply "an international policy, based on national independence, international cooperation, the anti-imperialism fight, and the effective support for movements fighting for independence or liberation of their country." Article 92 of the Constitution of 1976 confirmed its solidarity with struggling populations: "for political and economic liberation, [their] right to self-determination and to independence."[3]

On the international scene, the conference of the Heads of State and Governments of the Organization of African Unity (OAU) meeting in Cairo on July 21, 1964, favoured the "principle of inviolability" of African borders, declaring that "all member States are committed to respecting the borders existing at the moment they attain independence" (Jouve 1984). This declaration is a prohibition imposed on all member states from expressing any territorial claim or changing the colonial frontier to the detriment of another state. For African leaders, this imperative relates to any territorial claim from another state or any secessionist movement coming from within a state that would question the borders resulting from decolonisation (Benmessaoud 1989). From the principle of the concept of the inviolability of borders, Algeria also recognises the right of peoples, including the Sahrawi, to self-determination in accordance with UN Security Council Resolutions, such as Resolution 1514 (XV) of the United Nations on December 14, 1960. That resolution consecrates the principle of self-determination and independence of the colonised peoples, reiterated in Resolution 2229 of the General Assembly held on December 20, 1966.

At the conference held in Nouadhibou, Mauritania on September 14, 1970, the heads of state of Algeria and Morocco declared that, "After a thorough study of the situation prevailing in the Spanish Sahara, they decided to intensify their close collaboration to hasten the decolonization of this region, in accordance with the resolutions of the United Nations" (Benoist-Méchin 2010: 238).

Based on these historical and legal facts, Algeria's support for the Sahrawi cause represents a clear link to its own experience, and perhaps a sense of duty to support similar causes. Consequently, and in some respects counter to its own interests, Algeria endorsed the decisions of international jurisdictions, calling for the implementation of the United Nations settlement plan for referendum on self-determination agreed upon by Morocco and POLISARIO following the ceasefire in 1991. In pro-Moroccan circles, however, the Algerian position regarding the Sahrawi issue is viewed more pessimistically as a means to harm the Cherifian kingdom and to serve Algeria's stakes; for its part, Morocco seeks to persuade its allies to acknowledge that the occupation of Western Sahara is an existential matter for the monarchy.

The geopolitical implications of Algeria's role

Part of the tension that undermines the resolution of the Sahrawi conflict is Morocco's persistent call to negotiate directly with Algeria as an active party to the conflict. Algeria, however, fails to comprehend Morocco's invitations to negotiations, as it does not view itself as a directly interested party. Morocco's efforts to negotiate directly with Algeria are not only based on Rabat's assertion that Western Saharan nationalism is a fiction invented and maintained by Algeria, but also because Algeria's influence, strength, and geopolitical relations represent a real obstacle to the growing influence of Morocco, particularly on the international stage.

Algeria finds itself at the geographical crossroads of three of the strategic regions in the world: the Arab world, Africa, and Europe. Its seven land borders penetrate deeply into regional affairs, and it has the economic and financial assets to support its policies. With a territory of nearly 2.4 million km^2 and a growing demography (+1.8% per year, reaching 41.3 million inhabitants at the end of 2017), Algeria boasts the fourth largest Gross Domestic Product of the African continent (219.45 billion USD early 2018) and the second highest GDP per capita in North Africa, behind Libya.[4] With respect to the rest of Africa, Algeria has the largest reserves of gold and currency, is the third largest African economy in terms of GNP (267 billion USD), the third largest oil exporter after Nigeria and

Angola, and Africa's leading natural gas exporter. Despite the negative impact of the global fall in the price of hydrocarbons since mid-2014, the international position of the country remains relatively comfortable. In January 2017, Italy was Algeria's largest export destination, taking 17.74% of Algerian sales abroad, followed by Spain with 14.15%, the United States 12.73%, and France 11.40%. Imports arrived mainly from China, with a share of 21.53%, followed by France 8.94%, Italy 8.07%, and Spain 6.68%.[5] According to the *2018 Global Firepower Index*, Algeria's military strength is second only to Egypt in Africa and 23rd worldwide. Algeria ranks 10th in comparative military expenditure, with 3.3% GDP, in comparison with Morocco's 4th place at 5% GDP. Algeria also leads the fight against terrorism in Africa; it has strengthened its defence as well as its security ties with the United States, which counts on Algeria's local influence to stabilise the Sahel-Saharan region and eradicate the transnational threat of terrorism (Zoubir 2018b). Despite some friction with France, the European Union also has sought to reinforce its collaboration with Algeria as part of its efforts to contain the clandestine immigration into Europe.

In terms of neighbouring countries, its relations with Morocco are the most tumultuous and bellicose. Just 1 year after its independence, Algeria was at war with Morocco (The War of Sands 1963),[6] and was involved in the armed conflict in 1976 over Western Sahara. Since then, the issue of Western Sahara has only served to aggravate relations, leading to regional instability, a costly arms race and the absence of regional integration. This has of course had negative repercussions on the economic development of the region and on the Arab Maghreb Union founded in 1989, which has remained ineffective since its inception (Zoubir 2000). Morocco sought to exploit Algeria's situation during the 1990s when Algeria faced a quasi-civil war: "For Hassan II there was an opportunity to hinder its path [referendum process], or at least slow it down, in anticipation of the evolution of events in Algeria that would lead to new alliances and, perhaps, to the regional equilibrium in favour of propitious monarchy" (Lagdaf 2013, 118). In 1994, Algeria closed its border with Morocco in response to the latter's decision to impose a visa on Algerian citizens for security reasons. Algeria then demanded the settlement of the Western Saharan conflict before it would accept Morocco's request for the border to reopen (Zoubir 2010).

The Western Saharan conflict would not have carried the same intensity were it not for the interests of regional and international powers in the area, either seeking to maintain the *status quo*, or by supporting Morocco or the Polisario Front. Indeed, geopolitical and other very specific interests determine the differing positions and policies surrounding the Sahrawi conflict. France, for example, cannot provide openly unconditional support for Morocco on the Western Saharan conflict as the political, economic, socio-cultural, and security implications weigh just as evenly with Algeria as they do with Morocco. Despite Henry A. Kissinger's statement in December 1975 that, "we have no interest in the problem [Saharan issue], as such,"[7] the same can be applied to the United States. US relations with Algeria have always been ambiguous, notably because of Algeria's support for the revolutionary movements in North and South America. The US condoned Morocco's occupation of Western Sahara during the Cold War, due partly to Algeria's superior relations with the former USSR during the same period (Zoubir 2009). Algeria's tactical advantage in the fight against terrorism since the 2000s, however, overturned the situation immediately following the 9/11 terrorist attacks on American soil in 2001. Since then, Algeria has become a strategic partner of the US in security matters.

During Morocco's long absence from the Organisation of African Unity and its successor, the African Union,[8] Algeria continued to build its diplomatic strength through consistency and continuity. But since becoming a member of the African Union in 2017, Morocco has sought to break Algeria's dominance by gathering support, especially from the former French colonies, for its cause against the Sahrawis. The success of this remains far from certain while the African Union Charter continues to recognise the right of the Sahrawi people to self-determination and the inviolability of borders. For the US, France (Tarek 2019), and Spain, which support the Moroccan project for Western Sahara, Morocco remains a privileged partner due to economic, cultural, commercial, financial, strategic, and other reasons specific to each nation (Zoubir 2018a). While Algeria does not enjoy similar support from these nations, it retains a relatively high level of strategic importance, which, combined with its sphere of influence and diplomatic and military cohesion, provides it with enough flexibility to support the principle of self-determination of the Sahrawi people without fear of reprisal. Similarly, the two permanent veto powers in the Security Council, France and the US, must also pay heed to Algeria's geopolitical importance in their strategic affairs, even if they support Morocco in its endeavours. Algeria's commercial relations with its many trading partners and its economic and military independence represent major assets that allow it to assert its policies regarding the Western Saharan cause without ambivalence, despite Morocco's close relations with several powers, including France and the US.

The stakes of the Western Saharan conflict

To appreciate the dynamics of the Sahrawi conflict, we need to return to the circumstances that prompted Morocco to turn the Sahrawi issue into a matter of national importance. Following Morocco's independence, the Alawite monarchy plunged into a power struggle, and the new King had to make concessions to certain political parties, including the nationalist movement led by the Istiqlal party for its historical role beside the Sultan in the country's independence campaign. In 1961, following the death of King Mohammed V, the succession of Hassan II to the throne changed the balance of power; the new king excluded the *Istiqlal* party and its political allies from any decision-making processes. In 1965, with the support of the Moroccan Royal Army, Hassan II suspended the constitution and parliament and assumed full political power.

The opposition, far from weakened, then organised two failed coups in 1971 and 1972, and a further attempt in 1973, which seriously dented the monarch's power and sense of security (Willis & Messari 2005).

After losing the support of the political class and then the army, Hassan II had to find a way to legitimise his rule, save the monarchy, and ensure the support of the population. In an attempt to keep his army at a safe distance and to some extent compete with the vast expanse of the Algerian territory, he adopted parts of the famous thesis of Istiqlal's Allal Al-Fassi, for a "Greater Morocco" which included Western Sahara, Mauritania, part of Algeria, and of Mali. In 1958, Mohammed V accepted this vision (Ameyar 2000, 43), giving Al Fassi's ambitious ideas official national legitimacy (Bastide 1977, 47), and later consolidating them in a White Book that the Moroccan government published and adopted in 1960 (Sadouk 1982, 53).

The initial justifications for the expansion were derived from Islam. The *Sherifian* State was the oldest constituted state in the region that felt obliged to free all neighbouring Muslim and Arab territories from foreign control and integrate Dar El Islam, the community encompassing the Umma (nation, community), based on the "Jus religionis" (Gardet 1954, 22–26). It constitutes a territory with shifting borders that includes any Muslim territory expressing its wish to join the Muslim community (Flory 1957, 76–77). The Moroccan power therefore developed a politico-religious discourse that referenced the Islamic institution of central power, the caliphate, which prevailed in the lands of Islam until the early twentieth century (Gardet 1954, 164). What seems to be missing from the thesis for a "Greater Morocco" by Allal Al Fassi is any cultural or historical foundation. According to P.C. Renaud, it seems more an attempt to rewrite history:

> To support this fabulous claim, which would make Dakar a sub-prefecture of Rabat, Al Fassi wrote in his way, history of the Sherifian State. Until the establishment of protectorate, Morocco's Sultans were to rule beyond the Draa, over Mauritania and reaching Niger. (…) It would be the French who artificially cut off Morocco from its empire. What Al Fassi omits to say, is that the incursions of Moroccan dynasties had the brevity of lightening. The adventure would end in blood each and every time. The Moorish warriors, who neither saw themselves as Moroccan nor Senegalese—having their own traditions and lifestyle—would repel the invader descending Fez or Marrakech. (Renaud 1993, 64)

Exactly a day after Operation Swab-Hurricane, which was heavily supported by the Royal Armed Forces of the French-Spanish troops, Mohammed V claimed the "Moroccan" Sahara without, however, referring to specific territories. In a speech on February 25, 1958, in M'Hamid, a small village in the Zagora region of Morocco, he declared that: "We solemnly proclaim that the actions for the return of our Sahara will continue, as part of the respect of our historical rights and in accordance with the will of its inhabitants" (Barbier 1982, 79). By 1969,

Morocco had renounced most its territorial claims with the exception of Spanish Sahara, for which Morocco intensified its efforts, calling on its allies to help persuade the international community, including the United Nations and the OUA, of the legitimacy of its claims (De Froberville 1996, 44).

In addition to the major mobilisation for a national cause inspired by the greatness of Morocco, there are several other relevant factors to consider. The Western Saharan territory inherited from Spanish colonialism covers 266,000 km² in the northwest of the African continent. The western edge of this territory includes a 1,100 km coastline overlooking the Atlantic Ocean and facing the Canary Islands archipelago. Even though the official data regarding the territory's natural wealth is incomplete due to the political situation (Karmous 2002), the natural resources of Western Sahara are clearly covetable, as is the strategic position of the territory.

In terms of security, Morocco had suggested in the past that the Spaniards should support its claim on Western Sahara in order to prevent the region from embracing communism through the Polisario Front and socialist Algeria, which would have been deleterious for Spain and the Canary Islands. Today, in an entirely different regional and international context, Morocco justifies its sovereignty over the territory as being necessary to prevent it from falling under the control of fundamentalists such as the Islamic State, as well as to curb alleged Sahrawi involvement in contraband operations and all manner of trafficking. It is clear that these constitute attempts to persuade its allies and the international community of a common goal, and perhaps form a military coalition on a scale that the Western Saharan allies could not possibly match. This would almost certainly force the allies to abdicate and concede the annexation of Western Sahara to Morocco, all under the guise of preventing and suppressing terrorism in the Sahel. While all of these factors combine to give a better idea of the importance and interest of the Sahrawi territory to the Moroccan monarchy, analysts remain convinced that the monarchy's principal motive is to mobilise Moroccan public opinion around a common national cause that could guarantee national unity and stability for the monarchy. After the second attempt (August 16, 1972), through a propaganda campaign pointed at external enemies and threats to Morocco, Hassan II had successfully mobilised the Moroccan army—which was beginning to show signs of dissidence towards his reign—in order to protect the borders against possible enemy invasions. At the same time he rallied the political class and public opinion to his cause.

Algeria and the question of Sahrawi Refugees

The lengthy period of over 45 years of struggle and exile has moulded the general opinion of the Sahrawi people, who speak of an ongoing solidarity with Algerians, even if there are few official sources that document this bond.

The National Archives in Algiers contain large volumes of documentary material on the history of contemporary Algeria, and it is surprising how the documentation concerning the Algerian liberation struggle seems intertwined with certain characteristics of the Sahrawi people's push for self-determination. Several Sahrawi intellectuals maintain that the Algerian Revolution symbolises the fight against colonialism in Africa and Latin America. They also insist that the momentum continues, even if it is no longer characterised by the political landscape of the initial decolonisation period, and many of the countries born out of that process have now repositioned or adapted themselves to a context that might be defined as neo-colonial.

Representatives of the Polisario Front often refer to the Algerian contribution in official speeches. In a recent conference entitled "Africa and Bouteflika, 60 years of friendship and cooperation between Algeria and Africa," the Ambassador of the Sahrawi Republic to Algeria, Abdelkader Taleb Omar, highlighted the role that Algeria has played in the liberation and development of Africa. He argued that this is reflected in Algeria's support for the Sahrawi people, who have benefited from the protection of the nation's borders for 43 years (Cited in Sahrawi Press Service 2018). There are many other testimonies that echo this sentiment. Outside of the political and diplomatic contexts, many people of all backgrounds and education levels often speak of real examples of solidarity that confirm the bond that the Sahrawi people have built with Algeria and its people.

Several scholars, including the editor of the present book, have addressed the events concerning the relationship between Algeria and Western Sahara from a political and regional perspective.[9] However, one aspect of this story, spanning more than 40 years, remains unexplored. The narration and accounts usually highlight three main elements: solidarity, political affinity, and trust. The first aspects that emerge revolve around safety and mutual trust: Algeria welcomed tens of thousands of refugees following Morocco's invasion of Western Sahara in 1975, when Morocco and Mauritania divided the spoils of their conquest. It was indeed an unprecedented scenario as, until then, the Sahrawis had been fighting European colonisation. In the mid-1970s, the international context reflected the Cold War logic of blocs favouring the interests of their allies. The US protected Arab monarchies in opposition to Arab nationalist regimes, and Algeria, which was in the throes of building its own nation state, embodied the non-aligned countries struggling for self-determination against imperialism. Algeria's support for the Western Saharan cause represented a natural political extension of the values and principles rooted in independent Algeria.

The story of the relationship with Algeria began at the most critical moment of the Sahrawi war against Morocco and Mauritania. A witness describes apocalyptic scenes reminiscent of the televised events of the Vietnam War: "When Morocco bombed the temporary refugee camps inside Western Sahara (Um Adriga, Tifariti, Amgala, al-Galta), with napalm and white phosphorus, the Algerians opened their borders to those fleeing the Moroccan invasion. The Sahrawis were given real and immediate protection through the supply of tents, blankets, food and water." The witness emphasised the permanent aspect of this solidarity and trust, serving as an example in a region that is rife with displaced populations and conflicts deriving from its colonial heritage and from newly defined African borders. Indeed, "Algeria also reserved a part of its territory for the Sahrawi authority to host the refugees, and this area is not accessible to Algerian authorities or citizens without the permission of the Polisario Front authority" (Interview March 2018).

The extent of this solidarity and of providing a Sahrawi jurisdiction inside its borders instead of simply assimilating the newcomers into Algerian society, constitutes an important element for the preservation of Sahrawi national identity. In addition, it is not a restrictive measure, as the Sahrawis are free to circulate in other parts of Algeria. We might refer to this novel form of cohabitation as the temporary administrative sovereignty of an ethnic group inside a sovereign host state. It involves taking a political position that President Houari Boumedienne (1965–1978) summarised as follows:

> The politics of our country is clear; we are not against Morocco, never. We are not against Mauritania, never. However, we have helped and will help the Sahrawi people. When the Sahrawi people refused to be slaughtered—tens of thousands of people were threatened with extermination—they took up arms to defend their country. People say that Algeria is helping: yes, we are helping! People say that Algeria created the problem, our position is clear, we have not hidden it, we have recognized the provisional government of the Sahrawi people, we have not hidden this, history shall be our judge, it is a position that we took.[10]

Support for the Sahrawi cause was not limited to solidarity and assistance, as the Algerians continue to demonstrate firm commitment to the decolonisation process. Algerian diplomatic activity continues to support the Sahrawi Arab Democratic Republic and other liberation movements around the world. "Because of this arduous political commitment, Algeria was subjected to forty years of pressure and boycotts by Morocco and its allies in order to force it to abandon the Sahrawi cause; but it has all been in vain" (Interview June 2018).[11]

During the years of armed conflict, Algeria supported the Polisario Front with weapons and military training, while most of the exiled generation studied in Algeria. Today, the second generation of Sahrawi born in the desert and culturally raised in Algerian cities has come of age. A diplomat who arrived as a young boy with the first refugees recalls with some emotion:

> Algeria opened the doors of all its hospitals to treat the Sahrawi patients wounded in war, free of charge. Algeria also took care of the Sahrawi children and enrolled them in its schools, without asking anything in return; the same for students who were educated and continue to study in faculties and university courses. Algeria economically, technologically and scientifically sustained the institutions of the Sahrawi state in exile (Interview August 2018).[12]

The most important aspects of this relationship delve deeper than politics into critical factors surrounding the coexistence between a host country and its guest, such as freedom and trust, even providing Algerian passports so Sahrawi refugees could travel uninhibited. Indeed, as one Sahrawi put it, "the Algerian passport is Algeria's biggest investment in the freedom of the Sahrawis."[13] Trust continues to represent the fundamental element that guarantees freedom of movement for Sahrawi refugees throughout Algerian territory and almost anywhere else in the world with an Algerian identification document (humanitarian passport). This provision also acknowledges the Polisario Front authority, which is the guarantor for the Sahrawi population, ensuring that Sahrawi youth do not succumb to the appeals of international terrorism.

There is a constant risk of presenting the Sahrawi conflict as involving only Algeria and Morocco, and thus removing the political and physical presence of the Sahrawi people from the equation. Morocco, which has persistently challenged Algeria's hosting of the exiled Sahrawi state in Algerian territory, indeed continues to highlight Algeria's involvement in the conflict. First, Morocco defined the refugee camps as prison camps: former Moroccan Prime Minister, Saad Eddin Othmani, called on Algeria to "take responsibility for the conflict over Western Sahara and the situation of Sahrawi refugees in Tindouf camps" (echoroukonline.com 2018). This contradicts the reality that the Sahrawis enjoy freedom of movement, which has even been confirmed by international organisations such as Amnesty International and Human Rights Watch. Furthermore, Morocco has sought to open negotiations with Algerian representatives only, to the total exclusion of Sahrawi participation.[14] During the 73rd session of the UN General Assembly, Algeria's Foreign Minister, Abdelkader Messahel, expressed Algeria's support for the efforts of the UN General-Secretary and his personal envoy regarding Western Sahara; but added: "the solution of the Sahrawi issue can only be achieved through direct and unconditional negotiations between the parties to the conflict, Morocco and the Polisario Front" (echoroukonline.com 2018).

Conclusion

Algeria's support for national liberation causes and the right to self-determination stems from the nation's own history and experience and forms the basis of its foreign policy. It is a position that draws little from traditional schools of thought and theories in international relations, where an individual state's own interest is paramount. The Moroccan occupation of Western Sahara continues while the international community fails to find a solution. In this context, Algeria has been the protector of the rights of the Sahrawi people, insisting for more than four decades that the Sahrawis have the right to determine their own future. Morocco also has its own turbulent history, and internal frictions spurred the monarchy to find solutions to a simmering political, domestic dissidence that threatened and still occasionally threatens the longevity of the crown. Morocco, under king Mohamed VI, insists that negotiation with Algeria is the only way to resolve the Sahrawi conflict, while Algeria refuses to accept this role. Morocco refutes Algeria's disinterest in having an active role in the Sahrawi conflict; Algeria on the other hand, has stubbornly insisted on the preservation of regional stability and observance of international law.

Notes

1 "Tripoli Program": A document created in 1962 in Libya by the National Liberation Front (FLN), which defined the future roadmap for an independent Algerian state. "This document was the product of the last meeting of the wartime. FLN before simmering interrelate rivalry flared into tragic violence. (...) It criticized the Evian Accords and its neo-colonial character and by inference the elite who negotiated it" (Naylor 2006, 429).

2 The Soummam Congress was a secret meeting held by FLN on August 20, 1956, in the Soummam Valley. "With this congress, (...) the Algerian Revolution changed its nature. The long (twenty-day) debates culminated in a well-defined program, the structuring of the FLN-ALN (National People Army), and the affirmation of the primacy of political over military action and of the domestic scene over the exterior" (Stora 2001, 60).

3 These same principles are perpetrated in full in the 1996 Constitution amended in Articles 25, 26, 27, 28.

4 In 2016, during the civil war in Libya, Algeria actually had a higher GDP than Libya, totalling US$ 14,955 Purchasing Power Parity.

5 Algeria's Foreign Trade Statistics, National Center for Informatics and Statistics, January 2017, General Directorate of Customs, Algerian Ministry of Finance.

6 For a dispute over the borders, in the Figuig region to the northeast of Tindouf, as Morocco presumed that Algeria was to give it this territory, which it did not claim during its independence, to Morocco in return for its support for the Algerian Revolution. The OAU brokered a ceasefire between the two parties.

7 SECRET/NODIS/XGDS, Memorandum of Conversation, 01853, 1975/12/17, Declassified: Authority NNDOO9029, 7/27/00. www.*waronwant.org*/attachments/kissinger-boutaflika.pdf, accessed December 5, 2010.

8 Morocco left the OAU in 1984, following the Sahrawi Arab Democratic Republic membership of the organisation.

9 For more information about the political, social, and economic issues about the Western Sahrawi conflict, see, Hodges (1983); Lippert (1985); Lippert (1992).

10 President Haouari Boumedienne talking about Algeria's position on the conflict of Western Sahara (1977), accessed April 25, 2018. https://www.youtube.com/watch?v=-6HFUx-IqNo.

11 Interview with a Sahrawi diplomat, 6/22/2018, via Skype.

12 Interview with Muhammad, August 15, 2018, Smara, refugee camps.

13 Interview with Fatima M., diplomat Sahrawi, Enna, Italy, June 18, 2018.

14 Boumedienne saw this as a risk not only for the Sahrawi cause, but also for the very definition of the anticolonial role of Algeria: "The Moroccan monarchy wants to convert the conflict into a dispute between Algeria and Morocco, to hide its defeat, because it is a critical situation. Moroccan politics, or the politics of the Moroccan monarchy, is currently in an uncomfortable position in the Sahara, and it is trying to convert the situation into an Algerian-Moroccan conflict. We did not want this conflict, but we will accept it if it is imposed upon us. And as the policy of expansion, through force, steel, and fire failed in Western Sahara, it will certainly fail against the Algerian people." Former Algerian President Haouari Boumedienne talking about Algeria's position on the conflict of Western Sahara (1977), accessed April 25, 2018, https://www.youtube.com/watch?v=-6HFUx-IqNo.

References

Ameyar, Hafida. 2000. *Sahara occidental: Que veut l'ONU?* Alger: Casbah Editions.

Barbier, Maurice. 1982. *Le conflit du Sahara occidental.* Paris: L'Harmattan.

Benoist-Méchin, Jacques. 2010. *Histoire des Alaouites (1268–1971).* Paris: Perrin.

Byrne, Jeffrey James. 2016. *Mecca of Revolution: Algeria, Decolonization, and the Third World Order.* Oxford: Oxford University Press.

Central Intelligence Agency, 30 June 1978. Review of IIM, "The Conflict in the Western Sahara." Reference: NI IIM 77-008J of June 1977. Approved For Release 2007/03/06: CIA-RDP79R00603A00250010000-6 https://www.cia.gov/library/readingroom/docs/CIA-RDP79R00603A002500100001-6.pdf.

Chikhaoui, Arslan. 2015. *Paradigmes de la politique étrangère de l'Algérie.* Tunis: Friedrich Ebert Stiftung.

Damis, John. 2007. "The Western Sahara dispute as a source of regional conflict in North Africa," in Halim Barakat, (ed.), *Contemporary North Africa* (Washington, DC: CCAS, 1985), pp. 139–140, Cited in Zoubir, Yahia H. 2007. "Stalemate in Western Sahara: Ending International Legality," *Middle East Policy*, 14, 4.

De Froberville, Martine. 1996. *Sahara occidental: la confiance perdue.* Paris: L'Harmattan.

De la Bastide, Henri. 1977. "La guérilla du Sahara occidental," *Le Spectacle du Monde*, n°185.

Flory, Maurice. 1957. "La notion de territoire arabe et son application au Sahara. *in Annuaire Français de Droit International*, 3(1), 73–91.

Gardet, Louis. 1954. *La cité musulmane, vie sociale et politique.* Paris: Coll. Etudes musulmanes, Librairie philosophique, J. Vrin.

Henache, Dalila. 2018. (September 26). "A Battle between Algeria, Morocco in the United Nations' Corridors." https://www.echoroukonline.com/a-battle-between-algeria-morocco-in-the-united-nations-corridors/ accessed September 27, 2018.

Jacobs, Michael D. 2012. "Hegemonic Rivalry in the Maghreb: Algeria and Morocco in the Western Sahara Conflict." University of South Florida Graduate Theses and Dissertations. https://scholarcommons.usf.edu/cgi/viewcontent.cgi?article=5 282&context=etd.

Jouve, Edmond. 1984. *L'Organisation de l'unité africaine.* Paris: PUF.

Karmous, Afifa. 2002. *La légalité des contrats de prospection des ressources naturelles du Sahara occidental: les limites du droit international.* Paris: Fondation France Libertés.

Lagdaf, Souadou. 2013. *L'insuccesso del processo di pace nel Sahara Occidentale: protagonisti e responsabilità. POLO SUD*, vol. 3.

Mundy, Jacob. 2010. "Algeria and the Western Sahara Dispute," *The Maghreb Center Journal*, Issue 1. https://maghrebcenter.files.wordpress.com/2011/07/maghrebcenter-journal-mundy_algeria-w-sahara.pdf.

Naylor, Phillip C. 2006. *Historical Dictionary of Algeria.* Lanham, Maryland: Scarecrow Press, Inc. Official site of the presidency of the Algerian democratic and popular republic: http://www.el-mouradia.dz/francais/symbole/textes/soummam.htm https://www.youtube.com/watch?v=-6HFUx-IqNo. www.waronwant.org/attachments/kissinger-boutaflika.pdf.

Renaud, Patrick-Charles. 1993. *Combats sahariens, 1955–1962.* Paris: Editions Jacques Grancher.

Ruiz Miguel, Carlos. 2004 (May 10). "El 'gran acuerdo' sobre el Sàhara: anexiòn y antiamericanismo." *Colaboraciones* n° 83. http://gees.org/articulos/el-gran-acuerdo-sobre-el-sahara-anexion-y-antiamericanismo.

Sadouk, Omar. 1982. *L'affaire du Sahara occidental dans le cadre du droit international et des relations internationales*. Alger: Office des publications universitaires (OPU).

Sahrawi Press Service. 2018 (July 15). "The Sahrawi Ambassador to Algeria praises Algeria's role in helping the Saharawi people (translated from Arabic)." July 12, 2018. http://www.saharawi.net/?p=30713 (accessed July 15, 2018).

Stora, Benjamin. 2001. *Algeria 1830–2000: A Short History*. Ithaca and London: Cornell University Press.

Tarek, B. 2019. (May 4). "Les trois actes hostiles de la France envers l'Algérie sous Bouteflika," *Algérie patriotique*, https://www.algeriepatriotique.com/2019/05/04/pourquoi-lalgerie-doit-imperativement-redefinir-ses-relations-avec-la-france/.

Tredano Benmessaoud, Abdelmoughit. 1989. *Intangibilité des frontières coloniales et espace étatique en Afrique*. Paris: Bibliothèque Africaine et Malgache.

Willis, Michael and Messari, Nizar. 2005. "Analyzing Moroccan foreign policy and relations with Europe." *The Review of International Affairs*, 3(2), (2003), 152–172.

Zoubir, Yahia H. 2000. "Algerian-Moroccan relations and their impact on Maghribi integration." *The Journal of North African Studies*, 5:3, 43–74. doi:10.1080/13629380008718403.

Zoubir, Yahia H. 2009. "The United States and Algeria: Hostility, Pragmatism, and Partnership," in Looney, Robert (Ed.), *Handbook on US Middle East Relations*. London & New York: Routledge, pp. 219–236.

Zoubir, Yahia H. 2010. "Le conflit du Sahara occidental: enjeux régionaux et internationaux." https://www.sciencespo.fr/ceri/fr/search/apachesolr_search/zoubir

Zoubir, Yahia H. (2018a). "Conflit du Sahara Occidental: Manœuvres géopolitiques et facteurs de blocage," in Boulay, Sébatsien & Francesco Correale, Eds. *Le Conflit du Sahara Occidental*, Presses de l'Université François Rabelais. Paris: Presses Universitaires François Rabelais, pp. 123–144.

Zoubir, Yahia H. 2018b. "Algeria and the Sahelian quandary: The limits of containment security policy," in Ghanem, Dalia, R. Barras Tejudo, R. G. Faleg & Y. Zoubir (Eds.), *"The Sahel: Europe's African Borders," Euromesco Joint-Policy Paper*, pp. 70–95. https://www.euromesco.net/wp-content/uploads/2018/03/EuroMeSCo-Joint-Policy-Study-8_The_Sahel_Europe_African_Border.pdf.

INDEX